DIVINE IMPASSIBILITY AND THE

MYSTERY OF HUMAN SUFFERING

D1598164

Divine Impassibility and the Mystery of Human Suffering

Edited by

James F. Keating and Thomas Joseph White, O.P.

WILLIAM B. EERDMANS PUBLISHING COMPANY

GRAND RAPIDS, MICHIGAN / CAMBRIDGE, U.K.

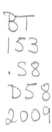
© 2009 Wm. B. Eerdmans Publishing Co.
All rights reserved

Published 2009 by
Wm. B. Eerdmans Publishing Co.
2140 Oak Industrial Drive N.E., Grand Rapids, Michigan 49505 /
P.O. Box 163, Cambridge CB3 9PU U.K.

Printed in the United States of America

15 14 13 12 11 10 09   7 6 5 4 3 2 1

Library of Congress Cataloging-in-Publication Data

Divine impassibility and the mystery of human suffering /
edited by James F. Keating and Thomas Joseph White.
    p.   cm.
Includes bibliographical references and index.
ISBN 978-0-8028-6347-8 (pbk.: alk. paper)
    1. Suffering of God — Congresses. 2. Suffering —
Religious aspects — Christianity — Congresses.
    I. Keating, James.   II. White, Thomas Joseph, 1971-

BT153.S8D58   2009
231'.4 — dc22

                2009015433

www.eerdmans.com

for

Avery Cardinal Dulles (1918-2008)

in gratitude for his service to theology

Contents

Contents

Acknowledgments

The majority of the essays in this volume derive from presentations originally given at a theological conference at Providence College, March 30-31 of 2007, one bearing the same title as this volume. The editors, who organized the conference, would like to thank all those who encouraged and supported this event: Dr. Patrick Reid, the chair of the department of theology at that institution, the faculty and staff of Providence College, and in a particular way, Fr. Brian Shanley, O.P., who helped to give the event its initial impetus.

In addition we would like to thank Sandra Keating, for her good humor, patience, and thoughtful reflection, during the many hours in which the theological question of divine impassibility was discussed in her living room or kitchen. Gary Culpepper was of great assistance through his constant advice and willingness to read carefully the manuscripts for the book. Brethren of the Dominican Province of St. Joseph were of great support and assistance during the planning and editing of this book, and in particular to Thomas Joseph White in his requests for time to work on the project. Fr. Charles Morerod, O.P., of the French journal *Nova et Vetera,* kindly gave us the permission to translate into English an essay by his confrere Gilles Emery, O.P.

Finally, we would also like to thank the contributors to this volume for their efforts on behalf of the conference and the essays alike. The reflections that they offer us herein are of great depth and wonderful interest. We are grateful that they were able to so easily accommodate our desire to produce a worthwhile book of theology on such an important theme. May their varied (and sometimes conflicting) accounts of the mystery of God lead us to reflect anew and more deeply on the gift that is redemption, and on the glory that pertains to God.

James F. Keating
Thomas Joseph White, O.P.
Feast of the Triumph of the Cross, 2007

Introduction: Divine Impassibility in Contemporary Theology

James F. Keating and Thomas Joseph White, O.P.

To speak of divine impassibility is to speak of the question of whether or not God suffers, and if so, in what way. Classically, Christian doctrine affirms that God is beyond the reach of both suffering and evil in his very deity. That is to say, in his transcendent divine nature God does not suffer. Yet this classical doctrine has been subject to intense criticism in modern theology.[1] Persons such as Karl Barth, Sergius Bulgakov, John Cobb, Jean Galot, Robert Jenson, Eberhard Jüngel, Jürgen Moltmann, and the Open Theists would all tell us — in significantly different ways — that the God of the Bible is not an impassible deity but one who suffers along with the creation he loves. In particular, they argue that if God suffers in Christ, this occurs not only by virtue of God's human nature taken up in the incarnation, but in fact in God's very being, in a history which he shares with us, and in some qualified but real sense, in his very nature. The notion of God himself suffering in Christ has enjoyed significant acceptance both in academic theology and popular spiritual literature in recent decades.[2] Nonetheless, despite the widespread prevalence of such a view, one also increasingly finds that affirmations of the traditional doctrine of divine impassibility have begun

1. The best treatment of the early history of the move away from impassibility classically defined remains J. K. Mozley, *The Impassibility of God: A Survey of Christian Thought* (Cambridge: Cambridge University Press, 1926). Commissioned by the Church of England to investigate and report on what was recognized as a significant development in Christian theology, Mozley presents a thorough and sympathetic treatment of those theologians who argue that some reconsideration of impassibility is necessary.

2. Ronald Goetz, "The Suffering God: The Rise of a New Orthodoxy," *Christian Century* 103 (1986): 385-89.

to resurface, and the discussion they have generated is quite animated. Why is there a stirring of such movement over a doctrine that so many believed one could dismiss as a dead letter?

Initially, it seems fair to say that the framework in which actual debate is set is most fundamentally soteriological in nature. The classical (patristic and medieval) doctrines of the impassible God can be seen (not exclusively but above all) as teachings that were meant to safeguard the divine transcendence and its inalienable prerogatives. God in himself is unaffected by creation: we depend upon him, and not the inverse. Because he is not conditioned by anything created that might alter his identity, consequently, he cannot be said to suffer. The modern debate, however, has shifted primarily onto the terrain of providence and "theodicy," and approaches ontological questions primarily from this angle. If human beings suffer so intensely throughout human history, how is God involved in this mystery? Since we suffer, should we not say that God suffers as well? However, if God is free from the limitations implied by our suffering because he is the Creator, what does this imply about his capacity to save us? These sorts of questions seem to animate the discussions of those who are willing to entertain some form of suffering in the deity of God, such as Jürgen Moltmann, process theologians, and Open Theists, as well as recent impassibilists such as Thomas Weinandy and David Bentley Hart. In other words, renewed debate concerning impassibility takes as its starting point the theological problematic of how we are to understand the nature of God in relationship to the fact of human suffering and the gospel's proclamation of its defeat in Jesus Christ. How is a doctrine of divine impassibility or divine suffering related to the redemption of human beings in their suffering? This is the fundamental issue that focuses into one the essays in this volume.[3]

In certain ways, then, the debate concerning divine impassibility is moving into a new phase. In the wake of modern criticisms of the doctrine of impassibility, those who would uphold the tradition are obliged to entertain a new set of challenges, and yet defenders of the classical doctrine have also posed exacting criticisms to the recent proponents of the suffering of God. The question today is certainly not "Does God suffer in virtually the

---

3. The majority of the essays in this volume derive from presentations originally given at a theological conference at Providence College, March 30-31 of 2007, one bearing the same title as this volume.

same ways human beings do?," but, rather, "Must not God in some way be free from suffering and evil if he is to be able to save us?" Or how does the divine identity of Christ assure a presence of God in the world that is capable of transcending the "inevitability of suffering"? And conversely, the question is not first and foremost, "Must we affirm philosophically that God as the Creator is incapable of suffering?," but "What role does the suffering of God in history play in order for God to compassionately redeem the world?" In the now well-known words of Moltmann: "Were God incapable of suffering in any respect, and therefore in an absolute sense, then he would also be incapable of love."[4] Might we wish to qualify our understanding of "divine impassibility" in light of the arguments of recent "passibilists" such as Moltmann? If God is impassible on account of his divinity, then in what sense is this the case and in what way is it not?

Here we shall attempt to give a brief, introductory reflection on the state of the question by signaling three central dimensions of the debate: that pertaining to classical metaphysics, the issue of the continued theological relevance of Chalcedonian Christology, and the centrality of theodicy, or the question of providence. In so doing, we will attempt to delineate the shape of some of the conflicts, but also to detect some of the potential points of compatibility between various authors in this field, especially those represented in this volume. The goal of this brief introduction is primarily descriptive. However, we think that various points of convergence amidst the diverse perspectives of the interlocutors represented in this volume indicate possible resolutions to the question of how the classical doctrine of impassibility might be interpreted today. While such solutions are only "tentative," and inherently controversial, we shall not hesitate to allude to some of them suggestively.

I. Metaphysical Dimensions of the Question

Christianity and Hellenization

Twentieth-century reflection on the passibility of the divine life of God presupposes a critical scrutiny and even fundamental questioning of the

---

4. Jürgen Moltmann, *The Crucified God: The Cross of Christ as the Foundation and Criticism of Christian Theology* (San Francisco: Harper & Row, 1974), p. 230.

"classical attributes" of God as conceived by pre-modern Christianity as well as classical (Hellenistic, patristic, and medieval) philosophy. May or should a doctrinal presentation of Christianity today attempt to articulate a doctrine of God as unconditioned by creation in his simplicity, perfection, non-mutability, timeless eternity, omnipotence, impassibility, and so on? Modern revisionist interpretations of the classical "divine attributes" tradition presuppose that these latter notions are "arbitrary" or at least imperfect historical accretions not essential to the true core of Christian belief. In so doing they accept the validity of a key distinction between the biblical conception of God and the extra-biblical, philosophical conceptions stemming from (primarily Greek) ancient authors, which were introduced progressively into the Christian tradition. In this respect they are the inheritors of nineteenth- and early twentieth-century historical studies which contrasted fundamental Judeo-Christian beliefs with the gradual "Hellenization" of early Christian doctrine that took place in the post-Apostolic period.[5]

Adolf von Harnack in particular articulated a highly influential and controversial version of this thesis. For Harnack, the first five centuries of Christianity were a time in which a distinctly biblical understanding of God and human ethics was gradually interwoven with and obscured by an "extraneous" Hellenistic philosophy, as well as a Latin institutionalism.[6] Accordingly, various classical dogmas can be seen retrospectively as an arcane mixture of both biblical and non-biblical substances. It is the task of modern genealogical study of dogma, therefore, to recapture the former in

5. Concern for the wisdom of expressing biblical ideas through the categories of Greek philosophy is almost as old as Christianity itself, e.g., Arius, Tertullian, Peter Damian, Bernard of Clairvaux, Martin Luther. This concern was connected to historical studies, however, in the nineteenth century, especially in Germany. The most influential nineteenth-century warning against "Hellenization" from within Protestant Christianity was Albrecht Ritschl's *The Christian Doctrine of Justification and Reconciliation*, 3 vols. (Edinburgh: T. & T. Clark, 1900).

6. See for instance Adolf von Harnack, *History of Dogma*, vols. 1-4 (New York: Dover, 1961), vol. 1, pp. 41-136; pp. 47ff.: "The Church doctrine of faith, in the preparatory stage, from the Apologists up to the time of Origen, hardly in any points shows the traces, scarcely even the remembrance of a time in which the Gospel was not detached from Judaism. . . . The attempts at deducing the genesis of the Church's doctrinal system from the theology of Paul will always miscarry; for they fail to note that to the most important premises of the Catholic doctrine belongs an element which we cannot recognize as dominant in the New Testament, viz. the Hellenic spirit."

contra-distinction from the latter. In doing so, modern historical method is invested with a kind of theological mission: to allow for a contemporary reappropriation of the "essence" of Christianity delivered from its pre-modern obsolescence, as well as some of its ancient mythological trappings. For Harnack, metaphysical affirmations implicit in classical dogmatic for-mulations such as those of the Councils of Nicea and Chalcedon fall within the scope of those traditional teachings in need of "reinvented" signifi-cance.[7] Consequently, the perennial significance of a pre-Hellenized Christ is uncovered only through a reflection on the pre-doctrinal, pre-metaphysical historical Jesus, his religion and ethics.[8] While many of the modern theologians who question classical impassibility reject Harnack's "low Christology," they nevertheless retain elements of his genealogical narrative as regards ancient philosophy, with its suspicion as concerns the a-biblical character of ancient notions such as "impassibility."

Recently, however, the thesis of a biblically extraneous Hellenization of Christianity has also been contested in important ways by the very gene-alogical method Harnack himself sought to employ. Martin Hengel, for example, has analyzed extensively the ways in which Hellenistic philosoph-ical concepts were assimilated into second-temple Judaism long before the advent of the early Christian movement.[9] These notions not only perme-ated pre-Christian Jewish literature such as the Septuagint translation, *Ben Sirach,* or the book of *Wisdom,* but, most significantly, colored the Jewish thought-world of Jesus and the evangelists.[10] Pope Benedict XVI has re-

---

7. Harnack, *History of Dogma,* vol. 3, pp. 39-59; 222-24.

8. See in particular, *What Is Christianity?* (New York: Harper & Row, 1957). Of course this dichotomous separation between the religiosity of the historical Jesus (with its perma-nent significance) and the post-biblical dogmatic apparatus which can today be reinter-preted finds important historical precedent in thinkers such as Schleiermacher and Ritschl. It was to find a distinctly "Catholic" expression in thinkers associated with the modernist controversy, such as Loisy.

9. See, above all, Martin Hengel, *Hellenism and Judaism: Studies in Their Encounter in Palestine During the Early Hellenistic Period* (Philadelphia: Fortress Press, 1974).

10. On the Hellenistic influences on the Septuagint translation of the Hebrew Bible, see C. T. Fritsch, *The Anti-Anthropomorphisms of the Greek Pentateuch* (Princeton: Princeton University Press, 1943). For provocative hypotheses on the influence of Hellenized wisdom literature on the early Jesus movement and the NT, see Ben Witherington III, *The Christol-ogy of Jesus* (Minneapolis: Fortress Press, 1990); *Jesus the Sage: Pilgrimage of Wisdom* (Min-neapolis: Fortress Press, 1994); *The Many Faces of the Christ* (New York: Crossroad, 1998); Martin Hengel, *Studies in Early Christology* (Edinburgh: T. & T. Clark, 1995).

cently argued that such biblical reformulations of Hellenistic thought provide sound foundations within the context of Christian revelation for a synthesis of faith and human philosophical reason, and in some cases "they are developments consonant with the nature of faith itself."[11]

Furthermore, as Paul Gavrilyuk has recently demonstrated, non-Christian Hellenistic religions and philosophies of the patristic period did not maintain a shared consensus on the topic of divine impassibility.[12] While significant strands of Greek religious thought asserted that divinity necessarily entails *apatheia,* others affirmed just as strongly the suffering of God, or the gods. Thus, when the early Christian doctrinal tradition employed philosophical language for God, they frequently did so within a distinctly theological context precisely in order to contrast the biblical notion of God with the mythological characteristics of pagan deities. Consequently, the patristic assertion of divine impassibility resists being reduced to "Hellenization" but must be seen as a profoundly complex, even paradoxical, reality. Patristic authors such as Cyril of Alexandria and Pope Leo I could claim that the Christian God became man and suffered in Christ, yet simultaneously maintain that it was the "the impassible God" who suffered in Christ.[13] That is to say, the God who was in the crucified Christ reconciling the world to himself retained by virtue of his divine nature the prerogatives of his inalienable transcendence as Lord. When the Fathers delineated a conception of divine impassibility, it was, according to Gavrilyuk, because they claimed to discover such a perspective in Scripture itself.[14] In sum, future discussion of impassibility must go beyond any

11. See Benedict XVI, Regensburg Address, September 12, 2006: "Faith, Reason and the University: Memories and Reflections," available at http://www.vatican.va/holy_father/benedict_xvi/speeches/2006/september/documents/hf_ben-xvi_spe_20060912_university-regensburg_en.html.

12. See Paul L. Gavrilyuk, *The Suffering of the Impassible God: The Dialectics of Patristic Thought* (Oxford: Oxford University Press, 2004), particularly pp. 21-63.

13. See in this respect Cyril's *Ad Nestorium,* 8, anathem. 2 and 3; *Ep.* 10.1 (*ACO* 1.1.1.110-12) and his *Adversus Anthropomorphitas,* as well as Leo's *Ad Flavian.*

14. Gavrilyuk, *The Suffering of the Impassible God,* p. 150: "The attribution of human emotions and experiences to God is regarded by the biblical authors themselves as a problem of anthropomorphism, not necessarily an advantage over non-anthropomorphic descriptions of God. Cyril was keenly aware of the problem of anthropomorphism. . . . He understood that to affirm without qualification that the divine nature was passible was to open a Pandora's box of theological problems. . . . Divine impassibility had its proper function in the framework of patristic negative theology and was not intended to rule out all emotion-

simplistic contrast between Greek metaphysical notions and biblical categories and ask again whether the affirmation of impassibility in the Fathers is something "extraneous" to the distinctly biblical conception of God or its implication. When Cyril of Alexandria or Leo the Great employed such "philosophical" categories to discuss the passion of Christ, did they subvert or illuminate something proper to the mystery?

Post-Kantian Metaphysics and Post-Hegelian Theology of God

What is clear today, at any rate, is that Harnack's historical observation about the inescapable influence of philosophy in ancient theology can be universalized. Some kind of ontological interpretation of the scriptural witness is present within any dogmatic formulation in any age and serves as a dimension of its self-expression.[15] Christian theology is inevitably metaphysical; the issue is how it is so. Yet to realize this fact only accentuates the acuity of the question of the perennial relevancy of the "classical attributes" of God. The philosophy the Fathers sought to come to grips with in order to explicate divine transcendence no longer enjoys wide acceptance. For in the world of modern and contemporary philosophy, the Kantian critique of classical metaphysics (or at least of what Kant took to be classical metaphysics) has had a profound and enduring impact, even in those philosophical domains where his own theses are disputed. Accordingly, in an intellectual environment in which the "recovery" of metaphysical thought seems plagued by difficulties, any commitment to decidedly pre-modern understandings of divine transcendence is bound to entail risks and encounter suspicion bordering on incredulity. Is it not necessary

---

ally coloured characteristics of God or God's involvement in creation. For Cyril, both qualified divine impassibility and qualified divine passibility were necessary for a sound theology of incarnation. The affirmation of impassibility was a way of protecting the truth that the one who became incarnate was truly God. Admitting a qualified passibility secured the point that God truly submitted himself to the conditions of the incarnation."

15. The organic connection between understanding and proclaiming the Christian faith and philosophy has been defended cogently within Protestant theology by Wolfhart Pannenberg; cf. "The Appropriation of the Philosophical Concept of God as a Dogmatic Problem of Early Christian Theology," in *Basic Questions in Theology*, vol. 2, trans. George H. Kehm (Philadelphia: Westminster Press, 1971), pp. 119-83; *Theologie und Philosophie: Ihr Verhältnis im Lichte ihrer gemeinsamen Geschichte* (Göttingen: Vandenhoeck & Ruprecht, 1996).

to translate classical Christology into a post-Kantian, post-critical intellectual motif, precisely to preserve the perennial significance of Christian thought? Perhaps this exercise in modern reappraisal of the deposit of faith is the opportunity for a more scriptural reappropriation of the classical Christian doctrines of Nicea and Chalcedon. Here again, one might seek to promote a "high" Christology even while maintaining that the Kantian critique has closed the doors permanently to a pre-modern metaphysical stance.[16]

It is at this juncture that the influence of a Hegelian metaphysics of divine becoming in history has proven of central significance. In an age of metaphysical skepticism, a number of theologians believe that it is necessary to rearticulate coherently a Christian doctrine of the analogy between God and the world such that the metaphysics of divine transcendence is intelligible in contemporary parlance. Yet here the Christian tradition now confronts the "alternative" ontology of Hegelianism, which has greatly influenced modern Protestant theology. For Hegel, history is composed of the ongoing dialectical process whereby opposites are rhythmically taken up into synthesis. This process is simultaneously in some way constitutive of the divine itself. God himself becomes in and through history, a history of dialectic, in an almost musical interplay of thesis, antithesis, and synthesis.[17] Modern Protestant thinkers such as Barth, Jüngel, Moltmann, and Jenson have not hesitated to draw on this distinctively historical (even dialectical) conception of God's being in selective ways in order to think about the character of God's suffering in Christ.[18]

---

16. Bruce McCormack in his *Karl Barth's Critically Realistic Dialectical Theology: Its Genesis and Development, 1909-1936* (Oxford: Clarendon Press, 1995), pp. 43-49, 129-30, 155-62, 218-26, 245-62 has noted various elements of epistemological realism that Barth took from Kant, emphasizing these over and against more skeptical forms of neo-Kantianism that were prevalent in Germany in the early twentieth century. Simultaneously, however, it is easy to see that Kant's skepticism with regards to the project of any philosophical theology (as "onto-theology") harmonizes nicely with Barth's early theological polemic against the tradition of the *analogia entis* in Catholic theology.

17. See in particular with respect to God's historical becoming in Christ's being, his death and non-existence, and his resurrection, *Lectures on Philosophy of Religion*, vol. 3. More generally, see the studies of Emilio Brito, *La Christologie de Hegel: Verbum Crucis* (Paris: Beauchesne, 1983), and Hans Küng, *The Incarnation of God: An Introduction to Hegel's Theological Thought as Prolegomena to a Future Christology* (Edinburgh: T. & T. Clark, 1987).

18. See Eberhard Jüngel, *God as the Mystery of the World: On the Foundation of the Theology of the Crucified One in the Dispute Between Theism and Atheism* (Grand Rapids:

In Christ, God elects to truly suffer and die in himself (his own deity), but also subsequently reconcile us with himself so as to definitively overcome suffering and death (which are in some sense his antithesis).[19] His shared history with us is the source of salvation, since it allows our history to participate in God's own history of victory over evil. In the wake of such notions, in what newly qualified sense ought Christianity to continue today to promote the idea of a God who is simple, perfect, immutable, eternal, omnipotent, and so on?

One way forward can be seen in the limitations that such post-Kantian theologians themselves place on the notion of the "historicity of God." In effect, if the theologian cannot maintain unequivocally the transcendence and distinction of God with respect to temporal history, then a seeming identification of God and creation ensues. Concerned to avoid such an outcome, Robert Jenson, for example, has insisted upon the necessity of some kind of analogical likeness-in-differentiation between God's own history and the temporal history of creation. Even if God is only known in and through his self-revelation as a radically historical being, he is also known as one whose identity "precedes" creation and is not as such dependent upon it. To speak in Barthian terms, the *logos ensarkos* (or the incarnate history of the Son) reveals the trinitarian life of God, but it presupposes both the ontological and logical priority of the *logos*

Eerdmans, 1983); Moltmann, *The Crucified God,* especially pp. 249-66; and Robert Jenson, *Systematic Theology,* vol. 1 (New York and Oxford: Oxford University Press, 1997). Of course, none of these thinkers embrace in any real sense a purely Hegelian ontology and insist that divine involvement in history is an expression of God's freedom, yet all of them have both assimilated and transformed noteworthy conceptual motifs from Hegel's thought.

19. See, for instance, Jenson, *Systematic Theology,* vol. 1, pp. 66, 219-21: "The Lord's resolve to meet and overcome death and the constitution of his self-identity in dramatic coherence are but one truth about him. For if death-and-resurrection occurs, this is the infinite dramatic crisis and resolution, and so God's own. Since the Lord's self-identity is constituted in dramatic coherence, it is established not from the beginning but from the end, not at birth but at death, not in *persistence* but in *anticipation.* The biblical God is not eternally himself in that he persistently instantiates a beginning in which he already is all he ever will be; he is eternally himself in that he unrestrictedly anticipates an end in which he will be all he ever could be." . . . "Death is time's ultimate act. Normal gods transcend death by immunity to it or by being identical with it. The triune God transcends death by triumphing over it, by the Son's dying and the Father's raising him again. . . . The one God is an *event;* history occurs not only in him but as his being. . . . God is the event of the world's transformation by Jesus' love, the same love to which the world owes its existence."

asarkos, the Word of God in the immanent life of the Trinity. God is himself ontologically distinguishable as God from the creation in which he is revealed.[20]

Similarly, though not identically, Bruce McCormack has argued that the biblical revelation itself indicates the structure of a likeness between God and the world in the being and history of Jesus. Following a significant theme in the work of Karl Barth, McCormack advances the claim that the human actions of Jesus are themselves indicative of the inner life of the triune God. The abasement and humility of the man Jesus in history are revelatory of the inner life of obedience and self-emptying which exist in the eternal Son of God. If not, McCormack reasons, then Jesus cannot be truly considered a self-revelation of the one God. Yet this revelatory significance of Jesus must not be conceived in such a way so as simply to identify the Son of God ontologically with the historical process which is the life of Jesus. God makes himself known in and through time, death, and suffering while remaining inexorably transcendent and free with respect to the constraints of creaturely being.[21] In this sense, the revelation of God itself makes apparent to Christian theology a certain *differentiation* amidst likeness (or analogy) proper to the historical world of time and the immanent

20. Jenson has criticized the notion of the filial "pre-existence" of Jesus as God in his *Systematic Theology* (pp. 138-44), yet he maintains (p. 141) the affirmation of the ontological priority of the generation of the divine *logos* from the Father with respect to the historical manifestation of the Son in history as Jesus. He also affirms the existence of an irreducible analogy of being (or likeness despite difference) between God and creation made manifest in Christ (pp. 225ff.). Simon Gathercole ("Pre-existence, and the Freedom of the Son in Creation and Redemption: An Exposition in Dialogue with Robert Jenson," *International Journal of Systematic Theology* 7, no. 1 [2005]: 38-51) has raised questions concerning the logical coherence of Jenson's treatment of God as simultaneously temporal and transcendent of created temporal history. Jenson's position would seem to orient itself toward the affirmation of some form of an "analogy" of temporality between God and creation.

21. See "Karl Barth's Christology as a Resource for a Reformed Version of Kenoticism," *International Journal of Systematic Theology* 8, no. 3 (2006): 243-51; 248-49: "God does not cease to be God in becoming human. *Kenosis* . . . is by addition and not by subtraction. Nothing proper to deity is 'left behind' when the 'Son' takes on the form of a servant. . . . For the Barth of CD IV/1, the 'self-emptying' or 'humiliation' of the Son is not, in the first instance at least, a this-worldly, historical activity on the part of the Logos who has already become incarnate. For the 'humiliation of the Son' in time has its root in the humility of the Son in eternity — which means that it has its root in the eternal relation of the Son to the Father . . . what the Son does and therefore is in time finds its ground in what he does and therefore is in eternity."

life of God. History is the locus of revelation, but the triune God is not thereby reducible to the historical process per se.[22]

Economic and Immanent Trinity: A Theological Analogy of Being

These reflections lead us toward one potential resolution of these matters recently proposed by David Bentley Hart. Hart has argued that any coherent attempt to discuss the economic unveiling of the immanent Trinity in our historical sphere must rely (at least implicitly) upon a differentiation between the immanent life of the transcendent, triune God and the economic manifestation of his triune identity. This differentiation-in-likeness suggests an inevitable "analogical interval" between God and his historical manifestation in the world, such that the former cannot simply be reduced to the latter in any instance of the divine economy. Correspondingly, Hart has argued that any identification of the *immanent* life of the triune God with the successive temporality of the created order (or an analogical envisaging of the former in terms of the latter) inevitably fails to uphold a necessary Christian affirmation of the transcendence of God with respect to creation. To speak in Heideggerian terms, if God is in some sense constituted by the events of history, then God is "merely" an ontic reality among other ontic realities, a finite supreme being acting amidst a finite scale of forms, and in turn, he is being conditioned by these latter.[23] If this logic

22. Consequently, McCormack, like Jenson, wishes to affirm the logical and ontological priority of the *logos asarkos* with respect to the incarnate Word. Nevertheless, the former is only known in and as the latter. This raises the question of how, for McCormack, the divine election of man in Jesus Christ is related to God's trinitarian identity. In writings in recent years he has argued that the historical life, suffering, and death of Jesus are in fact *constitutive* of the Son's eternal being — but constitutive as a consequence of a free and unconditioned decision by the Father. This decision is made freely by God eternally, and is one that the Son obeys or "receives" both eternally and in time. See on this point McCormack's "Grace and Being: The Role of God's Gracious Election in Karl Barth's Theological Ontology," in John Webster, ed., *The Cambridge Companion to Karl Barth* (Cambridge: Cambridge University Press, 2000), pp. 99ff. See also the criticisms of McCormack's position by Paul Molnar, *Divine Freedom and the Doctrine of the Immanent Trinity: In Dialogue with Karl Barth and Contemporary Theology* (Edinburgh: T. & T. Clark, 2002), and "The Trinity, Election and God's Ontological Freedom: A Response to Kevin W. Hector," *International Journal of Systematic Theology* 8, no. 3 (2006): 294-306.

23. See David Bentley Hart, *The Beauty of the Infinite* (Grand Rapids: Eerdmans, 2003), p. 165: "The God whose identity subsists in time and is achieved upon history's horizon —

holds, however, an ultimately "passible" deity is merely a being among other beings, and cannot be coherently conceived as the ground and condition of possibility for all temporal beings in the world. Consequently, he is no longer one who is absolutely free to redeem the world.

Where do all these reflections lead us? Essentially, they leave us with a question. The theologians aforementioned (Jenson, McCormack, Hart) argue that some form of a Christian ontological distinction between the immanent Trinity and the economic manifestation of God in history is necessary. Yet, what role should the classical language of "impassibility" play in maintaining such a distinction? Only a transcendent God who can act upon the very existence and nature of beings can assure us in turn of his eschatological victory over evil. Correspondingly, the transcendent power and love of God must provide the basis for Christian soteriology if we are to properly interpret the proleptic value of the resurrection of Christ. It is in the latter that the *definitive* victory of God over evil has been made manifest. Clearly, then, God is not merely a being in the world subject to historical suffering as all others are. He is not subject to death as we are, in an inevitable powerlessness. Yet to safeguard this affirmation, must Christian theology maintain the classical doctrine of divine *apatheia* as regards God's own immanent trinitarian life? Is this necessary so as to safeguard adequately the unquestionably biblical affirmation of his transcendence and goodness? This is a question that multiple essays in this volume seek to treat, albeit with differing conceptual results.

---

who is determined by his reaction to the pathos of history — may be a being, or indeed the totality of all beings gathered in the pure depths of ultimate consciousness, but he is not being as such, he is not life and truth and goodness and love and beauty. God belongs to the system of causes, even if he does so as its total rationality; he is an absolute *causa in fieri*, but not a transcendent *causa in esse*. He may include us in his story, but his story will remain both good and evil, even if it ends in an ultimate triumph over evil. After all, how can we tell the dancer from the dance? The collapse of the analogical interval between the immanent and economic Trinity, between timeless eternity and the time in which eternity shows itself, has not made God our companion in pain, but simply the truth of our pain. . . . Only a truly transcendent and 'passionless' God can be the fullness of love dwelling within our very being, nearer to us than our inmost parts, but a dialectical Trinity is not transcendent — truly infinite — in this way at all, but only sublime, a metaphysical whole that can comprise us or change us extrinsically, but not transform our very being. . . . Theology must, to remain faithful to what it knows of God's transcendence, reject any picture of God that so threatens to become at once both thoroughly mythological and thoroughly metaphysical, and insist upon the classical definitions of impassibility, immutability, and non-successive eternity."

II. The Suffering of God in Christ and the "Two-Natures" Doctrine

The Contested Legacy of Cyril and Chalcedon

A second question significant for a renewed consideration of the doctrine of impassibility pertains to the interpretation of the classical Christology of the Councils of Ephesus and Chalcedon. In light of modern criticisms of the doctrine of divine *apatheia,* what is the abiding significance of a Cyrillian Christology of the hypostatic union, and of the Chalcedonian theology of the "two natures" of Christ? In what ways might these classical theologies either facilitate or render obscure our reflection on the contemporary question of the suffering of God?

Thomas Weinandy and Paul Gavrilyuk have recently demonstrated the subtlety of patristic reflections on God's suffering, particularly with respect to the mystery of the incarnation of God in Jesus Christ. Here, both of these authors impress upon us the centrality of the thought of Cyril of Alexandria, the fifth-century champion of the theology of the "hypostatic union."[24] In effect, Cyril's bold and insightful use of the communication of idioms sought to underscore the unicity of the subject in Jesus Christ. It is the one subject of incarnation — the Word incarnate — who is scourged, mocked, and crucified, *and* who simultaneously upholds the world in being by his wisdom and power. "For God was in humanity. He who was above all creation was in our human condition. . . . The immaterial one could be touched; he who is free in his own nature came in the form of a slave; he who blesses all creation became accursed. . . . life itself came in the appearance of death. All this followed because the body which tasted death belonged to no other but him who is the Son by nature."[25] To rephrase this idea summarily by a succinct restatement of Constantinople II, canon 10: "One of the Trinity was crucified."

Ought not this classical theology oblige us to say something about the "passibility" of God in Christ? Did God not himself become the subject of suffering and torment through the mystery of his own human historicity?

---

24. See in particular, Thomas Weinandy, *Does God Suffer?* (Notre Dame: Notre Dame University Press, 2000), pp. 172-213; Gavrilyuk, *The Suffering of the Impassible God,* pp. 135-75; as well as J. J. O'Keefe, "Impassible Suffering? Divine Passion and Fifth-Century Christology," *Theological Studies* 58 (1997): 39-60.

25. Cyril of Alexandria, *On the Unity of Christ,* trans. J. A. McGuckin (Crestwood, N.Y.: St. Vladimir's Seminary Press), p. 61.

On this score the Christian tradition is unanimous. Yet this same tradition, beginning with Cyril himself, also sought to qualify such affirmations by recourse to a no less important claim that in Christ "the divine nature" remained transcendent of all evil.[26] In its Chalcedonian formulation (influenced not a little by the theology of Leo the Great), this way of thought stipulated that God suffered in the Son "by virtue of his human nature" even while remaining unconditioned by suffering and change "by virtue of his divine nature." This opened up the path toward the classical notion that God suffers personally, in the Word made flesh, yet he can do so only by means of his humanity. His divinity is free from the constraints of suffering not because of its indifference or absence of compassion, but due to the pure actuality of God's goodness and love, which can in themselves know no diminution. Divine *apatheia* is not apathy, but a characteristic of the plenitude of the divine nature as unblemished love.[27]

This "two-natures" Christology, however, has faced some significant and interesting challenges in contemporary christological reflection. Most noteworthy on this score is the reflection of Jürgen Moltmann, who suggests that the "abstract" Chalcedonian theology of the two natures of Christ can and ought to be abandoned today (or realistically rethought) precisely because it suggests an apparently inevitable "moral distance" between God and his creation.[28] This alterity is in fact the conceptual residue of a non-biblical ontology, inherited from Hellenistic sources. Classical Chalcedonian theology, in this view, is imprisoned by a portrayal of the deity insufficiently receptive to the biblical understanding of God's compassion and solidarity. It is because God reveals to us "what" he is *precisely and only in the crucifixion* that we can understand in turn that he *is* truly "capable" of radically identifying with our suffering, even in his very being, "essence," and inner life.[29] To

---

26. The statements of Cyril to this effect are many. See, for example, "God's Word is, of course, undoubtedly impassible in his own nature and nobody is so mad as to imagine the all-transcending nature capable of suffering; but by very reason of the fact that he has become man, making flesh from the Holy Virgin his own, we adhere to the principles of the divine plan and maintain that he who as God transcends suffering, suffered humanly in his flesh" (*De symbolo*, 24, trans. L. Wickham, *Cyril of Alexandria: Select Letters* [Oxford: Clarendon Press, 1983], p. 123).

27. This point has been made by David Bentley Hart, "No Shadow of Turning: On Divine Impassibility," *Pro Ecclesia* 11 (Spring 2002): 184-206.

28. See Moltmann, *The Crucified God*, pp. 214-15.

29. Moltmann, *The Crucified God*, pp. 202-3: "When the crucified Jesus is called the 'image of the invisible God,' the meaning is that *this* is God, and God is like *this.* . . . The nu-

fail to acknowledge this is to remain theologically insensitive to the true character of the personal union of God with humanity in Christ.[30] The qualifications of the "two-natures" theology of divine suffering only serve to suspend adherence to the mystery by means of artificial abstractions.[31] Moreover, such abstractions as employed in the mainstream Chalcedonian tradition often contain traces of a latent "Nestorianism," problematically dualistic in character.[32]

What should we say about this theological criticism of the Chalcedonian "solution" to the mystery of divine suffering in light of a renewed consideration of divine impassibility? It is clear that if one were to cease to employ the two-natures distinction altogether, certain problems would inevitably arise. For example, if the unity of the persons of God in classical theology is primarily conceived of by means of a concept of their shared nature, in the absence of a two-natures Christology, it tends to be conceived of in terms of their distinctly *personal* roles in salvation history. But this in turn raises up the specter of "tri-theism," since the

---

cleus of everything that Christian theology says about 'God' is to be found in this Christ event. The Christ event on the cross is a God event.... So the new christology which tries to think of the 'death of Jesus as the death of God,' must take up the elements of truth which are to be found in *kenoticism*.... It cannot seek to maintain only a dialectical relationship between the divine being and human being, leaving each of these unaffected.... That means that it must understand the event of the cross in God's being in both Trinitarian and personal terms. In contrast to the traditional doctrine of the two natures in the person of Christ, it must begin from the totality of the person of Christ and understand the relationship of the death of the Son to the Father and the Spirit.... From the life of these three, which has within it the death of Jesus, there then emerges who God is and what his Godhead means. Most previous statements about the specifically Christian understanding of talk about 'the death of God' have lacked a dimension, the Trinitarian dimension."

30. The background of Moltmann's Christology in Luther's theology is explored in Dennis Ngien, "Chalcedonian Christology and Beyond: Luther's Understanding of the *Communicatio Idiomatum*," *The Heythrop Journal* 45, no. 1 (2004): 54-68.

31. See *The Crucified God*, pp. 244-47, as well as the more moderate questioning of the "two-natures" tradition by Jenson in his *Systematic Theology*, vol. 1, pp. 127-38.

32. Jenson (*Systematic Theology*, vol. 1, pp. 131-32) argues that the distinction in Leo's *Tome* of divine and human *operations* in the one Christ leads implicitly to a semi-Nestorian distinction of agents, or subjects. Jenson's argument is based in part, however, upon a questionable interpretation of Leo's Latin. "Agit enim utraque forma cum alterius communione quod proprium est" does not mean "each nature *is agent* of what is proper to it" (p. 131), but "each 'form' acts in communion with the other in accordance with what is proper to it." Contextually, Leo is speaking here about Christ as one subject being simultaneously "in the form of God" and the "form of a servant" (Phil. 2:6ff.).

persons of God are distinct in the historical economy but in no clear way immanently one in themselves. Monotheism is thereby rendered conceptually unstable.[33] To avoid such instability, one is again compelled to think about ways in which the actions and sufferings of the man Jesus in his humanity are in fact revelatory of his transcendent nature, his divine life shared with the Father and the Holy Spirit. But this is to wade into the waters of the central topic of modern trinitarian theology: How does the historical cross of Christ reveal to us the trinitarian life of God? What correlation is there between the human actions of Christ and the divine nature? How do the human obedience, suffering, and dereliction of Christ reveal to us the mystery of intra-trinitarian life "eternally" present in the Father, Son, and Holy Spirit?

In this volume, christological essays by Gilles Emery, Gary Culpepper, Bruce McCormack, Trent Pomplun, Paul Gondreau, and Bruce Marshall all offer interpretations of the incarnation and paschal mystery in such a way as to broach directly these delicate contemporary questions. Emery, Pomplun, Gondreau, and Marshall seek above all to illustrate the resources that lie within a "classical" two-natures account of the life of Christ. Meanwhile, Culpepper and McCormack seek to reinterpret in various ways the two-natures tradition in a contemporary kenotic mode, illustrating the modern prerogative to locate the ultimate revelation of God's trinitarian life precisely in the suffering and dereliction of Christ. The issue of the "ontological correlation" between the natures of Christ is therefore acutely underscored. In what way should contemporary theology seek to construe the relationship between the human and divine activities of God in Christ?

---

33. In what is a clear reference to Moltmann, McCormack ("Karl Barth's Christology as a Resource for a Reformed Version of Kenoticism," p. 247) writes: "Recent theology has made much of the idea of divine suffering; indeed, there are many who would like to understand God as in some sense the subject of the human sufferings of Jesus. One way to get to this goal — the most popular route at present — is to follow Hegel in making a direct identification of the second person of the Trinity with the human Jesus, thereby jettisoning the two-natures Christology. . . . Such an identification is certainly capable of generating *differentiation* in the divine life. What it cannot deliver is an adequate conception of *unity* in the triune life of God. A direct identification of the second person of the Trinity with a human being must inevitably give rise to a conception of the members of the Trinity as three distinct 'subjects' (each equipped with its own mind, will and energy of operation). . . . Such a conception is 'tritheistic' by any early church definition of the term. . . ."

Aporia Surrounding the "Two-Natures" Christology

If we are to maintain that God suffered in Christ by virtue of his human nature and physical historicity, this need not signify an end to profound enigmas surrounding the event of God's suffering in Christ. For if this event transpires in and to the person of the Son of God, then the suffering and death of God transpire in fact in his very person, in *who* he is eternally.[34] In some real sense, then, every Chalcedonian theologian must wish to affirm that historical suffering truly has occurred within God. It is due to this mysterious truth that Thomas Weinandy and Paul Gavrilyuk, for example, are willing to speak about a "qualified passibility" of God in the Word incarnate. Weinandy appeals to Aquinas's ontology of the divine *esse* of Christ in order to explore this idea.[35] It is because all that transpires to Christ in history subsists in the person of the Word, in his very being and existence, that these facets of his history can be truly said to be his.[36] This *res nova* of the incarnation does indeed "import" into God the attributes of human change, misery, and perdition. Yet for Weinandy it is also because the Word is himself impassible as God that he can in turn act in and through the mystery of his historical suffering and death to redeem and restore "from within" the human condition.[37]

---

34. Cyril of Alexandria, *De Symbolo*, 31: "Do you allot the suffering to human being alone, fending it off from God the Word to avoid God's being declared passible? This is the point of their [the Nestorians] pedantic, muddle-headed fictions" (trans. L. Wickham, *Cyril*, p. 131).

35. In *Does God Suffer?*, Weinandy writes (p. 200): "Because the incarnational 'becoming' is *kath hypostasin*, according to the person, it can actually be said then that the person of the Son of God is truly born, grieves, suffers and dies, not as God, *but as man,* for that is now *the new manner in which the Son of God actually exists*" (emphasis added).

36. Weinandy, *Does God Suffer?*, pp. 206-8. Examples of Aquinas's doctrine of the personal *esse* of Christ are to be found in *Summa Theologiae* III, qq. 2; q. 6, a. 6; q. 8, a. 6; q. 16 and 17; *Summa Contra Gentiles,* IV, c. 34. *ST* III, q. 6, a. 6: "The grace of union [of the Word with the human nature] is the personal being itself *(ipsum esse personale)* that is given gratis from above to the human nature in the person of the Son." *SCG* IV, 34: "The body of that man is the body of the Word of God. So it is right to say that the Word of God — and God — suffered, was crucified, died, and was buried." (Translations by the English Dominican Province in *Summa Theologica* [New York: Benzinger, 1947], and Charles O'Neil, *Summa Contra Gentiles* IV [Garden City, N.Y.: Doubleday, 1957].)

37. Weinandy, *Does God Suffer?*, pp. 161, 209: "The trinity of persons subsist in relation to one another, as the one God, with their love for one another fully and completely actualized. They are immutable and impassible in their love for one another, not because their love is static or inert, but because it is utterly dynamic. . . . The immutability of God, far from be-

This leads us to a question, however. If God is in fact willing to suffer in and through his human physical, emotional, and psychological states, then what correspondence does this suggest between his human expression of suffering *in love* and his transcendent divine character as one whose goodness is "fully active" or "inalienable"? Surely there must be some real analogy between the two? Is it possible to identify a kind of correlation between the biblical parables of the "passionate God" in the Old Testament who suffers because of his people, and the transcendent perfections of God which these metaphorical expressions are clearly meant to denote? Most especially, does the "outer" suffering of God on the cross reveal the "inner" presence of an intense love in God himself, one that we might describe by the similitude of "vulnerability"?

Mystics such as Catherine of Siena have not hesitated to speak simultaneously both of the unchanging perfection of God's purely actual goodness, and of the vulnerability of God, who is "wounded" by human betrayal.[38] In the twentieth century it was Jacques Maritain who revised this manner of speaking with his notion of a perfection in God's charity and undiminished actuality which is conceptually unnamable, yet which must correspond analogically to what in us are the afflicted passions of love in the presence of evil.[39] While Thomas Weinandy has suggested that this theological motif is compatible with a classical Christian understanding of divine impassibility, Gilles Emery argues (in an essay we have reproduced in this volume) that it is not.[40] In his essay below, Gary Culpepper reinter-

---

ing a stumbling block to the Incarnation, is actually its prolegomenon. It is only because the Son is able to remain immutably himself, as a subsistent relation fully in act, that he is able to come to exist as man, and thus be truly passible as man."

38. St. Catherine in her *Dialogue* speaks in the person of Christ: "It was this human nature in which I was clothed that suffered in me, the Word. But because the two natures are fused with each other, the eternal Divinity took to itself the suffering I bore with such burning love. . . . I showed this in the opening up of my side [on the cross]. There you find my heart's secret and it shows you, more than any finite suffering could, how I love you." (Trans. S. Noffke [New York: Paulist Press, 1980], p. 139.) St. Catherine insists upon the immutable goodness and pure actuality of God, which cannot be attained by any finite disorder (see, for example, pp. 90, 91, 147), even as she claims that God the Holy Spirit *Himself* "weeps" for sin, in and through the members of the Church (p. 169).

39. See Jacques Maritain, *"Un grand problème,"* in *Approches sans Entraves, Œuvres Complètes,* vol. 13 (Fribourg and Paris: Editions Universitaires and Editions Saint Paul), pp. 837-57.

40. See *Does God Suffer?,* pp. 166-67, for Weinandy's qualified acceptance of Maritain's ideas.

prets Maritain in a more radically "passibilist" sense, in contradistinction to the views of Emery. It is of central importance in any renewed treatment of a Christology of the "two natures" of Christ to investigate the ways in which the suffering of the man Jesus are emblematic of his eternal character as the Son, of the divine life which resides within him. To do so, however, would require that one respect the "analogical interval" between God and creation, such that created characteristics are not problematically associated with the immanent life of God. How should these two principles be balanced when it comes to speaking about the "wound of love" in the person of the Son?

Perhaps here we might conclude these reflections by designating a paradox in need of further exploration. The greater the abasement of Christ in his passion, the more the greatness of God's kenotic love is revealed. If one conceives of the two natures of Christ as distinguishable yet analogically coordinated, then the sufferings of the human nature manifest and reveal the perfections of the divine nature without being reducible to the latter. Yet the authentic and inalienable character of Christ's love as God's love is manifest *most intensively* in the voluntary suffering and agony of the Son's crucifixion. Following Walter Kasper, might we not ask if the category of divine "freedom for love" is especially applicable here?[41] One need not oppose a *theologia crucis* and a *theologia gloriae* if the glory of the transcendence of God is a glory of love, and if this glory shines forth above all on the cross of Christ. In this case, Christ's kenotic self-offering in his death reveals God's complete identification with our humanity — and yet hidden within this event is also the victory of a divine transcendent love which becomes fully manifest only in the resurrection. This simultaneity of God's suffering and his transcendent, loving freedom leads us from the mystery of the cross into the question of God's eschatological victory over evil. How does God decide, in Christ, to overcome evil? That is to say, Christology is inextricably wed to theodicy, or perhaps to speak more traditionally, to the designs of God's providence.

41. Consider the thought-provoking words of Walter Kasper from *The God of Jesus Christ* (New York: Crossroad, 1989), p. 195: "God's self-emptying, his weakness and his suffering are not the expression of a lack, as they are in finite beings; nor are they the expression of a fated necessity. If God suffers, then he suffers in a divine manner, that is, his suffering is an expression of his freedom; suffering does not befall God, therefore, rather he freely allows it to touch him. He does not suffer, as creatures do, from a lack of being; he suffers out of love and by reason of his love, which is the overflowing of his being."

III. Human Suffering, Divine Impassibility, and Theodicy

As noted above, no contemporary treatment of divine (im)passibility can fail to mention the seemingly fundamental question of the relationship between God's own suffering and the suffering of human beings. The primary motivation for jettisoning or seriously modifying the classical doctrine of impassibility has been the belief that it is unable to account for what Christianity must say concerning God's response to the mystery of human suffering. Yet, to bring the question of God's relationship to human pain and misery into focus is to recapitulate the foregoing sections within a more ultimate light. What is the relation between God's capacity for (or transcendence of) suffering and his ethical goodness? How does this relationship bear itself out in the mystery of the suffering of Jesus with and on behalf of humanity? The topic of impassibility inevitably confronts us with the question of God's posture before evil and the suffering it brings. Both those who uphold divine impassibility and those who wish to qualify it are required to respond to the questions of God's response to historical evil.

Here the influence of the modern Lutheran tradition must once again be underscored. For contemporary thinkers such as Jüngel, Moltmann, and Jenson who reject the "moral distance" they believe is implied by classical treatments of divine impassibility (albeit in differing ways), God's historicity, suffering, and death in his deity are the necessary preconditions for the redemption of the human being. Taking seriously the essential truth of a traditional theology of the "hypostatic union" for these thinkers means taking seriously not only the historical character of God's very being, but also the entry into the being of God of suffering, death, and nonexistence. This historical becoming of God's own being is a "precondition" of sorts for his christological redemption of man from the powers of evil.[42]

---

42. Consider Jüngel's affirmations (*God as the Mystery of the World,* pp. 346-47, 219): "Where the economic doctrine of the Trinity speaks of God's *history* with man, the immanent doctrine of the Trinity must speak of God's *historicity.* God's history is his coming to man. God's historicity is God's being as it comes (being in coming). We must ponder this seriously if we want to take God's history with man seriously as an event in which God is God. In the process, of course, the immanent doctrine of the Trinity, which considers the historicity of God, must take seriously that God is *our* God. . . . In that God identified himself with the dead Jesus, he located nothingness *within* the divine life. But by making for nothingness a place within divine being, God took away from it the chaotic effect of its phantomlike at-

In other words, God's solidarity with us in passibility is an essential element of both his own true identity as God, and of his soteriological triumph over evil. Humanity not only has a divine companion in its suffering, but it is precisely God's freely chosen involvement in the full depths of suffering through the cross of the Son that brings salvation.

As David Bentley Hart has pointed out, however, questions do arise concerning both the ontological and ethical adequacy of this popular theological motif. If God is (or becomes) who he is only in and through a historical subjection to suffering and death in his own being, then the immanent Trinity risks being identified in some sense with the Christian economy (or vice versa).[43] Something like a "theopanism" results in which God is portrayed as a kind of "ontic" being of limitation situated amidst other beings, even while he is the principle of their cohesion (the "supreme being") through whom they have their internal narrative coherence.[44] What ethical ramifications follow from the affirmation of such a "historical life" within God? According to Hart, if God is indeed determined in his identity by the becoming of his very being among us as a subject of historical evil, then suffering and death, and even moral malice are in some sense "ontologically necessary" in order for the Christian God to be God in Christ.[45] While the modern unequivocal affirmation of the suffering of God was originally intended to acknowledge the compassion of God with regards to all human suffering, Hart raises the serious possibility of this approach implicating God in the very existence and severity of the evils

---

traction. . . . God is one who can bear and does bear, can suffer and does suffer, in his being the annihilating power of nothingness, even the negation of death, without being annihilated by it. In God nothingness loses its negative attraction and thus its annihilating effect."

43. See Hart's "No Shadow of Turning: On Divine Impassibility," pp. 188-93. The criticism is restated by Weinandy in this volume with regard to the theology of Jenson. Jenson in turn offers an important defense of his own position with respect to this criticism.

44. Hart, "No Shadow of Turning: On Divine Impassibility," p. 190.

45. Hart, "No Shadow of Turning: On Divine Impassibility," p. 191: "As many of the fathers would have argued, a God who can by nature experience finite affects and so be determined by them is a God whose identity is established through a commerce with evil; if the nature of God's love can be in any sense positively shaped by sin, suffering, and death, then sin, suffering, and death will always be in some sense features of who he is. Among other things, this means that evil must enjoy a certain independent authenticity, a reality with which God must come to grips, and God's love must — if it requires the negative pathos of history to bring it to fruition — be inherently deficient, and in itself a fundamentally reactive reality. Goodness then requires evil to be good; love must be goaded into being by pain."

suffered by humanity since they become in some sense constitutive of the identity of God. Accordingly, the rejection of impassibility in the cause of greater divine involvement in suffering ends up ironically giving evil an ultimate divine sanction.

However one responds to Hart, it would seem that Christian theologians must be prepared to maintain that in some unmitigated sense God is absolutely transcendent of creation — and of creation's evils — even in the midst of the divine economy. However, to acknowledge his transcendence with regard to the mystery of evil in creatures is also to accept a return to classical ontology in some steadfast fashion and a confrontation with formidable metaphysical and theological enigmas it has created for Christian theologians and believers throughout history. For while classical theology has attempted to alert us to the mystery of God's necessary transcendent omnipotence in the face of evil, it has also generated not a few serious difficulties with regard to the problem of God's actual causality, human freedom, and the permissions of evil. If God is not a being among beings but the origin of all beings, then what is his relationship to those beings that originate from him when they fall far from God, conceal the truth, and commit serious sin or murder? If human suffering (and the suffering of God) are in some way related to the original misuses of human freedom through sin, then what relationship ought we to postulate between the "impassible" goodness and freedom of God (a God who is truly transcendent) and the finitude of human beings who have freely fallen away from his goodness?

The question has of course been ferociously debated in the western Christian tradition, notoriously by Augustine and Pelagius, Calvinists and Armenians, Banezians and Molinists, and in a host of less remarkable instances.[46] Does an affirmation of the pure actuality of God as the primary cause of creation necessarily entail some kind of implicit determinism with respect to human moral evil? Does evil occur only as the result of an "antecedent permissive will" in God, by which God decrees "prior to any foreseen demerits" to allow the creature to fall into sin, in view of its subsequent punition and damnation (or redemption)? And if so, does this avoid making the impassible God the implicit author of human suffering and evil *precisely because he transcends suffering and evil?*

---

46. See in this respect the informative historical studies by Henri Rondet, *The Grace of Christ* (New York: Newman Press, 1968); Stephen Duffy, *The Dynamics of Grace: Perspectives in Theological Anthropology* (Collegeville, Minn.: Liturgical Press, 1993).

Here Jacques Maritain's twentieth-century "protest" against any form of monotheistic "determinism" and the controversies it spawned within Thomism are of immediate relevance. For what Maritain perceived (or thought he perceived) as the deterministic character of a certain school of Baroque Thomism led him to answer "no" to the first of the above-mentioned questions, "yes" to the third, and therefore "no" to the second. In other words, Maritain thought that one could understand God as the unique cause of all created existence and liberty, while avoiding determinism as an outcome. Correspondingly he maintained that the absolute causality of God need not and must not entail that God is responsible *in his transcendence* for the creaturely occasions of moral evil. As a consequence, the French philosopher developed his particular theory of the "innocence" of the transcendent God who sustains in being all created free agents, even when they misguidedly refuse his inspirations and "movements" of grace. God in his omnipotence, therefore, "permits" moral evil, even as it contradicts in some real sense his divine will for the salvation of spiritual creatures.[47] The important debate this theory gave rise to is still of great relevance. For there are two extremes in Christian theodicy which are still prevalent: an Augustinian theory of reprobation of human beings "prior to their foreseen demerits" and an Origenist theory of the universal recapitulation of all *(apokatastasis panton) despite* their demerits. In both cases, the determination of each human being before God (whether "before" or "after" sin) is ultimately dependent only upon the infinite will of God, the final arbiter of the mystery of human freedom. Evil and its conse-

---

47. See in particular Maritain's *Existence and the Existent* (New York: Vintage Books, 1966), *God and the Permissions of Evil* (Milwaukee: The Bruce Publishing Co., 1966), *The Sin of the Angel* (Westminster: Newman Press, 1959), and the complementary work by Charles Journet, *The Meaning of Evil* (New York: P. J. Kenedy, 1963). Important criticisms of Maritain's ideas were offered by Jean-Hervé Nicolas in his essays "La permission du péché," *Revue Thomiste* 60 (1960), vols. 1, 2, and 4 (pp. 5-37; 185-206; 509-46), as well as in his later article, "La volonté salvifique de Dieu contrariée par le péché," *Revue Thomiste* 92 (1992): 177-96, where he largely embraces Maritain's way of thinking. More recently, Steven A. Long in his "Providence, liberté et loi naturelle," *Revue Thomiste* 102 (2002): 355-406, has developed criticisms similar to those of the early Nicolas. See also the critique of the Maritainian position by Gilles Emery in his chapter "The Question of Evil and the Mystery of God in Charles Journet," in *Trinity, Church and the Human Person* (Naples, Fla.: Sapientia Press, 2007). A theological defense of the Maritainian position has been offered by Thomas Joseph White in his "Von Balthasar and Journet on the Universal Possibility of Salvation and the Twofold Will of God," *Nova et Vetera*, English Edition 4 (2006): 633-66.

quences, in each case, seem to somehow lose their seriousness — or even their reality — in the face of eschatology. Human freedom — and the suffering that has resulted from its misuse — risk being seen "in the end" to have been as if nothing before the all-determining prerogatives of the transcendent actuality of God.

Should theology rehabilitate, then, the admission of an ontologically autonomous state in the creature before God? Here the modern Hegelian motifs and the more scholastic viewpoints of Molinism would seem to coincide felicitously in affirming such autonomy.[48] Perhaps in God's own history, he is both determined by others as well as determining. Is God progressively altered by reactions to human beings even as they are themselves molded by his prerogatives? Such thoughts lead down the road toward process theology, Open Theism, and so many other attempts to revive the theories of a good but in some way limited, or self-limiting, God who calculates "strategically" with respect to the future of creation.[49]

Given the failure of any of these options to gain widespread acceptance amongst theologians, it is perhaps best to return to the main route of classical ontology and seek perspective there where it is to be found traditionally: in the metaphysics of participation. This is the argument of David Hart in this volume. Following the reflections of several contemporary Thomists, he argues that God is rightly understood by Aquinas as the transcendent source of a participated but real human agency, which is distinct

48. For a vigorous recent defense of the Molinist construal of divine government, see Thomas P. Flint, *Divine Providence: The Molinist Account* (Ithaca and London: Cornell University Press, 1998).

49. Reflections of this sort have arisen within American evangelicalism surrounding the so-called "Open Theism" movement. In an effort to fashion a more biblical and less "Hellenistic" view of God, and one that better protects God from any complicity with evil, the Open Theists have argued that the Christian God allows the free will of his creatures to determine aspects of human history, but only as part of God's overall plan to redeem his creation in Christ. Prominent works by Open Theists include John Sanders, *The God Who Risks: A Theology of Providence,* 2nd rev. ed. (Downers Grove, Ill.: InterVarsity Press, 2007); Clark Pinnock, *The Most Moved Mover: A Theology of God's Openness* (Grand Rapids: Baker, 2001), and Gregory A. Boyd, *God of the Possible: A Biblical Introduction to the Open View of God* (Grand Rapids: Baker, 2000). For criticisms of this approach see *Bound Only Once: The Failure of Open Theism,* ed. Douglas Wilson (Moscow, Idaho: Canon Press, 2001); Bruce W. Ware, *Their God Is Too Small: Open Theism and the Undermining of Confidence in God* (Wheaton: Crossway Books, 2003), and John Frame, *The Doctrine of God: A Theology of Lordship* (Phillipsburg, N.J.: P. & R. Publishing, 2003).

from him, always being received from him, and yet simultaneously self-determining.[50] In this case, all that is in the creature is truly given by God, with the important exception of moral evil. Precisely in virtue of the "gift" of its capacity for moral self-determination, the creature can freely defect from God's desire for its good, even while depending upon God for its being. One can attach to this idea the traditional Augustinian notion that to act out evil in freedom is (on some level of one's being) to diminish one's existence. Such a perverse use of autonomy (alas in no way rare) is permitted by God and insofar as it exists even sustained in being by him despite its destructive import. The irreducible horror of evil is that it occurs in spite of and over and against the prerogatives of God's will, even if it does not occur as something "outside" the scope of his omnipotence and creative agency.[51]

Thinking this way allows one, we believe, to maintain with integrity a twofold truth: sin and suffering have entered the world through the initiative of the creature, such that there is even a real possibility of final loss (damnation) which threatens every human being. Yet the God of Jesus Christ is a God of divine innocence who wills the salvation of all. He has no complicity with moral evil, even when he mysteriously upholds in being freely disobedient creatures. His transcendence of all evil is most manifest, however, not simply when he maintains creatures in being, but rather when he kenotically enters into the mystery of human suffering himself. Here the triumph of his resurrected life demonstrates the absolute prerogatives of divine love — in all its transcendence and splendor — against the backdrop of a fallen but redeemed human world. We conclude this volume with the theological and spiritual reflections on this theme by Avery Cardinal Dulles. His wizened and balanced meditation on the human condition examines the scope of potential responses to the mystery of suffering, and centers ultimately on the perspective that is proper to the Christian.

---

50. See in this respect the works of Bernard Lonergan, *Grace and Freedom* and *Gratia Operans,* in vol. 1 of *The Collected Works of Bernard Lonergan* (Toronto: University of Toronto Press, 2000); David Burrell, *Freedom and Creation in Three Traditions* (Notre Dame: University of Notre Dame Press, 1993); Brian Shanley, "Divine Causation and Human Freedom in Aquinas," *American Catholic Philosophical Quarterly* 72, no. 1 (1998): 99-122.

51. See the complementary argumentations to this effect by David Hart in his *The Doors of the Sea: Where Was God in the Tsunami?* (Grand Rapids: Eerdmans, 2005).

Conclusion

These comments are overarching and introductory. The authors we have presented in this volume have each worked for many years in sustained ways on the challenging issues that we have briefly alluded to above. Clearly their contributions cannot be considered final moments in what is bound to be a continuing contemporary conversation. However, taken together they exemplify, we believe, a new moment in the ongoing quest to do conceptual justice to the nature of the God revealed in Jesus Christ considered in light of the mystery of human suffering. Although there is no shortage of disagreement, each author demonstrates a desire to get beyond a mere trading in affirmations of the traditional teaching of divine impassibility and curt dismissals of it. Rather, the debates into which their essays initiate us are instructive for their subtlety and make clear that much is at stake in the treatment of "impassibility" in contemporary Christian doctrine. One cannot approach the issue on a profound level without at once touching upon central themes of ontology, classical Christology, and the Christian doctrine of providence. To seek to understand better God and the mystery of suffering therefore obliges us to think more clearly about a dense constellation of Christian theological positions. These doctrinal "puzzle pieces" must be moved in contiguity with one another incessantly, and affect the interpretation of one another reciprocally. Moreover, the question of how God relates to human suffering is an acutely existential question, affecting deeply how we face adversity with faith, both in our own lives and — perhaps more poignantly — in the lives of others. To reflect theologically on the question of the suffering of God, then, is to think seriously theologically. And this is one way (one among others to be sure, but a central one all the same) to acknowledge integrally, in the depth of our person, the God revealed in Jesus Christ. Let this be our task above all.

The Immutability of the God of Love and the Problem of Language Concerning the "Suffering of God"

Gilles Emery, O.P.

Both contemporary theology and the preaching associated with it seem to accord an ever-increasing place to the theme of the "suffering" of the triune God.[1] In various places this theme has also found its way into liturgical ceremonies (I have had the experience myself) where new hymns glorify God for his suffering, or celebrate the "separation" of the Father and the Son on the cross. This puts into question in profound ways the traditional affirmation of the immutability and impassibility of God.

In previous years the passibility of God has been discussed in conjunction with criticisms of the classical divine attribute of immutability. In contemporary theology it seems to have acquired for numerous theologians the status of a fundamental axiom. The theme of the "passion" of God is inscribed, in effect, into the very foundations of discourse concerning the mystery of the triune God and Jesus Christ. This has occurred in an increasingly expansive way, and beyond confessional distinctions. Without revisiting in detail the criticisms of this trend which can be posed from a metaphysical perspective,[2] and without entering into a profound theological consideration of human suffering, I propose to sketch out here some of the principal stages of the teaching of the Church (I), then examine certain

---

1. A previous version of this essay appeared in *Nova et Vetera* (French edition) 74 (1999): 5-37, entitled, "L'immutabilité du Dieu d'amour et les problèmes du discours sur la 'souffrance de Dieu.'" It has been translated by Thomas Joseph White with the generous permission of the editors of that journal. This translation includes citations from French or Latin sources rendered into English, unless otherwise stated.

2. See in particular Jean-Hervé Nicolas, "Aimante et bienheureuse Trinité," *Revue Thomiste* 78 (1978): 271-91.

aspects of the uneasiness that the traditional teaching elicits today (II). After this I will describe various forms of reflection developed by contemporary theologians (III), in order to discuss them in light of the teaching of St. Thomas Aquinas (IV).

I. A Christological and Trinitarian Doctrine

The articulation of a doctrine of divine *immutability* obviously does not constitute a novelty in the history of theology, particularly within the context of christological and trinitarian reflection. That such is the case is apparent from a consideration of the origins of the dogmatic teaching of the Church. It is important to note in this respect the constancy of the teaching of the Church: divine immutability is a traditional doctrine to the extent that it is part of the *tradition* of the faith of the Church. In demonstrating this constancy, I would also like to recall some of what is at stake in the patristic teaching.

When the Fathers gathered in council at Nicea in 325 to affirm the Catholic faith in the true divinity of Christ, they firmly excluded the idea that God might be "subject to change and alteration." The first ecumenical council explicitly rejected the Arian doctrine of a "becoming" of the Son ("there once was when he was not"), and it equally excluded the idea of an "alteration" and of a "change" in the Son of God as such. Arius had appealed to biblical texts showing the weaknesses of Jesus (hunger, thirst, sadness, etc.) in order to reject the eternity of the Son and his equality with the Father.[3] In the wake of Nicea, St. Athanasius of Alexandria made a noteworthy distinction between, on the one hand, that which belonged to Christ as the Word of the Father, and, on the other hand, "the infirmities ascribed to Him because of the flesh" he took from Mary.[4]

The affirmation of the Fathers at Nicea had the merit of possessing a clarity equal to that of Arius's thought: if the Son does not possess the immutability that is proper to the one and eternal God, then he must in fact be a creature. Confronted with a heresy that affirmed precisely the

3. Norman P. Tanner, ed., *Decrees of the Ecumenical Councils,* 2 vols. (Washington, D.C.: Georgetown University Press, 1990), vol. 1, p. 5.

4. St. Athanasius, *Orations Against the Arians* III, 29-35 (*PG* 26, 385-97); see Lewis Ayres, *Nicaea and Its Legacy: An Approach to Fourth-Century Trinitarian Theology* (Oxford: Oxford University Press, 2004), pp. 111-14.

non-eternity of the Son and that understood his generation as a kind of becoming (non-eternity → becoming → creaturehood), the affirmation of the impassibility and immutability of the Word in his divine nature became a central tenet of orthodoxy. The council presupposed here a reflection that the Apostolic Fathers and Apologists had already clearly formulated, based on their reading of Scripture: God, being perfectly transcendent, is impassible *(apathes)* and possesses a perfect freedom. Creation and the incarnation do not alter his immutability. Yet, just as the affirmation of divine incomprehensibility is not to be equated with irrationality, so God's immutability should not be thought of as inactivity: God acts by a voluntary impulsion from within rather than being swayed from without. The immutability that is proper to God guarantees precisely the *transcendence* and the *perfection of his free action*.[5] The rejection of "Arian" anthropomorphism regarding the generation of the Son further developed and deepened this reflection.

From this point on in conciliar history one can observe a consistent affirmation of divine *immutability* and *impassibility*, which are both seen to be connected with faith in the triune God and with the incarnate Son. In A.D. 382, shortly after Constantinople I, while a new synod in the imperial city was explicitly affirming the consubstantiality of the Holy Spirit, a Roman council indicated what is key for understanding the passion of the Word: "If anyone says that in the passion of the cross it is God himself who felt the pain and not the flesh and the soul which Christ, the Son of God, had taken to himself — the 'form of a servant' which he had accepted as Scripture says [cf. Phil. 2:7] — he is mistaken."[6] This dogmatic canon from the *Tome of Damasus* honors fully the true passion of the incarnate Word: this passion is ascribed to him by virtue of his human nature and not by virtue of his divinity, which remains transcendent of suffering. (This implies that it is necessary to distinguish between the *person* and the *natures* of the incarnate Word.) The clarifications adduced by later councils further developed this same structure of understanding.

Similarly the Second Letter of St. Cyril of Alexandria to Nestorius recognized that "by nature the Word of God is of itself incorruptible

---

5. George L. Prestige, *God in Patristic Thought* (London: SPCK, 1952), pp. 6-9.

6. Denzinger, #166 (*Enchiridion symbolorum definitionum et declarationum*, ed. Henricus Denzinger and Adolfus Schönmetzer, Editio xxxvi emendata [Freiburg im Breisgau: Herder, 1971], p. 69).

(aphtartos)." It was ratified and "canonized" as an authentic expression of the Catholic faith by the Council of Ephesus in 431. If one must "confess" unequivocally that the Word of God suffered, it is because "the Impassible *(ho apathes)* was in a passible body." The Catholic faith affirms that the Word suffered because the Word made the flesh "his own," by virtue of the "hypostatic union." Recalling the indispensable distinction between the (divine) nature of the Word and his humanity (the "flesh"), St. Cyril (and Ephesus) indicates that which the Word assumed for us (the "flesh," the passion, death) and simultaneously reasserts clearly the theological reason for the impassibility of the Word as regards his divinity: "For the divine, being without a body *(asomaton)*, is impassible *(apathes)*."[7]

In the western tradition, this conviction is equally manifest, as is witnessed some years later in the *Tome to Flavian* of St. Leo the Great: God is by nature immutable *(incommutabilis)* and impassible *(impassibilis)*. By the assumption of human nature, "The God who knows no suffering *(impassibilis Deus)* did not despise becoming a suffering man *(homo passibilis)."* St. Leo states clearly that the incarnation took place in the *person* of the Son, so that "the proper character of both natures was maintained" *(salva igitur proprietate utriusque naturae),* which implies that the divine nature did not lose its impassibility.[8]

Substantially the same teaching is found in the Council of Chalcedon in 451. Deepening the expression of the doctrine of the two natures in the one person of Christ, Chalcedon wards off the danger of a division of the two natures (Nestorianism), but rejects also the monophysite confusion of those who "fantastically suppose that in the confusion the divine nature of the Only-begotten is passible *(pathetes)."*[9] Following St. Leo, the dogmatic definition affirms that "the property of both natures is preserved," in such a manner that the divine nature and the human nature are united "with no change" *(atreptos)* in the person of the incarnate Son.[10] One should not be

---

7. Council of Ephesus, Second Letter of Cyril to Nestorius, in: *Decrees of the Ecumenical Councils,* vol. 1, p. 42. (I slightly modified this translation.) On this, see the remarkable study of Paul L. Gavrilyuk, *The Suffering of the Impassible God: The Dialectics of Patristic Thought* (Oxford: Oxford University Press, 2004); cf. my review in *Revue Thomiste* 107 (2007): 154-57.

8. St. Leo the Great, Letter to Flavian, in *Decrees,* vol. 1, pp. 78-79.

9. Council of Chalcedon, "Definition of the Faith," in *Decrees of the Ecumenical Councils,* vol. 1, p. 84.

10. Council of Chalcedon, "Definition of the Faith," in *Decrees of the Ecumenical Councils,* vol. 1, p. 86.

astonished, then, that Chalcedon expressly "expels from the assembly of the priests those who dare to say that the divinity of the Only-begotten is passible *(pathetes)*."[11]

The interpretation of Chalcedon by Constantinople II in the sixth century clarified the orthodox sense of the formula of the Scythian monks: "One of the Holy Trinity suffered." The union of divinity and humanity in Christ does not occur within the natures, but is accomplished in the hypostasis, in such a way that the properties of each nature remain what they are, without confusion. It is truly the person (hypostasis) of the Son who has suffered, but *according to his passible flesh,* as St. Cyril said. It is at this same level — that of the hypostasis — that the communication of properties (or "communication of idioms") transpires. Likewise, it is in this way that one must interpret the pronouncement of the Church: "Our Lord Jesus Christ, who was crucified in his human flesh, is truly God and the Lord of glory and One of the Holy Trinity."[12] The "theopaschite" controversies led to a clarification, then, of the orthodox understanding of the passion of the incarnate Son: the divinity did not suffer and the Son never ceded the impassibility of his divine nature. But for our salvation, the *person* or *hypostasis* of the Son suffered *by virtue of the human nature he had assumed.* Impassible according to his divinity, Christ the Son of God suffered in his flesh.[13]

At the end of the councils of antiquity, the Third Council of Constantinople (680-681) taught that one must recognize two "operations" and two wills in Jesus Christ: an operation and will which are divine, and an operation and a will which are human. This teaching condemned christological "monoenergism" and "monotheletism" by drawing the logical conclusions of Chalcedon's doctrine as regards the integrity of the humanity of the incarnate Son. In the message that the Third Council of Constantinople addressed to the emperor in order to present to him its decision, the council explained that it is necessary to recognize in Christ a human will *distinct* from his divine will for two principal reasons: (1) so as not to abolish that which is essential for our salvation, that is to say the integrity and

---

11. Council of Chalcedon, "Definition of the Faith," in *Decrees of the Ecumenical Councils,* vol. 1, pp. 85-85.

12. Second Council of Constantinople, Anathema 10, in *Decrees of the Ecumenical Councils,* vol. 1, p. 118.

13. Jean Chéné, "Unus de Trinitate passus est," *Recherches de Science Religieuse* 53 (1965): 545-88.

action proper to the humanity of Christ, (2) "and so as not to attribute passions *(ta pathe)* to the divinity."[14]

The affirmation of the immutability and impassibility of the divinity (of the divine nature) qualifies conjointly the totality of the eight first ecumenical councils shared by East and West, recognized today by both the Catholic Church and the Orthodox Churches. This doctrine fully accepts those biblical expressions that attribute to God sentiments and emotions, and demonstrates that in fact divine immutability must be upheld in order to properly interpret these biblical expressions. It seems to me difficult to justify the idea that patristic thought promotes a doctrine of "divine passibility" that one must place *alongside* the doctrine of divine impassibility, that is to say, as an *alternative* to the doctrine of divine impassibility.[15] Rather, one must recognize in the doctrine of divine impassibility a constant teaching, as Paul Gavrilyuk has shown. It plays a key role in interpreting integrally the biblical teaching concerning the activity of God and his profound engagement with our world.[16] At any rate, one can perceive how profoundly the Church has accepted a doctrine of divine impassibility by considering her progressive understanding of both the operation of each nature in Christ (with the attribution of the natures to the hypostasis because of the union), and the consubstantiality of the three divine persons. Synthesizing the reflections of this tradition at the end of the patristic age, John Damascene explains:

14. Council of Constantinople III, Address to the emperor Constantine IV, in *Sacrorum conciliorum nova et amplissima collectio,* ed. Joannes Dominicus Mansi, curantibus Ludovico Petit et Ioanne Baptista Martin, vol. 11 (Paris-Leipzig: H. Welter, 1901), col. 664. Cf. Francis Xavier Murphy and Polycarp Sherwood, *Constantinople II et Constantinople III* (Paris: Editions de l'Orante, 1974), p. 321.

15. Such an interpretation (which is disputable in my opinion) has been upheld by Jürgen Moltmann, *The Trinity and the Kingdom of God: The Doctrine of God* (London: SCM Press, 1981) pp. 21-25; Dominique Gonnet, *Dieu aussi connaît la souffrance* (Paris: Cerf, 1990), pp. 30-37. Cf. Henri Crouzel, "La passion de l'Impassible. Un essai apologétique et polémique du IIIᵉ siècle," in *L'homme devant Dieu: Mélanges offerts au P. Henri de Lubac,* vol. 1 (Paris: Aubier-Montaigne, 1963), pp. 269-79; Hans Urs von Balthasar, *Theo-Drama: Theological Dramatic Theory,* Vol. V: *The Last Act,* trans. Graham Harrison (San Francisco: Ignatius Press, 1998), pp. 216-23; François Varillon, *La souffrance de Dieu* (Paris: Le Centurion, 1975), pp. 46-48.

16. Gavrilyuk, *The Suffering of the Impassible God,* pp. 47-63. The author speaks on this subject of "impassibility as an apophatic qualifier of divine emotions." It seems to me, however, that impassibility does not play merely an "apophatic" role. I will return to this below.

The Word of God itself endured all in the flesh, while his divine nature which alone was passionless remained impassible. For since the one Christ, who is a compound of divinity and humanity, and exists in divinity and humanity, truly suffered, that part which is capable of passion suffered as it was natural it should, but that part which was void of passion did not share in the suffering. . . . Observe, further, that we say that God suffered in the flesh, but never that his divinity suffered in the flesh, or that God suffered through the flesh.[17]

A brief survey of the teaching of the Church after the ancient councils permits one to see that a continuous affirmation of the doctrine is accompanied by a new concern to defend the faith when confronted with the dangers of pantheism. Two historical events merit particular attention in this respect: the councils of Lateran IV and Vatican I. In 1215, at the beginning of the Constitution, *Firmiter,* the Fourth Lateran Council lists immutability among the divine attributes *(Deus . . . incommutabilis . . . Pater et Filius et Spiritus Sanctus).*[18] Immutability is ascribed equally to the Father, to the Son, and to the Holy Spirit. The three divine persons are considered here in their simplicity and single essence *(simplex omnino),* guaranteeing their perfect consubstantiality. In this way, Lateran IV recognizes that the three persons are one and the same "reality" *(res).* The council thus circumvents the tritheism that was suspected to be present in certain formulas of Joachim of Fiore, as well as some pantheistic notions that sprang up within spiritual movements affirming the unity of God and the world.[19]

The reassertion of this doctrine occurred at Vatican I in different circumstances, but it was animated by an analogous concern. Divine immutability, as the text of *Dei Filius* and the canons that follow it show, is affirmed especially in order to underscore the *essential distinction between God and the world* ("God . . . must be declared to be in reality and in es-

17. St. John Damascene, *De Fide Orth.* III, 26 (cf. *PG* 94, 1093-96), trans. S.D.F. Salmond, *Nicene and Post-Nicene Fathers,* vol. 9 (Oxford: James Parker, 1899).

18. *Decrees of the Ecumenical Councils,* vol. 1, p. 230.

19. See Raymonde Foreville, *Lateran I, II, III, IV* (Paris: Editions de l'Orante, 1965), pp. 280-86. Among others in the beginning of the thirteenth century, Almaricus of Bène and David of Dinant stand out for their famous "pantheistic notions," for which they were commonly reproached, e.g., "God and the universe are one," "the world is God"; cf. St. Thomas Aquinas, *Summa theologiae* I, q. 3, a. 8: Here Thomas Aquinas rejects the notion that one might identify God with the formal principle of all things, or that one might consider God as primary matter.

sence [*re et essentia*] distinct from the world"), and in order to show the *transcendence* of the God who is "supremely happy in himself and from himself." The council rejects pantheism not only in its extreme versions, but also in its more subtle forms. It refuses the notion that God might acquire a greater perfection or a greater happiness from creation or by means of action within the world. The idea that God, by his engagement with the world, might be subject to becoming, and the claim that God "constitutes" the world in and through his own self-determination, are also criticized.[20] From the perspective of the council, the affirmation of divine immutability is deeply related to the transcendent *simplicity* and perfect unity of God (as at Lateran IV), and denotes the unconditioned *freedom* and *gratuity* of the act of creation. The conciliar text considers in particular creation, but the affirmation can be extended to the whole of the works of God in the world (creation and grace).

This brief consideration of the teaching of the Church in various councils manifests three principal ideas which incorporate the doctrine of divine immutability: (1) the perfect *consubstantiality* of the three persons in their divine unity, (2) *the union without mixture and without confusion* of the divinity and the humanity in the person of Christ (his consubstantiality with the Father and the Holy Spirit is not ruptured by the truth of his incarnation and his passion), and (3) *the simplicity and transcendence* of the three divine persons in their action of creation and redemption. These acquisitions of the tradition are essential notions that must guide theological reflection. Correspondingly, this survey of the teaching of the councils of the Church suggests that if one abandons the affirmation of divine immutability and impassibility, a rupture with the tradition is inevitable.

---

20. *Decrees of the Ecumenical Councils*, vol. 2, pp. 805-6 and 809-10. The fourth canon denies that "the divine essence, by the manifestation and evolution of itself, becomes all things," and that "God is a universal or indefinite being which by self-determination establishes the totality of things." Though the council does not mention any particular author, its critique of pantheism pertains to theological doctrines notably influenced by Spinoza, Hegel, and Schelling; cf. Hermann J. Pottmeyer, *Der Glaube vor dem Anspruch der Wissenschaft: Die Konstitution über den katholischen Glauben "Dei Filius" des ersten Vatikanischen Konzils und die unveröffentlichen theologischen Voten der vorbereitenden Kommission* (Freiburg: Herder, 1968).

II. Uneasiness in the Face of Divine Immutability

Numerous factors contribute today to a widespread intellectual discomfort with the traditional doctrine of divine immutability. I will limit myself here to noting three "themes" that appear in diverse forms with various authors. This schematic grouping, then, is not composed of detailed argumentations, but is simply meant to sketch out the general horizon of the question.

1. Philosophical Influences

A first theme concerns the question of the encounter between philosophy and biblical teaching. Often one reproaches the traditional doctrine for having adopted pagan, non-biblical representations of God in an insufficiently critical manner. Here one habitually cites Plotinus and Proclus on this subject, but also Aristotle (the "unmoved mover") and Plato. The assimilation of this philosophical heritage by the Christian theological tradition is criticized for having led to an affirmation of the self-sufficiency of God, his simplicity and immutability, in such a way as to obscure the "living God" of the Bible. In the latter we witness a vitality, a mercy, and interaction in history even to the point of the offering of the Son on the cross. If the father of the parable narrated in Luke 15 is moved to pity in his heart for the prodigal son, is this not the very expression of the feelings that God experiences toward sinners whose salvation he so passionately desires? Behind the critique of the thesis of divine *apatheia*, often it is the conception of God as "substance" that one finds is most contested.[21] The critique extends sometimes to a more radical level, to the "metaphysics of being" as such, for which one proposes to substitute a "metaphysics of becoming." This philosophical debate, at times articulated in very learned ways,[22] is also frequently reproduced in a truncated, popularized form so as to establish the suffering of God: "In the order of

---

21. See, for example, Moltmann, *The Trinity and the Kingdom of God,* pp. 10-12 ("God as Supreme Substance"); Gisbert Greshake, *Der dreieine Gott: Eine trinitarische Theologie* (Freiburg: Herder, 1997), pp. 340-49.

22. See Hans Küng, *The Incarnation of God: An Introduction to Hegel's Theological Thought as Prolegomena to a Future Christology* (Edinburgh: T. & T. Clark, 1987), pp. 518-25 and 530-38.

being, suffering is an imperfection. But in the order of love, suffering is the seal of perfection."[23]

To avoid the peril of a problematic anthropomorphism, some theologians seek help from the philosophical resources of Hegel, whose thought is considered advantageous in this domain in at least two ways. First, his theory of the self-expression of Absolute Spirit is employed to express the mutually constitutive relationship that God undertakes with history. Second, Hegelian thought allows one to conceive of a divine self-differentiation with a distinctly trinitarian structure in such a way so as to contrast the trinitarian God precisely with the conception of God as "immovable." Among other passages, a text from the *Encyclopedia of the Philosophical Sciences* (1830) on the concept of Spirit *(Begriff des Geistes)* seems to clearly illustrate this idea:

> Christian theology, too, conceives of God, that is, of Truth, as spirit *(Geist)* and contemplates this, not as something quiescent *(nicht als ein Ruhendes),* something abiding in empty identicalness but as something which necessarily enters into the process of distinguishing itself from itself, of positing its Other, and which comes to itself only through this Other, and by positively overcoming it *(durch die erhaltende Aufhebung)* — not by abandoning it. Theology, as we know, expresses this process in picture-thinking by saying that God the Father (this simple universal or being-within-self), putting aside his solitariness, creates Nature (the being that is external to itself, outside of itself), begets a Son (his other "I"), but in the power of his love beholds in this Other himself, recognizes his likeness therein and in it returns to unity with himself; but this unity is no longer abstract and immediate, but a concrete unity mediated by the moment of difference; it is the Holy Spirit which proceeds from the Father and the Son, reaching its perfect actuality and truth in the community of Christians.[24]

One can readily perceive in this brief text the connection of multiple aspects of the question that concerns us: divine immutability is replaced

---

23. Varillon, *La souffrance de Dieu*, p. 71: "Dans l'ordre de l'être, la souffrance est une imperfection. Dans l'ordre de l'amour, elle est le sceau de la perfection."

24. *Hegel's Philosophy of Mind: Part Three of the Encyclopaedia of the Philosophical Sciences (1830),* trans. William Wallace (Oxford and New York: Clarendon Press, 1971), p. 12. Cf. G. W. F. Hegel, *Werke,* vol. 10: *Enzyklopädie der philosophischen Wissenschaften,* ed. E. Moldenhaur and K. M. Michel (Frankfurt am Main: Suhrkamp, 1970), p. 23. On Hegel's trinitarian thought, see Greshake, *Der dreieine Gott,* pp. 136-41.

by a constitution of the divine through a dialectical process of differentiation. This is expressed in manifestly trinitarian language referring to the
divine processions and the "economy" (i.e., creation and history). Recourse to Hegel requires that theologians maintain certain critical reservations, but one cannot fail to detect his influence behind the progressive
"historicization" of God in contemporary thought. His ideas also affect a
good number of kenotic theologians (we will consider some examples below) and those who posit a "becoming" in God.[25] In a related domain, Hegelian thought has had an equally important influence upon certain theological positions concerning the "immanent Trinity" and the "economic
Trinity," at times in a radical fashion. Piet Schoonenberg, for example, illustrates our theories in a striking manner. For him, the economic relations of the Trinity (the relations of the triune God with the world and
with human beings) *are,* in a rigorous sense, the immanent relations of the
Trinity such that the Father, the Son, and the Holy Spirit must be characterized *first and foremost* by their relations with us and only in turn by their
mutual relations. For it is within the economic Trinity alone, that is to say,
in God's historical action, that God appears as tri-personal. Yet, if we abstract from the history of salvation, is God a Trinity in himself? The very
question of whether the trinitarian being of God exists independently of
the history of salvation is dismissed in the name of divine dipolarity; of the
relationship between the immutability of God and his free self-
determination we can know nothing.[26]

On another level, the idea of a God engaged in becoming is very present in the *process theology* inspired by Alfred N. Whitehead, which applies
to God the notions of act and potency (consciously repudiating the non-
composition and immutability of God). In continuity with his philosophy
of science, Whitehead distinguishes between a "primordial nature" and a
"consequent nature" in God.[27] While the primordial nature of God is

25. See Küng, *The Incarnation of God,* pp. 538-58. Küng presents a very interesting pan-
orama of the influences of Hegel upon other authors: kenotic theologies of the twentieth
century, D. Bonhoeffer, K. Barth, K. Rahner, H. U. von Balthasar, E. Jüngel, J. Moltmann, etc.
On the question of the immutability and the eternity of God, see Emilio Brito, "Dieu en
mouvement? Thomas d'Aquin et Hegel," *Revue des Sciences Religieuses* 62 (1988): 111-36;
Emilio Brito, *Dieu et l'être d'après Thomas d'Aquin et Hegel* (Paris: Presses Universitaires de
France, 1991), pp. 157-80.

26. Piet Schoonenberg, "Trinität — Der vollendete Bund," *Orientierung* 37 (1973): 115-17.

27. Alfred N. Whitehead, *Process and Reality: An Essay in Cosmology* (Cambridge: Cam-

"conceptual" and "actually deficient," the consequent nature of God is "determined" and "fully actual." This dipolar theory implies a "passage" of the actuality of things in God's nature, in which "the complete adjustment of the immediacy of joy and suffering reaches the final end of creation."[28]

We must avoid drawing comparisons that are superficial. Influences of a philosophical kind upon theologians are often quite nuanced, and ideas are frequently reworked in a critical manner within original, new syntheses. Nonetheless, it is also fitting to pay close attention to the dialectical resources put to work within various theories of divine passibility.

2. The Relational Character of the Covenant

Divine immutability seems problematic to many Christians on a theological and spiritual plane, especially when one considers the relational character of the covenant that God sustains with his children. Can this notion permit us to give an authentic account of the "partnership" between God and human beings (i.e., his people, the Church, sinners saved by his mercy)? This criticism focuses in particular upon the scholastic and Thomist doctrine of the *relation between God and the world:* the relation is "real" from the side of creatures *(relatio realis),* while it is one "of reason" from the side of God *(relatio rationis).* The Thomistic doctrine affirms that the action of God always precedes that of creatures. God is the transcendent cause of the relations we maintain with him. Many authors — and

---

bridge University Press, 1929), p. 488: "Thus, analogously to all actual entities, the nature of God is dipolar. He has a primordial nature and a consequent nature. The consequent nature of God is conscious; and it is the realization of the actual world in the unity of his nature, and through the transformation of his wisdom. The primordial nature is conceptual, the consequent nature is the weaving of God's physical feelings upon his primordial concepts." Also on p. 494: "The consequent nature of God is the fulfillment of his experience by his reception of the multiple freedom of actuality into the harmony of his own actualization. It is God as really actual, completing the deficiency of his mere conceptual actuality." Concerning the influence and consequences of this thought (God's self-actualization and co-constitution through the world), see from a critical perspective, William J. Hill, *Search for the Absent God: Tradition and Modernity in Religious Understanding* (New York: Crossroad, 1992), pp. 80-91, 109-11, and 128-41.

28. Whitehead, *Process and Reality,* p. 495: "It is in this way that the immediacy of sorrow and pain is transformed into an element of triumph. This is the notion of redemption through suffering, which haunts the world." Cf. pp. 488-89 and p. 494.

some quite influential — suspect, however, that this idea would not be faithful to the teaching of the Bible, nor to the theological formulations of the Fathers of the Church.[29] For some theologians this doctrine of the relation means "the end of an authentic reciprocity between God and man," since it makes God "indifferent" to our sufferings and prayers. Without positing a "real receptivity" in God, can we authentically envisage a relation and communion of true covenantal *partners?* Can we rightly acknowledge the dialogical structure of revelation and of salvation?[30]

This set of issues raises two questions. The first, which is not unimportant, concerns the experience of faith and piety: Can one pray to an immutable God, invoking him in supplication? Theology cannot ignore this question stemming from the spiritual life. The second question — which is more theoretical (and apologetic) — concerns the origins of contemporary atheism, that is to say, the criticism of "theism" and "deism" of the seventeenth and eighteenth centuries which paved the way to atheism. If the confession of immutability seemed necessary in the past for fear of compromising the transcendence of God, is this concern still appropriate today? For many of our contemporaries, in effect, the chief concern is not to preserve recognition of the transcendence of God. The difficulty resides rather in the idea of a God who does not suffer.[31]

3. The Passion and the Death of Christ

The third and most theologically decisive difficulty concerns trinitarian and christological doctrine with respect to the interpretation of the passion and death of Christ on the cross. Following the teaching of the councils and the Fathers that I sketched out above, "classical" theology has insisted upon the unity of the person of Christ and the duality of his natures: the passion and suffering of Christ are experienced by the *person* of the

29. Balthasar, *Theo-Drama*, Vol. V: *The Last Act*, p. 222 (with an explicit reference to St. Thomas Aquinas). Cf. Küng, *The Incarnation of God*, pp. 531-32.

30. Johannes B. Brantschen, "Die Macht und Ohnmacht der Liebe. Randglossen zum dogmatischen Satz: Gott ist unveränderlich," *Freiburger Zeitschrift für Philosophie und Theologie* 27 (1980): 224-46, here at 225 and 232.

31. Gonnet, *Dieu aussi connaît la souffrance*, pp. 11-12. Several questions are posed here: that of the possibility of access to truth, the contextual character of preaching, the "functionalism" of theological discourse, etc.

Son in virtue of his *human nature.* Yet many authors believe that this interpretation is insufficient, and propose instead to understand Christ's suffering as a "trinitarian event." It is necessary, then, to understand the passion of Jesus in light of a drama affecting the trinitarian relations themselves, such that his passion is related to a "suffering of the Father" who sacrifices his Son, and to the *pathos* of the Holy Spirit. (I return to this idea below.) This interpretation is present at the heart of much of contemporary trinitarian reflection, which is itself conducted in the light of the crucifixion of Christ. It insists upon the properly personal character of the events of the history of salvation, manifest in the Father, Son, and Holy Spirit. In truth, it also confronts theology with the most serious challenges. For such an interpretation requires a profound transformation of the central notions of classical metaphysics (simplicity, eternity, immutability) and of trinitarian doctrine (the unity of the three persons). It does so because it conceives of the historical passion of Christ, and even of the entirety of the divine work of creation and redemption, as a distinctly divine intra-trinitarian "event." Depending upon the interpretation, this event frequently implies intra-divine suffering, or *pathos,* and self-emptying or *kenosis.*

III. The Suffering, Self-Emptying, and "Pathos" of the Triune God in Contemporary Theological Discourse

Faced with these questions, what response is required? Contemporary theological writing offers a variety of answers. In considering principally the speculative aspects of the question, I would like to delineate here, as key examples, some theoretical options that have been proposed by authors seeking alternatives to the traditional doctrine.

1. *Jürgen Moltmann: The Atoning Pain of God*

The work of Jürgen Moltmann, stemming from the tradition of the Reformation, surely represents one of the most radical attempts to develop theological language of the suffering of God.[32] For Moltmann, the patristic

---

32. Cf. Dennis W. Jowers, "The Theology of the Cross as Theology of the Trinity: A Critique of Jürgen Moltmann's Staurocentric Trinitarianism," *Tyndale Bulletin* 52, no. 2 (2001):

affirmation of divine immutability offers no more than a comparison: it signifies not that God is immutable in himself, but only that God is not changed in the same way that the creature is. Accordingly, God is not alterable due to constraint but only through the freedom of his love.[33] The axiom that structures his reflection is that of a strict *theologia crucis:* God only reveals himself under his contrary. The theologian may discover God only in the identification that transpires between God and the passion of Christ. The work of Moltmann, which takes inspiration from that of Karl Barth, is equally informed by a unique vision of theodicy: his theology of the cross and of the Trinity, as well as his doctrine of "divine suffering," seeks to recover the true identity of the Christian faith in reaction against the developments of modern western European "theism," and in the wake of the decline of continental idealism (the "death of God").

Moltmann introduces "kenosis" into his portrayal of the Trinity in a radical fashion. "Jesus' death cannot be understood 'as the death of God,' but only as death *in* God."[34] The interpretation is guided by a Johannine theme: "God is love" (1 John 4:16). Moltmann proposes a trinitarian interpretation of the phrase: "God is love" means that God "constitutes his existence in the event of his love"; "[h]e exists as love in the event of the cross." That which was experienced in the death of Christ was an event between God and God. On the cross, the Son was abandoned by the Father, and the Father's heart was pierced by the witness of the Son's love. "In the cross, Father and Son are most deeply separated in forsakenness and at the same time are most inwardly one in their surrender."[35] The death of Christ is not interpreted in light of the dogma of Chalcedon (in which the death is attributed to the hypostasis by virtue of the human nature), but enters into the very relation of the Son toward the Father, person to person. A key af-

245-66. See also the critical analysis of Moltmann by Jean Galot (Galot is, however, favorable toward a doctrine of divine suffering as common to the three persons): Jean Galot, "Le Dieu trinitaire et la passion du Christ," *Nouvelle Revue Théologique* 104 (1982): 70-87. From a Thomistic perspective: Jean-Hervé Nicolas, "Aimante et bienheureuse Trinité," *Revue Thomiste* 78 (1978): 271-92.

33. Cf. Jürgen Moltmann, *The Crucified God: The Cross of Christ as the Foundation and Criticism of Christian Theology* (London: SCM Press, 1974), pp. 229-30; *The Trinity and the Kingdom of God,* p. 23: "In Christian theology the apathetic axiom only really says that God is not subjected to suffering in the same way as transient, created beings."

34. Moltmann, *The Crucified God,* p. 207.

35. Moltmann, *The Crucified God,* p. 244.

firmation (which we will encounter later in Adrienne von Speyr, with other nuances) summarizes this idea: the relinquishing of the Father's name in Jesus' death cry is "the breakdown of the relationship that constitutes the very life of the Trinity."[36] The kenosis of the cross implies an *annihilation* of the Trinity, to the extent that the relations between the persons are destroyed: "If the Father forsakes the Son, the Son does not merely lose his sonship. The Father loses his fatherhood as well. The love that binds the one to the other is transformed into a dividing curse."[37] This interpretation (which is erroneous in my opinion) is guided by a vision of the cross wherein the Father abandons the Son to a "descent into hell," in such a way that the Son himself experiences the punishment of reprobation. This idea originated in the fifteenth century and was developed by Luther and Calvin.[38] Following them, Moltmann maintains that Christ "exchanged places" with us in our guilt and thus took upon himself the suffering of damnation. The theories of Moltmann, which refer explicitly to Luther, are unambiguous: on the cross, Jesus experienced "the absence of God the Father"; "Jesus endures the God-forsakenness vicariously." "It is *the experience of hell,* as the young Luther so emphatically stressed in his theology of the cross."[39] And because Moltmann abandons here the Chalcedonian distinction between the two natures of Christ, this implies that "Christ's suffering on the cross is human sin transmuted into the atoning suffering of God."[40] "What he suffered is his special *divine* pain."[41]

As concerns the Holy Spirit, he participates as well in the kenosis and suffering *("pneumatologia crucis").* The Spirit's descent upon Jesus at his baptism is seen as a "*self-restriction* and *self-humiliation* of the eternal Spirit"[42] such that Moltmann can affirm the "progressive *kenosis* of the Spirit, together with Jesus."[43] Moreover, the kenosis ("self-emptying") of

36. Moltmann, *The Trinity and the Kingdom of God,* p. 80.
37. Moltmann, *The Trinity and the Kingdom of God,* p. 80.
38. Cf. Léopold Sabourin, "Le bouc émissaire, figure du Christ?", *Sciences Ecclésiastiques* 11 (1959): 45-79. Sabourin shows that this interpretation first appears in the fifteenth century, particularly in Denys the Carthusian (+ 1471).
39. Jürgen Moltmann, *The Spirit of Life: A Universal Affirmation* (London: SCM Press, 1992), p. 65 and p. 136.
40. Moltmann, *The Spirit of Life,* p. 136.
41. Moltmann, *The Spirit of Life,* p. 136.
42. Moltmann, *The Spirit of Life,* p. 61.
43. Moltmann, *The Spirit of Life,* p. 62.

the Spirit appears as the precondition for the self-humiliation of the Son. "We may conclude from this that the story of the suffering of the messianic Son of God is the story of the suffering of God's Spirit too."[44] On Golgotha, "the Spirit suffers the suffering and death of the Son, without dying with him."[45] The cross of Jesus, then, is an event of suffering for the entire Trinity. "It is a single movement of love, welling up out of the Father's pain, manifested in the Son's sufferings, and experienced in the Spirit of life."[46]

This has important consequences for one's notion of God as well as for understanding the divine economy. What we mean by "God" is the unity of the dialectical history of the Father, Son, and Spirit on the cross, a history full of tensions. By "God," we denote not a nature, nor a person, but an "event" *(Geschehen):* "The event of the love of the Son and the grief of the Father from which the Spirit who opens up the future and creates life in fact derives."[47] One is no longer reflecting upon a history governed by God, who intervenes in that history, but rather upon a "history within God." The key to this understanding of the suffering of God is that "it is only through suffering that [love] acts creatively and redemptively for the freedom of the beloved."[48] Thus this system is motivated chiefly by theodicy. Faced with the absolute self-determination of God in his Lordship — such as it is presented by Karl Barth — Moltmann attempts to make room for human freedom, which he sees as threatened by the idealism of an absolute Subject. The latter idea leads to atheism. "Freedom can only be made possible by suffering love."[49]

The difficulties with this theory are particularly acute and underscore the principal problems posed by any theory of the suffering of God if it is carried through to its final logical consequences. The problems here stem from the philosophical resources Moltmann draws upon (e.g., dialectical thought, tensions in God, the historicization of God, an opposition between being and freedom), but also from his theological interpretations. Among these, one might mention the exclusive primacy of the cross, the radicalization of the kenotic interpretation of redemption, infernal tor-

---

44. Moltmann, *The Spirit of Life*, p. 64.
45. Moltmann, *The Spirit of Life*, p. 64.
46. Moltmann, *The Spirit of Life*, p. 137.
47. Moltmann, *The Crucified God*, p. 247.
48. Moltmann, *The Trinity and the Kingdom of God*, p. 60.
49. Moltmann, *The Trinity and the Kingdom of God*, p. 60.

ments inflicted upon Christ, a "functional" interpretation of trinitarian language, and the eradication of the distinction between the eternal being of the Trinity and God's action within the economy. Moltmann attempts to provide an explanation of suffering, but he does so through divinizing suffering and rendering it eternal, as an event that is constitutive of the divine persons.

2. *Sergei Bulgakov: Sophia and Kenosis*

Theologies of divine kenosis must not be confused with theologies of the "suffering of God." Effectively, the affirmation of trinitarian kenoticism does not necessarily imply the affirmation of the suffering of God. Within the context of modern theology, the theme of "divine kenosis" usually signifies that God in his action undergoes a "self-diminution" or a "self-emptying." However, theologians who affirm the "suffering of God" often present their reflection against the backdrop of a divine kenoticism. This is why, even while one must take care not to confuse the notions of "kenosis" and "suffering," it is important to investigate certain theological motifs involving divine kenosis.

Among the currents of twentieth-century thought that emphasize divine kenosis, a place of priority must without doubt be given to Slavic Orthodox thought, which has had an important influence on many Catholic and Protestant authors. It is fitting to allude here to the philosophy of Nikolai Berdyaev, whose (simultaneously philosophical and theological) theories of "theandricism" gave rise to the theme of the *Lamb immolated before the foundation of the world* (combining Rev. 13:8 and 1 Pet. 1:19-20).[50] Among theologians, it is probably the Russian Sergei Bulgakov who has given the doctrine of "trinitarian kenosis" its most striking formulation.

The thought of Bulgakov concerning divine kenosis is related to his original and complex conception of *Sophia,* Wisdom, which is simultaneously *divine* under one aspect and *created* under another. The divine Wisdom, which is the divine itself (the "non-hypostatic essence"), is the idea

---

50. See Xavier Tillette, *Le Christ des philosophes: Du Maître de sagesse au divin Témoin* (Namur: Lessius, 1993), pp. 430-37. The author notes the influence here of Jacob Boehme, in whose thought one discovers already the concept of a "divine dipolarity." The influence of Berdyaev, in turn, upon Jürgen Moltmann is quite remarkable (*The Trinity and the Kingdom of God,* pp. 42-47: "The Tragedy in God").

that governs all of the workings of God.[51] In God, Sophia is God himself; in the created world, it establishes the basis for the development of the creature, and is related to the condition of historical becoming or of a process. Heavenly Sophia and created Sophia are distinguished then by their condition, but they are identical in their content and in their basic foundation. This principle of "sophianity," which excludes a pantheistic confusion of God and the world, explains the conformity that exists between the world and God, the conformity that renders possible the incarnation. The Logos, who possesses by nature the divine Sophia, enters by means of the incarnation into the process of the created becoming of Sophia.

The first economic action of kenosis occurs in the creation, which is conceived as an overflowing of the life of God by a voluntary self-diminution, a metaphysical kenosis with respect to the divinity itself.[52] "The kenosis in creation of God who is the Holy Trinity signifies his self-diminution with respect to his absoluteness. The absolute God, correlated with nothing but himself, becomes correlative with something outside himself."[53] This kenosis consists in the passage from the immobility of the Absolute toward the becoming of the relative; he who is only absolute and not relative becomes relative by the creation. "The absolute God, who exists in himself, self-contained in his absoluteness, self-sufficing in his majesty, abandons this state and establishes in dependence upon his own absolute being a relative creaturely being."[54] The consequence, following the principle of "sophianity," is that we can no longer conceive of "God" without the world, because the notion of "God" is a relative one.[55]

This divine kenosis in creation is first of all that of the Father and of his "sacrifice of love."[56] The Son also undergoes a "self-diminution" in the act of creation. The Word is "immolated" through creation, in identifying with

51. See Sergei Bulgakov, *Sophia: The Wisdom of God* (Hudson, N.Y.: Lindisfarne Press, 1993).

52. See Serge Boulgakov, *Du Verbe incarné: L'Agneau de Dieu,* translation from the Russian by Constantin Andronikof (Lausanne: L'Âge d'Homme, 1982), pp. 48-49. Creation is presented here as a "kenosis of the divinity."

53. Sergius Bulgakov, *The Comforter,* trans. Boris Jakim (Grand Rapids: Eerdmans, 2004), p. 219.

54. Bulgakov, *Sophia: The Wisdom of God,* p. 60.

55. Bulgakov, *Sophia: The Wisdom of God,* p. 60.

56. Bulgakov, *The Comforter,* p. 219: "This self-relativization of the Absolute is the sacrifice of God's love for this other, which He Himself creates out of nothing."

it in order to become within it "the Word of all and within all."[57] This kenosis by the Father is in effect directly related to the Son and the Holy Spirit: "The kenosis of the Father consists in the fact that the Father, who reveals himself eternally in the Son and the Spirit in the divine Sophia, reveals himself in creation — also through the dyad of the Son and the Spirit — in the *creaturely* Sophia."[58] Sanctification, in its principle, is therefore rendered possible by the kenotic presence of Sophia within the created order, who disposes the creature to the action of sanctification. As for the Holy Spirit, his kenosis consists in the creaturely Sophia. "The Holy Spirit, Who is the fullness and depth of Divinity, diminished Himself to *becoming* in His revelation in the creaturely Sophia. . . . The Father, in sending the Spirit in the creative 'let there be,' restrains the Spirit's force and fullness, as it were — if only by the fact that He manifests them in time, in becoming."[59]

It is, however, in the incarnation and in the passion of the Word that the theme of kenosis takes on its full stature. "The kenosis of the Son consists in the fact that He, who is *all* in creation, diminished himself to the human form of being in the divine incarnation, became the God-Man, entered the world as the lamb of God, sacrificed on Golgotha in the fullness of time."[60] Bulgakov refuses recourse to the affirmation of the immutability of God; this notion is of no help since creation and providence imply a relation between God and the world that is "active and reciprocal." It is necessary to recognize therefore (through a reinterpretation of christological perichoresis and the theandric action of Christ) that *the divine essence participates* in the passion of Christ.[61] This affirmation must be nuanced, since the theory is complex. On the one hand, Bulgakov maintains firmly the inviolate permanence of the divine nature, since the kenosis of the Son in the economy of salvation does not affect the being of the Trinity.[62] The Son retains the divine nature, but without its glory (through a divine sacrifice). In

---

57. Boulgakov, *Du Verbe incarné*, p. 49; cf. p. 50: "The Son, the Lamb of God, is eternally 'immolated' through the creation of the world [. . .]." [Translation by the editors.]

58. Bulgakov, *The Comforter*, p. 219.

59. Bulgakov, *The Comforter*, pp. 219-20.

60. Bulgakov, *The Comforter*, p. 219.

61. Boulgakov, *Du Verbe incarné*, pp. 189-90.

62. Bulgakov, *Sophia: The Wisdom of God*, p. 63: "Nothing new is introduced for God by the life of the world of creatures." Cf. p. 89: "It is essential to realize that, contrary to the various kenotic theories of Protestantism, our Lord in his abasement never ceased to be God, the second person of the Holy Trinity."

this sense, the "immanent Trinity" is untouched by the kenosis of the Word, for this kenosis only exists in the "economic Trinity."[63] Yet on the other hand, Bulgakov rejects the idea that the divine nature of Christ, on the cross, is impassible. The impassibility of the divine nature seems incompatible with the "theanthropic" life of the Word incarnate. Bulgakov believes that such a notion of impassibility is a useless or even erroneous product of abstraction. The patristic theory of the impassibility of the divine nature must therefore be "rethought" with the self-diminution of Christ taken as a starting point. In virtue of the perichoresis of the natures in Christ, the divinity of our Lord, while being different from his flesh, participates spiritually in the sufferings of the flesh. For, following Bulgakov, the divine nature cannot fail to suffer if its hypostasis is subjected to suffering.[64] This is why the cross of Christ also engages the other divine persons in a kenotic participation. The mystery of Golgotha takes place in heaven in the heart of the Father — this heart which is the Holy Spirit.[65] It is the "sacrifice of the Father" who offers his only Son in the Holy Spirit.

On the subject of the "sacrificial kenosis of the Father," Bulgakov makes some extremely strong statements that seem to suggest a "mutual exile" of the divine persons and, in a certain sense, a crucifixion of the Trinity. Bulgakov explains that the Father deprives himself of the Son: the Father, at the cross, is without the Son (the Father no longer has a Son), and the Son is without the Father (the Son no longer lives in union with the Father).[66] The crucifixion of the Son sent by the Father becomes, then, their common crucifixion. It is the *crucifixion of the Trinity*. In the human crucifixion of the Son and the divine co-crucifixion of the Father, the very Love of the Father and the Son, the Holy Spirit, is co-crucified.[67]

It seems that there is in Bulgakov's theology a kind of dipolarity concerning divinity and immutability. On the one hand, God, in his plenitude of being, cannot be limited; this divine plenitude cannot be modified. Yet on the other hand, the divine plenitude can be limited, not from without, but by the free will of the divinity. In this way, following Bulgakov, God is immutable in his being (by himself) but can limit or "diminish" this plenitude of life by refusing for himself his own beatitude. It seems to me that

63. Boulgakov, *Du Verbe incarné*, p. 153 (on the kenosis of the Son: pp. 139-74).
64. Boulgakov, *Du Verbe incarné*, p. 188; cf. p. 184.
65. Boulgakov, *Du Verbe incarné*, p. 189.
66. Boulgakov, *Du Verbe incarné*, pp. 288-89.
67. Boulgakov, *Du Verbe incarné*, p. 289.

this dipolarity is based upon the — very modern! — dipolarity of being and freedom. In my opinion, the juxtaposition is problematic and perhaps constitutes one of the fundamental difficulties in Bulgakov's thought. "To attribute to God immobility and immutability in the way that He lives out His nature lessens His absoluteness and His aseity, because one thereby affirms that a necessary law exists for God himself."[68]

It is not easy to formulate a precise judgment concerning a doctrine so complex. Louis Bouyer offers one that is suggestive: "Essentially the most critical thing one can say is that it envelops a series of intuitions of an exceptional depth within a system that is dangerously ambiguous, where divine transcendence appears to be constantly threatened, with the supernatural basis of the revelation riddled by rationalism, or rather, by an impenitent idealism."[69] The theme of the mutual exile of the persons on the cross suggests, in my opinion, a failed comprehension of the mystery of redemption. As for the manner of distinguishing between the being and life (or action) of God, it seems to me to raise equally formidable difficulties concerning divine simplicity.

3. Hans Urs von Balthasar: Kenosis and Substitution

Kenoticism informs Balthasar's understanding of the mystery of Christ and of the Trinity quite profoundly. Here I will only give a brief sketch of some elements that concern the Trinity and the cross of Christ. In his *Theodramatik,* Balthasar presents an important survey of the theme of the "pain of God." In a vast philosophical and theological fresco, Balthasar explores the perspectives of Jean Galot and Jacques Maritain, whom I refer to below.[70] And yet it is the influence of Bulgakov that I would like to underscore, in

---

68. Boulgakov, *Du Verbe incarné,* p. 148. [Translation by the editors.]

69. Louis Bouyer, *Le Fils éternel: Théologie de la Parole de Dieu et christologie* (Paris: Cerf, 1974), p. 465. [Translation by the editors.] Bouyer notes in particular, alongside the Slavic influences, that of Hegel (p. 463). On the kenoticism of Bulgakov, see Paul Henry, "Kénose, V. Théologie de la kénose," in *Supplément au Dictionnaire de la Bible,* vol. 5 (Paris: Letouzey et Ané, 1957), col. 144-56. (See also col. 136-44 on the Lutheran, Anglican, and Orthodox precedents for this doctrine.)

70. Hans Urs von Balthasar, *Theo-Drama: Theological Dramatic Theory,* Vol. V: *The Last Act,* trans. Graham Harrison (San Francisco: Ignatius Press, 1998), pp. 212-46: "The pain of God."

considering other works of Balthasar. In effect, Balthasar borrows from Bulgakov many central elements of the theology of kenosis (kenosis in the Trinity, in creation, and on the cross), "while avoiding his sophiological excesses."[71] At the heart of his multifaceted theory is the thesis of the "selflessness *(Selbstlosigkeit)* of the divine persons."[72] The ultimate presupposition of the divine kenosis is the selflessness of the divine persons within the Godhead; it is the basis for the first economic kenosis that lies in creation, and for the second and truest kenosis, that of the cross. Two aspects of the thought of Balthasar seem to me all-determining in this regard: first, his radical interpretation of the dereliction of Christ on the cross; second, the divine foundation for the "trinitarian event" of the cross, inscribing kenosis within the heart of the eternal Trinity.

The Swiss theologian finds in the immanent life of the Trinity the ground of the world process (including the crucifixion), in such a way that this life is neither a formal process of self-communication in God (Rahner), nor entangled in the world process (Moltmann). Following Bulgakov, he understands the eternal generation of the Son by the Father (the "immanent Trinity") as "an initial 'kenosis' within the Godhead that underpins all subsequent kenosis": "The Father strips himself, without remainder, of his Godhead and hands it over to the Son."[73] Inherent in the Father who begets the Son from all eternity is "an absolute renunciation" *(ein absoluter Verzicht)* to be God for himself alone; the Father by love "lets go of his divinity" *(ein Losslassen des Gottseins).* The eternal act of the Son's generation by the Father is grasped as "the positing of an absolute, infinite distance" *(die Setzung eines absoluten, unendlichen Abstands)* within the Godhead itself, a "distance" that contains and embraces all the other "distances" that are possible within the world ("including the distance of sin"). Proceeding from the Father and the Son, as "their subsistent 'We,'" the Holy Spirit maintains "the infinite difference" *(die unendliche Differenz)* between the Father and the Son, and he

71. Hans Urs von Balthasar, *The Glory of the Lord: A Theological Aesthetics,* Vol. VII: *Theology: The New Covenant,* trans. Brian McNeil (San Francisco: Ignatius Press, 1989), p. 213.

72. Balthasar, *The Glory of the Lord,* Vol. VII: pp. 213-14. On the influence of Bulgakov upon the Balthasarian doctrine of the kenosis (inner-trinitarian life of God, creation and cross of Christ), see also Hans Urs von Balthasar, *Mysterium Paschale: The Mystery of Easter,* trans. Aidan Nichols (Edinburgh: T. & T. Clark, 1990), p. 35.

73. Hans Urs von Balthasar, *Theo-Drama: Theological Dramatic Theory,* Vol. IV: *The Action,* trans. Graham Harrison (San Francisco: Ignatius Press, 1994), p. 323.

Gilles Emery, O.P.

bridges this difference, since he is the Spirit of both. The kenosis of God in the covenant and on the cross, then, is based upon this "initial kenosis" *(Ur-kenosis, Urkenose)*. The thought of Balthasar rests upon a knife edge. On the one hand, he criticizes and rejects all fashionable talk of "the pain of God" (Moltmann). Yet on the other hand, by recourse to negative theology and to a complex theory of language concerning God, Balthasar posits an event *(ein Geschehen)* that happens within God. It is worthwhile to note the form this kenotic language takes: the eternal generation of the Son is explained in terms of a "separation of God from himself" *(Trennung Gottes von sich selbst, Trennung von Vater und Sohn)*. For it is only from within this trinitarian separation, for Balthasar, that other separations can take place: in creation, the history of salvation, and even those that are most alienating and painful. The "emptying" *(Entleerung)* of the Father's heart is the original trinitarian "drama," which constitutes the condition of possibility for the drama that unfolds between God and the world.[74]

The question of the suffering of God finds its response in this trinitarian kenosis: "There is something in God that can develop into suffering."[75] The trinitarian kenosis is the ground or starting point *(Ansatzpunkt)* of what can become suffering *(Leiden)* when "the recklessness with which the Father gives away himself" encounters a freedom that refuses this magnanimity.[76] In this way, Balthasar avoids identifying the being of God with an intra-worldly process, and safeguards the transcendent freedom of God with respect to his economic kenosis. He also rejects any separation of the being and the freedom of God, yet he bases the origin of the drama of suffering within the eternal processions of the persons.

It is in light of this primordial trinitarian kenosis that Balthasar understands the act of the cross, where the entire Trinity is involved. There the Son suffers his passion, the Father abandons the Son, and the Holy Spirit is involved in this act "by uniting them now only in the expressive form of the separation."[77] The passion does not merely affect the person of the Son in his human nature, but also changes the Son *in his personal relation to the Father,*

74. Balthasar, *Theo-Drama,* Vol. IV, pp. 319-28. For the precise vocabulary, I have followed the original German edition: *Theodramatik,* Dritter Band: *Die Handlung* (Einsiedeln: Johannes Verlag, 1980), pp. 297-305.

75. Balthasar, *Theo-Drama,* Vol. IV: *The Action,* p. 328.

76. Balthasar, *Theo-Drama,* Vol. IV: *The Action,* pp. 327-28; *Theodramatik,* Dritter Band: *Die Handlung,* p. 305.

77. Balthasar, *The Glory of the Lord,* Vol. VII, p. 214 (with a reference to Bulgakov).

50

and correspondingly affects the relation of the Father to the Son in their *separation*. At the heart of this trinitarian interpretation of the suffering of Christ, Adrienne von Speyr — who Balthasar follows — goes so far as to say that on Good Friday, the Trinity (who took part in the abandonment of the Son) finds itself, so to speak, "destroyed" *(zerstört)* in itself.[78] This interpretation of the dereliction of Christ, which is quite complex, is intimately related to the theme of substitution or representation *(Stellvertretung),* to which Balthasar accords a central place.[79] Jesus becomes the subject of divine wrath and as such suffers that estrangement from God that is the result of sin and its punishment. Jesus, who is sinless and bears the total sin of the world, takes the whole experience of hell *(poena damni)* upon himself, and goes through hell (as the place of God's absence) by substitution.[80]

The vision of Balthasar appears, in certain respects, quite grand. Yet there is a major problem with his understanding of the substitution and dereliction of Christ, and in the retrospective projection of this understanding onto the life of the Trinity itself. This trinitarian doctrine of the redemption, formulated in a dialectical manner, does not seem to be based upon a solid foundation within the Catholic theological heritage.[81] The attribution to Christ of the sufferings of hell is a tradition of the late middle ages, transmitted by the theologies of Luther and Calvin,[82] and involves, in my opinion, insurmountable difficulties. Only sin *separates* one from God.

78. Adrienne von Speyr, *Erde und Himmel: Ein Tagebuch,* Zweiter Teil: *Die Zeit der Grossen Diktate,* ed. Hans Urs von Balthasar (Einsiedeln: Johannes Verlag, 1975), p. 157. For more details on the theme of the participation of the three divine persons in the suffering of the cross, see Thomas R. Krenski, *Passio caritatis: Trinitarische Passiologie im Werk Hans Urs von Balthasars* (Einsiedeln: Johannes Verlag, 1990), pp. 257-76 and 318-20.

79. On the complexities and ambiguities of the Balthasarian theory of *Stellvertretung,* see the critical study of Michele M. Schumacher, "The Concept of Representation in the Theology of Hans Urs von Balthasar," *Theological Studies* 60 (1999): 53-71.

80. Cf. Balthasar, *Mysterium Paschale,* pp. 161-76.

81. I would maintain my reservations despite the broad acceptance that this doctrine receives on the part of numerous theologians, as notably witnessed, for example, by the work of the International Theological Commission: "No matter how great be the sinner's estrangement from God, it is not as deep as the sense of distance that the Son experiences vis-à-vis the Father in the kenotic emptying of himself (Phil 2:7), and in the anguish of 'abandonment' (Mt 27:46)." In *International Theological Commission of the Roman Catholic Church: Texts and Documents, 1969-1985,* with a Foreword by Joseph Cardinal Ratzinger (San Francisco: Ignatius Press, 1989), p. 202. This kind of affirmation is disputable to say the least, and invites the theologian to develop a critical reading!

82. See above, note 38.

How, then, could the supreme act of the charity of Christ effectuate such a separation? The difficulties affecting trinitarian theology are no less important: the choice of a dramatic presentation leads one to understand the unity of the three persons in terms of a dialectical event of distance.[83] According to this understanding, which is organized around the concepts of kenosis and substitution, trinitarian doctrine seems to be oriented unilaterally from — or towards — the dramatic interpretation of the cross.

4. Jean Galot: The Suffering of God

In the world of French-speaking theology, Jean Galot has been instrumental in developing the principal themes of a doctrine of the "suffering of God."[84] His reflection is based upon the passion of the Son, the "passion of God," which he employs to critique the "minimalist" interpretations of scholastic theology. Despite his criticisms of Bulgakov, whose kenotic doctrine he finds unacceptable due to its "depersonalization" of the Son on the cross, Galot retains from Bulgakov the theme of annihilation.[85] While he rejects the Lutheran thesis of the infernal torments of the Son, Galot seeks to understand the dereliction of the Son not only in his humanity but also in his divinity, in the divine intimacy of the Son with the Father.[86] His treatment of the subject matter has the advantage of designating clearly key dimensions of the debate: theological language, metaphysical foundations, and the consequences of this doctrine for trinitarian theology.

Concerning the first point, Galot explains that suffering is not to be attributed to God only metaphorically, but in the proper sense of what it means to "suffer." "God truly suffers."[87] When one affirms that God suffers,

---

83. See the enlightening analysis of Bernhard Blankenhorn, "Balthasar's Method of Divine Naming," *Nova et Vetera*, English Edition, 2 (2003): 245-68. Balthasar develops an interpretation of the divine names that differs from that of the classical tradition, and transforms notions such as separation or suffering into analogical perfections that exist in God in another mode.

84. Jean Galot, *Dieu souffre-t-il?* (Paris: Lethielleux, 1976). More recently, Jean Galot has restated his theory of the divine suffering of the Father, in: *Notre Père qui est Amour* (St.-Maur: Parole et Silence, 1998), pp. 107-12.

85. Galot, *Dieu souffre-t-il?*, pp. 45-46.

86. Galot, *Dieu souffre-t-il?*, p. 56.

87. Galot, *Libérés par l'Amour: Christologie III* (Paris: Parole et Silence, 2001), p. 251.

it is necessary to understand this language analogically, based upon a real similitude between God and the creature. Suffering occurs in God in his most essential reality. This suffering is just as real as that which we term "suffering" in human experience. "We affirm a basic resemblance between the suffering that we know by experience and that which has been revealed to us as belonging to God as savior."[88] There is, then, an "analogy" in the strict sense. Yet one also perceives here that the fundamental note of *diversity* — which is constitutive of analogy and without which univocity results — is marginalized by Galot. According to this author, then, one must recognize in God "personal subjection to pain" *as* in a human being.[89] The metaphysical problem immediately arises: How might one attribute to God, in his divinity, the experience of evil? A solution is inevitably offered (in terms that seem to echo Bulgakov's doctrine) by recourse to a kind of divine dipolarity. Galot in effect distinguishes between (1) the life that is necessary to God, his impassible nature, and (2) his gratuitous love, the free decision of the divine persons who choose to create a world and expose themselves to suffering. The suffering of God is only possible within the "domain" of God's freedom. It does not transcend the distance between the love of God and the necessary being of God: "The God who suffers remains the impassible God. There is no contradiction between these two aspects of God, because impassibility is a property of the divine nature, while suffering only affects the loving freedom of the divine persons with regard to human beings."[90]

A dipolarity of this sort is indispensable in order to affirm a true and real suffering in God without rejecting the affirmation of divine immutability. The problems that it evokes, however, seem to me insurmountable. In order to avoid a contradiction, Galot introduces into God himself a gulf that destroys the fundamental principle of divine simplicity. But is this not itself in fact another form of contradiction? In addition, one might well doubt that the distinction (in God himself) between an "ontological" love and a "freely given" love is capable of shedding light on the depth of God's love for creatures since it suggests a separation between the eternal love that God has

88. Galot, *Dieu souffre-t-il?*, p. 149; cf. p. 166.
89. Galot, *Dieu souffre-t-il?*, p. 148. The Thomist conception of analogy, as Maritain understands it for instance, is deemed "too narrow."
90. Galot, *Dieu souffre-t-il?*, p. 166. See also Jean Galot, *Libérés par l'Amour*, p. 252. This disjunction of concepts presupposes a real difference in God himself between love which is necessary to the divine essence and love which is freely chosen or freely given in relations with human beings; cf. *Dieu souffre-t-il?*, pp. 160-61.

for himself (which is impassible) and his freely given love for creatures (which suffers). By contrast, according to Thomist doctrine, it is in loving himself that God loves creatures. It is by the Holy Spirit in person that the Father and the Son love one another eternally *and* love us.[91] Under this aspect, the Thomist doctrine of divine simplicity and immutability permits one to better demonstrate the depth of love that God has for his creatures.

On the third point, Galot develops his understanding of the suffering of God from a trinitarian perspective that emphasizes in particular the person of the Father. Before reflecting on the suffering of the Son in his passion, he invites us to consider the suffering of the Father, which has two dimensions: (1) the act by which the Father offers his Son as a sacrifice, (2) the act by which the Father receives the redemptive offering of the Son. "In the act of offering his suffering to the Father, Christ expresses and reveals the suffering of the Father himself."[92] The Father initiates the sacrifice in his own person and, therefore, following the order of the persons, he is the first to suffer. The spiritual and pastoral preoccupation of Galot is evident: "If the Father himself suffers, the face of suffering is changed."[93] This fact should be duly noted: the trinitarian doctrine of "theopathy" seeks to help the faithful accept and transform their sufferings in light of the love of the Father. It constitutes then a "response" to the question of human suffering. Not only did the incarnate Son suffer; the Father also suffers with us.

Without returning to the metaphysical difficulties mentioned above, it is necessary to note here a problem that arises concerning the redemptive incarnation. If the Son has taken upon himself our human condition, is this not in order to liberate us from evil *by the assumption of a human nature?* (The assumption of a passible nature by one who is impassible allows us to participate in his immortal life.) If the Father sends his Son, is this meant to free us from suffering through the passion of the Son in his flesh, or is it meant to reveal that the Father suffers in his divinity with us? Language concerning the suffering of the Father, in preaching in particular, carries with it a serious risk: it seems to suggest that the suffering of the Son in his humanity *does not suffice* to enlighten us concerning the mystery

---

91. Aquinas, *ST* I, q. 37, a. 2.

92. Galot, *Dieu souffre-t-il?*, p. 191; cf. pp. 202-4. See likewise: Jean Galot, *Découvrir le Père: Esquisse d'une théologie du Père* (Louvain: Editions Sintal, 1985), pp. 111-21; Jean Galot, *Père, Qui es-tu? Petite catéchèse sur le Père* (Versailles: Editions St.-Paul, 1996), pp. 77-79: "The Father's experience of suffering."

93. Galot, *Dieu souffre-t-il?*, p. 203.

of suffering, and that consolation must therefore be found in the suffering of the Father himself.

5. Jacques Maritain: An Unnamable Perfection

As a disciple of Thomas Aquinas, Maritain does not partake of the dialectical influences that we have previously discussed. Nor do notions of kenoticism appear in his writings. His contribution to this debate merits great attention, however, because it offers a reflection of undeniable profundity. His perspective was also adopted by Charles Journet.[94] The essential reflection of Maritain is found in his short but dense treatise with the title, "A Great Problem," located within an essay on theological knowledge.[95]

Maritain's reflection takes as its point of departure the Thomistic teaching on the divine names. He distinguishes very clearly the names that are attributed to God by metaphor (names implying in their very notion a limitation incompatible with divine perfection), and the perfections that are attributed to God in a proper sense by analogy (being, wisdom, love, etc.). According to Thomistic doctrine, proper analogy implies that the names we use in order to speak about God have a twofold aspect: (1) there are the perfections themselves that these names signify *(perfectiones ipsae significatae)*, and (2) their mode of signification *(modus significandi)*. The perfections that we signify (the first aspect) exist in God as such, and they exist more properly in God than in creatures. These perfections are predicated first and foremost of God, and subsequently to creatures. They belong primarily to God himself and to creatures by way of participation. When we consider the second aspect, however (the "mode of signification"), no name is "properly" attributable to God, because all of the words that we use imply a mode of signification that is proportioned to creatures.[96] The mode of our intellectual knowledge and the mode by which our language signifies are both determined by the mode of being of created things. Our consideration of God and our words for naming God remain bound to the mode of being of our sensible world, the mode from which we take our knowledge.

---

94. See Gilles Emery, *Trinity, Church, and the Human Person: Thomistic Essays* (Naples, Fla.: Sapientia Press, 2007), pp. 253-58: "The 'Mysterious Suffering' of God."

95. Jacques Maritain, "Quelques réflexions sur le savoir théologique," *Revue Thomiste* 69 (1969): 5-27, here at 14-27.

96. Aquinas, *ST* I, q. 13, a. 3.

For example, when we call God "wise," we signify a perfection that really exists in God. However, the reality signified by this word surpasses our concept of "wisdom." "By the term 'wise' applied to man, we signify some perfection distinct from a man's essence, and distinct from his power and existence, and from all similar things; whereas when we apply the term 'wise' to God, we do not intend to signify anything distinct from his essence, or power, or existence." The name "wisdom," therefore, must be grappled with according to the rules of analogy and not in a univocal fashion. "When this name 'wise' is applied to a man, it circumscribes in some degree and comprehends the thing signified; whereas this is not the case when it is applied to God; it leaves the thing signified as uncomprehended *(relinquit rem significatam ut incomprehensam),* and as exceeding the signification of the name."[97] This Thomist doctrine of analogy fully respects the incomprehensibility of the divine. Maritain underscores this rigorously: if one forgets this rule, he or she will think of God in an unworthy fashion.

Maritain pushes this doctrine of St. Thomas higher and to its furthest point when reflecting on mercy. When St. Thomas analyzes the distress that is tied to mercy, he explains that the merciful person is the one who is affected by the distress of another, who feels sorrow for the misery of another "as if it were his own misery."[98] Compassion consists in this: "He who loves looks upon his friend as another self, and counts his friend's hurt as his own."[99] This is why the merciful man acts: he provides a remedy for another's misery out of love, "as if for his own misery." As regards God, St. Thomas explains, he does not experience mercy inasmuch as it is a passion tied to the sensible appetite (because of the immateriality and immutability of God): God is not afflicted *in himself,* but he is merciful *in his effects,* in the activity of his love for the creatures he loves. Following St. Thomas, then, "mercy is sovereignly *(maxime)* attributable to God, but according to the effect produced *(secundum effectum)* and not according to a passion which is suffered *(non secundum passionis affectum).*"[100] Maritain recognizes the perfect truth of this doctrine, which distinguishes suffering out of mercy for another (passion) and the remediation of the suffering of the other (effect). However, in recalling the gospel's teaching on the mercy

97. Aquinas, *ST* I, q. 13, a. 5.
98. Aquinas, *ST* I, q. 21, a. 3.
99. Aquinas, *ST* II-II, q. 30, a. 2.
100. Aquinas, *ST* I, q. 21, a. 3.

of God, he adds: "Yet that leaves the mind unsatisfied." Is it not necessary to attribute mercy to God in a way that is just as "proper" as our attribution of love to God? "Should we not say of mercy, then, that it exists in God according to what it *is,* and not only according to what it *does?*"[101] In response, Maritain proposes to acknowledge mercy in God as a perfection of his being, "but in the state of perfection for which there is no name: an unnamable glory or splendor which implies no imperfection, in distinction, then, from what we call suffering or sadness. It is something for which we have no idea, or concept, no name which might be properly applicable to God."[102] We change here from the incomprehensibility of God to perfections that are "without name" and "unnamable," perfections that are not only "innominatae" but also "innominabiles."[103] The suffering that is intrinsic to the human experience of mercy would be, then, related to our imperfection, our participation in this "unnamed and unnamable" perfection of God, who is undiminished in his plenitude of being, his immutability, and his beatitude.

These observations of biblical and metaphysical origin apply equally to a consideration of the anthropological order. Maritain rightly notes that in our human experience, the suffering of love is not an entirely negative reality. It is not only a privation, but contains a positive and noble element as well, which is bountiful and precious, in short, a perfection. This nobility transposed analogically would find its "mysterious exemplar" in God. For in God all is perfect; beyond all that is humanly conceivable, a divine exemplarity of merciful suffering must exist as a dimension of the beatitude of God.[104] Two allusions to the thought of Raïssa Maritain demonstrate her influence upon this proposal worked out by Jacques Maritain. In fact, one can find in *Les grandes amitiés* the intuitions developed by the philosopher in his essay on theological knowledge. There Raïssa affirms that the capacity to suffer constitutes a perfection for a created being. Like Léon Bloy in his *Le Salut par les Juifs,* she suggests the presence in God of "something corresponding" to our suffering, "a sort of glory of suffering" that must affect our contemplation of the abandonment of Christ on the

101. Maritain, "Quelques réflexions sur le savoir théologique," pp. 16-17: "Et cependant cela laisse l'esprit insatisfait [. . .]. Ne devrait-on donc pas dire de la miséricorde qu'elle se trouve en Dieu selon ce qu'elle *est,* et non pas seulement selon ce qu'elle *fait* [. . .]?"

102. Maritain, "Quelques réflexions sur le savoir théologique," p. 17.

103. Maritain, "Quelques réflexions sur le savoir théologique," p. 15.

104. Maritain, "Quelques réflexions sur le savoir théologique," p. 17 and pp. 21-22.

cross, who did not cede his beatitude even there. It is necessary, then, Raïssa continues, that "this mysterious perfection in the suffering of the creature" exist in God "under a form that no human name can name."[105] These are, very precisely, the intuitions that Jacques Maritain seeks to give an account of theologically.

This reflection of Maritain is indisputably of an exceptional depth. It is the penetrating expression of a thought that seeks to acknowledge in God, not suffering properly speaking, but that which takes on the form of suffering and pain in the human nature assumed by the Word, and within our human experience. It evokes a question, however: Is this noble, bountiful, and precious element of mercy present in the suffering of love something other than the very charity of God? When we employ the word "mercy," does this not signify precisely *the incomprehensible love of God* in its bountiful activity (in its effects in creatures who suffer from evil)?

In other words, if one removes from God all privation and evil, as Maritain surely does, what is the pure perfection that is contained in love which suffers in order to overcome suffering? What is the "core element" signified by the notion of mercy and love? It seems that here we find ourselves in a dilemma that Maritain's thought does not arrive at resolving, except by recourse to his obscure notion of the "unnamable." (1) Either God suffers in reality as the word "suffering" signifies, and he therefore experiences affliction in his very being, which Maritain clearly refuses to affirm, or (2) the merciful God does not undergo affliction and suffering in himself (and not because of a privation or defect, but by virtue of his eminent perfection). In this case, it is his love that we speak of: *a love at work to help others in their affliction.* If one appeals to the doctrine of divine names, which Maritain takes from St. Thomas, I think it is difficult to understand how this "unnamable perfection" — as an uncreated exemplar of suffering love — can denote for us anything other than the plenitude of divine charity at work in the world to liberate human beings. We can indeed name it,

---

105. This passage from *Les Grandes amitiés* (ch. 7) is cited by Jacques Maritain in the article we have examined here (p. 24); cf. Jacques et Raïssa Maritain, *Oeuvres complètes*, vol. 14 (Fribourg: Editions Universitaires; Paris: Editions St.-Paul, 1993), pp. 791-92. The reflections of Raïssa are introduced by the evocation of the sufferings of the Virgin at la Salette, which Maritain knew of through Léon Bloy. Above, in referring to the *Journal* of Raïssa, Maritain has already alluded to the mystery of Jesus crucified as "an image of the Father offended by sin" ("Quelques réflexions sur le savoir théologique," p. 21). The influence of Léon Bloy here is manifest and particularly striking.

then, even while knowing that its mode of existence and its reality in God remain incomprehensible for us.

IV. Elements of Reflection in Thomas Aquinas

1. *The Simplicity of God*

The thought of Thomas Aquinas concerning God is guided by his central affirmation of God's simplicity. In the *Summa Theologiae*, simplicity is the first divine attribute studied, and the consideration of the other properties of God and his action depends upon it.[106] The affirmation that God is "simple" signifies that God is exempt from the internal composition that characterizes the whole domain of the created order. While creatures are riddled with composition (act and potentiality, essence and existence, substance and accident, form and matter, genre and species, whole and part, etc.), God alone transcends all such combinations. Absolute simplicity, then, is an *exclusive* property of God alone, and relates to the affirmation of the *divinity* of God. This property pertains to the immanent being of God *as well as his action in the world.* God does not enter into composition with creatures. This norm is especially true in the incarnation of the Son: in the union of God and man in Jesus, the highest union of God with a creature, the divine nature remains *distinct* from the human nature. In other words, the affirmation of divine simplicity takes into account that God the creator and redeemer in fact *acts as God* in his action as creator and the exercise of his providence.[107] This acknowledgment of his simplicity excludes the possibility of the dipolarity we have encountered above in certain theologies of kenosis or of the "suffering" of God. It also provides the foundation for the affirmation of divine immutability.

In his *Summa Theologiae* as in his other works, Thomas Aquinas treats divine simplicity in the context of "that which concerns the divine essence."[108] From an epistemological point of view, according to St. Thomas,

---

106. Aquinas, *ST* I, q. 3. After the existence of God (q. 2), the consideration of all of the divine attributes is dependent upon divine simplicity, which governs the treatise on God. See Serge-Thomas Bonino, "La simplicité de Dieu," in *Istituto San Tommaso: Studi 1996*, ed. Dietrich Lorenz (Roma: Pontificia Università San Tommaso, 1997), pp. 117-51.

107. *ST* I, q. 3, a. 8; cf. q. 13, a. 7.

108. *ST* I, q. 2, Prologue.

one is concerned here with a teaching that is biblical and therefore revealed. Yet it is also one that philosophical reason can grasp by its own resources. We should not be misled, however, by the organization of the material or the importance that St. Thomas accords here to human reason acting by its own natural light. In effect, as I will indicate below, divine simplicity is directly related to the trinitarian doctrine of God, from the beginning of the treatise on "that which pertains to the distinction of persons." The same preoccupation is manifest from the first article of Aquinas's treatise on creation onward.[109] This means that for St. Thomas the simplicity of God is one of the fundamental elements of *Christian* discourse concerning God. It would be mistaken to perceive therein an alien import from philosophy (even if, for Aquinas, a healthy philosophy can and should affirm the simplicity of God). Rather, we are concerned here with a truth of the biblical faith itself, which human reason can also discover (under another light). Thus, the recognition of the simplicity of God and of his incomprehensibility is one of the fundamental elements of a Christian culture that respects the mystery of the triune God. Divine simplicity was emphasized by the pro-Nicene Fathers of the fourth century in order to account for faith in the Trinity, and belongs to what Lewis Ayres has described as a "pro-Nicene culture." This is the culture that nourished the philosophical and theological reflection of St. Thomas as well: "For pro-Nicenes God is non-composite: God has no parts, is incapable of division, and is not composed of a number of elements. In other words, God is simple. . . . Pro-Nicenes . . . assume God to be the only truly simple reality. . . . The generation of the Son and the breathing of the Spirit thus occur within the bounds of the divine simplicity."[110] The action of God in the world is characterized by the same property: God reveals himself and acts as he truly is, that is to say, as one who is absolutely simple.

2. God Is Immutable

In his most beautiful passages on the merciful love of God and the fullness of God's revelation in Jesus Christ, Thomas Aquinas still absolutely rejects the notion that there is any change in God. This is based for him upon a biblical doctrine, which philosophical reflection can give an account of, on

109. *ST* I, q. 27, a. 1, obj. 2 and ad 2; q. 44, a. 1.
110. Ayres, *Nicaea and Its Legacy*, pp. 278-82, here at 281.

its own respective level. It is necessary to note that in his interpretation of biblical texts,[111] Thomas never separates the essential immutability of God, on the one hand, from the immutability of the fidelity of God in the economy of salvation on the other. The "economic" affirmations concerning immutability lead one to acknowledge, as the basis for this economy, the immutability of the being of God. Thomas Aquinas also accepts divine immutability as a solemn teaching of the Church: the Fourth Lateran Council in 1215 had in fact confessed that God is immutable *("incommutabilis")*.[112] We should recall that divine immutability was especially emphasized by St. Augustine, who discovered therein a fundamental and determinate element of the true knowledge of God.[113]

On a speculative level, recognition of the *immutability* of God unfolds from the recognition of his *simplicity* in a necessary way. In order to give an account of Scripture, Thomas notes here three convergent paths of reflection which are very compelling. The first stems from the doctrine of pure act, already established through an examination of divine simplicity. The perfection of the actuality of God excludes any potency (potentiality) such as change would necessarily imply. Second, all change implies, in the reality that changes, a stable element that remains and another element that varies: that is to say, a composition, which simplicity excludes necessarily. The third argument is taken from the infinity of God's perfection, which is to say from the absolute plenitude of God. A change requires the acquisition of something new, the introducing of something that was not there before. To deny immutability signifies that God acts or finds himself in movement in order to acquire something he was previously lacking, and this would shatter the plenitude and perfection of being that pertains to him.[114]

---

111. There are two biblical passages that St. Thomas appeals to most frequently in this regard: "For I the Lord do not change" (Mal. 3:6), and "the Father of lights with whom there is no variation" (James 1:17). See, for instance, *ST* I, q. 9, a. 2, sed contra; *Super Primam Decretalem* (Leonine edition, vol. 40 E, p. 32).

112. *Decrees of the Ecumenical Councils*, vol. 1, p. 230. St. Thomas commented on this text (see the preceding footnote). In our own time, the confession of divine immutability has been reaffirmed by the First Vatican Council, and subsequently by the Catechism of the Catholic Church, promulgated by John Paul II: see *Decrees of the Ecumenical Councils*, vol. 2, p. 805; *Catechism of the Catholic Church*, 202.

113. See, for example, St. Augustine, *De Trinitate* V, 2, 3. Cf. Ayres, *Nicaea and Its Legacy*, pp. 366-81 (Augustine on God's simplicity, immutability, and immateriality).

114. *ST* I, q. 9, a. 1. The First Vatican Council (Constitution *Dei Filius*, ch. 1) suggests the

Based upon these presuppositions, the theological vocabulary of St. Thomas — like that of the Fathers — accepts the attribution of "motion" to God ("God moves himself," *movet se ipsum*), but does so in a "non-proper" sense, which implies a twofold clarification. First, the idea of a "self-motion" of God stems from a Platonic manner of speaking. This "motion" must be understood in a broad sense to designate "operation" *(operatio)*, but not in the sense of movement and change.[115] The operation of God, being identical with the very being of God in his essence (divine simplicity), is beyond all movement. Second, biblical expressions that denote a "motion" of God toward creatures (God "descends" toward his creatures) must be understood in terms of the efficient and exemplary causality of God. God acts in the world by producing effects that participate in his perfection. Here, then, Thomas both assimilates and "neutralizes" a central theme of neo-Platonic thought, that of procession from ultimate principles.[116]

Like simplicity, immutability in the strict sense is a property which is exclusively divine,[117] that is to say, a property of God insofar as he transcends all creatures. Immutability is a characteristic of *God insofar as he is God*. Immutability characterizes God in his radical differentiation from all that which is not God and which is subject to alteration. To deny this property of God (or to attribute it to a creature in an absolute fashion) results in the negation of the essential distinction between God and the world. Considered from this perspective, the affirmation of divine immutability is entirely consistent with biblical teaching concerning the transcendence of God as creator and redeemer.[118]

---

same coherence between *simplicity* and *immutability,* closely associating the two attributes: "Qui cum sit una singularis, simplex omnino et incommutabilis substantia spiritualis" (*Decrees of the Ecumenical Councils,* vol. 2, p. 805). For a more comprehensive presentation of Aquinas's teaching, see Serge-Thomas Bonino, "L'immutabilité de Dieu," in *Istituto San Tommaso: Studi 1997-1998,* ed. Giacomo Grasso and Stefano Serafini (Roma: Pontificia Università San Tommaso, 1999), pp. 73-95.

115. *ST* I, q. 9, a. 1, ad 1. The same remark should be applied to today's use of the language of "event" when referring to God.

116. *ST* I, q. 9, a. 1, ad 2.

117. *ST* I, q. 9, a. 2: "Solus Deus est omnino immutabilis." This article offers an engaging analysis of the kinds of mutability in the created world.

118. See Michael J. Dodds, *The Unchanging God of Love: A Study of the Teaching of St. Thomas Aquinas on Divine Immutability in View of Certain Contemporary Criticism of This Doctrine* (Fribourg: Editions Universitaires, 1986).

3. Divine Immutability, Divine Names, and Analogy

The affirmation of divine immutability makes use of analogical language about God and observes the epistemological norms of the divine names. We cannot know the essence of God *(quid sit)* — which remains for us incomprehensible in the strict sense of the word — but rather, what God is not *(quid non sit)*. This is why the treatise on the divine attributes, in which immutability is located, is concerned with "how God is not" *(quomodo Deus non sit)*.[119] The divine reality signified by our language, as Maritain recalled, is not circumscribed by our minds, because our concepts denote the mode of existence of perfections in our created world; divine reality remains incomprehensible for us. This trait is more acute in the case of immutability, since we are dealing here with a negative concept. We exclude from God *(remotio)* the mutability that is constitutive of the creature. This does not mean that all divine names can be reduced to having a merely negative sense. Thomas Aquinas is insistent upon the substantial content of absolute, affirmative names.[120] But when one affirms that God is immutable, this necessarily means that one *denies* of God that which we experience of realities in our world. There is truly a *perfection* entailed, but one that belongs only to God: it is "absolutely proper to him to be immutable." The affirmation of immutability, then, is metaphysically and theologically indispensable and is a constitutive element of our recognition of the transcendence of God. This is why divine immutability must not be understood simply in reference to various partial "absences" of change in our world, that is to say, according to the mode of certain forms of incorruptibility in creatures (for example, the incorruptibility of the human soul).

The manner in which God is immutable is entirely different from the hardness of a rock that resists change. The immutability of God *is not the projection upon the infinite of any form of created stability.* The divine mode of immutability, as concerns its very reality, escapes us, because it is the immutability of the pure actuality of God, indicative of his plenitude of being, love, and beatific life.[121] Instead of positing a suffering that God

---

119. *ST* I, q. 3, Prologue; cf. q. 2, Prologue. On this, see Emery, *Trinity, Church, and the Human Person*, pp. 53-54.

120. *ST* I, q. 13, a. 2.

121. It seems to me important to underscore this when faced with the accusation of anthropomorphism(!) sometimes raised against the doctrine of the impassibility of God; cf.,

possesses in a mode that is unique to himself (thereby running the risk of considering pure suffering as a transcendent perfection), Thomas Aquinas invites us to understand *divine immutability itself* as a transcendent perfection of the creator, with a mode profoundly different from that of created perfections. Its reality surpasses all that we could conceive of. It is evident that any theory of divine immutability suggesting that God is indifferent to his creatures would be more disastrous than one that attributes suffering to him. Yet divine immutability when rightly understood does not signify indifference: it is an excess of love and of joy.

The positive and luminous face of divine immutability is the *transcendent simplicity* and *pure actuality* of the triune God. The doctrine of pure act prevents us from conceiving of this immutability as a cold abstraction. Faced with the question: "Can an immutable God still love?," the doctrine of pure act denies any tendency to consider divine immutability as an incapacity or as a lack of life. If God does not change, this is not due to a defect, but because of a "surplus." If God does not suffer, this is not due to an absence, but by virtue of his plenitude without composition, by the eminent "intensity" of his being which cannot acquire perfection because it *is* this perfection, beyond all acquisition, or realization in a potentiality that would accede to its actualization. God exists without movement. One could also say, perhaps more correctly, that his plenitude surpasses all actualization, *"surpasses all mutability"* (*"excedit omnem mutabilitatem"*).[122]

4. Impassibility and the Vital Activity of God

The affirmation of divine impassibility unfolds from the recognition of the simplicity of God, in particular his *incorporeality,* and his immutability. First of all, a clarification is required concerning the language of the "passion" and "pathos" of God, or his "passionate" love for human be-

---

for example, Varillon, *La souffrance de Dieu,* p. 18. One has to ask inversely: Is it not instead univocal thought that bears the greatest responsibility for contemporary difficulties with divine immutability? The essential distinction between God and the world is a basic theme of analogical theology. No property is found in the creature according to the same *ratio* or according to the same mode as it is found in God.

122. Aquinas, *Super Primam Decretalem* (Leonine edition, vol. 40 E, p. 32).

ings.[123] St. Thomas analyzes this language critically, and it is necessary to understand the reason for this on a twofold level.

The first level has to do with the very notion of a "passion." It concerns the fundamental anthropological distinction between, on the one hand, the properly spiritual activity of man, and on the other hand, the sensible activity of the human being. This distinction does not establish a separation, certainly, for our voluntary (spiritual) activity is related to our sensible "appetite." St. Thomas notes that the human will exerts an influence of motion by means of the sensitive appetite. Consequently, the proximate principle of motion for our corporeal movements is our sensitive appetite, and thus the activity of the sensible appetite is always accompanied by bodily change. St. Thomas explains: "This is why activities of the sense appetite, insofar as they are bound up with bodily changes, are called passions *(passiones),* which is not the case with activities of the will."[124] Following John Damascene, St. Thomas defines passion in this way: "Passion is a movement of the sense appetitive power."[125] St. Thomas distinguishes clearly between (1) spiritual affection or "intellectual affection" *(intellectiva affectio),* which does not imply passion, and (2) emotion or "sensitive affection" *(sensitiva affectio)* which is necessarily accompanied by a passion with a corporeal change *(transmutatio corporalis).*[126] In and of itself, passion for St. Thomas does not have the modern connotation of a violent sentiment that is contrary to reason. Here one ought to resolutely resist any suspicion that Aquinas is somehow distrustful of the passions.[127]

---

123. See, for instance, Varillon, *La souffrance de Dieu,* p. 54 ("there is no greatness without passion"); Galot, *Dieu souffre-t-il?,* pp. 105-18 ("The compassion of the Father"); Balthasar, *Theo-Drama,* Vol. V, p. 221: "'Pathos' in the Impassible God"; etc.

124. *ST* I, q. 20, a. 1, ad 1. For the distinction between the will as an "intellectual appetite" and the sensible appetites, see also *ST* I, q. 82, a. 5. The application of the term "intellectual" to the will obviously must not be interpreted in the sense of a dry rationalism. It qualifies the will as a faculty that is properly spiritual, an inclination of a being who is intelligent toward its proper operations and its proper end.

125. *ST* I-II, q. 22, a. 3, sed contra: "Passio est motus appetitivae virtutis sensibilis in imaginatione boni vel mali." This definition comes from Nemesios of Emesa, *De natura hominis,* ch. 15; see Emil Dobler, *Indirekte Nemesiuszitate bei Thomas von Aquin* (Fribourg: Universitätsverlag, 2002), pp. 32-35 and 112-13.

126. *Summa contra Gentiles,* Bk. I, ch. 89. The difficulties of attributing the "affective passions" to God are discussed here in detail.

127. This has been demonstrated in superb fashion by Paul Gondreau, *The Passions of Christ's Soul in the Theology of St. Thomas Aquinas* (Münster: Aschendorff Verlag, 2002).

The movements of sensation, sentiment, or emotion are considered not that they might be repressed, but because St. Thomas proposes that they be inscribed within the virtuous activity of man.[128] It remains the case, however, that because they are grounded in our faculties of sensation, the passions depend upon corporeality.[129]

This leads us to a second level of reflection concerning the attribution of affections to God. Unless one changes the meaning of terms (and not without the risk of profound ambiguity), the preceding explanations furnish a fundamental reason for the absence of "passion" in God. We have already encountered this reasoning above in St. Cyril of Alexandria and St. John Damascene: God is not subject to passion *because he is incorporeal.* Passion is not only excluded from God in some particular form that it could take, but "passion *(passio)* is excluded in God by reason of its genus," that is to say, because the very notion of a passion pertains to sensible affection, *without which there is no such thing as a passion.*[130] God does not submit to passions, but he is *life (vita)* in the highest sense of the word. God is wisdom and love: he exerts by himself not only his operation, free from all external determination from passions, but he *is* this same operation of wisdom and love.[131]

Based upon this, can one extract the notion of a corporeal modification that is proper to the passions, and retain uniquely the notion of the impulsion of the appetite itself, in order to attribute to God affections that *in a human being* take on the modality of a passion? St. Thomas explains that this depends upon the specific object of the passions. Effectively this question — of the attribution to God of names signifying a sensible passion — requires a precise analysis that considers two elements: the corporeal modification that every passion implies (the "material" aspect), and the specific object of the aforementioned passion, or the appetite itself (the "formal" aspect). Under the first aspect (the "material" aspect), no passion can be attributed to God. Under the second aspect, St. Thomas responds, one must distinguish two modalities. (1) According to their formal aspect certain passions do not meet the conditions required for proper language concerning

---

128. See Servais Pinckaers, "Les passions et la morale," *Revue des Sciences Philosophiques et Théologiques* 74 (1990): 379-31.

129. *ST* I-II, q. 22, a. 3: "Passio proprie invenitur ubi est transmutatio corporalis."

130. *Summa contra Gentiles*, Bk. I, ch. 89.

131. *ST* I, q. 18, a. 3: "Vita maxime proprie in Deo est." *Summa contra Gentiles*, Bk. I, ch. 98.

God, and one cannot therefore attribute them properly to God. This is not only due to their generic character as passions, but also due to their specific notions (for example, the affliction of deeply felt sorrow, which pertains to the notion of mercy). Here St. Thomas gives the example of sadness, which implies the idea of the experience of evil, or of desire *(desiderium),* which suggests an idea of a good that is not yet possessed. Applied to God, these names of passions are metaphorical. They are attributed to God due to the effects they denote ("propter similitudinem effectus") and according to the spiritual affections to which they are attached. It is in this sense that the Bible speaks of the *mercy* of God who comes to the aid of human misery, or of the *sadness* of God, which denotes his love that is unrecognized by men. Otherwise put, God *himself* is affected by the misery of his creatures, admittedly not *in* himself, but *in the effects* of his merciful love. (2) But according to this same formal aspect, other passions imply no imperfection or privation unworthy of God. This is the case, for example, with love and with joy. Emotions of this second kind (love, joy) are then attributed properly to God, "yet, as we have noted, in him they are passionless."[132] They exist in God in an immaterial mode.

These explanations can be joined to the distinction between the "intellectual affections" and the "sensible affections." The names that signify "sensible affections" cannot be attributed to God properly, but by metaphor. Meanwhile, the names that signify spiritual or intellectual affections (affections without passion) are employed in proper discourse concerning God.

Let us return to the example of compassion or mercy. Mercy can occur in two forms: (1) *the union of friendship* ("unio affectus, quod fit per amorem"), in which a friend looks upon the evil incurred by his friend as his own; (2) *passionate union,* in which the affliction of those near to us penetrates us.[133] The second form cannot be attributed to God except by metaphor. As for the first form, it can be recognized in God, not in the sense that compassion would entail some form of divine pain, but according to a proper analogy that signifies the *active love of God:* "Love is the sole reason for God's mercy, for he loves us as something of himself."[134]

---

132. *ST* I, q. 20, a. 1, ad 2; *Summa contra Gentiles,* Bk. I, ch. 89. On *compassion,* see IV *Sent.,* d. 15, q. 2, a. 1, qla. 1, ad 4.

133. *ST* II-II, q. 30, a. 2.

134. *ST* II-II, q. 30, a. 2, ad 1: "Deus non miseretur nisi propter amorem, inquantum

These observations are not meant to discredit metaphorical language, or place it under suspicion. Such language is abundantly present in Scripture and plays an essential role in our human approach to God. We can and we *must* make use of metaphors to speak of God. They are *necessary and useful* ("propter necessitatem et utilitatem"), St. Thomas explains, because they are proportioned to our human condition. "It is natural for man to reach intelligible things through sensible things."[135] Metaphors must also be welcomed rightfully into the heart of theological argumentation: biblical metaphors and parables as well are not properly part of the spiritual sense of Scripture but are truly part of its literal sense (and it is beginning from the literal sense that the theologian makes his arguments). St. Thomas also recognizes that metaphorical language has a great value in the practice of negative theology: metaphors give us an awareness of the transcendence of God, as we know less "what he is" than "what he is not."[136] In extending these reflections of St. Thomas we can apply to the mercy and compassion of God what the Dominican theologian says on the subject of "symbolic" language. Such language is fittingly used to speak of God because divine truth transcends our reason. Symbolic expressions provide faith with a language that is appropriate not because the reality of God is irrational, but because it surpasses our reason.[137] These observations, however, take on their meaning and value *only* in light of a clear distinction between properly analogical language and metaphorical language. Otherwise, one surrenders to an anthropomorphism that predicates attributes of corporeality to the divine nature.

5. The Immutable Life of the Holy Trinity

The trinitarian theology of St. Thomas differs from conceptions of God that understand the divine processions according to the mode of an intra-trinitarian kenosis (Balthasar). It also permits us to avoid understanding the processions as a dialectical event (Moltmann). St. Thomas treats the

---

amat nos tanquam aliquid sibi." On this, see Marie-B. Borde, "Un Dieu souffrant?" in *Le mystère du mal: Péché, souffrance et rédemption*, ed. Marie-B. Borde (Toulouse: Editions du Carmel, 2001), pp. 261-75.

135. *ST* I, q. 1, a. 9, resp. and ad 1.
136. *ST* I, q. 1, a. 9, ad 3.
137. I *Sent.*, Prologue, a. 5, ad 3.

notion of "procession" following the norms of analogy that we have discussed above. In created realities, a "procession" implies movement and change. This is why St. Thomas proposes that we interpret intra-trinitarian procession in light of the notion of *"operation"* (immanent operation), that is, that perfect act in which the divine reality is maintained without movement *(motus)* and without change *(mutatio)* in the proper senses of the words.[138] The notion of "communication" *(communicatio),* based upon the doctrine of act (a being "communicates" itself by virtue of its act), permits us to understand this operation in a coherent way. God, being pure act, can and must be thought of as sovereignly "communicable." The communication of the divine being in its purity implies no "dispossession," nor "loss," nor "abandonment" of a divine privilege which the Father surrenders. The paternal act of generation, and the reception of divine plenitude by the Son, must be understood as identical with pure actuality. The paternal act of the communication of the divinity, and the filial act of the reception of the divinity by generation, designate the same operation but under different relations.[139]

The immense advantage of the analogy of origin by mode of intellect (the generation of the word) and by mode of will (the procession of love) is to permit one to conceive ever so modestly, but without contradiction, the real immanent procession of a person within the immutable, divine plenitude. (Without this, theology can *affirm,* but it cannot *manifest* the truth.) The generation of the Word and the procession of the Holy Spirit can then be conceived as an "operation of life" *(operatio vitae),* for the supreme degree of life resides in spiritual (immaterial and immanent) activity of the intellect and will, and this can be affirmed of God by means of indispensable correctives provided by theological analogy theory.[140] In ad-

---

138. I *Sent.,* dist. 4, q. 1, a. 1, resp. and ad 1. Cf. St. John of Damascus, *De fide orthodoxa* I, ch. 8.

139. I *Sent.,* dist. 20, q. 1, a. 1, ad 1: "Generatio significat relationem per modum operationis. . . . Una enim et eadem operatione Pater generat et Filius nascitur; sed haec operatio est in Patre et Filio secundum aliam et aliam relationem." The fact of being begotten does not imply any "passivity" in the Son. To be begotten is an action. And when one says that the Son "receives the divine nature from the Father," this "reception" refers to a pure relation of the Son to the Father: this is the relation of origin.

140. *Summa theologiae* I, q. 27, aa. 1-3; cf. I *Sent.,* dist. 13, q. 1, a. 1. *De rationibus fidei,* ch. 3: "God is of a spiritual or intellectual nature, indeed beyond every intellectual nature. So generation should be understood *as it applies to an intellectual nature*" (emphasis mine).

dition, for St. Thomas, the "processions" (generation of the Son, spiration of the Spirit) signify personal relation by mode of operation. These "personal relations" constitute the persons: the persons *are* the relations insofar as they subsist. The doctrine of "subsistent relations" permits one to make simultaneously manifest the real distinction of persons and their perfect identity with the divine essence. Clearly, this theological account posits no distance between the divine persons, and it does not evoke any self-emptying within the Trinity.[141]

6. Real Relations and Relations of Reason: Is the Immutable God "Indifferent" to His Creatures?

As already stated, for St. Thomas the relations of the creature to God are real relations, while the relations of God to the creature are relations "of reason." In spite of the criticisms mentioned above,[142] this doctrine seeks to take into account the truth of the action of God and the immutable transcendence of God. It presupposes first that one recognizes the "real relation" in creatures as a categorical reality. The real relation that St. Thomas indicates when discussing creatures and God is not a "transcendental relation" which would be identical in some way with the very essence of created things. (This manner of thinking is characteristic of much modern religious thought.) Rather, it is an accident (a predicamental relation) that affects and modifies the creature in its ontological consistency.[143] This relation is not understood in a conceptualist (nominalist) way as existing "between" things, but rather exists *within* things. Apart from this starting point, Thomistic thought becomes unintelligible. If, when considering the connection between God and creatures, St. Thomas recognizes a "real relation" in creatures and a "relation *of reason*" in God, it is because God and the world "do not belong to the same order of things," that is to say, "God is altogether outside the order of creatures" (*extra*

141. On this, see Gilles Emery, *The Trinitarian Theology of St. Thomas Aquinas,* trans. Francesca Murphy (Oxford: Oxford University Press, 2007), pp. 51-150.

142. See above, note 29.

143. Aquinas, II *Sent.,* dist. 1, q. 1, a. 2, ad 4: "Est quoddam accidens in creatura, et sic significat quamdam rem, non quae sit in praedicamento passionis, proprie loquendo, sed quae est in genere relationis." Cf. *ST* I, q. 45, a. 3; Emery, *The Trinitarian Theology,* pp. 86-88.

totum ordinem creaturae).[144] It is also *for this very reason* that God can act in all creatures, in the depth of the being of each one! The thesis of a two-fold real relation (a real relation in the creature but also in God) implies the insertion of the being of God into the order of created realities. In addition, it limits the extent and depth of divine action.

The affirmation of a "relation of reason" in God with regard to the world does not *in any way* imply that God is somehow "indifferent" or "disinterested" in his creatures. First of all, the real relation of the creature toward God has its foundation precisely in the operation of God which is identical with his very being. (The action of God in the world is God's essence, with a relation "of reason" with regard to creatures.)[145] This accounts for the absolute *priority* of God and his action, and the properly *divine* character of the activity of the Trinity in the world. For St. Thomas, a profound understanding of God's transcendence does not separate thinking about God from thinking about the world or human beings. Rather, it shows and ensures the gratuity of divine action in the world, by showing the depth at which the world's bond to God is rooted within God. This founds the participation of creatures in the divine life, and ensures the total liberty of the action that God exercises in the world on behalf of creatures. Still more, the fruits of God's activity in the world (creation, the exercise of providence, salvation) have their source and rationale in the eternal, immanent activity of God: it is by the *same wisdom* that God knows himself and knows us; it is by the *same love* that God loves himself and loves each of his creatures.[146] One does not take God's action seriously by allowing his relations to the world to condition him, but, rather, one discovers the source of the economy by contemplating the transcendent being of God in itself.

Second, if the being of God is not modified by his relation to the world, this is in virtue of the plenitude of act which he is, an act to which nothing can be added, not because of a defect, but because of a superabundant plenitude. The understanding of creation as a *relation* appears therefore to be particularly fruitful: the creation is not a "restriction" of God who would limit himself or give place to the creature through effacing himself (kenosis), but rather it is the *gift of a participation in God* by a free

144. *ST* I, q. 13, a. 7.
145. Cf. *ST* I, q. 45, a. 3, ad 1.
146. *ST* I, q. 14, a. 5; q. 19, a. 2. This implies that the love of God for his creatures is always *creative:* "Amor Dei est infundens et creans bonitatem in rebus" (*ST* I, q. 20, a. 2).

71

decision of divine superabundance. The conception of creation as a relation also permits one to grasp the trinitarian foundations of divine action in the world (the creative causality of the trinitarian relations).[147] Faith seeking understanding discovers in the immutability of God, then, the foundation for God's absolutely gratuitous generosity. God does not create so as to acquire a good that he lacks, but acts freely in order to communicate a participation in his own perfection. God is sovereign in his "liberality," acting in the sovereign gratuity of his love.[148]

This doctrine manifests that God is superior to the relation that we have toward him, *because he is the cause of the latter.* The life of his creatures is infinitely "important" to him: he precedes it and provides for it. According to St. Thomas, the divine will is not attracted toward or determined by a good that is found in the creature, but itself *creates* this good. God does not "re-act": he *acts.* Human actions, the prayers we address to God for example, are not meant to "bend" the will of God, or make him change. Rather, prayer is a *response* to the activity of God which is always primary, following his providential plan.[149] We do not pray in order to modify the course of providence, but to obtain by our cooperation with the work of God that which God has prepared in such a way that this might be accomplished by means of prayer. It is in this sense that St. Thomas invites us to understand the "dialogue" of man and God: in this dialogue the word of man is always a *response,* an active response that seeks to enter into the fulfillment of the divine will. It is necessary to emphasize the profoundly biblical character of this doctrine. This viewpoint leads to a spirituality of listening, of acceptance, and of cooperation with God who always "precedes" his creature. This is why God remains immutable in his relation with human beings: his relation to us is that of his *action which is always creative,* even to the point of the gift he makes of himself.

7. The Passion of the Impassible in Our Passible Nature

These reflections find their center and their summit in the theological understanding of the mystery of the passion and resurrection of Christ. The

---

147. See Emery, *The Trinitarian Theology,* pp. 338-59.
148. *ST* I, q. 44, a. 4; cf. I *Sent.,* dist. 18, q. un., a. 3.
149. *ST* II-II, q. 83, a. 2.

"greatest union," that of human nature with the divine nature in the person of the incarnate Word, does not shatter divine immutability.[150] The *novelty* that occurs in the incarnation comes from the *humanity of the Word:* this humanity is united to the plenitude of the divinity. The Word assumes it in order to accomplish the mystery of our redemption in a passible nature. In light of the preceding explanations, St. Thomas conceives of the hypostatic union as a coupling of non-symmetrical relations. This relation is "real" in the human nature, which receives a modification by its union with the divinity, while it is a relation "of reason" in the divine nature, which undergoes no change.[151] "Quia igitur unio relatio quaedam est, per mutationem creaturae Deus dicitur de novo factus homo, scilicet unitum in persona humanae naturae."[152] This is why it is important to emphasize that in Christ the union of God and man does not take place in the natures, but indeed in the person or hypostasis (Chalcedon). The kenosis of the Son in the incarnation *(exinanitio)* does not entail a limitation of his divine nature nor a self-diminution of his natural divinity, but rather the assumption of a human nature in its condition of indigence. In this abasement, by virtue of the "economy" *(dispensatio)* of the divine plan, the *divine glory* was withheld so that it did not overflow into the body of the Lord, and the *glory of his beatified soul* was withheld so that it did not overflow to the other parts of the soul and to the body, "so that Christ might fulfill the mysteries of our redemption in a passible body."[153]

Following St. Thomas, the passion of the Word must therefore be understood in light of the Chalcedonian doctrine of the two natures of Christ, which remain distinct within the one person of the Word, so that "the property of both natures is preserved."[154] Impassibility, however, is a property of the divine nature. And therefore, by virtue of the union without confusion of the two natures, "the passion of Christ pertains to the *divine person* by reason of the *assumed nature,* but not by reason of the impassible divine nature," that is, "inasmuch as he was a passible man."[155] It

---

150. *ST* III, q. 1, a. 1, ad 1.

151. *ST* III, q. 2, a. 7.

152. *In Ad Rom.* 1:3 (Marietti edition, #37).

153. *ST* III, q. 45, a. 2; q. 46, a. 8; q. 54, a. 2; *In Ad Phil.* 2:7 (Marietti edition, #57).

154. *Decrees of the Ecumenical Councils,* vol. 1, p. 86. Thomas Aquinas recalls this teaching of Chalcedon at the beginning of his reflection on the question: "Should Christ's passion be attributed to his divinity?" (*ST* III, q. 46, a. 12).

155. *ST* III, q. 46, a. 12, resp. and ad 1 (emphasis mine).

is truly the person of the Son who suffers, but in his human nature. St. Thomas recalls here the doctrine of the Council of Ephesus (St. Cyril): the Word of God suffered *in the flesh* and was crucified *in the flesh*. This flesh is truly the flesh of the Word: it is in this sense that, with the Council of Ephesus, St. Thomas will speak of the "death of God" ("mors Dei, scilicet per unionem in persona").[156] The doctrine of Ephesus and Chalcedon furnishes a veritable *norm* for the christological reflection of St. Thomas much more so, it seems to me, than it does for the theologians of divine "pathos" and trinitarian kenosis. In light of these explanations, one should not be surprised to discover that St. Thomas considers the idea of a "kenosis" *(exinanitio)* of the Father or of the Holy Spirit to be "absurd" *(absurdum)*.[157]

I have emphasized above the trinitarian themes that the theologians of the suffering of God or of kenosis seek to promote (including the idea, in Moltmann and Adrienne von Speyr, of a "destruction" of the personal relations), and which, in these authors, influence to a great extent the language of "separation" of the Father and the Son on the cross. The trinitarian dimension of the cross of Christ is indeed present in St. Thomas's reading of the Gospels. However, his interpretation differs greatly from the conception of substitution that attributes to Christ the torments of hell. It also contains nothing of the idea of a punishment to appease the anger of an offended God. On the one hand, St. Thomas maintains that the personal relations of the three divine hypostases are not affected — how could they be modified? These relations *are* the divine persons themselves, identical with the immutable God in his plenitude. On the other hand, the Father offers his Son for us (cf. Rom. 8:32), not in separating himself from the Son, but in giving him with the highest impulse of the Holy Spirit: "he inspired in him the will to suffer for us, by filling him with charity."[158] "The reason why Christ shed his blood is the Holy Spirit, since it is by the Spirit's motion and instinct (that is, by charity for God and neighbor) that Christ did this. . . . This is why the Apostle says that he offered himself through the Holy Spirit."[159] The

---

156. *ST* III, q. 46, a. 12, ad 2. On St. Thomas's knowledge of the ancient councils, see Martin Morard, "Thomas d'Aquin lecteur des conciles," *Archivum Franciscanum Historicum* 98 (2005): 211-365.

157. *In Ad Rom.* 1:3 (Marietti edition, #35).

158. *ST* III, q. 47, a. 3, resp.; cf. ad 1.

159. *In Ad Hebr.* 9:14 (Marietti edition, #444): "Causam [ponit] quare Christus

charity of Christ on the cross is the plenitude of the gift of the Holy Spirit in person. This charity is indissociable from the *most profound union* of Christ, in his humanity, with the Father; the center of light which illumines the mystery of suffering. For St. Thomas, it is this *unifying charity* of Christ (which unites him so profoundly with his Father) that confers to his sacrifice its complete value. It is also what permits us to understand the theological meaning of the satisfaction and merit of Christ: he is the Head of the Church, and all graces proceed from him to the members of his Body, by virtue of the mystical union of Christ with his members, that is to say, insofar as "the Head and members are as one mystical person *(quasi una persona mystica)*."[160]

The theology of St. Thomas demonstrates, therefore, that the passion of Christ must be understood in light of trinitarian faith. It does this, however, without introducing the passion into the divinity of the Trinity, but rather in maintaining the Chalcedonian doctrine of the two natures of Christ even to its last consequences. This Chalcedonian perspective prevents human reflection from introducing a contradiction into the mystery. In the passion of Christ, who saves us by his love, the joy of the Trinity appears, revealing itself in the *mutual Love* of the Father and the Son, in order to associate us with this joy. Another great doctor of the Church, St. Francis de Sales, explains this in an enlightening way:

> You know that each thing rejoices when it produces its fruit. . . . If the joy of the woman is in giving birth to many children, how many subjects of rejoicing did Our Savior and Master have on the day of his Death and Passion, because it was through this that he was made father of all the children of men, and acquired for them grace for this temporary life, and glory for eternal life. It was not only *the day of joy* of our dear Savior, but also that of the *joy* of the eternal Father, the angels and of all the souls of the Blessed. But how could it be for the eternal Father, since he saw his Son die of natural death? Does it not seem to you that it is rather the day of his sorrow, and not his delight? My dear souls, it should cer-

---

sanguinem suum fudit, quia hoc fuit Spiritus Sanctus, cuius motu et instinctu, scilicet charitate Dei et proximi, hoc fecit. [. . .] Et ideo dicit *per Spiritum Sanctum obtulit semetipsum.*"

160. *ST* III, q. 48, a. 2, ad 1; cf. III, q. 19, a. 4: "mystice una persona."

tainly not appear to you like that. Reason shows us, because it was in this way that God gave the fruit of his justice, his charity and his mercy towards men. O God, what an act of obedience this is! What an excess of complaisance for the eternal Father, who had said at the baptism of Our Lord that he was his *beloved Son!*[161]

---

161. St. Francis de Sales, Sermon of vesture on Monday of the nineteenth week after the Pentecost (October 15, 1618). French text in St. François de Sales, *Oeuvres,* vol. 9 (Annecy: J. Niérat, 1897), p. 212.

"One Suffering, in Two Natures": An Analogical Inquiry into Divine and Human Suffering

Gary Culpepper

How does one speak of the identity and life of the God of Jesus Christ against the background of an awareness of the depth and extent of human suffering in the world? A dilemma faces anyone who ranges through the Christian literature on the question today: Does the Christian hope for redemption arise in connection with the belief in a God who suffers with us in our suffering? Or do doctrines of a suffering God entail an ultimate powerlessness in God to triumph over and vanquish our suffering? Perhaps, then, the God whose life exists beyond all suffering is our only sure hope for deliverance from the suffering of the human condition. Or do doctrines of an impassible God entail a divine inability to be moved by the suffering of another, or to enter into that suffering in a merciful and redemptive gesture of solidarity?

I will pursue two interrelated questions in this essay: (1) Is there, in any sense, suffering in the eternal life of the God of Jesus Christ?, and (2) Does the answer to this question shed any light on how Christians attempt to understand the cruel extent of suffering in the world they believe is created and providentially governed by God? The suffering and death of Jesus, the Son of God, who reveals the eternal identity of God and the mysterious truth about human suffering, will supply the focal point for insight into these difficult questions.

According to the teaching of the Council of Chalcedon, the suffering of the man Jesus can never be separated from the eternal life of the Son, and, as such, from the perfection of the eternal life of the Trinity. In this way, the logic of Chalcedon should lead faithful Christians to reject the simple proposition "God does not suffer." At the same time, the logic of

Chalcedon suggests to many Christians that God should be said to suffer, not according to his divine nature, but only in the human nature that is assumed by the divine person of the Son. The Christian affirmation "God truly suffers" has its basis, on this account, in the intimacy of the union of the person of the Son with Jesus' human nature and its capacity for suffering, and not in a capacity for God to suffer apart from the incarnation. This sort of qualified speech about "divine impassibility" signifies primarily (and rightly) that God's eternal life is not diminished by the divine act of uniting human modes of suffering with his own eternal form of life.

In the first part of this essay, I will explore an alternative trajectory of interpretation than the one outlined above. I will affirm that in the man Jesus, the Son of God, there is "one suffering, in two natures." This approach differs from a traditional view in that it does not seek to limit the attribution of suffering to the "human nature" of the Son, but explores the view that God suffers according to the divine nature as well, and that this suffering is the analogical basis for the suffering which Jesus and his followers willingly suffer in a distinctly human form. I will distinguish two senses in which God, according to the divine nature, can be said to suffer: (1) according to the eternity of the Creator's knowledge and love of a world wherein evil exists, and (2) in the relations that identify the divine persons.[1] In the second part of the essay, wherein the problem of human suffering is the focus, I will argue that human suffering "consciously and patiently endured"[2] is a creaturely participation in the eternal suffering of

---

1. I will argue for proper *analogical* attribution of suffering in God in such a way that a common *ratio* or middle term can be identified in the analogy and thereby avoid a merely equivocal or metaphorical form of predication. In this sense, I am dedicated to the standards for analogical predication articulated by Stephen A. Long, "Divine and Creaturely 'Receptivity': The Search for a Middle Term," *Communio* 21 (1994): 151-61, though I do not think his argument against predicating "receptivity" as a divine perfection challenges the substance of my argument.

2. To speak of suffering "consciously and patiently endured" is to introduce a specifically moral dimension into the analysis of suffering, one that encompasses forms of suffering that seem both commensurate with our personal fault ("punishment") and incommensurate ("the sufferings of the innocent or the just"). Speech about "patient endurance" has nothing to do, however, with quietism or other forms of acceptance of or indifference towards the destructive power of natural and moral evil. Suffering in the fully human sense, then, refers not only to enduring physical and emotional pain, or suffering ignorance and restrictions on freedom of choice, but enduring these things in some kind of hope that life can be otherwise, and that goodness is the ultimate reality, each of which call forth pro-

God, for whom the "distance" or "alienation" of the creaturely experience of suffering is eternally encompassed in God's own distinctive form of suffering love.[3]

At the heart of the discussion about suffering, human and divine, is the question of the relation between suffering and love. The shared Christian conviction that "God is love" (1 John 4:16) gives rise to conflicting interpretations of this doctrine. Among those who attribute suffering to the divine life itself, the very nature of love is said to require that the lover suffer, in some sense, the existence of the other in a relation of openness, receptivity, and vulnerability. Suffering understood as a form of openness and vulnerability to the other defines, according to this school, the very act of love as a form of existence that goes beyond an exclusive regard for the self.[4] The suffering of the Christian God of love, revealed in the suffering of Jesus' relations of openness and vulnerability to God and neighbor alike, is said to stand in sharp contrast with pagan views of an impassible God who only knows and loves the perfection of the divine life. The suffering of the man Jesus, on this account, reveals the eternal suffering of the

---

phetic forms of speech and action aimed at a final and decisive triumph over moral and natural evil.

3. The suffering that arises from the "difference" or "alienation" from God on the part of the creature fallen into or otherwise wounded by sin is encompassed (1) in the "difference" (intentional in God, real in its effects) which God suffers eternally in the distinction between God's antecedent and consequent providential will, and (2) in the suffering of the "difference" (real in God) or "alienation" of the Trinitarian persons in their existence as subsisting relations. In this latter point, I go against Thomas Aquinas's counsel (*Summa Theologiae* I, q. 31, a. 2) to avoid speaking of "difference" and "alienation" in the relations of the divine persons out of concern that one confuse this usage with a difference or alienation of *natures* on the pattern of Arianism. I think this concern is addressed if it is made clear that by "difference" is meant only "a relative opposition that subsists as the divine nature" and that "alien" refers to *alius*, "another he," or individual, and not *aliud*, which as indeterminate according to gender might be said of another nature (*ST* I, q. 31, a. 2, ad 4).

4. Two important twentieth-century sources of inspiration for what might loosely be called a "school" of Christian reflection upon a suffering God include Elie Wiesel, "For God's sake, where is God? . . . Where is He? This is where — hanging here from this gallows . . . ," in *Night*, trans. Marion Wiesel (New York: Hill & Wang, 2006), p. 65, and A. N. Whitehead, "God is the great companion — the fellow-sufferer who understands," in *Process and Reality* (New York: The Free Press, 1978), p. 351. For the purposes of this essay, I will take Jürgen Moltmann — "a God who is incapable of suffering is a God who cannot be involved" — in *The Crucified God* (New York: HarperCollins, 1991), p. 222, to be representative of this school of thought.

God who is moved by love for suffering creatures in the love of the Father for Jesus, the crucified Son.[5] This account, however, meets with considerable resistance from Christians who argue that the attribution of "suffering" to the eternity of God risks confusing God's life with the life of a being whose existence is embodied, emotionally divided, and subject to constant change in moods, that is, with the life of the pagan divinities whose existence is readily exposed as an anthropomorphic projection of the finite human self.

The Meaning of the Verb "to Suffer"

The verb "to suffer" admits of a complex range of significations.[6] It is important to sort through these before inquiring more deeply into the question of divine and human suffering and their relation. In present-day English usage, the concept of suffering is nearly always associated with something negative, a deficiency in well-being, and especially that deficiency which is felt as emotional or physical pain.[7] Such pain can arise through the loss of physical health, or through the loss of something or someone dear to us, threatening relations in which our very identity has been formed through habits of affection, knowledge, and love. Humans are not the only animals to suffer in these ways, but human suffering is compounded by the specifically human form of consciousness of suffering

---

5. God is moved by love for the suffering of creatures in the movement of the love of the Father for the suffering and crucified Son, who represents a suffering humanity and recapitulates the history of human suffering in his person. In the eternity of the triune providence of God, the crucified Son sent out of love for humanity is the only Son whom the Father knows and loves.

6. Much of what is developed here relies upon the entries for "passion, *n.*" and "suffer, *v.*" in the Online Edition of the Oxford English Dictionary.

7. Thomas Weinandy, whose work I will treat below, restricts the meaning of both "passion" and "suffering" to the experience of embodied beings who, through the action of an external force, undergo change at the level of physical or emotional sensation. In this way, Weinandy embraces the practice of Aquinas and his followers, such as Gilles Emery, who similarly limit the concept of "passion" and "the passions." In this line of thought, the doctrine of "divine impassibility" is a simple corollary of the doctrine of the pure spirituality of God according to his divine nature, as Weinandy argues in *Does God Suffer?* (Notre Dame: University of Notre Dame Press, 2000), pp. 38-39. Unlike Emery, Weinandy does shift at times, however, to speech about God's love as the most passionate form of love.

in such circumstances. The uniquely human way of suffering ignorance (leading to anxiety about the future, regrets over the past, or existential and religious questions about identity and meaning in the present), together with consciousness of restrictions on freedom of choice, action, or mobility (preventing us from doing the kinds of good things we might desire to do), all intensify the human experience of suffering. All of these things can be suffered as the consequence of personal moral fault, but they can also be suffered in the absence of such fault, and hence there arises the consciousness of "innocent suffering." The awareness of such "innocent suffering" brings additional, heightened forms of suffering, especially in the context of belief in a good and providential God.

But "to suffer" has a second, broader, philosophical meaning that is not limited to the negative, defective, or painful. One can suffer good things as well as bad. In this second sense of the term, suffering is defined as "undergoing or enduring the action of another upon oneself" or "existing as the object rather than the subject of an action." The Latin root of the word "suffer," *sub-ferre,* connotes a "bearing" or "receiving" of the action of another person or thing, and can include as well the notion of allowing or permitting the action of the other in a stance of voluntary receptivity.[8]

The noun "passion" is a closely related concept. The Greek *pathos* can refer either to a painful emotion (provoked by experience of a certain literary form, a typical Greek use of the term) or, more broadly, to the state of existing as the (unstable) object of an action in contrast to existing as a relatively more stable agent (as employed in the Greek contrast between *pathos* and *ethos*). The same is true of Latin and Anglo-Norman usage, though here the word "passion" comes to refer particularly to both the literary recounting of the death of Jesus and the physical and emotional suffering he endured in the historical event itself. "Passion" also retained in the English language, however, the more generic sense of "being acted upon by another," and would come to be used to speak of particular ways of being moved by another, as in a "passionate love," whether the passion is in accord with reason or does violence to it (the latter sense being the more modern usage). In the philosophical anthropology of medieval scholasti-

8. For example, Mark 10:14 in the King James Version reads "suffer the little children to come unto me." In this way, my argument for God's eternal "suffering" can at certain points be compared to W. Norris Clarke's argument that "receptivity" is properly predicated of God by way of analogy. See W. Norris Clarke, "Person, Being, and St. Thomas," *Communio* 19 (1992): 601-18, and "Response to Long's Comments," *Communio* 21 (1994): 165-69.

cism, the meaning of the term "passion" increasingly was restricted to changes in the sensible appetite with its links to physiological change, and its use denied to name the spiritual change or movement of the intellect and will by another.[9]

In this essay, I will employ the verb "to suffer" in its most general signification, "to be moved by another," and suggest that if the concept of "passion" be employed as well, it be understood in light of this more general usage. If "to suffer" in *this* sense can properly be said of God, then "the God of love" is not only one who *emanates* love in the impersonal way that the sun emanates light, but God is also said to *give* love to the other as a personal *donum,* including the *donum* of *misericordia,* because God is personally moved to love for the other through knowledge and love of the existence of the other.[10]

"To suffer" — in the sense of "to be moved by another" — typically entails two other elements, relation and change. A thing or person can suffer only insofar as it exists not solely in itself but in relation to something other than itself, by which it is being moved, whether spatially, emotionally, or spiritually. Insofar as the thing or person is moved, in its relation to the other, it is typical to say that it has changed, again, according to its location, or its emotional or spiritual state. The possibility of true, analogical speech about divine suffering will have to treat the question not only of whether God "is moved by another," but also whether — and if so, how — this movement involves "relation" and "change," or "motion," in God himself.

9. Aquinas, for example, cites John Damascene (*De Fide Orth.* II, 22) and adopts his view that "passion" refers properly to change in the sensible and not the intellectual appetite (*ST* I-II, q. 22, a. 3). Aquinas gives further precision to "passion" when he links it primarily to a form of receptivity mixed with the loss of a good (following the teaching on the "passions of sin" in Romans 7:5 in *ST* I-II, q. 23, a. 1), and in *ST* I-II, q. 23, a. 2 he associates passion with the appetitive and not the apprehensive part of the soul. In each of these ways, Aquinas dissociates himself from the more general usage employed by Denys, *Div. Nom.* ii, where he speaks of both learning and suffering divine things in the spirituality of the soul.

10. Aristotle envisions in the development of virtuous friendship the possibility of a relatively stable form of interpersonal love which overcomes the instability of *pathos* in the negative sense of the term. Though he saw that such friendship required "receptivity" to the good that transcends those who participate in the friendship, he did not, as far as I know, speak of "suffering" the good. The "good" is the final cause which draws friends together, such that there can exist friendship "in the good," but unlike Jesus, Aristotle did not conceive of a friendship *with* "the good," wherein "the good" is itself understood as "suffering" the reception of the existence of the other in purely actualized friendship.

Divine Suffering: The Position of Thomas Weinandy

We can now return to the question of whether, and in what sense, a Christian should speak of God as a being who suffers in the eternity of the divine nature. It will prove instructive to begin with an opponent of the view being proposed here. In a number of works, Thomas Weinandy declares himself "very reluctant" to speak of suffering in God "since 'suffering' when applied to God has traditionally meant, especially now within the contemporary theological context, . . . that God undergoes some passible change of state and that, as a consequence, he experiences some inner emotional distress or anguish."[11] Weinandy does not close the door completely on such speech, for he argues that if one understands the existence of God as pure act, and the persons of the Trinity as "subsistent relations fully in act," then one can affirm that "the persons of the Trinity are completely and utterly *passionate* in their self-giving to one another and cannot become more *passionate* for they are constituted, and so subsist, as who they are only because they have absolutely given themselves completely to one another in love."[12]

It seems to me, however, that Weinandy does not sufficiently clarify his use of the term "passionate" insofar as he can juxtapose speech about "dynamic and passionate love" and "love that is immutably and impassibly in act" in reference to the same God.[13] He does attempt to shed light on the issue when he writes that God is said to be "passionate" insofar as "his will is fully and wholly fixed on the good as loved."[14] But it is not at all clear what the term "passionate" *adds* to Weinandy's affirmation of the existence of God as purely actualized love for the good that is himself. He does not, as far as I can tell, affirm that God is passionate in the sense that God "is moved by another."

This indeterminate attribution of "passion" to the life of the eternal God is exposed further when Weinandy turns to the incarnation, wherein,

11. Weinandy, *Does God Suffer?*, p. 168.

12. Weinandy, *Does God Suffer?*, p. 125 (emphasis mine).

13. Weinandy, *Does God Suffer?*, p. 163.

14. Weinandy, *Does God Suffer?*, pp. 125-26. Weinandy adds "God is supremely passionate because he is supremely loving and he is both because both are fully in act since God as *ipsum esse* is pure act." Further, "God is impassible precisely because he is supremely passionate and cannot become any more passionate. God simply loves himself and all things in himself in the one act which he himself is" (p. 127).

following Cyril, he unfolds the meaning of the doctrine that the "[i]mpassible suffers in the flesh." Here Weinandy holds fast to the formula that "the Son of God suffered as man, though not as God."[15] Why does Weinandy deny suffering of God as God in this context, when he affirms the "passionate" love of the God who is *ipsum esse per se subsistens,* the Trinity of subsistent relations? Certainly Weinandy is right to reject the view that Jesus reveals God's eternal life, according to the divine nature, as one of enduring moments of *physical pain and emotional suffering*. But he does not seem prepared to explore any analogical possibilities for the attribution of suffering to God in his divine nature, despite his speech about the "passionate" nature of divine love.[16]

It is at this point that Weinandy seems to miss the deeper point of Moltmann's challenge, perhaps because he is rightly scandalized by the imprudence of the latter's deployment of a dialectical logic and rhetoric that can lead to more problems than they resolve.[17] Setting these problems aside for the moment, I wish to take up Moltmann's argument that "[w]ere God incapable of suffering *in any respect, and therefore in an absolute sense,*

15. Weinandy, "Does God Suffer?," *First Things* 117 (November 2001): 36; *Does God Suffer?,* p. 200. This formula, I think, opens the door to a separation of the existence of the man Jesus from the eternal Son if one does not give an account of how Jesus' suffering — his being moved by another — is assumed in the divine life of the Son who is the *hypostasis* of the man Jesus.

16. Weinandy does speak of the appropriateness of attribution to God of joy, delight, mercy, grief, and sorrow, which for us exist as emotions, insofar as these are "purged of the passible and emotional connotations found within human suffering." He refers to such attribution as "metaphorical" (p. 169). Perhaps Weinandy would ultimately disagree with my proposal that "suffering" or "to be moved by another" can be properly and analogically attributed to God as a divine perfection.

17. It must be understood that the deployment of a "dialectical logic" to unfold the Christian doctrine of God is rooted in a profound "paradigm shift" in Christian thinking that transforms the fundamental understanding of what it means to predicate things truly of God in finite human language. In this sense, the "logic" of speech about dialectical moments of negation and negation of negation in God may very well be nothing more than logical moments in our thought, ways in which we in our finitude conceptualize the life of a God who exists as an incomprehensible unity of what, from our point of view, appear as irreconcilable differences. In that sense, the very predication of "suffering" in God is from the start, in the dialectical paradigm, a "limit concept" that discloses more about the finitude of our understanding than it does the truth of God's eternity. Nevertheless, as a logic, it points toward a difference in human understanding of the God of Jesus Christ relative to human understanding of the other gods.

then He would also be incapable of love."[18] Moltmann seems at this point to insist on the distinctive Christian meaning of "love" as the "mercy" of God disclosed in the suffering and crucifixion of Jesus. He argues for this Christian difference against the background of the richness and pluralism of doctrines of divine impassibility in ancient Greek and Roman philosophy which, as efforts to articulate the ground of true moral freedom as love for the good, point far beyond what today we mean by "apathy" or "indifference."[19] Moltmann's central point here is that the *apatheia* of the God of Aristotle, or other cognate pagan attributes of divinity, despite their moral depth, fall short of the Christian understanding of the passionate nature of the God who is moved by another, and in this movement of love for the other both creates the world and sends his Son to suffer for the salvation of a fallen humanity: "Aristotle's God cannot love; he can only be loved by all non-divine beings by virtue of his perfection and beauty, and in this way draw them to him."[20] Moltmann does not retreat, as his critics might suggest, into the pre-philosophical world of Homer in his articulation of the suffering of God. Rather, he affirms the "passionate love" of God in dialectical relation to a doctrine of divine impassibility, but unlike Weinandy, Moltmann does not limit this passion or suffering to the human nature of Jesus: "The justifiable denial that God is capable of suffering because of a deficiency of being may not lead to a denial that he is incapable of suffering out of the fullness of his being, i.e., his love."[21]

But in precisely what sense, or senses, can suffering be predicated truly of the eternal God? I will pursue this question in two ways, looking, first, to the oneness of God as the Creator, and second, to the Trinity as three persons who subsist as relations to another.

The Suffering of God the Creator

The suffering of Jesus cannot be taken in isolation from the history of human suffering, or indeed, from the still more comprehensive perspective on creation as a cosmos freely given its existence, and providentially gov-

18. Moltmann, *The Crucified God*, p. 230.
19. Moltmann, *The Crucified God*, pp. 267-70.
20. Moltmann, *The Crucified God*, p. 222.
21. Moltmann, *The Crucified God*, p. 230.

erned, by God. It is at this level of analysis that the question of human suffering becomes the most radical and the most difficult: "Why, given the goodness and power of God the Creator, is there any suffering in the world at all, or such a surplus of suffering?"

I will adopt the view, following Aquinas, that it lies within the power of God to bring into existence a world other and better than the one that has been brought into existence (*ST* I, q. 25, aa. 5 and 6).[22] This doctrine communicates that the creation, in all of its particularity and individuality, is not a necessary emanation from God. As a corollary of this view, the fall of Adam into sin is in no way necessary when considered in light of the causal activity of the Creator or the limitations of the finite structures of the world as they are given existence by God.[23] In this account of the freedom and goodness of God's creative power, moral evil and its allied forms of suffering are caused wholly by the creature, through a defective use of human freedom.

The moral evil of the creature does not, and cannot, however, "thwart" the ultimate goodness of the creation that is caused, sustained, and providentially governed by God. As the one who gives creation existence *ex nihilo,* God does not in turn "depend" on the cooperation of creatures to actualize his ultimate aims for creation. For precisely this reason, God is said to permissively will moral evil and suffering as something that remains within the scope of the divine wisdom, goodness, and power to redeem. The causal, positive will of God for the creation is ordered only to the good of creatures, for the divine will to create is, in its very depth, a free overflow of God's eternal love of his own infinite good. Speech about God's permissive will, on the other hand, refers to the will to sustain the existence of fallen creatures, precisely out of love for the goodness that re-

22. Like Bruce McCormack, I affirm the transcendent freedom of God, but it is the triune God who is eternally free, and not a God whose freedom is somehow prior to his self-determination to exist as triune. See Kevin W. Hector, "God's Triunity and Self-Determination: A Conversation with Karl Barth, Bruce McCormack and Paul Molnar," *International Journal of Systematic Theology* 7, no. 3 (2005): 246-61 for a helpful survey of this issue.

23. I am articulating the position that it is consistent with the power of God to create a world of free human agents who only freely elect to do good through free choice, and are sustained and preserved in this freedom throughout the course of the history of the world. This is not to say that such a world coheres with the wisdom and goodness of God, for God in his wisdom and goodness has created the world that we know, i.e., the world of creatures who sin and for whom a Redeemer has been sent.

mains in them, and above all, the goodness which is their capacity to be converted by the grace of the Son. This "permissive will" in God is fittingly associated with that form of "suffering" known as the "divine patience," and it is precisely here, in God's permissive will, that God the Creator can be said to suffer, insofar as God suffers the creature's refusal of the goodness of his creative intentions, the refusal of what can be called God's antecedent will for the creation. This is the suffering that Jacques Maritain identified as the eternal "wound" in God.[24] The existence of this "wound" in God is real, not in the sense that it exists as a relation of real dependence of God upon the creature (that is, as a real *relation* in God), but insofar as it exists *intentionally* in the simplicity of God's eternal knowledge of and will for all created things. But in what sense then does this divine wound qualify as a form of suffering in the sense of "being moved by another"?

Speech about the divine permissive will of the Creator as a divine wound, it must be made clear, is in no way intelligible in Christian understanding apart from the eternal divine will to send the Son and Spirit into the world of moral evil and suffering in accord with God's providential plan.[25] In light of the unity of the orders of creation and redemption in

24. This eternal wound exists at the level of what Aquinas calls the divine "operations" of knowing and willing in God, which include, in the simplicity of the divine life, that knowing and willing which encompasses the history of the world and its suffering in God's providential government. Maritain writes ". . . sin deprives the divine will of something which it actually desired. . . . In his antecedent will, God wills that all men should be saved. . . . Sin does not only deprive the universe of something good, it also deprives God himself of something which was conditionally but really willed by him. . . . Moral defect affects God, though not in himself, but in the things and effects which he wills and loves. In this, God can be said to be the most vulnerable of beings . . . an invisible movement in the heart of a free agent is sufficient to wound him and deprive his antecedent will of something on this earth which it has desired and loved from all eternity, and which now will never be" (Charles Journet, *The Meaning of Evil,* trans. Michael Barry [New York: P. J. Kenedy & Sons, 1963], pp. 183, citing Maritain, *Neuf leçons sur les notions premières de la philosophie morale*).

25. The question of divine providence and divine permission of sin is a difficult one. Without engaging the issue in all of its complexity, I take Augustine's teaching in his *Enchiridion* (*Augustine: Confessions and Enchiridion,* trans. Albert C. Outler [Philadelphia: Westminster Press, 1955]) as a starting point for reflection: "For the Omnipotent God, whom even the heathen acknowledge as the Supreme Power over all, would not allow any evil in his works, unless in his omnipotence and goodness, as the Supreme Good, he is able to bring forth good out of evil" (#11); and, concerning God's wisdom, "For God judged it better to bring good out of evil than not to permit any evil to exist" (#27). The strength of Augustine's formula lies in its refusal to make evil an instrument of God's plan, for Augustine does not

God's eternal providence,[26] one must affirm the unity of the eternal suffering that is the divine patience of the Creator (the divine permissive will, the "wound" in the antecedent will of God) with the suffering of God the Son sent in the ministry of Jesus and his death upon the cross. In this unity, I will argue (in accord with Augustine's understanding of the divine permission of evil) that God knows and permissively wills the evil and suffering of the world in and through the Father's providential knowledge of the suffering of the Son. This approach permits the development of a perspective wherein the suffering of God can truly be said to be a "being moved by another," precisely in the Father's being moved by the knowledge of the Son who is united to the otherness of a creaturely human suffering that God permissively wills to exist in the man Jesus.[27]

The Suffering of God the Trinity

In the brief discussion on suffering above, it was noted that "to suffer," signifying "to be moved by another," entails relation of one to another. Christian reflection on the identity of the triune God discloses the existence of real relations in the divine eternity.[28] If one begins with the eternal relation

---

argue that God permits evil *so that* he might bring forth a greater good. For Augustine, the "good" which God will draw from the evil he providentially permits is the good that comes from the Redeemer sent as a consequence of sin to the human race.

26. Again, following Aquinas's doctrine of the simplicity of the divine act of existence, the act of God's knowing and loving, the processions of the Son and the Holy Spirit, the creation and providential government of the world, and the sending of the Son and Holy Spirit into the world are encompassed in the infinite simplicity and unity of God's eternal existence.

27. At this point, my reflection shares a certain affinity with Bruce McCormack's appropriation of Barth's doctrine of the eternal predestination of the man Jesus to exist as the Redeemer of humanity. See Bruce McCormack, *Karl Barth's Critically Realistic Dialectical Theology* (Oxford: Oxford University Press, 1995), especially chapter 11, "The Eternal Will of God in the Election of Jesus Christ," pp. 453-63.

28. I follow here Aquinas's development of Augustine's doctrine that God is most properly said to be "three persons in one nature." It is at this point that I depart — materially, at least — from Bruce McCormack in his predilection for the propriety of speech about the God who is "one subject in three modes of being." While I cannot explore the relative merits and limits of each approach here, it will suffice to point out that the whole of my approach to the eternal suffering of God depends on the understanding that speech about a "divine person" names a "subsisting relation," an *esse in* the divine nature and *esse ad* another divine person in the simplicity of divine existence and life.

between the Father and the Son, it can be said that the Father "suffers" the knowledge and love of the otherness of the Son, and, reciprocally, the Son "suffers" the knowledge and love of the otherness of the Father. The Father is, substantially, nothing other than this suffering of the relation to the Son, and the Son is, substantially, nothing other than the suffering of the relation to the Father. (This incomplete way of speaking will be rectified in speech about the Holy Spirit below.) This reciprocal suffering of the existence of the other is a suffering wherein each person is moved to love by the other.[29]

Faithful adherence to the Christian understanding of the Trinity requires at this point, however, a more complex formulation of the suffering involved in the reciprocal relations of the Father and the Son. The Father, who *is* the act of suffering a relation to the Son, is *moved by that other who is the Holy Spirit* in the knowledge of the other who is the Son. The knowledge of the Son is integral to the Father being moved by another, but the Holy Spirit is the person who is the motive force itself, the eternal Love which is suffered by, and moves, the Father in his knowledge of the Son. The Son also suffers the relation to and knowledge of the Father, and in this knowledge is moved, by the Holy Spirit, to love of the Father. This reciprocal suffering of the Father and the Son, and the suffering of each of the Love that is the Holy Spirit, who unites the Father and Son across the infinite distance of their relations of personal otherness, identifies the eternal identity of God.

This is the suffering that signifies perfection in the triune God, a perfection revealed in the history of the incarnate Son, whose history is inseparably united with that form of suffering which is privation and defect: "one suffering, in two natures." The "face" of the triune God who suffers eternally in love is manifest in the "face" of the man Jesus and his suffering, precisely in the absolute openness and vulnerability of the Son to the Love that is the Holy Spirit in Jesus' knowledge of his Father. This absolute openness and vulnerability opens Jesus to the depth of the suffering of humanity; and, in his knowledge of this suffering (identical with the knowledge connected to the divine permissive will) and its distance from the

---

29. Aquinas not only speaks of the divine persons, as subsisting relations, as an *esse ad,* but also, at *ST* I, q. 28, a. 1, elucidates the affirmation of real relations in God through the example of a "heavy body" existing in relation to the earth, whereby the heavy body is moved by another, the earth.

knowledge of the Father's intention for humanity (the divine antecedent will), Jesus suffers the Love that is the Holy Spirit for a suffering humanity. The infinite distance between the Father and Son in their personal otherness, united by the Love of the Holy Spirit which moves each to love the other, is infinitely greater than the horrible and terrifying difference, and all the suffering entailed by this difference, between God's love for the creation and the creature's negation of God's creative, antecedent will through moral evil.[30]

The crucifixion of Jesus is not the end of our history with God. The proper suffering of the Father is fully revealed when, in the Father's knowledge of the suffering of Jesus, he is moved by the Holy Spirit to send the Holy Spirit upon the Son who, unjustly executed, lies dead in the tomb. The Father's knowledge of the Son extends as well to the knowledge of Jesus' prayer from the cross for the forgiveness of the whole of a suffering humanity, and in this knowledge the Father is moved by the Holy Spirit to send the Holy Spirit to them as well, that they may see the divine mercy revealed in the suffering of God upon the cross, and come to share in this way of life. In this way, the Trinity communicates to creatures the good message that the suffering of God's eternal love is infinitely greater than the suffering that sin and death have brought into the world.

Attribution of suffering to the divine eternity, then, is rooted in the affirmation *that God is moved by another* in the reciprocal relations of Father, Son, and Holy Spirit. This affirmation can be sustained insofar as it is credible and defensible to take "being moved by another" to be the prime analogate of the verb "to suffer" in its analogical range of meanings. In this light, it is no longer appropriate, when speaking of the suffering of God in the person who bears the name Jesus, to restrict attribution of suffering to the human nature of Jesus. It becomes appropriate, analogically, to attribute suffering to the "divine nature" of the Son as well,[31] though this does

---

30. The truth of Balthasar's doctrine of Jesus' descent into the suffering of "God-abandonment" (*Mysterium Paschale: The Mystery of Easter,* trans. Aidan Nichols [Grand Rapids: Eerdmans, 1990], pp. 148-88), which grounds a hope for the salvation of all, has its basis in what I am calling the absolute suffering of the divine persons in their relation to the other.

31. I put "divine nature" in quotes here to draw attention to the "abstract" reality of the concept, insofar as speech about the "divine nature" is derived from a being given phenomenally to experience (through faith) as a unity of being (the man Jesus, the Son of God). The abstracted concept truly names the real, "the divine nature," in its own order of intelligibil-

not affirm that in God, according to the divine nature, there exists any defect, such as physical or emotional pain, all of which are proper only to the form of suffering found in creatures.[32]

To this point, I have attempted to show the appropriateness of analogical attribution of suffering on the basis of the belief that the divine persons are subsisting relations. But what about the concept of "change" that is typically associated with suffering, or more specifically, the "movement" integral to the concept of "to suffer" as "to be moved by another"? Some Christian thinkers, such as Moltmann, borrow from Hegel a dialectical logic which enables them to incorporate that aspect of suffering which is "change" or, in more precise Hegelian terms, that change which is negation, into the relation between the living God the Father and the crucified Jesus, the Son of God, which change is in turn taken up again in another change (a negation of the negation) into a higher eternal unity (which transcends all negation) through the power or Love that is the Holy Spirit. This conceptuality makes speech about "unchanging change" across opposite states of being possible, though it demands adherence to a dialectical logic which Hegel's opponents find more irrational than illuminating.[33]

---

ity, in distinction from that order of being which is created; but as abstract, the concept prohibits the possibility of a reification of the concept as a being that exists "separate from" the being given to human experience in the economy. The abstraction "logos asarkos" is a good example of a concept that names the real, e.g., the eternal existence of the Son considered in abstraction from the assumed human nature of the man Jesus, which abstraction directs human thinking to a consideration of the divine nature — the purely actualized existence and life — of the Son. But it is illegitimate according to the rule of biblical testimony to proceed, on the basis of abstracted concepts of a *logos asarkos,* to speak as if there existed a God who as Father does not eternally know the Son who unites to himself the man Jesus.

32. According to the more general signification of the verb "to suffer," one can suffer good or evil, and hence suffering can involve either joy or pain respectively, or both simultaneously, as exemplified by anyone who experiences delight in the consciousness that they are doing what is good despite the painful consequences of their actions. Accordingly, it is possible to abstract the concept of an "immanent Trinity" which suffers eternally without the defect of pain, and understand the crucified man Jesus, as one of the Trinity, as one who suffers both the joy of the consciousness of the love of the Father together with the pain of physical, emotional, and spiritual dereliction.

33. Christian thinkers (e.g., Wolfhart Pannenberg, *Systematic Theology,* vol. 1, trans. Geoffrey W. Bromiley [Grand Rapids: Eerdmans, 1988], pp. 388-91) who employ this conceptuality or logic often refer to the "eschatological future" as the moment in history when the Holy Spirit has reconciled all things in a Love which transcends all further negation, and identify the eternity of the triune God as the "Absolute Future" which has a "retro-

The dialectical conception of "unchanging change" is not the only route available in the history of Christian thought to speak of eternal motion in God. There exists as well an analogical form of affirmation of "unchanging change" or, better, "unchanging motion," in the pure actuality and eternity of the divine life. This unchanging motion encompasses the whole of the divine life — the processions in God, the creation of a diversity of beings, the sending of the Son and Spirit into the world, and the eschatological return of creation to the Father, through the Son, in the Holy Spirit. The predication of an eternal "being moved by another" in the life of the one God, said of God both in the relations of opposition that constitute the identity of the persons, and the eternity of the difference between the antecedent and consequent will of God in the simplicity of the operations of knowing and willing the creation (providence), have their basis in the affirmation of the "unchanging motion" that is the purely actualized life of the triune God.[34]

A final question arises in connection with an analogical attribution of suffering to God. In speaking of God the Creator, this suffering is not said directly of the divine essence, but of the eternal divine operations of knowing and willing in the difference between God's antecedent and consequent will for the creation.[35] This is a suffering of God "in his ef-

---

active causal power" in history. It is not possible to engage the merits and/or limits of such a logic for Christian theology in this essay.

34. Aquinas speaks of motion in the eternal life of God at *ST* I, q. 18, a. 3, ad 1. In this way, Aquinas parts ways with Aristotle's denial of change (both *metabolē*, "transformation," and *kinēsis*, "motion") in the intellect of God (*De Anima* III, 7; 431a6), and adopts the approach developed by neo-Platonists such as Porphyry and Proclus, adopted by Denys, and transmitted by way of Averroës, which identifies the intellectual motion in God as *proodos*. The identification of God's life as one of "unchanging motion" opens the way toward new analogical ways of understanding the relation between created time or history and divine eternity. The critical historical and philosophical work on this issue can be found in Stephen Gersh, *A Study of Spiritual Motion in the Philosophy of Proclus* (Leiden: Brill, 1973); see also Wayne Hankey, *God in Himself: Aquinas' Doctrine of God as Expounded in the* Summa Theologiae (Oxford: Oxford University Press, 1987), pp. 53-56.

35. In Aquinas, the distinction between "the divine essence" and "the divine operations" is logical, not real, and involves a subtle affirmation of the eternal unity of God's knowledge and love of himself with his knowledge and love of the world in and through his knowledge and love of himself, in such a way that the "world" is not a necessary emanation of his own "natural" triune existence, but is the free overflow of his self-diffusive goodness in the creation. On the significance and basis of this distinction in Aquinas, see Wayne Hankey, "*Ab uno simplici est nisi unum:* The Place of Natural and Necessary Emanation in

fects," though these effects display the difference between the antecedent and consequent will of God, that is, the divine suffering or permission of evil in the intentionality of God's eternity. This difference is revealed in its greatest intensity in the suffering of the man Jesus. Does this divine suffering "in the other," that is, in "the effects" of God's creation, participate in a more intimate mode of divine suffering, a mode which belongs to God's eternal essence? I have attempted to argue for the affirmative on this point. In speaking of the suffering of the eternal Trinity of persons, this suffering is said of the divine essence. It is important to clarify the point, however, that this analogical affirmation of suffering as a divine perfection is attributed directly to the persons, and only secondarily and indirectly to the divine nature.[36] This distinction is vital because the proponents of an impassible God rightly argue that the radical meaning of "divine love" does not entail an essential "receptivity" or "openness" in the divine nature towards a creation with its own reciprocal causal power over the Creator. For this reason, the proponents of the doctrine of divine impassibility reject the attribution of "receptivity" or any other form of suffering to the divine nature, and limit speech about "suffering" to created beings. This perspective justifies the qualified acceptance of a Christian doctrine of divine impassibiility. I have argued here that another perspective must also be put into play, and that is the perspective that arises out of the belief that the appearance of God in the economy, and especially in the suffering of the Son upon the cross, is the revelation of the eternal God. It is not that the suffering of the Son reveals that God is moved by the suffering of a creature, but rather that the suffering of a creature — the human nature of Jesus — reveals that the Father is eternally moved by the Son. In this revelation, the suffering of God is located precisely in the relations between the persons, and is said only indirectly of the divine nature (following the logic of the identity of the divine nature and the persons). Hence, an analogical suffering in the divine nature is posited, not on the basis of the reality of a real relation of God to the world, but in the reve-

---

Aquinas' Doctrine of Creation," in *Divine Creation in Ancient, Medieval, and Early Modern Thought: Essays Presented to the Rev'd. Dr. Robert D. Crouse,* ed. Willemien Otten et al., Studies in Intellectual History (Leiden: Brill, 2007), pp. 309-33.

36. The indirect attribution of suffering to the divine nature is a true and real attribution, because the Trinity of persons and the divine nature are an identity, distinct only according to our inability to think unity and Trinity in their simultaneity.

lation of the reality of the suffering of one person of the others in the relations that are the divine persons.[37] This is what is revealed in the suffering of the man Jesus, the eternal Son of God.

Christology and the "Analogy of Suffering"

The Christian experience of suffering is one informed by faith that God, in his wisdom and mercy, has sent his Son to share in the history of human suffering in all of its depth and extent. In this sense, Jesus enters into solidarity with human fallenness into the region of alienation from God, into the gap traversed by the difference between the antecedent will of God to save all human beings and the divine permission to uphold the existence of a sinful humanity. "For our sake he made him to be sin who did not know sin, so that we might become the righteousness of God in him" (2 Cor. 5:21).

The belief that the man Jesus suffered the pain of God-forsakenness in a depth and extent greater than any other man must nevertheless be qualified.[38] Jesus did not suffer all possible physical pain in his own body, e.g., he did not suffer broken bones as did the criminals hanging alongside him on the cross. Furthermore, Jesus did not suffer the pain of eternal damnation itself, if by this "hell" one means the pain suffered by one who descends into a conscious, free, and definitive rejection of the love of God.[39] But Jesus did suffer the pain of alienation from God due to sin more intensely than the whole of humanity collectively considered, precisely be-

---

37. One difference between my own position and that developed by Jenson, in his essay "Ipse pater non est impassibilis," has to do with how we each negotiate the *triplex via* of divine predication. On the attribution of "passibility" Jenson wants to say that (1) "God (the man Jesus) suffers," (2) "God does not suffer as we suffer (divine impassibility)," and (3) "God is not impassible (as we understand impassibility)." I agree with this set of propositions, but conclude, not with a negation of a negation, but the analogical affirmation "God does suffer" (though we do not comprehend the mode of this suffering, insofar as "subsisting relations" bespeaks of "impassible suffering"). The difference may or may not be substantive, though the sentences spoken at the conclusion of the *triplex via* do differ.

38. Aquinas, *ST* III, q. 46, a. 6, cites Lamentations 1:2, "Look and see whether there is any pain comparable to my pain" in support of the view that Jesus suffered more than any other man.

39. At this point, I part ways with Balthasar and his view that "Christ's suffering, the greatest one could conceive, was like that of the damned who cannot be damned any more" (*Mysterium Paschale*, p. 170).

cause of his unparalleled clarity of insight into the gap between the antecedent and permissive will of God for humanity, that is, between the goodness of the gift of the kingdom of God offered in his person and the incomprehension and rejection he met with in his ministry which characterizes the fallen human situation.[40] In the depth of this solidarity, Jesus truly represents the whole of the human race before God, and not in a merely extrinsic way, for Jesus the Son suffers interiorly an intense sorrow and grief in his knowledge of the depth of human suffering. In this way, the profound grief of the man Jesus reveals the eternal wound in the heart of God.

But what moves Jesus to enter so deeply into solidarity with humanity in its suffering? How is it that this terrible grief does not repel him, or crush him in the unbearableness of its weight? How, in other words, is the "eternal wound" not a fatal wound, the source of death itself rather than life? Aquinas, following Augustine, taught that the life of the man Jesus exists in union with the person of the eternal Son in such a way that he is enabled to bear pain and grief beyond the capacity of any other man.[41] This intuition points, I think, in the direction of the "analogy of suffering" that I have attempted to develop in speaking of "one suffering, in two natures" as a faithful unfolding of the Chalcedonian teaching on the person of Jesus, the Son of God. Jesus is drawn into suffering in solidarity with a fallen, God-forsaken humanity, not out of love for suffering self-abnegation itself, or any of its mystical variants (as in Albert Schweitzer's celebrated account of the nobility of Jesus' tragic will to power as would-be apocalyptic Messiah). Rather, the mercy of Jesus on display in his suffering solidarity with us is grounded in his eternal suffering of the knowledge of the Father, and his suffering of the Love that bursts forth from this knowledge as the person of the Holy Spirit. This eternal suffering of God is not a love of death, destruction, negation, emptiness, or self-abnegation, but is the fullness of the joy of divine knowing and loving in the oneness of an interpersonal communion of life.[42] The Father's will

40. Thus Aquinas's interpretation (*ST* III, q. 46, a. 6) of Jesus' quotation of Psalm 22.
41. *ST* III, q. 47, a. 1; *De Trin.* IV, 13.
42. Despite my defense above of Moltmann's line of questioning, I agree with Bruce Marshall (in his essay below) that Moltmann's interpretation of Jesus' God-forsakenness as "a separation and conflict within God himself" raises difficult questions for Christian reflection. The only possible way I could save Moltmann's language (and Pope Benedict XVI's, in *Deus Caritas Est*, #10, when he writes that "God's passionate love for his peo-

that Jesus suffer passively the sin of humanity upon the cross is the outward dimension, the dimension permitted by God, of the inner vocation and will of Jesus to exist as the Father eternally exists. This existence is the joy of a life of suffering the knowledge of the other, and, "being moved by another," to suffer the Love that bursts forth in this reciprocal knowing, the Person of the Holy Spirit.

According to Paul, the meaning of conscious endurance of suffering in human history comes to light in the thought of a participation in the suffering of the First-Begotten: "Now I rejoice in my sufferings for your sake, and in my flesh I am filling up what is lacking in the afflictions of Christ on behalf of his body, which is the church" (Col. 1:24). If the Love that is eternally God is itself a form of eternal suffering, then it becomes possible to understand human suffering, consciously and patiently endured, as an entrance, in the mode of human finitude, and under the circumstances of sin and its effects, into the divine form of suffering itself. The Son, sent into the far country, makes a place, in the power of the Spirit, for members of his body to "fill up what is lacking" in his suffering and in this way share in the joy of God's eternal suffering of knowledge and love in the Trinity, the One God.

---

ple . . . is so great that it turns God against himself, his love against his justice") is to speak of God's antecedent will for the salvation of all "turning against" his permissive will in the *novum* of the appearance of the Son in history. Also, I agree with Marshall when he cites Cyril to affirm that Jesus' obedience unto death "undoes sin": this is what I mean when I speak about the weight of sin not destroying Jesus (which is the case in Schweitzer's tragic mysticism). However, unlike Marshall's formulation of the matter — in which the incarnate Word does not undergo our abandonment, but "undoes" it — I argue that the Word does both, though his experience of abandonment is not identical to our own, for though he does experience the effects of our abandonment to sin in his flesh, his experience of spiritual abandonment is "intentional" (rooted in his knowledge of and love for an abandoned humanity) and not moral. Because the weight of abandonment does not destroy Jesus, God is truly said to be "impassible" insofar as his life is not threatened by the negative associated with human suffering. But, as Jenson points out, God is "not impassible" insofar as his life is not merely a negation of possibility. My own "analogy of suffering" is connected to an attempt to find language about God in the silence generated by Jenson's "not impassible," rooted, I hope, in the final words of Jesus, the Son, in his conversation with the Father on the way to, and upon, the cross.

Conclusion

The gain in developing this Christian grammar of suffering, human and divine, is more, I hope, than merely semantic.[43] I recognize, with Weinandy and Aquinas, the risk that such speech about "suffering" in God might be confused with the defective forms of suffering associated with physical and emotional change. If such confusion can be avoided, however, such a grammar will supply a faithful and coherent Christian way to speak of God's love as a form of suffering or "being moved by another" which avoids (1) a categorical denial of suffering in God, especially in connection with the form of love that is mercy towards sinful creatures; (2) too hasty a retreat into paradox or, as in Weinandy, an unclear attribution of "passion" to God's purely actualized love; and (3) the tendency to mix or confuse divine and human natures which could arise in the work of Jenson or McCormack.[44] In addition, the christocentric approach to the mystery of

43. William Hill, "Does Divine Love Entail Suffering in God?" in *Search for the Absent God*, ed. Mary Catherine Hilkert (New York: Crossroad, 1992), p. 161, comments that Rahner's formula, "God suffers not in himself, but in his other" may prove to be nothing more than a semantic device without real content. The proposal that I make is that God does suffer in himself, that is, directly in the otherness of the persons in their eternal relations to one another, and indirectly in the difference between the antecedent and consequent will, which difference is known in its greatest intensity in the knowledge of (objective and subjective genitive each apply here) the crucified God.

44. The agreement that I share with McCormack and Jenson is rooted, I think, in openness to rethinking the categories of eternity and time in light of the belief that God's life is one of infinite, unchanging movement. McCormack works this out in terms of a divine act of freedom that encompasses the whole of divine action in history, and Jenson through the development of speech about the "infinite temporality" of God inscribed in the "narrative time" of the biblical story. Though I cannot develop this point further here, I think that the Chalcedonian distinction of two natures remains important in our speech about the unity of the divine freedom or the infinite temporality of God's life. I agree that the distinction between two natures is abstract when speaking of Jesus in the unity of his person, and hence can never name two subjects. However, insofar as Chalcedon also wants to speak of Jesus as a representative man, as "one in being with us," language about Jesus must incorporate the real distinction between divine and human nature in order to make clear that Jesus represents our existence "in a human nature" created by the Creator, a nature adopted into the form of eternal life which is natural for the man Jesus as the eternal Son of God. The logic of our "adoption" is supported by the Chalcedonian doctrine, which, it should be recalled, affirms the unity of Jesus' person through the *negation* of our adverbial understanding of the hypostatic union of two natures in Jesus: not dividedly, not separately, not mixedly, not confusedly.

human suffering which I have attempted to develop here discloses innocent suffering, or suffering in faith, patiently endured, as the creaturely form of participation in the eternity of the joyous suffering of the divine persons in a way that sheds light on Jesus' willingness to enter into the Father's will that he suffer (Mark 14:36), and Paul's ability to find joy in his own participation in the suffering of the First-Begotten (Col. 1:24).

God and Human Suffering:
His Act of Creation and His Acts in History

Thomas G. Weinandy, O.F.M. Cap.

In this essay I want to return to two topics that I previously discussed in my book, *Does God Suffer?*[1] The first concerns the act of creation. What does the act of creation teach us about the nature of God? Moreover, through the act of creation what kind of relationship is established between God and all else? I will argue that, since it establishes the foundational relationship between God and creatures, the act of creation must govern, by metaphysical necessity, all possible subsequent interactions and relationships between God and creatures. Thus, the manner in which God interacts with human beings within time and throughout history and the ensuing consequences of such interactions is predicated, in the first instance, upon the nature of Creator/creature relationship established in the act of creation. The second topic I wish to discuss here is the significance of history. Why is history theologically important within the Jewish/Christian tradition? What is the nature of God's actions within time and how do such historical actions affect humanity? Likewise, do such divine historical actions bear upon the very being of God, that is, do they ontologically affect God in a manner that is constitutive of who he is, and so both launch and contribute to his own divine history as well?

I believe that it is in the correct understanding of these philosophical and theological issues that we are able to discern properly the manner in which God addresses the mystery of evil with its consequent human suffering. Moreover, a correct conception and articulation of these issues refutes false notions of God, erroneous expressions of his relationship to and

1. See *Does God Suffer?* (Notre Dame: Notre Dame University Press, 2000).

action within history, and so misguided portrayals of his association with and response to evil and the suffering it causes.

Robert Jenson: History as the Making of God and the Act of Creation

Before examining the act of creation and what it reveals about the nature of God, I want to outline R. W. Jenson's conception of God, his actions within history, and the manner in which God creates.[2] The reason for doing so is that Jenson illustrates a vigorous trend among many contemporary theologians. He purposely sets his thought over against what he considers a deformed traditional understanding of the biblical notion of God — conceived by the Fathers and finding its maturity in Aquinas — which sprang from a less-than-robust appreciation of the importance of God's historical actions. Here God is perfectly actualized, and, while he acts in history, his historical acts do not in any way determine the kind of God he is or is becoming. Jenson espouses, in contrast, an understanding of God whereby God both is ontologically affected by human history, such as enduring suffering in union with evil-afflicted humankind, and simultaneously actualizes himself within the historical process as he acts to overcome the evil that is the cause of such suffering. While such an understanding of God substantially deviates from the traditional Jewish/Christian notion of God, Jenson argues that the biblical narrative itself demands such an interpretation.

Even though Jenson offers a "new" conception of God and of his relationship to history, he does continue to advocate a traditional Jewish/Christian understanding of the act of creation, that is, that God brings into existence, *creatio ex nihilo,* something other than himself. Is such a traditional Christian understanding of the act of creation compatible with this novel notion of the Christian God? The answer resides in what it means to enact an act of creation. God must be that being capable of enacting an act of creation.

---

2. The reason that I have chosen Robert W. Jenson as my present dialogue partner is that his two-volume work on systematic theology was still to be published when I wrote my book, *Does God Suffer?* Moreover, he was a speaker at the conference that gave rise to this volume and so has contributed an essay to this volume.

To appreciate sufficiently Jenson's proposal, and so to allow adequately for a reliable critique, a fuller account of his arguments must be set down. His central thesis, which he advocates in the first volume of his *Systematic Theology,* is that God is not only ontologically affected by the course of human history but that he also ontologically actualizes himself, becomes who he is, through his actions within history. Jenson believes that this is totally in accord with and is actually mandated by the biblical historical narrative where God reveals who he is by identifying himself and his activity with particular historical events, the most decisive being the Exodus event in the Old Testament and the resurrection of Jesus in the New Testament.[3] Thus, "these blatantly temporal events belong to his [God's] very deity."[4] Because temporal events belong to the very being of God, he actualizes himself throughout the course of history. "The biblical God is not eternally himself in that he persistently instantiates a beginning in which he already is all he ever will be; he is eternally himself in that he unrestrictedly anticipates an end in which he will be all he ever could be."[5] God, through his free historical actions, becomes the loving Father of the man Jesus through the Holy Spirit and in so doing not only constitutes himself, who he fully is, but also triumphs over sin and death.[6] "For the doctrine of Trinity is but a conceptually developed and sustained insistence that God himself is identified by and with the particular plotted sequence of events that make the narrative of Israel and her Christ."[7]

In advancing such a notion of God and his actions within time and history, Jenson has abandoned the traditional Christian understanding of God in at least three significant ways. First, God is no longer eternal in the sense that he is timeless. Jenson sees such a notion as a remnant of Greek philosophy which the early church injudiciously incorporated into the biblical notion of God and in so doing distorted it.[8] "The biblical God's eternity is his temporal infinity. . . . The true God is not eternal because he lacks time, but because he takes time. . . . The eternity of Israel's God is his

---

3. See, for example, Robert W. Jenson, *Systematic Theology,* vol. 1, *The Triune God* (New York: Oxford University Press, 1999), pp. 12, 13, 42-48, 57-59, 63.

4. Jenson, *Systematic Theology,* vol. 1, p. 49.

5. Jenson, *Systematic Theology,* vol. 1, p. 66. See also pp. 64-65.

6. For Jenson, who God is and becomes is by necessity shaped and determined by the sinful history of humankind. See *Systematic Theology,* vol. 1, pp. 72-74.

7. Jenson, *Systematic Theology,* vol. 1, p. 60.

8. See Jenson, *Systematic Theology,* vol. 1, pp. 94-95.

faithfulness. He is not eternal in that he secures himself from time, but in that he is faithful to his commitments within time."[9]

Second, because God actualizes himself within time and history he is obviously not immutable and impassible. Again, Jenson argues that these attributes were inappropriately attributed to God by the early church because it uncritically adopted a Greek philosophical understanding of deity. Because the biblical narrative portrays God as being ensconced within time, he must participate in and so be affected by the changes, good or bad, that are constitutive of a history that comprises his own history.[10]

Third, God as a trinity of persons did not exist as such from all eternity. Rather, for Jenson, God comes to be who he is by acting in a triune manner within the course of history and so becomes trinitarian. Thus, to be faithful to John's Gospel, it should not be read so as to "conceive the pre-existence of the Son as the existence of a divine entity that has simply not yet become the created personality of the Gospels."[11] Rather, "[w]hat in eternity precedes the Son's birth to Mary is not an unincarnate *state* of the Son, but a pattern of movement within the event of the incarnation, the movement to incarnation, as itself a pattern of God's triune life."[12] The Son then is eternal insofar as God always foresaw and acted within history so as to ensure that he would fully identify himself with the man Jesus, in his life and death. Following Barth, Jenson holds that since "God *is* his act of choice, God in making his actual choice not only chooses that he *will be* the man Jesus; as the event of the choice, he *is* the man Jesus."[13] This culminates in the crucifixion, for the crucifixion must be perceived "precisely as Jesus' human doing and suffering, as itself an event in God's triune life. Its reconciling efficacy, most fundamentally and baldly stated, is that this is the event in God that settles what sort of God he is over against fallen creation."[14] Thus, Jesus acts in a manner that fully actualizes and so fully

---

9. Jenson, *Systematic Theology,* vol. 1, p. 217.

10. See Jenson, *Systematic Theology,* vol. 1, pp. 100-102, 104, 108, 110-13. For a refutation of this frequently misrepresented and misguided interpretation of the Fathers' use of the concepts of "immutability" and "impassibility," see my *Does God Suffer?,* pp. 83-113. See also Paul Gavrilyuk's fine study, *The Suffering of the Impassible God: The Dialectics of Patristic Thought* (Oxford: Oxford University Press, 2004), and his essay in this present volume.

11. Jenson, *Systematic Theology,* vol. 1, p. 139.

12. Jenson, *Systematic Theology,* vol. 1, p. 141.

13. Jenson, *Systematic Theology,* vol. 1, p. 140.

14. Jenson, *Systematic Theology,* vol. 1, p. 189.

identifies who God is, and as such he becomes the Son for he supremely images what God has become and now is, and so he himself is assumed into the historical actualization of who God has become and now is. The Holy Spirit, like the Son, is not a distinct timeless person within the Trinity for Jenson, but rather the freedom that allows the Father to be Father of the Son and the Son to be the Son of the Father. As such the Spirit is "the Goal of God's ways," that is, he is God's future.[15]

The theological vocation demands that one always attempt to bring a greater depth of understanding and clarity to the gospel. Jenson has taken his vocation seriously, but in his attempt to provide a deeper and clearer understanding of the gospel, particularly in his understanding of God as a Trinity and the nature of God's actions within history, has he stayed within the legitimate parameters of the gospel? Or, has he strayed into an alien terrain where the authentic gospel is incapable of surviving? Before addressing these questions we must first see how Jenson understands the act of creation.

While Jenson's conception of God is far from traditional, he wants to hold, nonetheless, that God is the Creator, and his view in this instance is quite traditional. In the second volume of his *Systematic Theology,* he states that "God *commands* the world to be, this command is obeyed, and the event of obedience is the existence of the world."[16] Or, as he states later:

> According to Genesis, at least as Judaism and the church have read it, "before" there is the creature there is God and nothing. Nor is this nothing of a kind that can be the antecedent condition of something. God speaking is the creature's only antecedent condition: as Philip Melanchthon formulated, "When things were not, God spoke and they began to be."[17]

This understanding of creation sounds very traditional and appears to be very straightforward. God being God, he has the ability, through the mere command of his voice (through the mere act of his will), to bring that which is other than himself, and which did not exist, into existence. However, while this position, seemingly, may possess the ring of authentic

15. Jenson, *Systematic Theology,* vol. 1, p. 161.

16. Robert W. Jenson, *Systematic Theology,* vol. 2, *The Works of God* (New York: Oxford University Press, 1999), p. 7.

17. Jenson, *Systematic Theology,* vol. 2, p. 12.

Christian doctrine, in the light of Jenson's own understanding of God, this traditional view of creation rings hollow. His view of God renders God impotent to create, and so his articulation of God as Creator is, as a consequence, philosophically, utterly naïve and, theologically, wholly inadequate. To clearly see why Jenson's conception of God denies God the ability to create, we must examine the nature of the act of creation and in so doing discern the kind of God that God must be if he is to create.

The Act of Creation as Revelatory of God

Here I want to recast Aquinas's argument found in his *De Ente et Essentia*. There Aquinas distinguishes, within finite beings, *ente* (being) from *essentia* (essence). In order for finite beings to exist they must be given *being,* for their essence or nature does not necessitate that they exist, and they of themselves cannot account for their own existence. Aquinas concludes that God must be "pure being" *(esse tantum)* or "being itself" *(ipsum esse),* for "being" is required if creatures are to be, and only a being who is "being itself" is able to bestow "being" upon others.[18] To reinforce what Aquinas concludes, I want now to highlight the nature of that "giving" or "bestowing" of "being," that is, the act of creation, for it is that "act of giving" which necessarily determines and so accentuates the ontological nature of God as "the giver."

When we survey the cosmos as a whole, we find that everything which exists is in potency to change — either to become more or less what it is (accidental change), or to cease to exist in the process of becoming something else (substantial change). It is this actualization of potency, this process of change that accounts for time and thus marks out history. However, this potential for change, whether accidental or substantial, must necessarily be constitutive of something that presently *is,* for if it did not exist it would not possess the potential to change. Thus, "change" is the process by which something is in act in one manner and, through an action of its own or by an action of another, is subsequently actualized in another manner. For example, Charles must exist as Charles in a certain actualized manner in order for him to change and so be Charles in a newly actualized manner. Thus, there is an ontological priority of "existence" *(esse),* that is, that something

18. For Aquinas's entire argument, see his *De Ente et Essentia*.

is and is in act in a certain manner, over that of "potency," what it could be by way of change, in that something possesses potency only insofar as it exists and is in act in a certain manner.

While the cosmos and everything in it exists, and so is in act in some manner with the potential to further change and so be in act in another manner, neither it as a whole nor the individuals within it are of such a kind that, following the truth expressed by Aquinas, what they are ontologically demands that they actually be; nor can they account for their own existence. While stars, dogs, human beings, etc., exist and are in act in a certain manner, there is nothing intrinsic in what they are that demands that they be or accounts for the fact that they actually do exist. However, since the cosmos and everything within it does actually exist and since existence is ontologically prior to potency, the act of creation is that act whereby something comes to be or exist and so to be in act in a certain manner with the consequent potential to be in act in another manner — either accidentally or substantially.

Because the act of creation is the bringing of something into existence, that is, that it be in act in a certain manner, that which brings something into existence must possess the ability to do so. That being would be God. However, as seen above, such ability cannot reside within a being which is in act in one manner and is capable of being in act in a subsequent manner through change, for such a being would possess the same contingent ontological status as everything else, and so could not be God. Rather, such ability to enact the act of creation can only reside in a being whose very nature is "to be," that is, to be "pure act," and as such is ontologically incapable of further enacting some self-actualizing or self-constituting potential after the manner of everything else that exists. It is precisely because such a being possesses no inherent self-actualizing potential that it does possess the positive potential to bring something other than itself into existence, that is, to be in act in some manner. Thus the very character of the act of creation reveals and so demands that God be "being itself" and so "pure act," for any other mode of existence, one which by necessity would possess self-constituting potential within its own actuality, would be incapable of performing such an act.

It is obviously true to say that God can create because he is almighty and all-powerful, but for him to be such demands that he exist in a certain manner. It is not just, as Jenson would seem to have it, that he possesses some undefined and indeterminate infinite amount of power, but rather he must possess this infinite power in a very specific and precise manner. From our analysis, the act of creation determines and so defines that to be almighty or all-powerful necessitates specifically that a being be "pure act," for "might" is power in act; and to be almighty demands that one simply be "pure act" and so possess the plentitude of power. Thus, God, as "being itself," creates by the pure act that he himself is because no other act than the "pure act" that he is is capable of so doing.

The Creator/Creature Relationship

Aquinas states: "Creation signified actively means the divine action, which is God's essence, with a relation to the creature."[19] We have seen that the act of creation is an action in which God acts by no other act than the pure act that he is. Thus, the act of creation does not bring about a change in God, for the act by which he creates is none other than the pure act that he is.[20] Moreover, this act of creation establishes the primordial relationship between God as Creator and everything else as created. This relationship both ontologically distinguishes God from creatures and simultaneously unites God and creatures in a manner that is singularly immediate, intimate, dynamic, and unbreakable. It is important that these unique aspects of the Creator/creature relationship be grasped as clearly as possible.

First, the act of creation establishes an ontological distinction between God and creation, in that the manner in which creatures exist is of a different ontological order than the manner in which God exists, and thus God cannot be numbered as one being among the many. As we saw above, all creatures exist in a manner in which change is inherent within their very mode of existence, in that they actualize self-constituting potential or become something else. Jenson and those of a similar mind, because they argue for a God who changes and so possesses potential after the manner of everything else, must conclude that God does not exist in an ontological order different from everything else. Yet, in so doing, they make it metaphysically impossible for such a God to create in the sense of bringing

---

19. *ST* I, q. 45, a. 3, ad 1.

20. While the act of creation demands that God act by no other act than the "pure act" that he is, our minds are incapable of conceiving the manner in which "pure act" acts, for our direct knowledge is limited only to actions of beings who are not "pure act."

something into existence, since the very act of creation does reveal and require that God not exist in such a manner but rather exists simply as *ipsum esse.* Thus, because God's nature is simply "being itself," he cannot be placed within any genus, for there is no other being that exists in such a manner and so possesses a like nature.

Contrary to Jenson's position, it is, therefore, ontologically impossible for God, in his manner of existing as God, as *ipsum esse,* to exist as a fellow member of the created ontological order. God and all else exist in two entirely distinct manners. Therefore, this ontological divide between God and creatures demands that what takes place within the ontological order of creation cannot wash back into God's own singular ontological order in which he alone exists. It is metaphysically impossible. Thus sin and evil, which have infected the created order and inflict much suffering, reside only in that order and do not affect, in any manner, the ontological constitution of God.

Second, while the act of creation radically distinguishes the divine order from the created order, yet the act of creation, likewise, binds God and creatures in an immediate, intimate, dynamic, and unbreakable relationship. (1) The relationship is immediate in that creatures exist only by being related to God as God is, that is, as he exists as *ipsum esse,* for only by being related to God as God is, as *ipsum esse,* can creatures exist. Thus, there are no mediating acts, such as between human beings (hugs, kisses, etc.), that unite God and creatures. In the act of creation God unites creatures to himself as he is in himself, for it is through that relationship that they come to be and continue to exist. (2) The relationship is therefore utterly intimate. While human beings may express their intimate union through mediating actions such as "kisses," those very mediating actions, precisely because they are mediating, equally distance the two persons from one another. Human beings are never able to unite themselves to one another as they are, but only through the expression of some mediating action. Because the act of creation unites creatures to God as God is, this relationship is uniquely intimate. (3) The immediate intimacy that is the act of creation is further enhanced when it is perceived that the relationship is act to act, and so supremely dynamic. The act *(esse)* by which a creature exists is such an act only because it is unmediatedly related to the pure act that God is. The Creator/creature relationship is an unmediated, intimate relationship between the pure act of God as *ipsum esse* and the act, the *esse,* by which the creature is. (4) The act of creation establishes an unbreakable bond between God and creatures because only by this unmediated, intimate, and dynamic relationship between the created act of existence and God's pure act of existence do creatures continue to be. If this relationship were ontologically severed, creatures would cease to be.

What we find then in examining the act of creation is an act that radically demarcates two distinct ontological orders, that of God and that of creatures, and therefore it is ontologically impossible for creatures to exist as God exists, and it is equally ontologically impossible for God to exist as creatures exist. Moreover, because God is "being itself" and thus "pure act," he is fully actualized, and so he cannot nor does he need to actualize himself within the created order of time, and so history cannot be constitutive of who God is. I have emphasized this because this is precisely what Jenson proposes — that God exists after the manner of creatures. By conceiving God as a being who actualizes himself within the course of human history, he has attempted to place God in an ontological position in which it is metaphysically impossible for God to reside.

I have also emphasized the immediate, intimate, dynamic, and unbreakable union established by the act of creation so as to highlight that, while God and creatures exist in radically distinct ways, yet this radical distinctiveness, far from disconnecting or separating them, as Jenson would imply, actually unites them in a manner that is unique to the act of creation. Thus, the act of creation that establishes that God and creatures abide in distinct ontological orders is the very same act that unites them in an unmediated, intimate, dynamic, and unbreakable bond of life.[21]

Before proceeding, there are two further aspects of this understanding of God and creation that need to be noted. First, it is evident, both from mere observation and from revelation itself, that created reality is *good* in that it exists. The primordial "good" is "to exist." Moreover, human beings innately, even in their fallen state, testify to the goodness of truth, justice, love, etc. Where do such virtues originate? The obvious answer is: from God. However, within human beings virtues are virtues only insofar as they are in act. Human beings are potentially just and only become just when they habitually enact just actions. Human beings are potentially loving persons and

---

21. For a fuller exposition of the act of creation and the kind of relationship it establishes between God and man, see my books, *Does God Change? The Word's Becoming in the Incarnation* (Still River, Mass.: St. Bede's Publications, 1985), pp. 88-96 and *Does God Suffer?*, pp. 113-46. In the latter book I examine the trinitarian nature of the act of creation.

only become such insofar as they habitually enact loving actions. We now have a situation similar to that of the need for the "act of existence." Because creatures are only potentially truthful, just, and loving, they are incapable of instantiating such virtuous potential within themselves. Only a being who is goodness fully in act, truth fully in act, justice fully in act, and love fully in act is capable of implanting such potential in something other than himself. If God were not love fully in act, then he would be, as are creatures, ontologically in need of being given it himself, but such an ontological need would, *ipso facto*, disqualify him from actually being God. Jenson, without any metaphysical defense, presumes that God is good, truthful, loving,, and just, but there is no inherent or necessary reason, philosophically or theologically, for him to be such, in Jenson's conception, since, according to him, God does not, from all eternity, instantiate such virtues fully in act. Only if God is "being itself," and thus inherently absolute goodness in act — for "to be" is "to be good" — is he capable of being truth, justice, love, etc. fully in act. Thus, the act of creation by which human beings come to be with the potential for development through change is the same act by which they are capable of being and becoming truthful, just, and loving.

Second, it should be evident at this point that to say that God is "being itself" and thus "pure act" means that he is immutable not in the sense of being static and inert, but rather that being "pure act" he is so dynamic that no further self-constituting action could possibly make him more dynamic. Moreover, for God to be impassible does not mean that he lacks the ability to love in all its various manifestations — admonition, kindness, compassion, forgiveness, etc. — but that because he is love fully in act, he does not need to be affected in some manner so as to be passionately aroused as human beings need to be in order to perform loving acts. God being fully in act demands that his love be fully in act, and so he is supremely fervent and attentive in his love.[22]

God and History

Having examined the importance of the act of creation for determining the nature of God and his relationship to creation, we can now turn to the importance of history and God's action within it.

22. For a more complete presentation on what it means for God to be immutable and impassible, see my *Does God Suffer?*, pp. 113-27.

Thomas G. Weinandy, O.F.M. Cap.

One of the motivating factors rousing Jenson and others to argue for a God who actualizes himself within the course of history — in so doing acquiring his own personal history — is that such an understanding appears to enhance, in accord with the perceived biblical narrative, God's immanence within history itself. His salvific actions would seemingly assume a superior importance within the human historical narrative. He looks to be a more immediate, dynamic, significant, and ultimately crucial player in the human drama that is being historically played out between the forces of sin and evil and those of justice, truth, and love. Moreover, the impression is given that God participates more directly in the vicissitudes of history and so co-suffers in solidarity with all of humanity. Within Jenson's view not only do we come to know who God is through his actions within the historical drama, but we actually witness in these actions the kind of God he is truly coming to be. What could possibly be more dramatic than to discover that God has become so loving that he has identified with the one who dies on the cross? "Why did Jesus have to die? Most directly stated: the crucifixion is what it cost the Father to be in fact — and not just in somebody's projected theology or ideology — the loving and merciful Father of the human persons that in fact exist."[23] God becomes the truly loving Father in actuality (in act) through the historical action of Jesus' death.

Such a conception of God, while metaphysically abrogated by the act of creation properly understood, is in itself absolutely devastating to the Jewish/Christian understanding of God and to the relevance of his actions within human history.[24] The significance of human history, from within a

23. Jenson, *Systematic Theology*, vol. 1, p. 191.
24. Jenson insists, as we saw, that his understanding of God actualizing himself historically is not only warranted by the biblical narrative but that the biblical narrative itself actually demands such an interpretation. If such were the case, why is it that the biblical narrative was never interpreted in this manner from the time of the early Fathers? It would seem a tad bit premature to conclude that the Church, for two thousand years, misunderstood and so misinterpreted the Bible on such central issues of faith as that of the Trinity, the incarnation and salvation, and that Jenson has ingeniously discovered, finally, the proper hermeneutical clue for conceiving a correct interpretation and understanding. While Jenson claims that he is merely a biblical exegete, in actual fact the basis of his exegesis lies not within the scriptural text itself but from within erroneous philosophical principles imported from without. He has overlaid the biblical narrative with a philosophical template that actually distorts the narrative.
For an excellent critique of Jenson's view that God constitutes himself within the his-

Jewish/Christian tradition, is not found in the annals of God becoming God. Rather, biblical history chronicles the immanent actions of the wholly transcendent, perfectly loving and all-powerful God by which history assumes a more than this-worldly historical significance. Through God's actions in history, history is given a purpose and terminus that exceeds the historical created order; history now leads to a trans-historical heaven, that is, sharing in the life and love of the Father by being conformed into the likeness of the glorified risen Christ through the power of the Holy Spirit. Therefore, God's actions are of supreme historical salvific importance precisely because they are performed by a God who transcends the historical, created order, and not merely by another actor from within the historical, created order. If God were merely another member actor within history, his actions could not bestow on history a meaning and goal that exceeded it, for he too would be subject to and so limited by the created historical order. Moreover, specific to our purposes here, if God were ensconced within the historical created order, it would then be impossible for him to act so as to conquer evil and the suffering it causes.

God's historical actions are to free humankind from sin and evil, and thus from the suffering that accompanies them and, simultaneously, to establish, by these same actions, a new or deeper relationship with him as he is, as the wholly other transcendent and all-loving God. If God existed as a member of the same ontological order as everything else, he too would be infected by the evil that resides within that order, would experience the suffering produced by it, and thus would also need to be freed from it. Moreover, whatever consequences God's actions might have, they would not establish a new kind of relationship with a transcendent all-perfect and all-good God, who is eternally all-loving, since God never did exist in

---

torical process, see David Bentley Hart, *The Beauty of the Infinite: The Aesthetics of Christian Truth* (Grand Rapids: Eerdmans, 2003), pp. 155-67. See also his article, "The Lively God of Robert Jenson," *First Things* 156 (October 2005): 28-34. Hart points out the devastating effect of Jenson's Hegelianism, whereby the immanent Trinity is collapsed into the economic "If the identity of the immanent Trinity with the economic is taken to mean that history is the theater within which God — as absolute mind, or process, or divine event — finds or determines himself as God, there can be no way of convincingly avoiding the conclusion (however vigorously the theologian might deny the implication) that God depends upon creation to be God and that creation exists by necessity (because of some lack in God), so that God is robbed of his true transcendence and creation of its true gratuity" (*The Beauty of the Infinite*, p. 157).

that manner and so cannot exist now or in the future in that manner. Let me illustrate these points by examining the two divine actions that play so prominent a role in Jenson's work.

The Event of the Exodus

In the Exodus, God, manifesting that he truly is the almighty, transcendent God who is, acted within history so as to free the Israelites from their slavery in Egypt. God's actions within history were able to free the Israelites from their geopolitical situation of slavery precisely because, as transcendent, he himself was not historically enslaved by the geopolitical situation but could freely act in a manner that was truly liberating. Moreover, he also acted, through the establishment of the covenant, so as to forge a new kind of relationship with the Israelites. He would truly be their God in a manner that differed from the kind of relationship he would have with the other nations. Equally, the Israelites would be his people in a manner that differed from the kind of relationship other peoples would have with him. Thus God's historical actions fashioned a relationship with the Israelites singularly intimate and dynamic, a relationship that would not have been possible if God, as transcendent and wholly loving, had not historically so acted. What we find here is not that God changes through his actions within history, but that through his historical actions a historical people now has access to God in a manner that was not possible prior to his historical actions. The historical importance of the action is not how the action enhanced God. He is not the beneficiary of his historical action. Rather, the Israelites were the beneficiary of God's historical action. Their history, as a nation and as individuals, was enhanced and changed by God's historical action. It was the beneficence of this covenant with the transcendent all-loving and all-merciful God that sustained the hope of the Israelites when they subsequently, as individuals and as a nation, were tragically confronted by their own sinful history and the historical tribulations and sufferings that accompanied it.

The Exodus event illustrates two important aspects concerning the nature of God and his actions within history. First, the ultimate mystery within the Jewish/Christian revelation, as biblically narrated, is that God, who wholly transcends the historical created order, can act within the historical created order, as he exists as the wholly transcendent God, without losing his wholly transcendent divinity in so doing. The beneficiaries of such historical actions are human beings in that, because of such actions, they are able to relate to God, as he actually exists as wholly transcendent, in a manner that was not possible prior to God's actions. Second, God's compassion is not defined by his ability to suffer in solidarity with human beings, but, as the Exodus event illustrates, in his ability to act so as to alleviate the cause of the suffering, and simultaneously to establish a relationship with himself that assures that future suffering is perceived in a new manner, that is, from within that new relationship.[25]

God's Definitive Antidote to Suffering: Jesus Christ

If the Exodus event illustrates God acting within the historical created order without losing his transcendent divine status, the supreme instantiation of this mystery is the incarnation. Here the wholly transcendent eternal Son of God, ontologically equal to the Father, came to exist as a historical man without loss of his wholly transcendent divinity, and, as such, performed historical human actions.[26] Both terms of this equation are of equal and necessary importance. These specific human actions, not divine

25. See Aquinas, *In Psalmos,* XXIV, 8 and *ST* II-II, q. 30, a. 4. For a fuller discussion of this point, see my *Does God Suffer?,* pp. 167-68.

26. Because Jenson disallows the eternal pre-existence of the Son, his understanding of the incarnation is erroneous. The Son does not come to exist as man, but rather, for Jenson, the Father merely identifies himself with (adopts) the man Jesus, who then reflects as "Son" the authentic identity of what the Father has now become. What Jenson forgets is the venerable adage articulated by the early Fathers and marshaled into service by Athanasius against the Arians: If the Father is eternally the Father, then the Son must be eternally the Son for if there ever was a time when the Son was not, then the Father would not be either. While Jenson refers to God as Father prior to the coming of Jesus as Son, there is no longer any theological justification for such a claim. In the end it must be admitted that Jenson does not uphold the Trinity, but a view that might at best be considered modalistic. God merely acts in a trinitarian pattern — the man Jesus being the image of what God has become and the Holy Spirit being God's power to actualize his future.

For a critique of Jenson's understanding of the pre-existence of Christ from a biblical perspective, see Simon Gathercole, "Pre-existence, and the Freedom of the Son in Creation and Redemption: An Exposition in Dialogue with Robert Jenson," *International Journal of Systematic Theology* 7, no. 1 (2005): 38-51; and from a systematic and philosophical perspective, see Oliver D. Crisp, "Robert Jenson on the Pre-Existence of Christ," *Modern Theology* 21, no. 1 (2007): 27-45.

actions, are salvific and they are salvific precisely because they were performed by the Son of God. It was these historical human actions of the Son
of God, his passion and death, that changed — not the personal being of
God, but human beings' personal relationship to him. Through his passion
and death, Jesus, as the Son incarnate, offered his life, by the power of the
Holy Spirit, as a loving sacrifice to the Father and so reconciled humankind to the Father. The cross, then, is not the manner in which God as Father, Son, and Holy Spirit becomes the all-loving God, for how could any
being become perfectly "all-loving" in the absolute sense of being "love" itself if he were not perfectly so by nature?[27] Rather, the cross is the supreme
expression of what God as Father, Son, and Holy Spirit is eternally, for only
if the persons of the Trinity are eternally all-loving would they possess the
love required to enact the drama of the cross each in accordance with who
they are — the Father who loved the world so much that he sent his only
begotten Son into the world; the Son who loved the Father and every human being so much that he was willing to be obedient to the Father even to
death on the cross; and the Holy Spirit in whose consummate love the Father sent the Son and in whose sacrificial love the Son offered his life to the
Father. Moreover, by raising Jesus bodily from the dead by the power of the
Holy Spirit the Father made possible for humankind a new and definitive
relationship with the persons of the Trinity.[28] Such a relationship with the
Trinity was not possible prior to the historical actions of Jesus' passion and
death and his subsequent action of sending forth the Spirit, as the risen
Lord of history. Thus, again, the beneficiary of these actions was not the
personal enhancement of God's manner of being but that of human beings. They are now able to live, within the historical created order, as children of the Father, in union with Christ the Son, through the transforming
indwelling of the Holy Spirit. Thus Christians are united to the persons of
the Trinity — as they themselves exist as the transcendent God. And so this

27. While the good angels and the saints in heaven become "all-loving," they do so from
within the limited capacity of their created natures. Being finite, their love merely reflects
the perfect infinite and eternal love that defines the very nature of God's absolute being.

28. The nature of the resurrection, as the triumph over the power of death and the glorification of Jesus' full humanity, requires a cause that exceeds the finite, the earthly, or the
historical, all of which by their nature are incapable of such an act, and all of which, moreover, have been enfeebled by sin and death. While the resurrection is an act within history, it
can only be performed by a being who transcends the historical and whose very nature is to
live and so be capable of bestowing life.

historical Christian life, lived on earth, is but the foretaste of its fulfillment in heaven.[29] It is this new and unique relationship that is the ultimate resolution to evil and the suffering that it causes.

By being united to the risen Lord Jesus and so becoming members of his body through the shared life of the Holy Spirit, Christians come to know God truly as their Father. Moreover, this relationship is a sure pledge that everlasting life and happiness, in union with the Trinity and all of the saints, is their certain goal, for all sin and evil, even death itself, are incapable now of severing this relationship; the very relationship itself is fount of the fullness of life and so the spring from which perfect joy flows. While in this life Christians can still suffer horrendous evils, they now do so in union with Christ their risen victorious head, who forever intercedes on their behalf before the merciful face of the Father. Moreover, Christians experience suffering within an ecclesial context, that is, in union with their fellow brothers and sisters here on earth and with the triumphant saints in heaven.[30]

The Christian gospel, then, is God's definitive response to the mystery of evil precisely because salvation in Jesus Christ unites us to the persons of the Trinity, in whom no evil and suffering reside but only perfect life and abundant happiness. If the Trinity itself were mired in the history of evil and the suffering it causes, as Jenson and others insist, then to be united to them would be of no consolation but rather the cause of absolute despair. It is only because the persons of the Trinity reside in an ontologi-

29. I have argued elsewhere that the persons of the Trinity are subsistent relations fully in act, that is, the Father is fatherhood fully in act in relationship to the Son and the Holy Spirit. The Son is sonship fully in act in relationship to the Father and the Holy Spirit. The Holy Spirit is love fully in act in relationship to the Father and the Son. See Thomas G. Weinandy, *The Father's Spirit of Sonship: Reconceiving the Trinity* (Edinburgh: T. & T. Clark, 1995) and *Does God Suffer?*, pp. 113-29. Because these relationships are fully in act, grace is that effect within the believer whereby he or she is related to the persons of the Trinity as they themselves exist and are related to one another. The Holy Spirit conforms believers into the likeness of the risen incarnate Son by uniting them to him and in so doing they become children, in him, of the Father. Since Jenson holds, as do many others, that God changes, the only way God can relate to human beings and they to him is through mediating acts that bring about change in God. These mediating acts may form a relationship, but their very mediation demands that the two terms are not related to one another as they fully exist in themselves.

30. For a fuller account of my understanding of salvation and its effects, as well as how Christians presently experience suffering in the light of this salvation, see my *Does God Suffer?*, pp. 214-86.

cal order distinct from that of the created order, and so are not contaminated with the malady of evil, that they, in their immutably all-consuming and perfect love, are able to so act in time and history as to unite us to themselves, thus freeing us from the wages of sin and rescuing us from the ravages of death. Christians now longingly anticipate the day when Jesus will return in glory so that those who are in communion with him will share fully in his risen glory and life. On that day every tear will be wiped away and the fullness of heavenly joy will commence.

Ipse Pater Non Est Impassibilis

Robert W. Jenson

I

What I hope to offer in this paper is a suggestion or two that may help to avoid stalemate between such supposedly antithetical groups as "passibilists" and "impassibilists" or "traditionalists" and "revisionists." And in this connection let me take occasion to regret that Fr. Weinandy chose to deliver his attack on my previously published proposals outside the framework laid down for contributors to the symposium. For who knows? Openness might have led to some rapprochement.

It would in general be good if we could get past polemics of the kind that determines for someone — without asking him — what he must *really* mean, in order then to denounce it. From Weinandy's paper, I will instance only one central case. He writes that according to me God "actualizes himself . . . through his actions within history." I have not said any such pseudo-Hegelian thing, nor do Weinandy's citations from my work entail the proposition. Or rather, they entail it if and only if one invincibly presumes as the conceptual framework precisely the construal of time and eternity that I want to overcome — that is, only by a remarkably comprehensive *petitio principii.* In response to the editors' gracious and repeated requests that I clarify a little the issue with Weinandy and those who in this matter are like him, I will add a few paragraphs here — but only with the urgent plea that the actual beginning of *my* concern in *this* paper is at the number II.

It was, is, and, until the Lord comes or the western church disappears, will remain a chief intellectual labor of the western church to respond to the profound questions posed by pre-Christian Greece's religious thinkers, and in responding to transform them.[1] Encountering the new gospel, they asked: What sort of "being" does this "Son of God" have? By what title is he "God"? What, indeed, do Christians mean by "being"? Or "God"? We have been working on answers ever since. The temptation that regularly besets us is fundamentalist longing to think that this conversation has come to a satisfactory rest at some point in the past, whether with the Fathers or Thomas or Luther or Barth or whomever, so that we are dispensed from its labors. Pointing out that this is indeed a temptation should not be regarded as an attack on the tradition; for — as especially much Catholic theology has recently insisted — the tradition is fundamentally the continuing enterprise itself, encompassing but never identical with its achievements to date.

Parmenides and Plato and Aristotle and the Stoics did not know the incarnation or the biblical distinction of creature from Creator; thus their vision of deity necessarily differed greatly from that of Scripture. For them, the great distinction was between the temporal world and the atemporal realm of deity, the latter conceived as an abstract sheer other. Plato's deity is the geometric point at the center of time's circular mobile, that as merely geometric is itself immobile. Aristotle's deity is an "unmoved" mover,[2] an utterly self-contained substance, that attracts and so moves temporal almost-substances precisely by its obliviousness to them and their temporal troubles. For both, deity is pure timelessness.

It is apparent that this theology and Scripture's portrayal of God cannot both be true. The great labor begun by the Fathers and carried on through the centuries has been so to converse with Greece's pre-Christian theologians, as to rejoice in areas of agreement, to be energized and enlightened by their insights, and to overcome their pagan assumptions about being and God. Is my "being" — what it means for me to be — persistence in what I am from the beginning, and so am timelessly, in the manner of the Greek thinkers? Is it not first anticipation of what I will be at the End, and so am *in via,* à la Paul? And if God is the Being of which my being is a participation, what then of him?

---

1. Adolf von Harnack notoriously taught several generations of theologians to suppose that what the Fathers were doing was the Hellenizing of the gospel, whereas what they in fact were working on was the Gospelizing of Hellenism.

2. Or movers. This theology can accommodate a relative polytheism.

My own attempt to carry on the work may prove to make a minor or
no contribution. But in the nature of the case *all* contributions — past,
present, or future — to this effort must be partial and incomplete, including those of the Fathers or Thomas or whomever; and to suppose that any
of them provides a sabbath rest leads to ideology, not theology. I confess
that in some critiques of my writing I detect yearning for such respite, and
discern more remainders of Greek paganism's construal of deity than is
tolerable at this stage of theological history — notably located in nervous
insistence on God's utter impassibility. I am moved to say, as a theological
hero of mine said of the neo-Arian devotees of impassibility:[3] "[L]et them
rather . . . find the mark of deity in endless futurity . . . ; let them guide
their thinking by what is to come and is real in hope rather than by what is
past and old."[4]

II

I return now to what I wrote for the symposium, the "suggestion or two"
announced at the beginning. Let me start with the simpleminded beginning of my own problem. If indeed the Christology is true whose slogan is
that "one of the Trinity suffered in the flesh," then the God here referred to
by "the Trinity" is not impassible, in any use of the adjective that would occur to a native user of Greek, Latin, or English — or at least not to any such
user who had mastered the relation of subject and predicate.

It is indeed important that the sentence ends with "in the flesh," but
this adverbial phrase — adverbial also in the Greek — does not displace
the subject-object relation: with or without "in the flesh" the subject of
"suffered" is God the Son/Logos. Until 325, theologians alarmed by the suffering the Bible attributes to God, could exploit the seeming need to *specify*
the deity of the Son over against that of the Father — who was taken to be
God without specification — so as to construe the Son as ever so slightly
less God than the Father, and so as one to whom the salvifically necessary
suffering could be assigned without alarm. But Nicea stopped that bolt-
hole. After Nicea the ground shifted, and from then until 451 the move was
to intimate — never more than that — that there are two persons in Christ

---

3. That was the real content of their "ungenerate."
4. Gregory of Nyssa, *Against Eunomius,* 1:672.

himself, one to be untouched God and the other to do the suffering. But
Chalcedon's "one and the same" plugged also this escape — or did where
the whole decree was taken seriously and not just its technical terminology
and one of its attachments. Cyril's famous *apathos pathoi* is on the right
track, and the subject of "suffers" remains the same also in this formulation. Let me add that the suggestions I will offer might well be taken as attempts to unpack Cyril's formula.

I am more or less aware of the subtle qualifications and real insights
involved in the tradition's sophisticated massaging of the notion of
impassibility. But in any sense of impassibility perceptible on the *face* of
the word, it will not do as an attribute of the God of Scripture and dogma.
The difficulty is that the face-values of the words we appropriate can creep
back into the structure and tone of our discourse.

There is another simplicity: neither can we say that the biblical God is
"passible." Jürgen Moltmann's theatrically suffering God, or the God of
"open theism," is no more biblical than his contradictory, and certainly no
more coherent with dogma. Pagan gods have sometimes been given to suffering. "The God whom men call Zeus," the abstracted deity of high Hellenic theology, could not suffer, but the actual old Zeus himself had his
Hera, and between Osiris's divine lot and that of Sisyphus there is little to
choose. Which is why none of that crowd is the Lord. If it is permitted to
mention Martin Luther here, his outrage at Erasmus was in considerable
part driven by insistence that God is not going to react to our bad behavior
by withdrawing his promises, that he cannot be affected in this way.[5] The
Lord can say by the mouth of Ezekiel that Israel's unfaithfulness has broken his heart (Ezek. 8:6) — which is certainly an affect. But throughout
Ezekiel's book the Lord's concluding insistence remains: without tenses, "I
am the Lord."

What then are we to do? We are of course dealing with paradox.[6] But if
someone asks "How do you *mean* this paradox?," it does not help simply to
repeat, "It is a paradox."

When both answers to a question posed between contradictories seem
wrong or both right, the question may be wrongly posed. That is the possibility this paper will explore. Perhaps, *in divinis*, "*x est passibilis*" is not the

5. Martin Luther, *De Servo Arbitrio*, WA 18:619.
6. And my own discussion of these matters in the *Systematic Theology* begins with
Melito of Sardis.

right contradictory to *"x est impassibilis."* Perhaps *"x non est impassibilis"* with the double negative is, *in divinis,* the precisely right stipulation.

III

My title is, of course, a famous line from Origen's homily on Ezekiel 16.[7] The two contexts are important: one is Ezekiel's allegory of foundling Jerusalem, and the other an argument Origen constructs. Origen stipulates "pity" as the *caritatis passio,* a dispositional affect necessarily present in anyone who displays *caritas,* as the Lord in Scripture does to his people. This affect must be in God, and indeed eternally antecedent in the Father, as the ground in God for involvement *in conversatione humanae vitae,* an involvement centering in the Son's *passio.* Hence not only the Son but *ipse Pater* is not-impassible. Origen constructs his argument as exegesis of Ezekiel's allegory[8] in which the Lord's pity is evoked as he, on his way to some unspecified destination, happens upon the discarded infant. That is, the Lord's pity appears during an incident on the divine way.

It is the notion of a divine way, and of a dispositional *passio* in God as the possibility of certain incidents on that way, that I suggest may be developed to offer some alleviation of our problem. Many, I think, of our difficulties stem from a subliminal supposition that passibility or impassibility would themselves be statically possessed — impassible! — characters of God.

Let us suppose that a narrative can be told of God's life with us creatures, that is true of God himself — that is, that the Bible and the doctrine of the Trinity are true to God. Narrative goes in waves, and its waves overlap and intersect in indefinitely many ways. Perhaps passibility and impassibility — and indeed other such abstractly stated attributes — appear with different waves of the narrative — or, as I will shortly suggest, with interactions between hyperbar levels of the narrative's music. Perhaps the question is not whether God is or is not impassibly possessed of the abstract character of impassibility, but where he is in his story with us. And it

---

7. Origène, *Homélies sur Ézéchiel,* ed. Marcel Borret, Sources Chrétiennes (Paris: Editions du Cerf, 1989), pp. 229-30. Since Origen's homilies are preserved only in Latin translation, we cannot always be sure what "the historical Origen" may have written. Here, I mean by "Origen" whoever is responsible for the text I adduce.

8. Which he does not allegorize, since it already is an allegory.

is indeed his story with us — the "economic" Trinity — that is the locus of our problem and of most of the following discussion; though we will come to brief evocation of the "immanent" Trinity.

Narrative time — that is, the time that actually obtains, the time traversed in Scripture's narrative — is neither linear nor cyclical, nor is it accommodated merely by talk about *kairoi* or such. Narrative time is the ordering of events by their mutual reference, and the narratively temporal extension of an event is thus its relation to other events in a set. Let us suppose a set of events A, B, C, and D. C may very well embrace A and B, and D be the event of the succession itself. Let us suppose a unitary subject of A, B, C, and D. Perhaps this subject may truly be said to be Y as the subject of D, but –Y as the subject of C, Y as the subject of A, and –Y as the subject of B.

And now let me make a main move of this paper. The pure actuality of narrative time can most sharply be seen in western music as it was from the sixteenth century through most of the twentieth. That music can be invoked in discussing such matters is of course not an original idea: when Augustine wanted to model the time of his confessional narrative, he turned immediately to the sequence of semantically empty sounds we call a melody.

Nor is it any accident that our music has this narrative character. What in the West we know as music appeared within a culture that supposed history was getting someplace, that it had a plot, and that plotted sequences — subplots — could therefore often be discerned also in shorter sequences than universal history. A piece of western music is the semantically emptied mode of such a sub-narrative — or even, in occasional Promethean intention, of the whole universal story. When the culture lost faith that history has a plot and subplots, our music promptly morphed into an antithesis of its original self.

Recommending theological attention to the way time works in western music, Jeremy Begbie[9] has pointed out that a western composition's total plot of tensions and resolutions has a bottom temporal level of meter-bars, and as many superimposed levels of ever more encompassing "hyperbars" — phrases, themes, movements, etc. — as the music's sophistication requires. What time it is in a piece of music thus depends on

9. Jeremy S. Begbie, *Theology, Music and Time* (Cambridge: Cambridge University Press, 2000), pp. 29-70.

which level of bars or hyperbars you are asking about. And — much to our point — thrusting bars or hyperbars at one level may, e.g., be embraced by dragging hyperbars at another level. Which then is the piece, vital or foreboding?

In Ezekiel's/Origen's story of God and foundling Jerusalem, was God passible when he felt pity for the exposed newborn Jerusalem? With Origen, we will have to say "Yes," since in fact he was affected and so manifested this dispositional property.[10] Was God impassible in his commitment to the wayward foundling? With Luther we will have to say "Yes," since at this level of the narrative's hyperbars he simply overrides all challenges to that commitment.

Is God, considered as the subject of his total history with us, impassible? By the testimony of Scripture, he is indeed — in any plausible sense of the word. Is God, happening upon a lost sheep, passible? By the testimony of Scripture he is indeed — in any plausible sense of the word. Is then God, abstracted from all such tales, passible or impassible?

But that last is a pseudo-question, since the abstraction cannot be performed on the biblical God. Which brings us to the trinitarian ground of all this — where some here were anyway sure I was heading.

Whatever we find to say about the "immanent" Trinity is derived from the revelation we call the "economic" Trinity, that is, from a certain constellation of bars and hyperbars in God's history with us. Both in that constellation and in the derivation, much that occurs in God's whole history with us, taken with all its notes and their sequences and other relations in bars and hyperbars, is omitted: e.g., the specific wording of the Son's prayer to the Father in John 17 is not revelatory of an inner-triune relation, is revelatory only of the occurrence of such a prayer — or anyway, this holds so far as we can know and so for the doctrine we can propound.

But while trinitarian doctrine is *derived* from the full biblical tale of his life with us, with all its levels and intersections of time-markings, and while the derivation elides a great deal, teaching about the immanent Trinity is not and must not be *abstracted* from the full tale. Whether or not a theologian thinks it wise to deploy the notions of narrative or history in an account of God's immanent life — analogously of course — if he is orthodox he cannot deny the hypostatic identity of one *persona* of the immanent Trinity with one *persona* of the saving history, and there-

---

10. Whatever it may mean to say that God has such-and-such a property.

fore cannot deny the hypostatic identity of the inner-triune relations, all of which have the Son as a pole, with narrative relations of the saving history.

IV

Thus there is in the immanent life of God something like what I have called narrative time. Or rather, there is in the immanent life of God that which narrative time is something like. In his immanent narrative time — begging permission to call it that — God to be sure transcends any conceivable "linear" time — as the partisans of divine impassibility rightly insist. *And* by the same token he also transcends any conceivable mere negation of our times — the negation on which partisans of divine impassibility seem to insist. If "eternal" is with the Greeks taken to mean simply "not temporal," it cannot be used of the real God.

The life of the biblical God cannot be located on any "time-line"; *that is,* it cannot be laid out on any story's bottom level of time-bars. Thus it makes no sense to ask what was happening "before" the inner-triune begetting of the Son, as was recognized at Nicea. And by the very same token, it makes no sense to ask what things in God were like "before" Mary conceived — even as it makes perfect and necessary sense to ask what eternity must be like for the Son to be born in time of a woman.

Nor can the biblical God be located at a point equidistant from all points on any time-line; our narrative/music does not circle endlessly around him. Thus the assertion that all points on any time-line are simultaneous for him, and the assertion that they are not simultaneous for him, are equally meaningless.

What then is the narrative time — or whatever you choose to call it — that God has in himself? It is marked out by the well-known "inner-trinitarian relations" — though perhaps the traditional list needs some additions. E.g., the Father begets the Son and is begotten by no one; here is a clear before and after — as those who lost at Nicea had insisted — which however can be plotted on no straight time-line — as those who won had insisted. After Nicea, we may take it as determinative for God's narrative time that the spatial language involved in all our images of time cannot constrain it. This does not mean God's time does not obtain; on the contrary, it means that it is the archetype of all times.

V

As the general assignment of our conference supposes, our attempts to construe the fact of providence are indeed a chief place where difficulties with God's impassibility/passibility impede our efforts. According to Thomas — whom I should doubtless forebear to cite in this company — God's universal knowledge and universal will are in such a sort one that God's foreseeing determines what is seen. He is the cause of all things *per suum intellectum,* and in this context that holds precisely with respect of their ordering to their good.[11] The pre/provision, moreover, extends to every item and single event of creation.[12]

It is apparent that this doctrine must provoke some questions. One is the so-called problem of theodicy. In my judgment, this problem is in this life insoluble: faith in God's universal ordering of creation to the good — i.e., to himself — will remain a great "Nevertheless . . ." until the final vision. Another is the question with which Thomas ends the *quaestio* just cited: *Utrum providentia rebus provisis necessitatem imponat.* This he disposes of elegantly and so far as I am concerned for good and all[13] — though folk do have some trouble keeping his answer in mind.

In my view, however, the really difficult question concerns the meaningfulness of petitionary prayer — which is, after all, the kind most recommended and practiced in Scripture. Suppose I pray for someone's recovery. If the Lord foresees from all eternity that my friend will/not recover, and if that foreseeing determines the event, and if he thus already knows what he ordains and ordains what he knows, what role does my petition have?

It is a question every pastor regularly encounters. And the answers offered are in large part evasions. Prayer undoubtedly "opens" the soul to God, but is the content of the utterance irrelevant to its benefit? Praying is undoubtedly salutary obedience to the Lord's command, but why this particular command in the first place? Petition is undoubtedly — and this has been my own mantra — the appropriate utterance of a creature to the Creator, but if we remain with this formalism how does that construe the Creator/creature relation? Not, I fear, conformably to Thomas's resolution of determinism.

11. Aquinas, *Summa Theologiae* I, q. 22, a. 1.
12. *ST* I, q. 22, a. 2.
13. *ST* I, q. 23, a. 4.

It is the "already" two paragraphs back that is the Jonah, for its appearance presupposes that God's history with us can indeed be laid out on a straight time-line, on a sequence of meter-bars without hyperbars, without phrasing or melody or development or . . . ; that is, it presupposes that "already" and "before" and their like are univocal when used of God's time with us. What, however, if the temporal relation between God's determination and my prayer is not exhausted in any one before-and-after? What if there is a section through the bar-and-hyperbar structure of God's time with us, in which his determination precedes my prayer, *and* one in which my prayer precedes his determination?

How does time work when in obedience to our Lord's command, we address God as "Father," and tell him how we children think the universe should go? With assurance that our opinion means something material to him, as it would to a good parent? We address this Father, after all, in unison with the One who by birth has that right, and who is himself one of the eternal Trinity whose joint knowledge and decision[14] determine the event. Prayer is *involvement* in Providence.

If prayer is anything less, it is simply a pitiful delusion. Perhaps if we were more straightforwardly to consider the biblical necessity of the two sentences just previous to this one, discussion of God's relation to our time, and so of his passibility/impassibility, would make more progress.

---

14. For will and intellect belong to nature, not hypostasis.

God's Impassible Suffering in the Flesh: The Promise of Paradoxical Christology

Paul L. Gavrilyuk

I. Paradoxical Christology as a Part of *Lex Orandi*

I cannot think of a more suitable occasion for discussing the topic that is before us than the season of Lent. During this time we are invited to purify our spiritual senses in order to enter into the mystery of Christ's passion so that we could share more fully in the reality of his resurrection. The hymnography of the Byzantine *Lenten Triodion* gives us much to ponder in this regard. On Good Friday the Orthodox Church sings:

> Today he who hung the earth upon the waters is hung
>   upon the cross.
> He who is king of the angels is arrayed in a crown of thorns.
> He who wraps the heaven in clouds is wrapped in the
>   purple mockery.
> He who in Jordan set Adam free receives blows upon his face.
> The bridegroom of the Church is transfixed with nails.[1]

The author of the hymn draws a sharp and deliberate contrast between the divine subject, identified as the Creator of the world, and the characteristically human experiences of humiliation, mockery, crucifixion, and death that this subject is made to endure. The same point is reempha-

---

1. "The Service of the Twelve Gospels," antiphon 15, in Mother Mary and Kallistos Ware, trans., *The Lenten Triodion* (South Canaan, Pa.: Saint Tikhon's Seminary Press, 2001), p. 587. This antiphon is also repeated during the Royal Hours (p. 609) and on Holy Saturday, Matins, Second Stasis (p. 637).

sized in different ways throughout the *Lenten Triodion*. Drawing upon the eschatological imagery of Matthew 27:45, 51-52, the hymnographer presents crucifixion as a great cosmic drama: "When the thief beheld the author of life hanging upon the cross, he said: 'If it were not God made flesh that is crucified with us, the sun would not have hid its rays nor would the earth have quaked and trembled.'"[2] Elsewhere the Byzantine hymnographers address Christ as "the crucified God" and speak of his "divine passion" and even of "God's death":

> And putting all our trust in it [the cross], we sing to Thee, our crucified God (σὲ τὸν σταυρωθέντα, Θεόν): Have mercy upon us.[3]

> We exalt thy divine Passion (τὰ θεῖα πάθη), O Christ, above all for ever.[4]

> By dying, O my God, thou puttest death to death through thine divine power (Θάνατον θανάτῳ, σὺ θανατοῖς Θεέ μου, θείᾳ σου δυναστείᾳ).[5]

These texts are not easily datable. The liturgists agree that the earliest strata of the *Lenten Triodion* belong to the sixth century, with the activity of the editors peaking during the ninth century and continuing for the next five hundred years. The bold theopaschitism of these texts is reminiscent of the paschal liturgical sermon attributed to Melito, the second-century bishop of Sardis. Compare, for example, Melito's description of crucifixion with the first quotation from the *Lenten Triodion:* "He who hung the earth is hanging; he who fixed the heavens has been fixed; he who fastened the universe has been fastened to a tree; the Sovereign has been insulted; God has been murdered."[6]

Elsewhere Melito (or another patristic author) marvels at the mystery of the divine kenosis and expresses his wonder in a set of the following antitheses: "The invisible is seen and is not ashamed, the incomprehensible is seized and is not vexed; the immeasurable is measured, and does not resist;

---

2. *Lenten Triodion*, pp. 86, 608; cf. Athanasius of Alexandria, *Ep.* 49.10: "For this reason it was that the sun, seeing its creator suffering in His outraged body, withdrew its rays and darkened the earth." Trans. A. Robertson, *Nicene and Post-Nicene Fathers*, 2nd series (Peabody, Mass.: Hendrickson), vol. 4, p. 574.

3. *Lenten Triodion*, p. 587.

4. *Lenten Triodion*, p. 532; cf. 229, 343, 368.

5. *Lenten Triodion*, p. 642.

6. Melito, *Peri Pascha*, 96.711-15.

the impassible suffers and does not retaliate; the immortal dies and takes it patiently; the heavenly one is buried, and submits."[7]

We find a similar pattern in the anaphora recorded in the late fourth-century liturgical manual known as the *Apostolic Constitutions:* "the judge was judged and the Savior was condemned; the impassible was nailed to the cross (σταυρῷ προσηλώθη ὁ ἀπαθὴς); the immortal by nature died; the life-giver was buried."[8] This appears to be the only surviving Eucharistic prayer to contain explicitly theopaschite language. I have shown elsewhere that the literary dependence of this part of the anaphora upon Melito's liturgical sermon is very plausible.[9] The anaphora of the *Apostolic Constitutions* VIII offers a particularly telling example of how the words of early paschal sermons found their way into the later Eucharistic prayers, thereby transforming the liturgy into a "Sunday pascha."

The hymns of the *Lenten Triodion,* composed almost a millennium after Melito's *On Pascha,* also echo the words of the bishop of Sardis: "without changing Thou hast emptied Thyself, and impassibly Thou hast submitted to Thy Passion."[10] The continuity between the paradoxical language of Melito and that of the *Lenten Triodion* is remarkable. Melito's liturgical sermon is the fountainhead of a homiletic tradition that was later crystallized in the hymnography of the Byzantine *Lenten Triodion.*[11] This homiletic tradition has tenaciously preserved in the worship of the Orthodox Church to this day the paradox of the impassible God's suffering in the flesh. The historical studies of divine (im)passibility have thus far largely ignored this rich hymnographic material. Recited every year during Lent, the theopaschite hymns continue to have a considerable impact upon the collective imagination of the Orthodox Christians.

Beyond Byzantium, the language of paradox also found its home in

7. Melito (?), frag. 13.14-19. Stuart G. Hall offers compelling arguments for Melito's authorship of this fragment in *Melito: On Pascha and Fragments* (Oxford: Clarendon, 1979), pp. xxxiv-xxxvii.

8. *Apostolic Constitutions,* VIII.12.33. The text is a part of the Post-Sanctus.

9. See my article "Melito's Influence upon the Anaphora of *Apostolic Constitutions* 8.12," *Vigiliae Christianae* 59 (2005): 355-76.

10. Canon ascribed to St. Kosmas (d. ca. 750), canticle five, in *Lenten Triodion,* p. 593.

11. This tradition is traceable through the works of Apollinaris of Hierapolis, in *Chronicon Paschale, Corpus Scriptorum Historiae Byzantinae* 16 (Bonn: E. Weber, 1832), vol. 1, pp. 13-14; Hippolytus of Rome, *Contra Noetum* 18; Ephrem the Syrian, *De crucifixione* II, III, IV; and Cyril of Jerusalem, *Catechesis* XIII, and other later authors, such as Proclus of Constantinople.

Syrian Christianity (for example, in the work of St. Ephrem the Syrian) and in the Latin West. One is reminded of the famous *Vexilla Regis*, commonly sung in the Roman Catholic Church on the Feast of the Exaltation of the Cross and during Lent:

> Abroad the regal banners fly,
> Now shines the cross's mystery:
> Upon it Life did death endure,
> And yet by death did life procure.
> [. . .]
> That which the prophet-king of old
> Hath in mysterious verse foretold,
> Is now accomplished, whilst we see
> God ruling the nations from a tree.[12]

Both *Vexilla Regis* and Byzantine hymns heighten the drama of Christ's death by reminding the worshipers that the Crucified One is God incarnate, and that by enduring death he has paradoxically abolished death. Other notable parallels may be found in the libretto of Johann Sebastian Bach's *Saint Matthew Passion*[13] and in Charles Wesley's hymn "O Love Divine What Hast Thou Done!"[14] It is remarkable that despite their considerable cultural and theological differences, Eastern Orthodox, Roman Catholics, Lutherans, and Methodists pray with a united voice, especially when they lift up their eyes to the Crucified God. Even if today the theologians may disagree on how to understand God's

---

12. *Vexilla Regis,* stanzas 1 and 4: "Vexilla Regis prodeunt;/fulget Crucis mysterium,/quo carne carnis conditor/suspensus est patibulo [variant reading followed in my translation: qua vita mortem pertulit,/et morte vitam protulit]. . . . Impleta sunt quae concinit/David fideli carmine,/dicendo nationibus:/regnavit a ligno Deus. . . ." The hymn is attributed to Venantius Fortunatus (530-609). Some changes, including the variant reading cited in square brackets, were introduced by Pope Urban VIII in 1632. The English translation is by Walter Kirkham Blount (d. 1717).

13. "Ah Golgotha, unhappy Golgotha!/The Lord of majesty must scornfully here perish,/The saving blessing of the world/Is placed as scorn upon the cross./Creator of both earth and heaven/From earth and air must now be taken./The guiltless must here die guilty./Thee pierceth deep into my soul/Ah Golgotha, unhappy Golgotha!" J. S. Bach in cooperation with C. F. Henrici, *Matthew's Passion.* First performed on Good Friday 1727 (1729?).

14. "O Love divine, what hast thou done!/The immortal God hath died for me!/The Father's co-eternal Son/Bore all my sins upon the tree./Th' immortal God for me hath died:/My Lord, my Love, is crucified!" Charles Wesley, *Hymns and Sacred Poems* (1742).

involvement in suffering, the prospect of unity is open in the Church's *lex orandi.*

God's appropriation of human suffering in the incarnation is one of the central themes of patristic Christology. The Fathers also assert with equal force that God is impassible. In contrast, there is a widespread tendency today to question the notion of divine impassibility. Many contemporary theologians hold that the assumption of divine impassibility renders early Christian discussions of God's participation in suffering problematic, if not altogether contradictory. Is this criticism justified? What precisely was at stake for the Fathers in affirming both that God is impassible and that in the incarnation God participates in human suffering? How did such paradoxical statements function in patristic discourse?

In this paper I will defend the coherence of paradoxical Christology. I will contend that the notion of what I call "qualified divine impassibility" is not only defensible, but *necessary* for a sound account of the divine incarnation. I will also point out the problems to which the abandonment of divine impassibility has led some modern theologians. I will argue that God is neither eternally indifferent to suffering, nor eternally overcome by it. Rather, there is eternal victory over suffering in God, manifest most fully through the cross and resurrection.

It should be noted that while rejecting divine impassibility, most contemporary passibilists acknowledge that considerable qualifications apply to the claim that God suffers. It would be worthwhile to explore the points of convergence between these more measured proposals and what I have called the paradoxical Christology of the Fathers (although I will not undertake such an exploration here).

II. The Scope of Modern Passibilism

In the last two hundred years the issue of God's participation in suffering has attracted an increasing amount of theological attention. In the nineteenth century the problem of the divine self-limitation in the incarnation became a focal concern first for the German theologians Gottfried Thomasius (1802-1875) and Wolfgang Gess (1819-1891) and later for the British kenoticists, such as Charles Gore (1853-1932) and Frank Weston (1871-1924).[15] In the early

---

15. Thomasius, *Christ's Person and Work,* in *God and Incarnation in Mid-Nineteenth*

twentieth century Russian theologian Sergius Bulgakov (1871-1944), whose works are now becoming increasingly accessible in the West, developed a deeply original and comprehensive kenotic account of divine agency, testing the boundaries of the Eastern Orthodox tradition.[16] In the United States, the process metaphysics of Alfred North Whitehead (1861-1947) provided the foundation for the dipolar theism of Charles Hartshorne (1897-2000) and his followers.[17] In the Reformed tradition Karl Barth's (1886-1968) treatment of kenoticism has recently been constructively reassessed by Bruce McCormack.[18] In the field of biblical theology, Abraham Joshua Heschel (1907-1972), Terence Fretheim, Richard Bauckham, and others developed a theology of divine pathos which aims at recovering the rich vocabulary of divine emotions present in the Bible.[19] Jürgen Moltmann's theology of the cross introduced the theme of God's identification with suffering humanity into political theology.[20] No contemporary discussion of theodicy, especially the so-called theologies after the Holocaust and Auschwitz, can avoid the issue of God's compassionate responsiveness to suffering.[21] In evangelical circles

---

Century German Theology, trans. Claude Welch (New York: Oxford University Press, 1965), pp. 31-101. For a survey of the nineteenth-century kenotic theories, including that of Gess, see Alex B. Bruce, *The Humiliation of Christ* (Grand Rapids: Eerdmans, 1955), pp. 144-52, and most recently, T. R. Thompson, "Nineteenth-Century Kenotic Christology: The Waxing, Waning, and Weighing of a Quest for a Coherent Orthodoxy," in C. Stephen Evans, ed., *Exploring Kenotic Christology: The Self-Emptying of God* (Oxford: Oxford University Press, 2006), pp. 74-112.

16. See my article "The Kenotic Theology of Sergius Bulgakov," *Scottish Journal of Theology* 58 (2005): 251-69.

17. Alfred North Whitehead, *Process and Reality: An Essay in Cosmology* (New York: Macmillan, 1929); Charles Hartshorne, *A Natural Theology for Our Time* (La Salle, Ill.: Open Court, 1967).

18. Bruce L. McCormack, "Karl Barth's Christology as a Resource for a Reformed Version of Kenoticism," *International Journal of Systematic Theology* 8 (2006): 243-51 and his contribution to this volume.

19. Kazoh Kitamori, *The Theology of the Pain of God* (Richmond, Va.: John Knox, 1965); Abraham J. Heschel, *The Prophets* (New York: Harper & Row, 1962); T. E. Fretheim, *The Suffering of God: An Old Testament Perspective* (Philadelphia: Fortress Press, 1984); Richard Bauckham, *God Crucified: Monotheism and Christology in the New Testament* (Grand Rapids: Eerdmans, 1998); William C. Placher, "Narratives of a Vulnerable God," *The Princeton Seminary Bulletin* 14 (1993): 134-51.

20. Jürgen Moltmann, *The Crucified God* (Minneapolis: Fortress, 1993); Paul Fiddes, *The Creative Suffering of God* (Oxford: Clarendon Press, 1988).

21. Elie Wiesel, *Night* (New York: Hill & Wang, 2006; originally published in 1958); Marilyn McCord Adams, "Redemptive Suffering: A Christian Solution to the Problem of

Clark Pinnock, John Sanders, and other proponents of Open Theism have called for a reconsideration of the notions of divine timelessness, foreknowledge, and sovereignty in light of what these theologians take to be the biblically based ideas of divine possibility and changeability.[22] To do justice to these proposals I would have to engage them one by one. For fear that we will not be finished before Easter, I will spare you such a discussion for the time being. I should emphasize that I do not see patristic understanding of God's involvement in suffering as in *all* respects antagonistic to the insights expressed in these proposals. It would be fruitful to produce a companion volume that would put these diverse approaches in conversation with patristic theology.

My sketchy map gives some idea of the vastness of the theological terrain that the participants of our symposium are invited to explore. The most comprehensive proposals include the following three dimensions:

(1) The suffering of God on the cross and, more generally, in the work of redemption;

(2) The suffering of God entailed by the act of and subsequent interaction with creation;

(3) Suffering as a feature of God's inner life, particularly as pertaining to the immanent Trinity.

The first dimension, God's suffering within the economy of salvation, usually constitutes the shared focus of discussion. Not all contemporary passibilists develop the second and third dimensions. The question whether eternal suffering can be ascribed to the inner life of the Trinity remains arguably the most controversial and speculative of all three.[23]

Evil," in Robert Audi and William J. Wainwright, eds., *Rationality, Religious Belief and Moral Commitment* (Ithaca & London: Cornell University Press, 1986), pp. 248-67; Sallie McFague, *Models of God* (Philadelphia: Fortress Press, 1987), p. 142; Nicholas Wolterstorff, *Lament for a Son* (Grand Rapids: Eerdmans, 1987); C. S. Lewis, *A Grief Observed* (San Francisco: Harper, 2001); Kenneth Surin, "The Impassibility of God and the Problem of Evil," *Scottish Journal of Theology* 35 (1982): 97-115.

22. Clark H. Pinnock, Richard Rice, John Sanders, William Hasker, and David Basinger, *The Openness of God: A Biblical Challenge to the Traditional Understanding of God* (Downers Grove, Ill.: InterVarsity Press, 1994); Clark H. Pinnock, *Most Moved Mover* (Grand Rapids: Baker, 2001); John Sanders, *The God Who Risks: A Theology of Providence* (Downers Grove, Ill.: InterVarsity Press, 1998).

23. There is much internal debate in the passibilist camp on this score. For a recent sur-

The common denominator of most passibilist proposals is the conviction that the heritage of patristic theology cannot be accepted in its entirety. Here again there is a spectrum of positions on just how far the revision of patristic theism[24] must be carried out. Some theologians, following Jürgen Moltmann and Clark Pinnock, call for a revolution in the Christian concept of God. The most far-reaching projects abandon theistic frameworks altogether and consequently reject most classical divine attributes, including omnipotence and omniscience, as well as the corollary doctrines of creation out of nothing and miracles. When engaging such projects it would be myopic to focus on the issue of divine suffering without first considering the underlying ontology.

More moderate proposals focus primarily on the criticism of divine impassibility and immutability as presumably the "weakest links" in the intellectual structure of the traditional theism. Even those Christian thinkers who find most features of the patristic theism defensible concede that the notion of divine impassibility is one of the most vulnerable aspects of patristic theology.[25] Analyzing these developments, particularly the widespread tendency to reject the concept of divine impassibility, Ronald Goetz spoke twenty years ago of "the rise of a new orthodoxy."[26]

I realize, therefore, that by defending the concept of divine impassibility in this essay I am swimming against a potent current of contemporary thought. I am not prepared to call this dominant trend a "new orthodoxy," since no Christian communion has yet endorsed passibilism officially. A consensus of contemporary theologians that emerged in the second half of the twentieth century is hardly a reliable barometer of doctrinal truth.

To be sure, I do not labor in heroic solitude (it would be a rather un-Orthodox and un-catholic thing to do). The concept of divine impassi-

---

vey of this debate see Sturla J. Stålsett, *The crucified and the Crucified: A Study in the Liberation Christology of Jon Sobrino* (Bern: Peter Lang, 2003), pp. 442-73.

24. The concept of what I here call "patristic theism" is introduced and defended in William J. Abraham et al., eds., *Canonical Theism: A Proposal for Theology* (Grand Rapids: Eerdmans, 2008).

25. Richard Swinburne, *The Coherence of Theism* (Oxford: Oxford University Press, 1993); Nicholas Wolterstorff, "Suffering Love," in T. V. Morris, ed., *Philosophy and the Christian Faith* (Notre Dame: University of Notre Dame Press, 1988), pp. 196-237.

26. Ronald Goetz, "The Suffering God: The Rise of a New Orthodoxy," *Christian Century* 103 (1986): 385-89.

bility has had several eloquent champions in our time, including this symposium's participants Fr. Thomas Weinandy and David Bentley Hart.[27] In addition, the philosophical work of Richard Creel deserves more attention than it has received.[28] *Consensus patrum* is another weighty reason to reassess the matter more closely.

III. Some Prevalent Misconceptions of Divine Impassibility

It has become common to dismiss divine impassibility on superficial etymological grounds. Patristic theology is falsely credited with a bleak view that God is apathetic, uncaring, unconcerned about the world, emotionally withdrawn, and in this sense impassible. Lucien Richard expressed a common climate of opinion when he wrote: "the acceptance of the apathetic God into classical Christology led to insoluble theological difficulties. Qualities such as pity, compassion and love appear incompatible with absolute 'immutability.'"[29]

In addition, the critics of divine impassibility unfailingly note that the Fathers drank from the poisoned wells of Hellenistic philosophy. Almost a century ago William Temple declared: "Aristotle's 'apathetic God' was enthroned in men's minds, and no idol has been found so hard to destroy."[30] Along similar lines, William Wolf noted that the Church Fathers "were deriving their definition of the changeless perfection and utter serenity of deity from Greek philosophical theology rather than from the revelation of the God and Father of our Lord Jesus Christ."[31] Modern theology of divine suffering is then presented as a long-overdue message of liberation from the shackles of heathen philosophy and idolatry.[32]

27. Thomas G. Weinandy, *Does God Suffer?* (Notre Dame: University of Notre Dame Press, 2000); David Bentley Hart, *The Beauty of the Infinite* (Grand Rapids: Eerdmans, 2004) and their contributions to this volume.

28. Richard Creel, *Divine Impassibility* (Cambridge: Cambridge University Press, 1986).

29. Lucian J. Richard, *A Kenotic Christology: In the Humanity of Jesus the Christ the Compassion of Our God* (Washington, D.C.: Catholic University of America, 1982), pp. 249-50.

30. William Temple, *Christus Veritas* (London: Macmillan, 1954), p. 269.

31. William Wolf, *No Cross, No Crown* (New York: Doubleday, 1957), p. 196.

32. One finds a similar rhetoric in Karl Barth's critique of both patristic Christology and Lutheran orthodoxy. See *Church Dogmatics* IV/1 (London: T. & T. Clark and Continuum, 2004), pp. 84-85, quoted by Bruce McCormack in his contribution to this volume. Fol-

This line of argument is a classical case of genetic fallacy. Surely the fact that a given idea, in this case the notion of divine impassibility, has been used by the Greek philosophers (or Sufi mystics, or the German idealists) does not discredit this idea automatically. Obviously the critic needs to establish that the ancient philosophers were *wrong* in claiming that God was impassible. Actually, the critic cannot even show that the philosophers agreed on this matter. The Epicureans taught that the gods had anthropomorphic emotions, but were unconcerned about the world. In contrast, the Stoics held the moral ideal of *apatheia* in high esteem. However, it would be logically odd to predicate *apatheia* to their material and impersonal deity. For the Peripatetics and later Platonists, divine *apatheia* was a corollary of incorporeality. As a minimum, the Fathers' adoption of impassibility involved a choice between these and several other options including the overly passionate gods of the Homeric pantheon and mystery cults. More importantly, the passibilist critic needs to establish that the Christian theologians borrowed impassibility from the pagan philosophers without quite baptizing it. I have argued elsewhere that it is in this regard that the passibilist objector is most obviously mistaken.[33]

One would search in vain for a patristic text in which divine impassibility means apathy or absence of concern for creation. Augustine, for example, was emphatic about distinguishing the Christian ascetic virtue of *apatheia* from insensitivity. In *The City of God* he asks rhetorically: "If *apatheia* is the name of the state in which the mind cannot be touched by any emotion whatsoever, who would not judge this insensitivity to be the worst of all moral defects?"[34] For Augustine, therefore, *apatheia* was anything but stone-heartedness. Following Justin Martyr and other early Christian writers, Augustine proposes that the resurrection state will be characterized by *apatheia,* understood as freedom from suffering and irrational impulses, as well as by joy and love. Most contemporary passibilists simply ignore this textual evidence and continue to identify divine impassibility with emotional atrophy.

---

lowing his contemporaries, Barth characterizes the claim that God is not affected by the experiences of the incarnation as a pagan idea, alien to the biblical understanding of God.

33. For the details of this argument, see chapter one of my study, *The Suffering of the Impassible God: The Dialectics of Patristic Thought* (Oxford and New York: Oxford University Press, 2004).

34. Augustine, *De civitate Dei* XIV.9; *Augustine: The City of God,* trans. Henry Bettenson (London: Penguin Books, 1984), p. 565.

In ascetical theology, *apatheia* refers to the state of the soul freed from the attachment to sinful thoughts and desires. According to Evagrius of Pontus, "the progeny of *apatheia* is *agape*."[35] Far from being an emotional zero, *apatheia* is the precondition of Christian love, purified of all self-centered desires. By analogy, divine impassibility in the sense of perfect control over emotional states, is a condition of divine love, mercy, compassion, and providential care. Unfortunately most contemporary passibilists continue to ignore this historical evidence and to interpret divine impassibility as emotional impotence and indifference.

In general I find the widespread contemporary tendency to draw ill-founded psychological and political implications from the metaphysical notions to be quite lamentable. Sartre famously felt nausea when pondering the idea of infinity.[36] Some contemporary theologians fail to imagine divine omnipotence in terms other than tyranny, absolute monarchy, or some equally detestable form of political government.[37] Such distortions become possible when divine omnipotence is erroneously and arbitrarily divorced from God's perfect goodness, love, and compassion. A God of infinite power who is at the same time wicked may justifiably be imagined as a tyrant and a veritable terminator. But the omnipotence of God cannot be separated from his perfect goodness, for in God all attributes are united in a union beyond description. There can be no better panacea from all forms of human idolatry, power grabbing, and tyranny than the overflowing goodness and the self-emptying love of the omnipotent God. A deity of limited power would be too weak to counter human usurpations of power and idolatry.

At times political theologians practice a similar hermeneutic of suspicion against other attributes of God. When a metaphysical term has no ob-

35. Evagrius of Pontus, *Praktikos,* 81. This Evagrian theme is developed by Maximus the Confessor, *The Four Hundred Chapters on Love,* I.2, I.81, IV.91.

36. Jean-Paul Sartre, *La Nausée* (Paris: Gallimard, 1938).

37. I should underscore that I concede that divine omnipotence could be imagined in these questionable ways. It would be historically naïve to deny that the term "almighty" has had complex political connotations in the collective imagination of Christendom. It is possible, for example, to look at the Byzantine icon of Christ Pantokrator and construe it as somehow issuing a blank check endorsement to the autocratic abuses of the imperial power. I am also not advocating a sterile claim that the notion of divine omnipotence is intrinsically apolitical. Instead I propose to read the icon of Christ Pantokrator as a reminder that the only absolute Lordship that the believers are to recognize is that of Christ, not of any earthly ruler.

vious political or psychological connotations, such a term is dismissed as too impersonal, static, and abstract (as opposed to being personal, dynamic, concrete, or relational). Apparently this approach is immensely effective rhetorically, since so many theologians deploy it as a "preemptive strike" to preclude any serious discussion of the concepts so attacked.

The impassible God has been called "the celestial Narcissus,"[38] "the self-protecting monarch,"[39] "the patriarchal ruler,"[40] "the eternal bystander" (Camus), and numerous other non-flattering appellations. I suppose that traditional theists could return the compliment by calling the God of modern passibilism the Perpetual Heavenly Masochist, the Feuerbachian Copy of the Suffering Humanity, the Idol of Self-Flagellating Theological Liberalism, or the Grand Phantasm of Victimhood Ideology (take your pick). In a recent article Christopher Insole psychoanalyzes the God of classical theism as a projection of the Cartesian self, and the God of modern passibilism as a projection of the Romantic self.[41] No matter how intellectually seductive such caricatures may be, they only distract from an in-depth analysis of metaphysical alternatives. I suggest a thorough purification of contemporary theological imagination through a heavy dose of mental *askesis*. To put it bluntly, not every passionate thought that invades one's theological mind when pondering divine perfections needs to be recorded in print. In the spirit of the third commandment, I think it is time to call for a moratorium on divine name-calling.

More seriously, it has been argued that the assumption of divine impassibility renders any account of divine emotions and involvement in the drama of human suffering highly problematic, if not altogether incoherent. I will meet this objection in two interrelated ways: (1) by distinguishing adequate and inadequate ways in which impassibility and other negative divine attributes have actually functioned in Christian theological discourse, and (2) by arguing that in order to be redemptive God's involvement in suffering must be marked by impassibility.

38. William Wolf, *No Cross, No Crown*, p. 196; cf. Pinnock, *Most Moved Mover*, p. 87.
39. Paul Fiddes, *The Creative Suffering of God* (Oxford: Clarendon, 1992), p. 1.
40. Elizabeth Johnson, *She Who Is* (New York: Crossroad, 1992), p. 247.
41. Christopher Insole, "Anthropomorphism and the Apophatic God," *Modern Theology* 17 (2001): 475-83.

IV. The Function of Divine Impassibility in Patristic Christology

How does divine impassibility actually function in patristic texts? As the hymnographic material cited in the beginning of this essay illustrates, the notion of divine impassibility commonly appears in the context of other apophatic markers of the divine transcendence, such as immortality, immutability, invisibility, incorporeality, incomprehensibility, uncreatedness, and the like. This implies that *divine impassibility is primarily a metaphysical term, marking God's unlikeness to everything in the created order, not a psychological term denoting* (as modern passibilists allege) *God's emotional apathy.* When Melito says that "the invisible [God] is seen" his point is that the God who is by nature unavailable to the ordinary senses (cf. John 1:18), under certain circumstances and for certain reasons makes himself visible (cf. Matt. 5:8; John 14:9; 1 John 1:1-3). Similarly, the uncreated God creates and reveals himself through creation. The incorporeal God manifests himself through material objects. As the Orthodox Church sings on Good Friday: "Today he who is in essence unapproachable, becomes approachable for me and suffers his Passion, delivering me from passions."[42] God is the Holy Other and in this sense "unapproachable." But God is also a caring Father and in this sense he makes himself approachable, when he chooses to do so.

If one rejects the attribute of divine impassibility on the grounds that there are instances of special revelation in which God is said to suffer, one will face similar difficulties in the case of all negative markers of the divine transcendence. It is a methodological mistake to isolate the concept of divine impassibility, as some contemporary passibilists often do, and jettison this concept without attending to a more general problem: How can the attributes of the transcendent Creator be reconciled with God's revelation under the finite conditions of the created order? I will touch briefly upon three complementary strategies for addressing this difficulty. (I cannot offer a detailed discussion of a general theory of religious paradoxes here.)

The first strategy is to construe the paradoxical statements as poetic devices conveying "insights through the clash of images, insights which could not be communicated in any other way."[43] Such a reading of paradoxes seems to be especially relevant for interpreting the antithetical lan-

---

42. *Lenten Triodion*, p. 576.
43. W. H. Austin, *Waves, Particles, and Paradoxes* (Houston: Rice University, 1967), p. 81.

guage of Melito and that of the later Byzantine hymnographers. The powerful juxtaposition of Christ's divine attributes ("he who held the earth upon the waters . . .") and his human experiences of suffering and death (". . . is hung upon the cross") in the Good Friday service is designed to bring in the hearts of the believers a sense of contrition, sorrow, gratitude, and wonder before the depth of God's self-abasement. On this reading, paradoxical language is a contemplative technique designed to direct believers' minds in prayerful meditation upon the mystery of God's crucifixion and death, the mystery which is ultimately beyond all human words and powers of expression. I am sympathetic to this understanding of the function of paradoxical language, as long as no rigid distinction is made between the allegedly purely affective language of poetry and prayer on the one hand and the language of philosophical theology on the other hand. When the Byzantine hymnographers sang praises to God they theologized; conversely, when the Fathers theologized, they continued to pray.

The second strategy is to take the proposition "the impassible suffered" as a particular case of what Ian Ramsey called the "paradox of the religious ultimate." This paradox consists mainly in recognizing the limitations of religious language: while on the one hand *some* predicates (not all) may be fittingly ascribed to God, on the other hand, from the standpoint of apophatic theology, *no* predicate can be applied to God because God does not belong to the same order of being.[44] Whatever appropriate qualifications one applies to the claim that God suffers, one is bound to acknowledge at the same time that God is impassible, because he transcends all suffering, just as he transcends everything else.

The third and last strategy is to construe God's impassible suffering as a special case of *coincidentia oppositorum*. Impassibility enables God to be involved in suffering to the fullest possible extent, in the manner that only God can. The critics of patristic theism object that the idea that God transcends suffering makes God apathetic and incapable of compassion. In fact, the exact opposite is the case. It is precisely because God infinitely transcends all human suffering that he is able to overcome our suffering and manifest true compassion. It is precisely because God has nothing at stake for himself in the experience of suffering, that he is able to love us so

44. Ian Ramsey, *Models and Mystery* (London: Oxford University Press, 1964). For a critique of Ramsey, see W. H. Austin, "Models, Mystery, and Paradox in Ian Ramsey," *Journal of the Scientific Study of Religion* 7 (1968): 41-55.

perfectly. If God chooses to participate in suffering, he is not overwhelmed by suffering. God retains his freedom and remains active in suffering. God's involvement in suffering is never meaningless, but is always purposeful, aimed at healing the misery of his creatures.[45]

Already in the third century Gregory Thaumaturgus (ca. 213–ca. 270) established most of these points in his treatise *To Theopompus, On the Impassibility and Passibility of God.* Gregory explained the voluntary character of Christ's suffering as follows: "For he in his sufferings continues as he is, voluntarily taking human sufferings upon himself, and does not suffer the pains which arise from human passions. For God is the one who is unharmed by every suffering, and it is his property always to remain the same."[46] God retains his freedom and immutability even in suffering. According to Gregory, God manifests his impassibility not by keeping aloof, but by the manner of his participation in suffering:

> We would not have known the impassible to be impassible if he had not participated in the passions and undergone the force of the passions. For impassibility eagerly rushed upon the passions like a passion, so that by his own Passion he might show himself to be the cause of suffering of the passions (*ostenderet se esse passionem passionibus*). For the passions were not entirely able to stand against the weight of the power of impassibility.[47]

Many philosophically minded pagans of Gregory's time found such a way of using impassibility to be quite objectionable, perhaps even verging on nonsense. They argued that it would be more fitting for the impassible God to dissociate himself from all involvement in human misery altogether. Gregory ascribes to his philosophical opponents a view that "God is turned towards himself and wallows in himself, with the result that he does nothing and allows others to do nothing."[48] Gregory proceeds to argue that a God who is unconcerned about his creation is weak (*infirmus*

---

45. This observation applies to God's direction of only certain kinds of evil. I am not arguing that God uses all suffering to bring about healing. I leave open the possibility of apparently and inexplicably gratuitous evil that God permits without directing.

46. Gregory Thaumaturgus, *Ad Theopompum,* 10, *St. Gregory Thaumaturgus: Life and Works,* trans. Michael Slusser (Washington, D.C.: Catholic University of America Press, 1998), p. 164.

47. Gregory Thaumaturgus, *Ad Theopompum,* 6, p. 158.

48. Gregory Thaumaturgus, *Ad Theopompum,* 15, p. 170.

est) and inactive. He goes so far as to say that "in God it would be a great passion *(passionem maximam)* not to care for human beings."[49] Similar to Augustine, Gregory sees divine impassibility and providential care not only as compatible, but as reinforcing each other. Here Gregory uses the term *passio* in the sense of a defect or fault, a connotation that is largely lost in the English term "passion." He also appears to make a point that a passionate person may be uncaring and selfishly absorbed in the realm of her own emotions. For example, the Greek Zeus was a very passionate god, but he was hardly compassionate. This point often escapes those contemporary theologians who think that to make God super-emotional and omni-relational is to secure divine compassion. God may indeed be relational, but so is the Devil. (I imagine that the Devil also has his emotional highs.) More to the point, divine affectivity and relationality must be carefully qualified before they can play a part in a sound account of divine compassion.

Gregory also argues that it would be unworthy of God to abandon his creatures to die in sin and ignorance without offering them any assistance. He compares the benevolent God of Christians to a physician, who "when he wants to cure those who are afflicted with grave illnesses, gladly takes upon himself hardships in his ministry to the sick, for he already looks forward to the joy which will be his from the recovery."[50] It is fitting for God *(theoprepes)* to participate in human suffering for the sake of healing. This therapeutic analogy and the teleological justification of the incarnate God's participation in suffering became commonplace in patristic literature.[51]

Gregory is aware of the fact that divine impassibility may be used in what I call an unqualified sense, which rules out any form of divine involvement in pathos. The later Platonists ascribed this kind of impassibility to the noetic realm.[52] The Gnostics, particularly those with Docetic sensibilities, claimed that since God was impassible it was both metaphysically impossible and morally unfitting for him to be involved in the evil realm of matter by assuming a despicable human body. More than a century later the Arians argued that since the unbegotten God was impassible, he could not possibly be ontologically equal to the suffering Logos. In the

---

49. Gregory Thaumaturgus, *Ad Theopompum,* 13, p. 168.

50. Gregory Thaumaturgus, *Ad Theopompum,* 6, p. 156.

51. Origen, *Contra Celsum,* IV.14, 15; *De principiis,* II.10.6; Gregory of Nyssa, *Contra Eunomium,* 3.4.724; *Oratio Catechetica Magna,* 14.16.

52. Plotinus, *Enneads,* III.6.1.

fifth century, to safeguard the notion of unqualified divine impassibility, the Nestorians insisted upon a sharp division between Christ's divine actions on the one hand and his human experiences on the other hand. Their profound theological differences notwithstanding, the Docetists, Arians, and Nestorians shared a common approach to divine impassibility. All three groups deployed divine impassibility in an unqualified sense, as a property that categorically excluded God's participation in any form of suffering. It is significant that the Church has rejected such a use of divine impassibility as flawed.

In response, the Church Fathers defended the reality of Christ's suffering against the Docetists, the fullness of the incarnate Son's divinity against the Arians, and the unity of his person against the Nestorians. For the Fathers, divine impassibility was quite compatible with God's providential care even to the point of participating in suffering. Contemporary theologians fail to understand the main thrust of patristic Christology when they reduce the contribution of the Church Fathers to a version of Docetism or Nestorianism. When the Fathers of the Fifth Ecumenical Council, following the insights of Athanasius and Cyril of Alexandria, affirmed that "one of the Holy Trinity suffered in the flesh," they intended to emphasize that God did not cease to be God when he had entered the conditions of human suffering. In a statement such as "the impassible suffered," divine impassibility functions as an indicator of the divine transcendence and as a marker of God's undiminished divinity.

Used adverbially, as in the expression of the Lenten Triodion "and impassibly thou hast submitted to thy passion," divine impassibility qualifies the manner in which God endures suffering. To read such statements in a Nestorian manner as saying that the divine subject is not affected by suffering in any way at all is to misinterpret them. When the Fathers spoke of God suffering impassibly, they wanted to stress that God was not conquered by suffering and that God's participation in suffering transformed the experience of suffering.[53] In the incarnation God made human suffering his own (ἰδιοποιήσις, οἰκείωσις) in order to transform suffering and redeem human nature. In the words of the *Lenten Triodion:* "Thou hast put to death the passions (πάθη) of my flesh by thy divine cross, and by thy Passion (πάθος) Thou hast given all men freedom from the passions (πάθη)."[54] Note an in-

---

53. Cyril, *Ad Nestorium*, III.6.
54. *Lenten Triodion*, p. 267.

tricate *jeu de mots* in this quotation: πάθος (singular) refers to the drama of the cross, whereas πάθη (plural) refer to sinful human desires. This word-play can only partially be conveyed in English.

Given the exegetical complexities of the term πάθος and its cognates, some contemporary scholars have argued that while the notion of divine *apatheia* may have played a valuable function in patristic theology, the notion should be best abandoned by the present-day theologians, because of its allegedly permanent association with apathy. I am in general against any historical insulation and domestication of patristic ideas, and in this particular case I could not disagree more. *Apatheia,* even in its least attractive Stoic form, has as much to do with apathy as amnesia does with amnesty. The claim that any talk about divine impassibility must be abandoned because the notion has been so often misunderstood is a classic case of an argument from abuse. No matter how powerful its rhetorical appeal, this argument is profoundly flawed. As even a sketchy discussion of divine omnipotence indicates, a similar set of interpretative difficulties besets a theologian in the case of just about any other divine attribute, including even such seemingly non-problematic concepts as love and compassion. It is misleading to isolate the concept of divine impassibility and to require that all of its possible uses be immune from criticism as a condition of the concept's viability. As I argued earlier, divine impassibility is not only compatible, but is actually a corollary of a proper understanding of God's love and providential care. In the final section I will address the difficulties to which the abandonment of divine impassibility has led those contemporary passibilists who make suffering a permanent feature of the inner life of God.

V. Problems with the Concept of Eternal Divine Suffering

Many contemporary theologians who claim that God suffers eternally tend to conceive of suffering as a permanent quality of divine love. I concur with the legitimate concern of these theologians that the account of God's love manifested on the cross must be continuous with the qualities of God's love vis-à-vis creation and that love which is shared by the persons of the Trinity. In the words of the nineteenth-century Russian theologian, metropolitan Filaret of Moscow: "The love of the Father is crucifying, the love of the Son is crucified, and the love of the Holy Spirit triumphs by the power of the cross."[55] However, against those who would eternalize divine suffering by making it a feature of the immanent Trinity (as, for example, Jürgen Moltmann and his followers do), I would contend that the love that is manifest on the cross embraces not only the suffering of all those abandoned by God, but also holds the power of the resurrection to transform and conquer all suffering, penetrating to the very depth of hell.

Tomorrow, on Lazarus Saturday, Christ will be weeping (liturgically speaking) at the tomb of his friend. In line with the theological insights of Cyril of Alexandria, the Fathers taught that the Weeping One was God incarnate himself. However, the Weeping One did not just stand at the tomb of Lazarus and continue weeping for all eternity, as some passibilists imagine. He has also raised Lazarus from the dead. The Weeping One triumphed over grief and mortality when Lazarus was resuscitated.

It follows that in order to be able to redeem, God must be more than a Whiteheadian "fellow-sufferer who understands."[56] A God who is merely a fellow-patient cannot help those who suffer. Divine compassion is far more than sentimental commiseration. The time will come when God will wipe away every tear from the sufferers' eyes (Rev. 7:16), as he had wiped away the tears of Mary and Martha by raising Lazarus from the dead. This means that tears, grief, and pain do not have the final word in the life of God, contrary to what the books under such titles as *The Tears of God* and *Theology and the Pain of God* would have us believe.[57]

Perpetual divine suffering has no purpose, except the perpetuation of misery. To postulate the unredeemed suffering in God, as some contemporary theologians tend to do, is to eternalize evil. Far from offering a compelling theodicy, the projection of humanity's suffering onto the inner life of God only compounds the problem of evil.[58] In this picture, which has an almost hypnotic hold on contemporary passibilists, the destructive nature of suffering is trivialized and falsely romanticized as something intrinsically valuable and redemptive. The victims of the Gulags and the

---

55. Quoted in Vladimir Lossky, *Spor o Sofii* (Moskva: Izdatel'stvo Sviato-Vladimirskogo Bratstva, 1996), p. 70; trans. mine.

56. Alfred North Whitehead, *Process and Reality,* 3rd ed. (New York: The Free Press, 1978), p. 351.

57. Wilfrid J. Harrington, *The Tears of God: Our Benevolent Creator and Human Suffering* (Collegeville, Minn.: Liturgical Press, 1992); Kazoh Kitamori, *Theology and the Pain of God* (Richmond, Va.: John Knox Press, 1965).

58. Cf. E. L. Mascall, *Existence and Analogy* (London: Longmans, 1949), p. 142.

Nazi concentration camps would cry out, if they could, against such a conception of God, for they have learned experientially that prolonged suffering destroys personhood, if it is not physically resisted and overcome spiritually. The Christian martyrs certainly did not suffer atrocious pain in this life so that they could go on enduring the same pain with God for all eternity. This would be a nightmare. Mortality and attendant misfortunes are by definition the features of this life, not of the life eternal.[59]

The theology of eternal divine suffering is a misguided and sentimental glorification of evil, despite the best intentions of those who proclaim it. The savior who suffers eternally himself stands in need of the other impassible Savior, who alone is capable of rescuing the impotent savior from his miserable fate. One may imagine that such an impotent savior would be so absorbed in the drama of his own suffering as to be incapable even of sentimental commiseration with his creatures.

In the spirit of patristic theology it would be appropriate to speak of God's eternal and decisive victory over suffering and death, a victory marked by impassibility, not of God's suffering for all eternity, associated with the rejection of impassibility. When modern passibilists (in many cases for good reasons) protest against the false triumphalism of *theologia gloriae,* they nevertheless do not sufficiently acknowledge that *theologia crucis* remains largely a theology of despair without the *theologia resurrectionis,* i.e., the message of God's decisive victory over death. In the words of the Orthodox Easter troparion: "Christ is risen from the dead, trampling down death by death, and upon those in the tombs bestowing life." Christ's suffering on the cross has universal redemptive value only if sin and mortality have been once and for all conquered by the power of the resurrection.

The Fathers, from Melito of Sardis to the anonymous hymnographers of the *Lenten Triodion,* have faithfully retained the paradox of the impassible God's suffering in the flesh. This paradox captures the vital tension between God's transcendence and undiminished divinity on the one hand and God's intimate involvement in human suffering on the other hand. God is impassible inasmuch as he is able to conquer sin, suffering, and death; and God is also passible (in a carefully qualified sense) inasmuch as in the incarnation God has chosen to enter the human condition in order

---

59. I am reminded of the words of the Eastern Orthodox funeral service: "With the Saints give rest, O Christ, to the soul of your servant, where there is no pain, nor sorrow, nor suffering, but life everlasting."

to transform it. God suffers in and through human nature, by taking human grief and sorrow into his life and making these experiences his own.

Some contemporary passibilists reject Chalcedonian Christology, which they wrongly interpret along the Nestorian lines of sharply distinguishing the sufferings of human nature from the actions of divinity. These theologians propose instead to predicate all suffering directly to Christ's divine nature. Consider the attendant problems of this position.

First, if God suffers for all eternity, then there is nothing uniquely redemptive about Christ's suffering on the cross. Incarnation becomes a pale copy of what God has been enduring for all eternity. Second, if all experiences of Christ can be predicated directly to God in his divine nature, in other words, if God as God undergoes human suffering exactly in the way that humans suffer, then the assumption of human nature will be completely superfluous. In this scheme human nature only duplicates the experiences that God has already undergone apart from humanity in his divine nature. Third, God's eternal suffering in the divine nature entails some form of permanent divine embodiment — an inescapable conclusion, which only a few modern passibilists would be prepared to defend.[60] If God already has a cosmic body, his assumption of an additional human body in the incarnation becomes unnecessary.[61] Finally, if within the framework of the incarnation suffering is predicated to God directly in his divine nature, then God no longer shares in the suffering of the assumed humanity, but rather suffers in complete separation from humanity. As Thomas Weinandy aptly pointed out, "ironically, those who advocate a suffering God, having locked suffering within God's divine nature, have actually locked God out of human suffering."[62] Taken together, these objections are too damaging to make the concept of eternal divine suffering viable.

60. See Marcel Sarot, *God: Passibility and Corporeality* (Kampen: Pharos, 1992).

61. It is possible to deflect these objections by arguing that the central significance of the cross consists in God's revelation of what he endures for all eternity. The problem with this move is that it shifts the function of Christ's atoning death from that which brings about reconciliation between God and humanity to that which solely manifests the already present reality of reconciliation and suffering, which supposedly exists in God for all eternity. Such an internalization of atonement has the overall effect of the supreme divine drama being accomplished outside of history. In my judgment, the theological problems created by this move far outweigh the valuable claim that there must be a continuity between God's inner life and God's actions ad extra.

62. Thomas G. Weinandy, "Does God Suffer?," *Ars Disputandi* 2 (2002): 11 [pagination lacking in the original], at: www.arsdisputandi.org.

VI. Conclusion

The central aim of Chalcedonian Christology was to keep Christ's divinity and humanity distinct, yet united. By blending the distinction between divinity and humanity as well as by attributing all human experiences of Christ directly to God, the contemporary passibilists have made the assumption of humanity in the incarnation superfluous at best and metaphysically impossible at worst. I repeat: God, as God, does not replicate what we, as humans, suffer. Yet in the incarnation God, remaining God, participates in our condition to the point of the painful death on the cross. Remaining impassible, God chooses to make the experiences of his human nature fully his own. For these reasons, the notion of divine impassibility needs to be recovered and more adequately integrated into the contemporary theological reflection on the mystery of God's involvement in the world's suffering.

Paradoxical Christology holds the potential of moving the discussion beyond the modern caricatures of the traditional understanding of impassibility, and *vice versa*, beyond at times too dismissive readings of the passibilist proposals by the champions of impassibility. Paradoxical Christology expresses in the language of prayer and symbol that which is so difficult to formulate adequately in the language of dogma.

To propose paradoxical Christology is not to revel in irrationality and incoherence. These old intellectual vices are still intellectual vices, despite all lauds sung to them by the high priests of postmodernity. My point is that the dissolution of the christological paradox, by those who reject either that God is in any sense impassible, or that God is in any sense passible, creates far greater theological conundrums than those presented by the admittedly problematic paradoxical language.

The intent of the paradoxical statements is to hold God's transcendence and undiminished divinity in tension with the divine care for creation and involvement in suffering. While paradoxical Christology provides for a considerable array of plausible kenotic models, such a Christology does rule out those approaches that exclude any notion of divine impassibility altogether.[63] Some critics may see the reticence of the

---

63. For an illuminating and nuanced critique of the main kenotic models, see Sarah Coakley, "*Kenosis* and Subversion: On the Repression of 'Vulnerability' in Christian Feminist Writing," *Powers and Submissions: Spirituality, Philosophy and Gender* (Oxford: Black-

hymnographers to specify just how precisely the impassible God participates in human suffering as theologically immature and question-begging.
I think the issue could be looked at in a different light. The strength of this
position lies in its apophatic reserve and breadth: to repeat, no one model
of God's involvement in suffering is endorsed as normative or binding,
while both divine apathy and unredeemed eternal suffering are decidedly
rejected. However God participates in suffering, he is neither eternally indifferent to suffering, nor eternally overwhelmed by it. Thus, the recognition of the irreducible paradox of the divine transcendence and immanence lying at the heart of the mystery of God's involvement in suffering
will provide a basis for achieving the future theological consensus on this
issue.

---

well, 2002), pp. 3-39. Coakley's concluding suggestions for how the imitation of Christ's vulnerability may be suitably appropriated in contemplative prayer are especially valuable. See
also her "Does Kenosis Rest on a Mistake? Three Kenotic Models in Patristic Exegesis," in
Exploring Kenotic Christology, pp. 246-64.

Divine Impassibility or Simply Divine Constancy? Implications of Karl Barth's Later Christology for Debates over Impassibility

Bruce L. McCormack

When it comes to reflection upon the problem of divine impassibility and/ or passibility, Karl Barth was something of a latter-day Cyril of Alexandria. Of Cyril, it has been said that Christology was the "driving force" of his entire theological vision; indeed, Christology provided for him "the central point to which and from which all other comprehensions run."[1] The same could be said of Barth, quite obviously. I would even take this a step further: if the central problematic faced by Cyril was to explain "how the existence of a soul in Christ could be reconciled with a single-subject Christology,"[2] then here, too, there is commonality, for Barth's central problem in Christology could be described in much the same way. Not surprisingly, the solutions offered to this problem by these theologians differ widely, as do the implications of those solutions for the concept of divine impassibility. Still, Barth does find in Cyril warrant for a christocentric approach to issues surrounding impassibility.

I mention all of this because Paul Gavrilyuk's fine study of patristic treatments of divine impassibility is somewhat marred, in my view, by its tendency to regard all modern objections to impassibility as standing somehow in the shadow of Adolf von Harnack's Hellenization thesis,[3] as

---

1. John A. McGuckin, *Saint Cyril of Alexandria and the Christological Controversy: Its History, Theology and Texts* (Crestwood, N.Y.: St. Vladimir's Seminary Press, 2004), p. 175.
2. McGuckin, *Saint Cyril of Alexandria*, p. 183.
3. Paul L. Gavrilyuk, *The Suffering of the Impassible God: The Dialectics of Patristic Thought* (New York: Oxford University Press, 2005), p. 3.

I dedicate this essay to Robert Jenson, in deep gratitude for all that he has taught me.

somehow lending support to what he calls "the Theory of Theology's Fall into Hellenistic Philosophy."[4] This simply won't do. Barth, for example, was quite critical of that theory.[5] And when he criticized definitions given to the concept of impassibility — in the ancient church on through the post-Reformation period — he did so on the grounds of Christology, by entering with love and respect into the same set of problems that once engaged a Cyril.

In what follows, I will begin with a brief survey of those passages in which the concept of impassibility appears in Barth's *Church Dogmatics*. I will then turn to his later Christology. I will argue on the basis of this Christology that there really is no room left for a truly meaningful use of the term; that what Barth finally affirms is simply God's "constancy," i.e., his fidelity to himself. I will also show how Barth's solution to Cyril's problem differs from Cyril's own and explain why that should have been the case.

I. Survey of Barth's Use of the Key Terms in the Debate

The English terms "impassible," "impassibly," and "impassibility" rarely appear in the *Church Dogmatics*.[6] Only seven instances can be found,

4. Gavrilyuk, *The Suffering of the Impassible God*, p. 5.

5. See Karl Barth to Rudolf Bultmann, 12 June 1928 in *Karl Barth — Rudolf Bultmann Briefwechsel, 1922-1966*, ed. Bernd Jaspert (Zürich: TVZ, 1971), p. 85; English translation: *Karl Barth — Rudolf Bultmann: Letters, 1922-1968*, trans. Geoffrey Bromiley (Grand Rapids: Eerdmans, 1981), p. 41: "It is . . . a fact that the defect of the old theology has never been clear to me at the point at which Harnack's *Dogmengeschichte* lays its finger, that the Platonism or Aristotelianism of the orthodox was not as such a hindrance to my . . . understanding of what was at stake and therefore to taking all kinds of old terminology into my own vocabulary without identifying myself with the philosophy that lies in back of them. . . ."

6. All references to the standard translation of the *Church Dogmatics* are to the translation by Geoffrey Bromiley. See Karl Barth, *Church Dogmatics*, trans. Geoffrey Bromiley et al. (Edinburgh: T. & T. Clark, 1936-1969) [hereafter abbreviated to "*CD*"]; Barth, *Die Kirchliche Dogmatik* (Munich and Zurich: Chr. Kaiser Verlag and TVZ, 1932-1967) [hereafter abbreviated to "*KD*"]. The reader should note that, in what follows: if I am citing the English text alone, I will refer simply to "*CD*." Where I am citing the German text alone, I will refer to "*KD*." If I am citing both editions, the English will come first if I am leaving the existing translation unchanged; the German text will be referred to first in those cases in which I have made some alteration of the English translation — whether a completely new translation or a minor adjustment.

along with two instances of untranslated Latin.[7] Of these nine uses taken together, only three are positive in the sense of bringing to expression some aspect of Barth's theology. Three are "neutral" in the sense that Barth takes up no clear stance for or against the conceptions described by these terms. Two are negative in that Barth is actively criticizing a specific conception of "impassibility." And one is a clear mistranslation — which leads us to a second significant point where usage is concerned.

Some comment should be made here at the outset about the fact that the English words "impassible," "impassibly," and "impassibility" do not always translate the same German words. Of the seven instances where these words appear in Bromiley's translation, one translates *Unbeweglichkeit;* two translate either *Unangerührtheit* or *unangerührten;* and two translate *unberührbar* and *Unberührbarkeit,* and one is a circumlocution for *"ohne jeden Affekt."* Allowing for some differences in nuance, the meaning of these terms adds up to the concept of a God who is "immoveable" and "unaffected" by anything outside of himself.

Here is the entire list, presented synoptically with due attention to context, meaning, and significance.

(1) *CD* II/1, p. 370

Here Barth is arguing against Schleiermacher's conception of the Whence of the feeling of absolute dependence. He writes "The source of the feeling of absolute dependence has no heart. But the personal God has a heart. He can feel and be affected. He is not impassible *(unberührbar)*." Clearly, what is in view here is the question of God's "affectivity." The German here is a bit more provocative in that it includes a term that Geoffrey Bromiley has omitted. The German says: "He can feel, *sense* and be affected. He is not untouchable." And it continues, "Not that He could be touched from the outside, by alien powers, so to speak. But also not in such a way that He could not touch and move Himself. No, God *is* touched and moved not as we are in our powerlessness but in power, in His own free power, in His innermost essence [*Wesen*]; affected and moved through Himself, i.e. open, ready, inclined to co-suffering with alien suffering. . . ."[8] The attribution of

---

7. Thanks are due here to Dr. Clifford Anderson of Princeton Theological Seminary, who used the search engine he created for the *Church Dogmatics* to chase down these uses for me.

8. Barth, *KD* II/1, p. 416.

an ability to "sense" *(empfinden)* to God is one of the peculiarities of Barth's theology that points strongly towards the incarnation as the basis for speaking about God. In any case, what we have here is a sharp denial of God's "untouchability" and a corresponding affirmation of his affectivity.

(2) *CD* II/1, p. 371

Here we have a clear case of mistranslation. Bromiley has "The impassibility of God cannot in any case mean that it is impossible for Him really to feel compassion." The word translated here "impassibility" is *Unveränderlichkeit* ("unchangeability" or "immutability").[9]

(3) *CD* II/2, p. 79

Here we have mention of a doctrine of impassibility that Barth clearly rejects. This time the object of the critique is the old Reformed orthodoxy, rather than Schleiermacher. Seen in context, Barth is illustrating the fact that the orthodox failed to treat election as an "integral part" of the doctrine of God. In Bromiley's translation, the passage reads: "There is a link here with the particular conceptions of the fathers and scholastics frequently touched on in the first part of our doctrine of God — a conception now appropriated afresh by the older Protestant orthodoxy. According to this conception God is everything in the way of aseity, simplicity, immutability, infinity, etc., but He is not the living God, that is to say, He is not the God who lives in concrete decision. God lives in this sense only figuratively. It is not something that belongs to His proper and essential life, but only to His relationship to the world. Basically, then, it may only be 'ascribed' to Him, while it is believed that His true being and likewise His true Godhead are to be sought in the impassibility which is above and behind His living activity within the universe." It is striking that, in this passage, Barth should say that God lives *in concrete decision* and that life in this decision is somehow "essential" *(wesentlich)* to him. In any event, the word translated "impassibility" here is *Unbeweglichkeit* — "immovability."[10] Whether Barth would still affirm a differently qualified form of "impassibility" than that which is characterized by immobility is a question that might seem to be left open by his rejection of the latter. But what-

9. Barth, *KD* II/1, p. 417. The term itself is set off in scare quotes to indicate that the meaning of it is being negotiated in this context.
10. Barth, *KD* II/2, p. 85.

ever form we tried to find in his writings could not contradict his explicit affirmation that God has his being in the concrete decision of election without causing problems for his conception here.

It is worth noting here that, for Barth, the fact that God lives in his concrete decision of election has implications for how one understands the doctrine of the Trinity. Barth says of the older Reformed orthodoxy: "They spoke here of the three Persons, of their relations one to another, of their common work directed outwards, without making clear to themselves what it means that this three-in-one essence neither exists nor is knowable as resting or moving purely *in itself,* that God is not *in abstracto* the Father, the Son and the Holy Spirit and that this three-in-one is the One but rather is all of these things in a definite relation and resolve: in virtue of the love and freedom which, in the bosom of His three-in-one essence, He has disposed of Himself from eternity to eternity."[11] What Barth establishes in this passage is a rule of thought. God may not be thought of as triune in abstraction from the concrete decision of election. Indeed, a three-in-one essence as resting or moving purely in itself *does not exist.* If ever it did exist, it certainly does so no longer. In any event, the triunity of God is a triunity over which he freely "disposes." It is a triunity *in this concrete decision* and, therefore, in a definite relationship to the world or it is not the one true God's triunity. If this is true of God's triunity, however, it is hard to think of "immovability" as anything other than a possibility that is unreal because never chosen.

(4) *CD* II/2, p. 163

Here we have a hint of the concept of *kenosis* which will be central to the Christology of IV/1. Barth asks (again in Bromiley's translation): "What was involved, then, when God elected to become the Son of Man in Jesus Christ?" And he answers, "In giving Himself to this act He ordained the surrender of something, i.e. of His own impassibility in face of the whole

---

11. Barth, *KD* II/2, p. 85. In German, the passage reads: "Man redete dort von den drei Personen, von ihrem Verhältnis untereinander, von ihrem gemeinsamen Werk nach außen, ohne sich klar zu machen, was es bedeutet, daß dieses dreieinige Wesen als rein *in sich* ruhendes oder bewegtes doch weder existiert noch erkennbar, daß Gott doch nicht *in abstracto* der Vater, der Sohn und der Heilige Geist und als dieser Dreieinige der Eine ist, sondern das Alles in bestimmter Beziehung und Entschließung: kraft der Liebe und Freiheit, in der er im Schoße seines dreieinigen Wesens von Ewigkeit her und in die Ewigkeit hinein über sich selbst verfügt hat."

world which, because it is not willed by Him, can only be the world of evil. In Himself God cannot be affected either by the possibility or by the reality of that will which opposes Him. He cannot be affected by any potentiality of evil. In Him is light and no darkness at all. But when God of His own will raised up man to be a covenant-member with Himself, when from all eternity He elected to be one with man in Jesus Christ, He did it with a being which was not merely affected by evil but actually mastered by it." The word translated "impassibility" here is *Unangerührtheit* — once again, something akin to "immovability."[12] The affirmation made here of a divine surrender of "immovability" is (once again) somewhat strange, given Barth's clear rejection of such a concept in #1 and the rule of thought established in #3. If God truly surrendered something that was *originally* his, then the revelation that took place in Jesus Christ could not have been the revelation of what God was originally but a revelation of God in an altered form. Barth's consistent opposition throughout his life to every version of kenotic Christology known to him militates against such a conclusion.[13] But, then, if the "surrender" in question took place in an eternal act, then Barth is here speaking of the surrender not of what God had been but of what he might yet have become had he not made the decision he did. In any event, the language found in this passage is typical of those kinds of passages in which Barth gives a nod to the tradition at a point in which it did not serve his purposes to do so. His real focus throughout is on the consequences of the act of surrender — not on what might have been. Still, this is the first of the instances I have counted as "positive" in that Barth at least seems to ascribe some sort of impassibility to God. That it is surrendered, however, is not to be missed.

(5) *CD* II/2, p. 166

Here we have the second of our positive uses of the word "impassible." God, Barth says, "could have remained satisfied with Himself and with the impassible glory and blessedness of His own inner life. But He did not do so." The word Bromiley has here translated "impassible" is *unangerührten* — more literally "unmoved."[14] Seen in context, Barth is here again suggesting that things might have been otherwise. God did not need to create

---

12. Barth, *KD* II/2, p. 178.

13. See, for example, Barth, *CD* IV/1, pp. 182-83; *KD* IV/1, pp. 198-99.

14. Barth, *CD* IV/1, pp. 181; *KD* IV/1, pp. 198-99.

human beings. He did not need to make them his partner in the covenant of grace. He did not need to redeem them. But here again, the affirmations made — however positive they may seem — are rendered ambiguous by the kinds of affirmation we saw in #3 above. Barth speaks here of a possibility *not* chosen by God, a possibility of a being which is *not* a being in the concrete decision in which God *lives*. Such a being, according to #3, neither exists nor is knowable.

(6) *CD* III/1, p. 395

Here we have a description of the God-concept found in Christian Wolff's 1719 work, "Reasonable Thoughts About God, the World, and the Soul of Man and of all Things Generally, Communicated to Lovers of the Truth." Wolff was, as is well known, an Enlightenment philosopher and theologian. Barth says of this God-concept, "Who and what is this God? He is the being which, like our own soul but perfectly, has the power plainly to conceive all worlds at once. He does so impassibly [*ohne jeden Affekt*] except for His pleasure in the well-being of the creature whose inner perfection has induced Him to confer reality upon it."[15] As Barth clearly is less than happy with this conception, we need not linger over it.

(7) *CD* IV/1, pp. 176-77

This passage appears in the context of what I would describe as a general introduction to the problem of speaking appropriately about the incarnation. It is not yet an attempt at an explanation, in other words, but an attempt to circumscribe a problem, to describe the conditions that create the decisive difficulties for understanding. It is in this context that our two Latin uses of the terms appear — one in a quotation from Irenaeus, one in a quotation from Melito of Sardis. Taken together, the two quotes make the same point that he who was almighty God made himself weak and impotent. Irenaeus expresses the point this way: "The invisible is made visible and the incomprehensible comprehensible and the impassible passible."[16] Melito has this to say, "The creature trembled, was horrified and said: what is this new mystery? The Judge is judged and remains still; the invisible is

---

15. Barth, *KD* III/1, p. 454. In German, the passage reads "Who and what is this God? The being which, similar to our own souls but in perfection, has the power to conceive of all worlds clearly all at once. He does this without any affect . . ." [*ohne jeden Affekt*].

16. *Invisibilis visibilis factus et incomprehensibilis comprehensibilis et impassibilis passibilis.*

seen and does not blush; the incomprehensible is comprehended and is not indignant; the immeasurable is measured and does not put up a fight; the impassible suffers and takes no revenge; the immortal dies and says not a word in response."[17] Wonderfully paradoxical sayings, obviously, and one of them — "the Judge is judged" — is made by Barth to be the heading of his treatment of the atoning work of Christ. But they do not amount to an explanation of any kind and for this reason I regard them as neutral, as speaking neither for nor against a doctrine of divine impassibility in Barth.

(8) *CD* IV/1, p. 187

We have before us here another of the apparently positive uses of "impassibility." In Bromiley's translation, the passage reads: "As God was in Christ, far from being against Himself, or at disunity with Himself, He has put into effect the freedom of His divine love, the love in which He is divinely free. He has therefore done and revealed that which corresponds to His divine nature. His immutability does not stand in the way of this. It must not be denied, but this possibility is included in His unalterable be-ing. He is absolute, infinite, exalted, active, impassible, transcendent, but in all this He is the One who loves in freedom, the One who is free in His love, and therefore not His own prisoner." The word translated "impassible" by Bromiley is *unberührbar* — literally, "untouchable."[18] As this passage appears in a section of the *Dogmatics* which will provide the central focus of the substantive section of this paper, I will postpone further discussion of it until then.

(9) *CD* IV/2, p. 68

The context is a consideration of the Reformed protest against the classical Lutheran understanding of the "communion" of Christ's two natures and the communication of attributes to which it was thought to give rise. In relation to this protest, Barth says, "It is a complete — if common — misunderstanding to attribute this protest to a barren intellectual zeal for the axiom: *finitum non capax infiniti,* and therefore for the impassibility

17. *Horruit creatura stupescens ac dicens: quidnam est hoc novum mysterium? iudex iudicatur et quietus est; invisibilis videtur neque erubescit; incomprehensibilis prehenditur neque indignatur; incommensurabilis mensuratur neque repugnant; impassibilis patitur neque ulciscitur; immortalis moritur neque respondet verbum.*
18. Barth, *KD* IV/1, p. 204.

[*Unberührbarkeit*] of the divine essence. In older Reformed dogmatics this axiom did not play the outstanding role attributed to it in later presentations."[19] I have classified this use of the term as "neutral" since Barth does not, in the context, take up a stance against the use of the term. But given that its meaning is "non-affectivity," it could just as easily have been classified as a negative use (on the basis of earlier protests against such a concept).

Taking a step back, we might usefully ask what we have learned from this survey. Two things above all: first, Barth emphatically rejects the concept of impassibility insofar as it is used to deny the affectivity of God. In fact, that is the *only* understanding of "impassibility" of which he has any real awareness. Second, the term has been employed by Bromiley in translation only three times in contexts that might seem to make its use at all positive. In none of these cases, however, is the term or the concept it represents the focus of Barth's attention. We do not find anything in Barth's writings like a sustained effort to elaborate a *doctrine* of impassibility. Even when positively employed, the term is used only in passing; the issue under discussion lies elsewhere. And the great probability is that it is descriptive simply of a road not traveled.

What I would like to show now is that Barth's later Christology leaves no room for a positive use of the term; that we would be better off speaking simply of the divine constancy. We turn then to Barth's later Christology.[20]

---

19. Cf. Barth, *KD* IV/2, p. 73.

20. I have argued elsewhere that development takes place in Barth's thinking about Christology between his treatment of that subject-matter in his doctrine of revelation in *CD* I/2 and his later treatment of the same problems in his doctrine of reconciliation in *CD* IV/1 and IV/2 especially. The development in question is largely a function of Barth's revision of the doctrine of election in *CD* II/2 and can best be described as a move from a Christology that allows the metaphysics of Chalcedon to stand for the time being (I/2) to a more historicized account that seeks to uphold the theological values which come to expression in the Chalcedonian Formula while rejecting its metaphysics. See Bruce L. McCormack, "Barth's grundsätzliche Chalcedonismus?", *Zeitschrift für dialektische Theologie* 18 (2002): 138-73. If I were ever to complete my intellectual biography of Karl Barth, by extending it to the end of his life, I would add to the four phases in the unfolding of his dialectical theology, a fifth phase devoted wholly to volume IV of the *Church Dogmatics* — both because it is only here that the moves made in *CD* II/2 received their final deepening and clarification and because the volume of reconciliation departs from the *loci communes* approach that had governed preceding volumes and established a highly systematic architectonic of its own. For the first four phases, see Bruce L. McCormack, *Karl Barth's Critically Realistic Dialectical Theology: Its Genesis and Development, 1909-1936* (Oxford: Clarendon Press, 1995).

II. The Way of the Son into the Far Country

Barth's treatment of the doctrine of the incarnation in *CD* IV/1 appears under the heading of "The Way of the Son of God into the Far Country." The section is divided into three movements: first, a description of the mystery to be explained followed, in the second and third movements, by the explanation. The second movement treats of the "outer moment" of the Son's obedience to the Father in time. The third treats of the "inner moment" of the Son's obedience to the Father in eternity. Since the "inner moment" provides the ontological ground for the "outer moment," the third movement is the culmination, so that all of the material spirals upwards into a reflection on trinitarian relations. I should point out that Bromiley's translation has the effect of making this structural feature of Barth's presentation less easily discernible, since he chose to eliminate the centered bold strokes by means of which Barth had originally set off the second and third movements from each other and from the initial description of the subject-matter to be treated.[21] In what immediately follows here, I will offer first a description of the problem, then turn to Barth's discussion of the "outer" and "inner" moments.

A. The Problem

Barth's starting-point, his point of entry into the doctrine of the incarnation, does not lie in the Chalcedonian dogma. It lies rather in the New Testament, in the recognition on the part of all of the writers of the "full and genuine and individual humanity of the man Jesus of Nazareth."[22] It is precisely as this concretely existing human that he was also understood by the writers to be "qualitatively different" from all other men and women; qualitatively different because he is acknowledged to be "their Lord and Lawgiver and Judge." "In attestation of this understanding of the man Jesus, the New Testament tradition calls Him the Messiah of Israel, the *kyrios,* the second Adam come down from heaven, and, in a final approximation to what is meant by all this, the Son or the Word of God."[23] It is *the man Jesus* who is said to be "by nature God."[24]

21. See Barth, *KD* IV/1, pp. 195, 210.
22. Barth, *CD* IV/1, p. 160; cf. *KD* IV/1, p. 174.
23. Barth, *CD* IV/1, p. 160; cf. *KD* IV/1, p. 174.
24. Barth, *CD* IV/1, p. 163; *KD* IV/1, p. 178.

But, then, if the man Jesus is God, then a problem announces itself. As Barth puts it, "The true God — if the man Jesus is true God — is obedient." It should be noted that the subject-referent is *still* the man Jesus, but from this point on it is the man Jesus *as God* of whom Barth speaks. What is said of him is said also of God. The true God is obedient. "The New Testament describes the Son of God . . . not only as the servant but also as the *suffering* servant of God. Not as One who suffers accidentally and incidentally, perhaps for the sake of testing and proving His conviction, perhaps for the sake of attaining a goal through struggle, perhaps as a picture, in a different way, of His glory, but as the One who suffers necessarily and, as it were, essentially. . . ."[25] This is not to say that he suffers against his will. "The story of Gethsemane . . . shows two things: first, that we have to do with His genuine human decision; and second, that it is a decision of obedience. He chooses, but He chooses that apart from which, being who He is, He could not choose anything else."[26] It is *as God* that the man Jesus suffers necessarily and, as Barth puts it, essentially; in all of his humanness. In the freedom proper to him as human, he suffers "necessarily."

Barth then proceeds to explain this "necessity" in terms of the divine election. All that takes place in Jesus' life, his passion, and his death takes place in fulfillment of God's covenantal dealings with Israel and, therefore, in fulfillment of the divine election. "The particularity of the man Jesus in proceeding from the one elect people of Israel, as the confirmation of its election, means decisively that the reconciliation of sinful and lost man has, above all, the character of a divine *condescension,* that it takes place as God goes into the *far country.* The Father who is one with the man Jesus His Son (John 10:30) is the God who years before was not too good, and did not count it too small a thing, to bind Himself and to obligate Himself to Abraham and his descendants, and to be God in this particularity and limitation — 'I will be your God.'"[27] The "necessity" in question must finally be understood in light of the fact that this man is God, that what takes place in him is the consequence of a divine act of condescension which was also an act of *Self*-limitation. For the Father-Son relationship between God and the man Jesus possesses an intimacy that the God-Israel

25. Barth, *KD* IV/1, pp. 179-80; *CD* IV/1, p. 164.
26. Barth, *CD* IV/1, p. 166; *KD* IV/1, p. 181.
27. Barth, *KD* IV/1, p. 184; *CD* IV/1, p. 168.

relation did not. ". . . [W]here in the Old Testament we find Israel, or the king of Israel, in the New Testament we find the one Israelite *Jesus*. He is the object of the same electing will of the Creator, the same merciful divine faithfulness. . . . Of course, what takes place between Him and the Father is incomparably greater and as God's Self-humiliation much more un-heard of than all that is designated by the Old Testament Father-son relationships. This one man is now — it is as if that Old Testament framework is fulfilled only immediately to be blown up — *the* Son of God who is *one* with the Father and, therefore, is *Himself God*. God is therefore now not only the electing Creator but also the elect creature, not only the gracious One but the One who receives grace, not only the One who commands but the One who is called to obedience and placed under obligation."[28] What is in view here, finally, is a "Self-limitation and Self-humiliation"[29] on the part of God.

Barth's description of the christological problem as it is announced in the New Testament entails a progression in thought. It begins with the man Jesus. It proceeds from the affirmation of this man's full humanity and his concrete place in history to his identification with God. Where the Chalcedonian Formula fixes its attention on two "natures" (so that the problem becomes the relation of the "natures" to the person of the union and to each other), Barth is preoccupied with *obedience* — indeed, with a *history* of obedience that is equated directly with the history of God. Thus it is not surprising that the progression in thought ends with the thought of a Self-limitation and Self-humiliation on the part of God. That is the decisive problem that Barth will now seek to resolve.

Before turning to Barth's resolution, it remains only to add — in order to complete our initial description of the problem — a word with regard to the *telos,* the goal of this Self-limitation and Self-humiliation. "'God sent His Son in the likeness of sinful flesh to condemn sin in the flesh' (Rom. 8:3). In the pregnant words of John 1:14, the Word became *flesh.* 'Flesh' in the language of the New (and earlier the Old) Testament is man under the divine verdict and judgment, whose existence — because he is a sinner — must perish before God, becoming nothing, hastening towards nothingness, being subject to death."[30] That the Word was made flesh

---

28. Barth, *KD* IV/1, pp. 185-86; *CD* IV/1, p. 170.
29. Barth, *KD* IV/1, p. 186; *CD* IV/1, p. 170.
30. Barth, *KD* IV/1, p. 180; *CD* IV/1, p. 165.

means that this man exists "under the wrath and judgment of the electing and loving God. . . . [W]hen the New Testament says of the *Son of God* that he became *man,* it has also said of Him that He stands under God's wrath and judgment. He breaks apart and is shattered on God. It could not be otherwise. It must be this way. His history must be a history of suffering."[31] That this man is God means that God has made his own this man's history of suffering. In the Old Testament, Barth says, the one who suffers stands over against God, under his judgment. In the New Testament, this element of standing over against is gone. "[I]t is God Himself who takes the place of those older sufferers and allows the bitterness of their suffering to fall upon Himself."[32] Indeed, it is only in the New Testament that we fully grasp what suffering and death mean "in that they become God's own work, in that God now gives Himself over into this most dreadful of all foreign spheres."[33] The problem has now been given its most pointed form.

B. The "Outer Moment" of the Son's Obedience

The language of "outer moment" and "inner moment" serves quite intentionally to bring the obedience of the Son in time and his obedience in eternity into the closest possible relationship. We are, in fact, dealing with one and the same act or event — viewed first from the standpoint of its outworking in time, viewed second from the standpoint of the eternal decision/act itself and its implications for the being of God. These are, thus, "moments" in the human comprehension of a single movement in the divine life. To regard them as such is of decisive importance for showing why it is that God does not cease to be God when he gives himself over to the human experiences of pain and suffering. It is in this context — in laying out the outline of the two movements to follow (the "outer moment" and the "inner moment") — that we find the Latin quotes from Irenaeus and Melito of Sardis which constituted the seventh instantiation of the term "impassibility" in my survey above. Seen in the context of the argument as a whole, the citation from Melito of Sardis serves as a foil. It is Melito's de-

---

31. Barth, *KD* IV/1, p. 191; *CD* IV/1, pp. 174-75.
32. Barth, *KD* IV/1, p. 191; *CD* IV/1, p. 175.
33. Barth, *KD* IV/1, p. 191; *CD* IV/1, p. 175.

scription of the incarnation as a *new* mystery which is the focus of Barth's critical scrutiny.[34] And, in fact, the demonstration that the mystery before us is precisely not a *new* mystery is the red thread that runs through the whole of Barth's treatment of both "moments." The mystery of the incarnation may be new to us, but it is not new to God; it is not an altogether new event in his being and life when it occurs in time — and that is why it involves God's being in no change. We turn then more directly to the "outer moment."

Barth's attempt to resolve the problem posed by New Testament Christology takes the form of a meditation on the mystery of the "deity of Christ" — a mystery which Barth defines in these words: "[t]hat God as God is able and willing and ready to condescend, to humble Himself." God *as God* is able and willing and ready. The "mystery" of the incarnation is finally the mystery of God's own deity. And the deity of God "is not the deity of some kind of divine essence equipped with all manner of supreme attributes. . . . *Who* the one true God is and *what* He is, i.e. what His essence as God and therefore His deity is, the 'divine nature' which, if Jesus Christ is true God, is also His nature — that we have to read off of the fact that as such He is also true *man* and therefore participates in *human* nature, on the basis of His becoming man, His becoming flesh, and what He did and suffered as man in the flesh. For . . . the mirror in which it becomes knowable and is known that He is *God* and that He is of the *divine* nature is precisely His becoming *flesh* and His existence in the *flesh*."[35] What Barth sets forth in this passage is, at a minimum, an epistemological principle. We have no other access to understanding the divine "nature," indeed, the very essence of God, than there where God exists in the flesh, under the divine verdict and judgment, under the sentence of death. But this is more than mere epistemology.

Barth's treatment of the "outer moment" is bracketed by two readings of the "Christ hymn" in Philippians 2. Seen in combination, these exegetical passages establish the point to be made in the second movement of Barth's exposition, viz. that God does not undergo change in becoming human. For Barth, the *kenosis* spoken of in Philippians 2:7 consists in a divine "renunciation of His being in the form of God alone."[36] The subject

---

34. See above, note 17.
35. Barth, *KD* IV/1, p. 193; *CD* IV/1, p. 177.
36. Barth, *CD* IV/1, p. 180; *KD* IV/1, p. 196.

who performs this act of "renunciation" is described as the "Word of God" or, more typically, simply as "God."[37] The effect of this decision is that being in the form of God is *not* God's "one and only and exclusive possibility."[38] God was not "bound to any such 'only.'"[39] He was able, willing, and ready to take on the form of the human. Without detriment to his deity, any "diminution or alteration of His Godhead," God had this other possibility, the possibility of existing in this "alien form."[40]

Now it might well seem, on the basis of what has been said thus far, that Barth's talk of the *addition* of a human nature leaves room for a being in the "form of God" which might still be dressed out in terms of supreme attributes. The epistemological principle might well be thought to have no ontological implications whatsoever. To restrict knowledge of the divine "nature" and essence to that which is made known in Christ might seem to mean that there is a mode of being and existence enjoyed by God above and prior to his eternal act of electing himself for suffering but that such a mode of being and existence is simply unknowable. In that case, we would have to make a distinction between God "in himself" and God "for us." It would be surprising, however, if it were so. For Barth also seems to think that what he is doing is something new — as is clear when he says, ". . . it is not enough to remain standing in the great line of theological tradition and, therefore, to reject all thought of a changeability or change of God in His presence and action in the man Jesus. What depends on this rejection is clear. If God is not truly and wholly in Christ, what sense can there be in talking about the reconciliation of the world with God in Him? There is, however, something very powerful and deeply astonishing about what we are daring to do when we say, without reservation or diminution, that God was truly and wholly *in Christ,* when we maintain His identity with this man. . . . This statement of identification may not be a mere postulate. . . . In calling this man the Son or the eternal Word of God and, therefore, in ascribing to this man in His unity with God divine essence, divine nature,

---

37. Barth begins the small-print section within which the reflection on Philippians 2:7 appears by speaking simply of "He": ". . . existing in the form of God, in full possession of it, freely disposing of it, emptied Himself. . . ." For the antecedent of the "He" one must look back to the preceding large-print paragraph where the subject is, alternatively, the Word of God, and God.

38. Barth, *CD* IV/1, p. 180; *KD* IV/1, p. 196.

39. Barth, *CD* IV/1, p. 180; *KD* IV/1, p. 196.

40. Barth, *CD* IV/1, p. 180; *KD* IV/1, p. 196.

this statement speaks not only and not first of Him but rather first and above all of *God*."[41]

What is new in Barth, I think, is that he has identified the *human* subject, Jesus of Nazareth, as God — and done so, as we shall soon see, on grounds other than those provided in Hegel's philosophy. More on that in just a moment. For now, let me just say that the problem which the identification of the human subject with God creates for Barth's understanding of God has to do with the concept of immutability. If the human Jesus is God, if the human subject is, as such, a divine subject (in a sense yet to be established), then God really does suffer and die. Where the question of immutability is concerned, we would have before us just two options. The first is the possibility just announced, that of driving a wedge between God in himself and God in the economy of salvation. Barth describes this option in the following words: "The Word becoming flesh, God's being human, His condescension, His way into the sphere of alienation, His existence in the form of a servant can be understood in such a way that in it, we have to do with a *'novum mysterium'* (the expression of Melito of Sardis would, in that case be understood strictly and literally); with that which is, from a noetic-logical point of view, an absolute Paradox, a pure antinomy; with that which is, from an ontic point of view, a cleft, a rift, an abyss in God Himself, between His being and essence in itself and His acting and effecting as Reconciler of the world created by Him. That is (or much rather appears to be) the *one* possibility."[42]

In favor of this option lies the fact it takes with radical seriousness the fact that, in the incarnation, God not only becomes a creature, but gives himself over to the human's contradiction of him — thereby placing himself under the judgment that rests on that contradiction. And that, Barth thinks, is all to the good. As he puts it, "The meaning of the incarnation is revealed in the question of Jesus from the cross: 'my God, my God, why have you abandoned me?' (Mk. 15:34)."[43]

And yet, Barth finds the results of this option simply intolerable. "But at this point what is meant to be supreme praise of God can in fact become supreme blasphemy. God gives Himself but he does not give Himself away or give Himself up in becoming a creature, in becoming human. He does

---

41. Barth, *KD* IV/1, pp. 199-200; *CD* IV/1, p. 183.
42. Barth, *KD* IV/1, p. 201; *CD* IV/1, p. 184.
43. Barth, *KD* IV/1, p. 202; *CD* IV/1, p. 185.

not cease in this condition to be God. He does not in this condition come into conflict with Himself. He does not sin when, in His unity with the man Jesus, He enters into the midst of sinners and takes their place. And when He dies in His unity with this man, death does not gain any power over Him."[44] If it were otherwise, if in doing any of this, "God set Himself in contradiction with Himself, how could He reconcile the world with Himself? What help would His deity be to us if, instead of crossing over the real abyss between us and Him precisely in His divinity, He left His deity even partially behind . . . ?"[45]

Barth's target in this passage is, as the context makes amply clear, modern kenoticism and Heinrich Vogel's Christology. But what he says here has ramifications for other positions as well. For Barth is here objecting to any view that would seek to make a distinction in content between God in himself and God in the economy of salvation. Classically, of course, the validity of such a distinction was taken for granted — with the consequence, I would say, that no one who embraced it could then uphold a single-subject Christology without either drifting *willy nilly* into Nestorianism or embracing some form or other of the absolute Paradox of which Barth speaks. I will have more to say on that subject in the next section. But it is important to notice that Barth's critique here also impacts Hegel and his followers in a negative way — which shows that Barth was not deceiving himself in thinking he was doing something new here. The Hegelians, of course, also began with an identification of the second "person" of the Trinity with the man Jesus. But they used this identification in order then to affirm that the death of Jesus meant a rift in the being of God. And that is precisely what Barth does *not* do. That Barth is inspired by Hegel is true; that his Christology in *CD* IV/1 is Hegelian is not.

The only remaining option, Barth says, is to affirm that in God "there is no paradox, no antinomy, no division, no unfaithfulness to Himself, and no possibility of it. . . . What He is and does, He is and does in complete unity with Himself." But you cannot successfully uphold this claim, Barth thinks, unless you begin where he does. If we think that God cannot experience death, that he is incapable of such things, then "our concept of God is too narrow, too arbitrary, too human, all too human. Who God is and what it means to be divine is something we have to learn where God has

44. Barth, *KD* IV/1, p. 202.
45. Barth, *KD* IV/1, p. 202.

revealed Himself and, thereby, His nature, the essence of the divine. And when He reveals Himself in Jesus Christ as the God who *does* such things, then it must lie far from us to wish to be wiser than He and to maintain that such things stand in contradiction to the divine essence."[46]

Where this second option is taken seriously, we will learn anew how to think about the being of God. God has acted in the freedom of his love, Barth says. He has freely elected himself to stand in the place of the human, under his own judgment and wrath, and to suffer and die there. In doing all of this, he has done that which "corresponds" to his divine nature. "His immutability does not stand in the way of this and must therefore not be denied. Rather, the possibility for all of this is included in His unchangeable essence. He is absolute, infinite, high, active, unaffected, transcendent, but in all of that, He is the One who *loves* in freedom, the One who is *free* in His love and therefore is not His own prisoner."[47] In my survey of the uses of the word "impassibility," I mentioned one positive use which, more than any other, might conceivably lead readers to think that Barth affirms a doctrine of divine impassibility. The passage I just cited is that passage. The word I translated "unaffected" is *unberührbar* — literally, "untouchable." I have translated it "unaffected" because it is being used to describe what God might have been had he not chosen to be God for us in Jesus Christ. It is descriptive, in other words, of a possibility that was never actualized — which can only be talked about, if at all, in terms of that which was rejected by God and put aside. The same holds true of the other two apparently positive uses of the term "impassibility" in the Bromiley translation. In each case, we are dealing with a less-than-real abstraction.

One last observation: earlier I said that Barth makes what appears to be a direct identification of the human subject, Jesus of Nazareth, with the divine subject. What Jesus does, God does; what Jesus experiences, God experiences. But identification should not be understood as reduction. Certainly, Barth comes right up to the edge of a direct equation of a human being, full stop, with the second "person" of the Trinity. That is the step taken by Hegel and his followers, but it is not finally a step that Barth takes. We turn then to the "inner moment" in order now, finally, to see Barth's resolution of the christological problem as that problem was envisioned by the New Testament writers.

---

46. Barth, *KD* IV/1, p. 203; *CD* IV/1, p. 186.
47. Barth, *KD* IV/1, p. 204; *CD* IV/1, p. 187.

C. The "Inner Moment" of the Son's Obedience

The necessity that some sort of distinction be made between the divine subject and the human "nature" of Jesus finds its ground in the fact that the divine subject pre-exists the birth of the human Jesus. That is as true for Barth as it ever was for the orthodox among the ancients — his apparent identification of the two notwithstanding. The old orthodoxy expressed this distinction by saying that the Logos remains other than his human nature, even as that human nature subsists in the Logos. And yet there is a problem in this formulation that must be addressed because it won't go away. Once you grant that the human Jesus had a soul (as all the orthodox did in the aftermath of the Apollinarian controversy), then what you have looks very much like a human *subject* — not just a human "nature" (understood as an abstract list of predicates proper to the human), but a thinking, willing, fully self-conscious, performative agent. As is well known, the recognition of that fact led Nestorius to posit a two-subject Christology. In order to maintain a single-subject Christology in the face of this pressure, Cyril carried out what I would myself call an "instrumentalization" of the human Jesus. Expressed more neutrally by John McGuckin: "The human nature is, therefore, not conceived as an independently acting dynamic (a distinct human person who self-activates) but as the manner of action of an independent and omnipotent power — that of the Logos; and to the Logos alone can be attributed the authorship of, and responsibility for, all its actions. The last principle is the flagship of Cyril's whole argument. There can only be one creative subject, one personal reality, in the incarnate Lord; and that subject is the divine Logos who has made a human nature his own."[48] The problem created by this solution finds its focus in the question as to whether a human nature which is simply used in this way can really be equated with a thinking, willing, fully self-conscious, performative agent. Based on McGuckin's reading of Cyril, I would have to say that such an equation is impossible. There is only one active agent, McGuckin says, and that agent is the Logos. The Logos even raises his own body from the dead[49] — which means that the instrumentalization of the human is complete. Not only does the Logos, as the sole active agent, act *through* his human nature, he even acts *upon* it.

48. McGuckin, *Saint Cyril of Alexandria*, p. 186.
49. McGuckin, *Saint Cyril of Alexandria*, p. 186.

Now Barth, too, wants a single-subject Christology. He too understands that the human Jesus had no independent *existence*. He affirms the doctrine of the *anhypostasia* and *enhypostasia* of Jesus[50] — which means that for Barth, too, the human Jesus has his being and existence grounded *in* the person of the Logos. But unlike Cyril, Barth treats Jesus as a thinking, willing, "performative agent" (my phrase) who has an independent *power of action. That* is the real point of difference from Cyril which McGuckin helps us to see so clearly. Cyril is motivated throughout by his soteriological commitment to a doctrine of theosis. Barth rejects any and every concept of divinization.[51] He is motivated by a concern for the integrity of Christ's humanity — and equally by a concern for divine immutability. How he accomplishes this is what I must now explain. But here, at the outset, I want simply to suggest that Barth shares with Cyril the problem of explaining how a single-subject Christology can be reconciled with the ascription of a soul to the human Jesus. Barth's approach to this problem — starting with the human obedience of Jesus — does not call that measure of shared interest into question. But Barth's solution to this problem is quite the opposite of Cyril's. Barth is, as we shall now see, a Cyril "in reverse."

Barth finds the ontological basis for his solution to the christological mystery in a novel understanding of the trinitarian relations of the Father to the Son and of the Son to the Father. The relation of the Son to the Father in eternity, above and prior to the act of creation, is a relation of humility. That the humility of the Son may not be restricted to an economy of salvation that is other and different from the Son's *true* mode of being is made clear when Barth says, "Not only may we not deny, much rather must we affirm and understand as *essential* to the being of God the offensive fact that there is in God Himself an above and a below, a prius and a posterius, a superiority and a subordination."[52] Or again: ". . . it is just as natural to God to be lowly as to be high, to be near as to be far, to be small as to be large, to be weak as to be strong. . . . In the servant form of His presence and action in Jesus Christ, too, we have to do with Him in His

50. Barth, *CD* IV/1, pp. 49-50, 91; *KD* IV/2, pp. 52-53, 100.

51. See Bruce L. McCormack, "Participation in God, Yes, Deification, No: Two Modern Answers to an Ancient Question," in Ingolf U. Dalferth, Johannes Fischer, and Hans-Peter Großhans, eds., *Denkwürdiges Geheimnis: Beiträge zur Gotteslehre. Festschrift für Eberhard Jüngel zum 70. Geburtstag* (Tübingen: Mohr Siebeck, 2004), pp. 347-74.

52. Barth, *KD* IV/1, p. 219; *CD* IV/1, pp. 200-201 (emphasis mine).

true deity. The *humility* in which He lives and acts in Jesus Christ is not alien but rather proper to Him. This humility is a *novum mysterium* for us. . . . For *Him*, however, it is no *novum mysterium*."[53] What is clear in these passages is that Barth finds the basis for upholding the divine immutability in an eternal humility of the Son. The humiliation of the Son in time finds its ground in an eternal humility so that the Son in time perfectly "corresponds" to the Son in eternity. That is Barth's argument for divine immutability. Less clear to most Barth researchers (in this part of the world, at any rate) are the ontological implications of saying that humility is *essential* to the Son.[54] What does it mean to say that humility and maj-

---

53. Barth, *KD* IV/1, pp. 210-11; *CD* IV/1, pp. 192-93.

54. My first attempt at laying out the ontological implications of Barth's doctrine of election are to be found in Bruce L. McCormack, "Grace and Being: The Role of God's Gracious Election in Karl Barth's Theological Ontology," in John Webster, ed., *The Cambridge Companion to Karl Barth* (Cambridge: Cambridge University Press, 2000), pp. 92-110. This is the place to acknowledge that the hidden conversation-partner throughout was Robert Jenson, whose critical questions to the "extra Calvinisticum" made me realize that I could not retain the latter unmodified. My essay on Barth's ontology was my way of answering a critical question posed to me in private conversation by Jenson. It is for that reason that I have chosen to dedicate this essay to him. My Cambridge Companion essay has provoked a debate, however, that shows every sign of gaining in strength. For criticisms of that essay, see Paul Molnar, *Divine Freedom and the Doctrine of the Immanent Trinity: In Dialogue with Karl Barth and Contemporary Theology* (London: T. & T. Clark, 2002), pp. 62-64, 81. Molnar's critique, which was centered principally on the question of whether my understanding of the logical relationship between election and triunity made creation "necessary" for God, was then addressed by Kevin Hector. See Hector, "God's Triunity and Self-Determination: A Conversation with Karl Barth, Bruce McCormack, and Paul Molnar," *International Journal of Systematic Theology* 3 (2005): 246-61. Molnar has responded with "The Trinity, Election and God's Ontological Freedom: A Response to Kevin W. Hector," *International Journal of Systematic Theology* 8 (2006): 294-306. That exchange was then followed by one between Edwin Chr. van Driel and myself. See Edwin Chr. van Driel, "Karl Barth on the Eternal Existence of Jesus Christ," *Scottish Journal of Theology* 60 (2007): 45-61; Bruce McCormack, "Seek God Where He May Be Found," *Scottish Journal of Theology* 60 (2007): 62-79. It should be noted that van Driel's reading of Barth is not Molnar's, though the questions he puts to me are similar. This debate has now also made its way into the evangelical world. See K. Scott Oliphint, "Something Much Too Plain to Say," *Westminster Theological Journal* 68 (2006): 187-202. I should add that I have also written a number of essays that have teased out the implications of my interpretation of Barth's theological ontology for other doctrines. See McCormack, "The Being of Holy Scripture Is in Becoming: Karl Barth in Conversation with American Evangelical Criticism," in *Evangelicals and Scripture: Tradition, Authority and Hermeneutics*, ed. Vincent E. Bacote, Laura C. Miguélez, and Dennis L. Okholm (Downers Grove, Ill.: InterVarsity Press, 2004), pp. 55-75; "The Ontological Presuppositions of Barth's

esty are equally basic, equally original to the being of God? It might *seem* to mean nothing more than that both exist as abstract possibilities, requiring only a decision to be actualized. But Barth goes a step further. He says, "If the humility of Christ is not only a behavior of the man Jesus of Nazareth, if it is the behavior of this man because there is . . . a humility grounded in the essence of God, then something else is just as grounded in the essence of God itself. According to the New Testament, the humility of this man is an act of *obedience*. . . . If, now, God is in Christ, if what the man Jesus does is, at the same time, God's own work, then this character of the self-emptying and self-humiliation of Jesus Christ as an act of *obedience* cannot be alien to God Himself. Rather, we have to recognize in it the inner side of the mystery of the divine nature of Christ and therefore the mystery of the nature of the one true *God. . . .*"[55] So not only is humility essential to God, but obedience is as well.

Now the difference between humility and obedience is the difference between that which might possibly be only a posture or attitude and that which is clearly a willed activity. To make the act of willed obedience *essential* to God is to suggest that the divine decision which sets in motion the economy of salvation is the act which *constitutes* God as God. So humility and majesty are not abstract possibilities that find their ground in a divine essence which is finally to be distinguished from both; rather, both belong to God essentially and, therefore, with equal originality. Barth's explanation of why this should be so takes us deep into his most mature reflections on the triunity of God.

"He is, as the Son, as the One who *submits* in *humility,* the same as what the Father is, as the One who *decrees* in *majesty.* He is, as the Son, in the *outworking* (in obedience!), the same as what the Father is, in the *Origin.* He is, as the Son, as the *Self-posited* God (or, as the dogma has it, as the Son generated in eternity by the Father), the same as what the Father is, as the *Self-positing* God (as the One who generates the Son from eternity)."[56]

Doctrine of the Atonement," in *The Glory of the Atonement: Biblical, Historical and Practical Perspectives,* ed. Charles E. Hill and Frank A. James III (Downers Grove, Ill.: InterVarsity Press, 2004), pp. 346-66; "*Justitia Aliena:* Karl Barth in Conversation with the Evangelical Doctrine of Imputed Righteousness," in Bruce L. McCormack, ed., *Justification in Perspective: Historical Developments and Contemporary Challenges* (Grand Rapids: Baker Academic, 2006).

55. Barth, *KD* IV/1, p. 211; *CD* IV/1, p. 193.
56. Barth, *KD* IV/1, pp. 228-29; *CD* IV/1, p. 209.

Barth's point in this passage is, above all, to lay stress on the singular identity of the divine subject — now in this mode of being, now in that one. His model of the Trinity is that of a single divine subject in three modes of being, a "Self-repetition"[57] in eternity. But notice the language he puts in the place of the traditional language of "generation." The Self-*posited* God is the same as the Self-*positing* God. This is Hegel-*like* language which, in the context in which it is employed, strongly suggests that the eternal "generation" of the Son is willed activity, indeed, that it is *purposive* activity. In fact, given that Barth makes the act of obedience to be *essential* to God's being, that is the only way this language could be taken. We might most accurately state Barth's position by saying that it is precisely the Father's command which posits the Son — and which thereby makes the Father to be *Father*. The Father commands — and in so doing posits himself over against himself in a modality of being (viz. humility) which makes him capable of responding in obedience. Therefore, there are not two divine acts "in" eternity, one in which God constitutes himself as triune and one in which he freely elects to be God "for us." There is only one divine act in eternity in which both of these things take place.

The preceding paragraph admittedly represents a wee bit of "smoothing out" of Barth's reflections. The truth is that I have introduced greater clarity and self-consistency into Barth than is to be found on the surface of his texts.[58] Barth can speak in ways that suggest that divine essence is presupposed by the eternal act in which God elects himself for incarnation, suffering, and death. And when he does, he speaks of it in terms of "freedom in love" — which seems also to imply the existence of God in triunity

---

57. Barth, *KD* IV/1, p. 224; *CD* IV/1, p. 205.

58. It has been my conviction, throughout the debate described in note 54 above, that the question I put to Barth in my Cambridge Companion essay was a question he did not put to himself in quite the same form. How else to account for the fact that passages can be found in the *Church Dogmatics* that lend support to both sides in the debate, so that each side is faced with the necessity of explaining the meaning of those passages that contradict their preferred reading? Seen in this light, Molnar's claim — "I never insist, as they [McCormack and Hector] do, that Barth must change his thinking so that my presentation of his views can be continuous with his" — rests on a considerable amount of naïveté. Every participant in this debate engages necessarily in a certain amount of "smoothing out" in their efforts to present a self-consistent proposal on the basis of Barth's writings. The difference between Molnar and myself is that I have freely acknowledged the fact all along, while he continues to deny it. See Molnar, "The Trinity, Election and God's Ontological Freedom," p. 295.

above and prior to the eternal act of election. Seen in the context in which such talk appears, Barth's reason for speaking in this way is clearly to secure the truth that God would be God without human beings. But there is something slightly improper — even abstract — about this. If God "essences" himself as Father, Son, and Spirit in the act of divine election and the history to which it gives rise, then a presupposed "essence" must constitute limit-language; something we must say in particular contexts but which always has something improper about it. The "smoothing out" that I have undertaken has the effect of shifting attention away from a *presupposed* divine "essence" in order to focus upon the act of "essence-ing." But I did this not in order to read my own views into Barth's texts but simply to make his solution entirely consistent with his goal; the goal, namely, of upholding the divine immutability. For nothing can more successfully safeguard the divine immutability quite like making the divine suffering in time to be the outworking of an eternal humility that is truly *essential* to God. That I have done this while also seeking to preserve the divine freedom is a strong witness to the fact that my interpretation of Barth at least has the advantage of securing *all* of the theological values Barth held most dear, i.e., divine suffering *and* divine freedom. The reader will have noticed, I hope, that such a conception leaves no room for divine impassibility. In the ancient world, divine immutability and divine impassibility were correlative terms. In Barth, they have been severed.

My only remaining task is to give some indication of how Barth also upholds a single-subject Christology.

D. Karl Barth's Single-Subject Christology

To provide a complete defense of the view I find in Barth would require close attention to the quite lengthy section from *Church Dogmatics* IV/2 entitled "The Homecoming of the Son of Man." That I cannot do. What I will do is to give you a sketch of Barth's solution to the christological problem with such supporting evidence as space will allow.

One way of expressing the christological problem is that of identifying the ontological conditions that make it possible to say that "what the man Jesus does, God does." This way of putting the problem has the advantage of bringing Barth into conversation with Cyril, since both believe that statement to be true. Cyril's explanation of how this statement could be true was, it will be remembered, to instrumentalize the human "nature," making it the tool of the single subject which he identified with the Logos. Barth's answer moves in the opposite direction — which might seem to mean that, for him, it is the man Jesus who is the single subject. How, then, can it be that what this man does, God does — *if* we are not to simply make a human being to be the second person of the Trinity (as Hegel and his followers did)? If, as I would maintain, "the man Jesus" is the performative agent of all that is done and experienced by the God-man, how then is this *not* a Hegelian reduction? The answer has to do, first, with Barth's understanding of the hypostatic union as a *history;* second, with his affirmation of the so-called *genus tapeinoticum* as the heart of a proper understanding of the "communication of attributes"; and third, with his understanding of the divine election as the ground of the mode of being we typically refer to as the second "person" of the Trinity.

First, then, the hypostatic union. With the ancients, Barth affirms that the "man Jesus" is a special creation, that he has his being and existence given to him *in* the being and existence of the Son of God. "God the Son is the acting Subject in this event."[59] But here already, a difference of opinion separates Barth from the ancients. The emphasis falls here on uniting as an ongoing activity by means of which the Son of God gives to the man Jesus being and existence in his own being and existence. Thus, the uniting is not an event that is complete in an instant, at the very beginning of the life of Jesus, but one that *continues* in the form of a history. The effect of this historicizing of the union is to call into question the abstractness of the Chalcedonian Formula, the "static center" between the great divine acts of virginal conception and resurrection which, classically, allowed the structure of the relationship between the Logos and his natures or between the natures themselves to be reflected upon without regard to the history of Jesus. Barth summarizes the move he has made in relation to Chalcedon this way: "We have 'actualised' the doctrine of the incarnation, i.e. we have used the main traditional concepts, *unio, communio* and *communicatio,* as concentrically related terms to describe one and the same ongoing process. . . . We have, in a sense, kept company with the older dogmatics in each of the three concepts, as in those of *exinanitio* and *exaltatio,* to the extent, that is, that they are all terms which speak of actions, *operationes,* events. But — thinking and speaking in pure concepts of movement — we

59. Barth, *CD* IV/2, p. 46; *KD* IV/2, p. 49.

have re-translated that whole phenomenology into the sphere of movement. And we have done this because originally the theme of it . . . is not a phenomenon, or complex of phenomena, but a history. It is the history of God in His mode of existence as the Son, in whom He humbles Himself and becomes also the Son of Man, Jesus of Nazareth. . . ."[60]

I turn, then, in the second place, to the concept of a *genus tapeinoticum*. The phrase *genus tapeinoticum* (literally the "genus of humility") refers to a logical possibility treated under the more general heading of the "communication of attributes" in post-Reformation theology. Whether it is instantiated in the ancient world or not is a question I would have to ask patristic scholars. The idea set forth in the phrase is that the union of divine and human in Jesus Christ has as at least one of its consequences a sharing by the divine in the being of the human such that human attributes are rightly ascribed to the divine. It was thus the polar opposite of the Lutheran *genus majestaticum,* which set forth the notion that the hypostatic union made possible a human participation in the divine attributes of omniscience, omnipotence, and omnipresence.[61] In any event, both Reformed and Lutheran theologians identified the *genus tapeinoticum* as a strictly logical possibility which they rejected. They held that the idea of an ascription of human attributes to God was unthinkable largely as a consequence of their commitment to a concept of divine immutability that was itself controlled by the notion of impassibility. It is precisely this idea that Barth chooses to take up.

Consistent with his historicizing of the hypostatic union, a union that is rooted ultimately in the divine election by God of himself for rejection and suffering, Barth speaks of the single act in which the Son of God turns continuously towards the man Jesus (uniting himself to him and giving him existence in his own being) as an *address* — an address that has ontological significance both for the human and for the divine. "We must begin with the fact that what takes place in this address is also and primarily a determination of divine essence: not an alteration, but a determination. God does not first elect and determine man but Himself. . . . He elects and determines Himself for humiliation. In so doing He does not need to become alien to Himself, to change

---

60. Barth, *CD* IV/2, pp. 105-6; *KD* IV/2, pp. 117-18.

61. This participation was qualified in the *Formula of Concord,* being limited in its full use to the state of exaltation. See "Epitome," Art. VIII, sect. 11 in Theodore G. Tappert, *The Book of Concord* (Philadelphia: Fortress Press, 1959), pp. 488-89; and "Solid Declaration," Art. VIII, sect. 9 in Tappert, p. 596.

Himself. The Godhead of the true God is not a prison whose walls have first to be broken through if He is to elect and do what He has elected and done in becoming man. In distinction from that of the false gods. . . . His Godhead embraces both height and depth, both sovereignty and humility, both lordship and service. It is only the pride of man, making a god in its own image, that will not hear of a determination of divine essence in Jesus Christ. The presupposition of all earlier Christology has suffered from this pride — from the fathers to both Reformed and Lutheran orthodoxy. This presupposition was a Greek conception of God, according to which God was far too exalted for His address to man, His incarnation and therefore the reconciliation of the world and Himself, to mean anything at all for Himself, or in any way affect His Godhead. In other words, He was the prisoner of His own Godhead."[62] It is in this context that Barth takes up the *genus tapeinoticum*. "We have already seen something of the anxiety of the Lutherans — who were at one with the Reformed in this — to dispel the thought of any *reciprocatio* in the union of natures in Jesus Christ, of any *genus tapeinoticum* corresponding to the *genus majestaticum*. The recollection of the *immutabilitas Dei* had for them the same effect as a Soviet veto [in the United Nations], and completely stifled any further thinking. It was with this anxiety on the one side that they tried to take up the thesis of the divinisation of the human nature of Jesus Christ on the other."[63]

Barth is not, on the other hand, advocating a divine mutability. In fact, it is his view that it is only a false understanding of immutability that calls forth a reaction in the form of an affirmation of mutability. "And when the 'Kenoticists' of the 19th century . . . attempted to think further in this direction, they could only oppose to the immutability of God a quite intolerable mutability. Even in the eyes of the Liberals (e.g. Biedermann) and the Ritschlians (e.g. Loofs) it appeared as if they were reducing all earlier Christology *ad absurdum*. What they were really reducing *ad absurdum* was the orientation of all earlier Christology by the profoundly unchristian conception of a God whose Godhead is supposed not to be affected at all by its union with humanity. . . . If we are to shake off the spell, and try to think of the Godhead of God in biblical, rather than pagan terms, we shall have to reckon, not with a mutability of God, but with the kind of immutability which does not prevent Him from humbling Himself and therefore

62. Barth, *CD* IV/2, pp. 84-85; *KD* IV/2, pp. 92-93.
63. Barth, *CD* IV/2, p. 85; *KD* IV/2, p. 93.

doing what He willed to do and actually did in Jesus Christ. . . . Even in the constancy (or, as we may calmly say, immutability) of His divine essence He does this and can do it . . . not only without violation but in supreme exercise and affirmation of His divine essence."[64] And finally, lest we get too excited about what all of this might mean for the divine freedom, Barth adds, "It is not that it is part of the divine essence, and therefore necessary, to become and be the God of man, Himself man. That He wills to be and becomes and is this God, and as such man, takes place in His freedom. It is His own decree and act. . . . [I]t is indeed a part of the divine essence to be free for this decree and its execution, to be able to elect and determine itself in this form."[65]

I would like to suggest that Barth's affirmation of the *genus tapeinoticum,* when seen in connection to his ascription of humility and obedience to God in his mode of being as Son, leads quite naturally to the following conclusion. The *only* act of the Son of God in relation to his humanity is the act in which he gives it existence in his own being and existence. All subsequent acts of the God-man made possible by *this singular act* are acts performed by the man Jesus. The *genus tapeinoticum* creates the possibility that the man Jesus should be the performative agent of all that is done by the God-human in his divine-human unity. But that possibility is itself grounded in the reality of the eternal *receptivity* of the Son of God vis-à-vis his human nature, a receptivity that is the consequence of that humility and obedience proper to his mode of being. Again, my suggestion is that the only act performed by the Son of God vis-à-vis his humanity is the act in which he gives it life in himself. All subsequent acts are performed by the man Jesus — and I would add, in the power of the Holy Spirit which descended on him at the Jordan.[66]

---

64. Barth, *CD* IV/2, p. 85; *KD* IV/2, p. 93.

65. Barth, *CD* IV/2, p. 85; *KD* IV/2, pp. 93-94.

66. In that Barth speaks of a "mutual impartation of divine and human essence in Jesus Christ," it is my view that he can mean nothing other than this. See Barth, *CD* IV/2, p. 76; *KD* IV/2, p. 83. For Barth, the "communication of attributes" runs in one direction only — talk of "mutual impartation" notwithstanding. What the man Jesus receives from the Son of God is not a share in divine attributes but simply *existence* — existence in the being of the Son of God. What the Son of God receives, on the other hand, are the "attributes" of the human Jesus. Or, more accurately expressed: through the perfect receptivity by means of which the Son relates to his humanity, he takes into his own life and makes his own all that the man Jesus does and all that happens to him.

Third and finally, this modality of being in perfect receptivity in relation to his humanity is a new mystery for us, but it is not a new mystery in God. Because Barth "collapses," if you will, the relation of "command" and "obedience" that structures the divine election into the eternal processions, the modality of receptivity vis-à-vis the man Jesus is not merely an economic relationship; it is rather that which constitutes God's second "mode of being" already in eternity-past. The second "person" of the Trinity is not a Logos *asarkos* considered in abstraction from the human "nature" to be assumed. The second "person" of the Trinity is the God-man.[67] So even in the act of hypostatic *uniting,* the "subject" who performs that action is the God-man, Jesus Christ in his divine-human unity. What happens in time in the historical enfleshment is simply the actualization in history of that which God has determined for himself from eternity and which, therefore, is already real in him.

We are now in a position to add a final refinement to our understanding of the christological "subject." The single subject is the one performative agent (the man Jesus), hypostatically united to the Son of God who gives him life in himself. The single subject, in other words, is neither the Logos *simpliciter* nor the man Jesus *simpliciter* but the God-human in his divine-human unity.[68] Though this might seem a rather complex way of

67. It is Barth's view that the identity of the One by whom all things are created in Colossians 1:16 is clearly identified in v. 20 as "Jesus Christ" — and not a Logos *asarkos.* The same pattern is observable, he says, in John 1 (where the Word which was in the beginning with God in v. 1 is identified as the "Word made flesh" in v. 14), as well as in Hebrews 1:2f. and 1 Peter 1:29. See Barth, *CD* IV/2, pp. 33-34; *KD* IV/2, pp. 35-36.

68. In his fine essay on the Chalcedonian character of Barth's Christology, George Hunsinger suggests that Barth "alternates back and forth, deliberately, between an 'Alexandrian' and an 'Antiochian' idiom." See Hunsinger, "Karl Barth's Christology: Its Basic Chalcedonian Character," in *Disruptive Grace: Studies in the Theology of Karl Barth* (Grand Rapids: Eerdmans, 2000), p. 135. Such a statement certainly witnesses to something I believe to be true. But in the form in which it is stated, it conceals more than it reveals — and can easily mislead. The truth resident in this statement is that Barth's single subject is the God-human in his divine human unity — a rather complex "single subject." It is that complexity (with all that pertains to the *genus tapeinoticum,* etc.) which accounts for the shifts in focus that occur from time to time in Barth's elaboration of his mature Christology. But I do not believe that Barth alternates between "Alexandria" and "Antioch" — either "deliberately" or unconsciously. It seems to me that the viewpoint on the basis of which he elaborates his Christology is consistent throughout. The problem, I think, is that Hunsinger's treatment of Chalcedon and, consequently, of Barth as well is insufficiently *material* in nature. The central terms in his analysis are the formal terms of "deity," "humanity," and "unity-in-

describing a *single* subject — perhaps even an impossible way to do so, since we are speaking of both God and the human at the same time — it is the fact that Barth, like Cyril, only has one performative agent that ensures that he has a single-subject Christology. Where you have but a single performative agent, there you have single-subject Christology, no matter how complex the ontological structure of that subject.

I said earlier that this is Cyril "in reverse," and now the reason for that claim can be made clear. Like Cyril, Barth has a single-subject Christology, i.e., he has but a single performative agent of the works of the God-man. But Barth is unlike Cyril in that the performative agent is the man Jesus. He is unlike Cyril in that he has a "humanization" of God by means of a *genus tapeinoticum* where Cyril had a "divinization" of the human by means of an instrumentalization of the human nature. The difference this makes, finally, is that whereas both can say "what Jesus does, God does," Barth alone is capable of saying without equivocation "what Jesus experiences, God experiences."

Though it lies beyond the bounds of this paper to discuss it fully here, I might add that the result of this Christology is a soteriology at whose center stands not a divinization theory but something rather more than that. If the single subject in Christology is the God-human in his divine-human unity, then the history of God (in which the divine "essence" is constituted) and the history of the royal human (in which human "essence" is constituted) are one and the same history. For believers to "correspond" then to the exalted humanity in Christ is to engage, as he did, in freely willed obedience. Where this occurs, there is a participation not only

---

distinction." "Extreme" Alexandrianism is then said to "stress Jesus' deity at the expense of his humanity" so that the union between the natures "obliterates their distinction." See Hunsinger, p. 134. The "extreme" Antiochian tendency moves in the opposite direction. It "stresses Jesus' humanity at the expense of his deity" so that the union of natures is not "internal to his 'person.'" "Deity" and "humanity" then fall apart, so that *unity*-in-distinction is called into question. Hunsinger sees Barth — in good Chalcedonian fashion, as he understands it — as engaged in a to-and-fro movement between idioms, which also enables him to preserve the "diversity of idioms" proper to the New Testament itself. My own conviction is that, with regard to "type," Barth is simply "Alexandrian" because he has a single-subject Christology. The fact that the "subject" is defined in historical terms, that divine essence and human essence are what they are in the history of the *one* God-human (a *single* history, by the way), makes Barth's account more complex than Cyril's, but it does not constitute a departure from the single-subject Christology which Cyril insisted upon in his debate with Nestorius.

in the history of the human Jesus but also (since the history of the human Jesus is the history of God), a participation in the history of God. And if it be true that this one history is constitutive of both divine and human "essence," then this participation is also, at the same time, a participation in the divine "essence." This is not a "divinization" theory, obviously, since it has set aside the "essentialism" of the ancient church and rejected its attachment to the idea that the Logos acts in and through and upon the human "nature" of Christ. It is, in fact, something rather more than a "divinization" theory, since it results in a human participation in the divine "essence."[69] In any event, Barth is as deeply ontological in his thinking about salvation as ever the ancient church was, but his ontology is thoroughly modern in character. For he has exchanged the substantialist understanding of the divine "essence" for an understanding that is historicized and actualized.

III. Evaluation

It is very tempting, when confronted with an idea that is really new, to seek to understand it in relation to that which is already known. And if the novelty has weight and seriousness, then an even greater temptation arises to understand it in relation to existing *heresies*. On the face of it, talk of an eternal humility of the Son can sound "subordinationist" or even Arian. There are, however, at least three reasons why the doctrine of the Trinity that finds its ground in Barth's Christology (as previously sketched) is not Arian. First, Barth does not hold that there was a "time" when the Son was not. Second, Barth has no interest in safeguarding the impassibility of the "high God" (to use the language of Arius). Third, and most decisively, Barth does not make the Son to be a different subject than the Father. Not only is the Son not a creature in any sense; he is the same as the Father, albeit in a different "mode of being."

Now given the final point, it might well appear that Barth has saved himself from Arianism only by placing himself squarely on the side of the modalists. But Barth is not a modalist either — for the following reasons.

69. For a full exposition of the problem of participation in Barth's writings, see McCormack, "Participation in God, Yes, Deification, No: Two Modern Answers to an Ancient Question" (cited in note 51 above).

First, Barth does not fail to distinguish adequately between the Father and the Son — a point of great importance where the modalism of Noetus and Praxeas is concerned. According to Thomas Weinandy and Paul Gavrilyuk, "the real issue was not that the Modalists attributed suffering to the Father, but rather that they failed to distinguish adequately between Father and Son. . . . Because the Son was seen as merely a different temporary mode of expression of the Father, it could be said that the Father became man and so suffered. Patripassianism was therefore condemned not out of an excessive fear of ascribing suffering within the Incarnation, but out of a desire to assure that it was the Son, and not the Father, who became man and suffered."[70] Gavrilyuk adds: "Noetus held that before coming to earth God was impassible, unchangeable, and immortal. During his ministry on earth God became passible, changeable, and mortal. Noetus conceived divine impassibility and passibility as temporary properties that mark out successive modes of God's existence."[71] But Barth's Christology does not lead to the notion of a merely temporary difference between Father and Son. The difference is a difference *in* the being of God — and therefore, an *eternal difference.* Thus Barth too has to say that the Son alone suffers. The idea that impassibility is surrendered in the becoming incarnate, so that the Son becomes something other than what he had been "in eternity" (with the Father), finds its modern analogue in nineteenth-century Lutheran kenoticism. Noetus's successor in the modern period is, above all, Wolfgang Gess, not Karl Barth.

But Barth is wrongly associated with the other ancient form of modalism as well, viz. that of Sabellius. Sabellius sought to preserve divine impassibility by distinguishing the divine subject from all three of his modes of appearance ("Father," "Son," and "Holy Spirit"). Barth's insistence on "modes of *being*," as opposed to "modes of appearance," was his way of opposing Sabellius. And this observation leads to a final thought.

It belongs to one of Barth's more significant insights that he saw the root of *both* subordinationism and modalism as lying in the same theological commitment, viz. the commitment to divine impassibility.[72] Neither

70. Thomas G. Weinandy, *Does God Suffer?* (Notre Dame: University of Notre Dame Press, 2000), p. 176; cited by Gavrilyuk, *The Suffering of the Impassible God,* p. 92.

71. Gavrilyuk, *The Suffering of the Impassible God,* p. 94.

72. "We can now see the error which is common to the subordinationist and the modalist presentation and solution of the problem. Both suffer from the fact that they try to evade the cross of Jesus Christ, i.e. the truth of the humiliation, the lowliness and the obedi-

Arius nor Sabellius could grant the possibility that God suffers. Arius handled the problem by making the Son a creature; Sabellius, by distinguishing the impassible divine subject from his modes of appearance. If Barth is right in this piece of analysis (and I think he is), then you cannot get to either subordinationism or modalism (in the historically recognized forms these heretical tendencies took) *without a prior commitment to divine impassibility.* And since Barth's later Christology leaves no room for divine impassibility, there is no way he could be guilty of either of these ancient heresies.[73]

The challenge to us created by Barth's theology is that all of our thinking about God, from first to last, must have a christological foundation. The problem with the concepts of "impassibility" and "passibility" is that *both* are metaphysical in nature. *Both* have a foundation other than Christology; "impassibility" in cosmology (a move that proceeds from the order perceived in the world to its First Cause — which is then dressed out in "attributes" derived through a careful application of the *via negativa* especially); "passibility" in anthropology (a move that proceeds from the human person to the divine person — which is then dressed out in "attributes" derived through a careful application of the *via eminentiae* especially). At the end of the day, impassibility and passibility constitute an altogether *this-worldly* dialectic, a dialectic between two decidedly *human* possibilities (viz. the possibilities of negative and positive qualifications of concepts formed by attention to realities other than Jesus Christ). The truth is that God transcends this dialectic. But a rightly ordered understanding of this "transcendence" will not be purchased by means of an

---

ence of the one true God Himself as it became an event amongst us in Jesus Christ as the subject of the reconciliation of the world with God. They evade it because they start from the assumption that it cannot be accepted as true. And they then err in their different ways as they try to escape the dilemma which they themselves have created, interpreting the obedient Christ either as some heavenly or earthly being distinct from God or as a mere mode of appearance of the one true God. Both damage and indeed destroy the nerve of the New Testament knowledge of Christ. Both solve the christological mystery by juggling it away, and for that reason both show themselves to be quite useless. They were both rightly rejected by the Early Church." See Barth, *CD* IV/1, pp. 199-200; *KD* IV/1, p. 218.

73. What Barth has accomplished is indeed innovatory. But if a would-be critic can only cope with his innovation by advancing an equally novel definition of the terms "subordinationism" and "modalism," then the critic too is an innovator. What this suggests is that nothing — but nothing! — can be decided in the debate created by Barth's christological critique of impassibility by the use of ancient labels.

apophatic gesture, a merely *conceptual* relocation of divine being above and beyond the dialectic of impassibility and passibility. It will only be purchased by a complete dissolution of that dialectic by means of sustained concentration on the God who suffers on the cross.

Conclusion

Karl Barth did not have a doctrine of divine impassibility. At most, what he had was the *concept* of a divine impassibility (understood strictly as non-affectivity) which, he says in a small handful of passages, was surrendered by God, put aside, rejected — a perfection that *might* have been God's, in other words, had he not chosen rejection, suffering, and death for himself. But what Barth's Christology makes amply clear is that this surrender was *not* the surrender of anything essential to God. Indeed, that which is *essential* to God is that which God has chosen for himself: a being in both majesty and humility, a being as omnipotent and impotent. Both are essential to God; therefore, both are equally original. So even to speak of the surrender of impassibility is to speak of the surrender of something that was never God's. Talk of "possibilities" which were never actualized is intended in Barth's writings only to underscore the freedom of God's self-determination to be a God "for us" in Jesus Christ. They are not considered as possessing reality in God's life. And so I say: Barth's stress on obedience (a freely willed activity) as determinative of that which is essential to God makes the exploration of such "possibilities" to be a forbidden exercise, an exercise in fruitless speculation that can only distract our attention from what God actually is in Jesus Christ. It is for this reason I say that Barth's Christology leaves no room for a doctrine of divine impassibility.

Now some might want to say: well, if the only conception of impassibility that Barth was able to envision is that of non-affectivity, then there is surely still room in Barth for the modified version held to by the Church Fathers. Paul Gavrilyuk would argue, for example, that it is only the heretics (Arius and Nestorius) who held to an absolute, unmodified concept of impassibility.[74] For the orthodox, the concept of divine impassibility "functioned as an *apophatic qualifier* of all divine emotions and served to rule out those passions and experiences that were unbecom-

---

74. Gavrilyuk, *The Suffering of the Impassible God,* pp. 141-44.

ing of the divine nature."[75] Such a use of the concept did not "preclude divine care or God's involvement in history."[76] And Cyril took all of this a step further by affirming that God does indeed suffer, albeit *humanly.* But it is precisely the use of the apophatic qualifier that signals the irremovable difference between the Fathers and Barth. Barth made no use of the pseudo-Dionysian *via negativa* in order to underscore the otherness of God's emotive life, as compared with our own. There is no apophaticism here. Barth preserves the element of un-likeness in the relation of God's emotions to human emotions through the careful application of a concept of immutability whose meaning is controlled by the christologically grounded doctrines of election and Trinity. And though Barth agrees with Cyril that God suffered *humanly,* his use of the *genus tapeinoticum* allows him to say this in a straightforward, un-paradoxical way not available to Cyril. And so, I repeat: Barth's later Christology leaves no remaining room for *any* doctrine of divine impassibility.

In conclusion, I would like to say just one thing. I am sure that the Christology I have set forth will not only be new to many; it may even be offensive. Certainly, it can be offensive to hear it suggested that some, at least, among one's theological heroes, were guilty of thinking more often in pagan terms than in biblical terms. If I have caused offense, I am deeply sorry for it. I have no wish to do so. And, in any case, I would like to create friends for Barth rather than enemies. But I had to risk giving offense. The reason is this: there is a trend in Barth scholarship in the English-speaking world to want to remove the offense by reading Barth as a "classical" theologian, one who stands not only formally in close relationship to Cyril (as I have it) but also materially.[77] And Barth himself does leave *some* room for such a reading.[78] But when you take all the elements I have laid out here

75. Gavrilyuk, *The Suffering of the Impassible God,* p. 16. Gavrilyuk adds, "With reference to the Christian God impassibility meant [for the orthodox] that he does not have the same emotions as the gods of the heathen; that his care for human beings is free from self-interest and any association with evil; that since he has neither body nor soul, he cannot directly have the experiences typically connected with them; that he is not overwhelmed by emotions and in the incarnation emerges victorious over suffering and death" (pp. 15-16).

76. Gavrilyuk, *The Suffering of the Impassible God,* p. 132.

77. This is done well (with due attention to textual evidence and the need for careful nuancing) by George Hunsinger in the essays contained in his collection, *Disruptive Grace.* It is done less well, in my view, by Paul Molnar in his book, *Divine Freedom and the Doctrine of the Immanent Trinity.*

78. Barth leaves room for such a reading when he says things like, "It is not that it is

together, when you consider that Barth made humility and obedience to be essential to God, I think you will see why I have read him as I did. The offense, therefore, remains. And the question is: What do we do about it?

My plea would be that the option I have sketched not be rejected out of hand, without thinking it through carefully in the light of Scripture and the tradition. I would like to suggest that ecclesially minded theologians have ample reason for calm and thorough consideration of this proposal. No ecumenically recognized council I am aware of has ever declared as dogma a particular understanding of the divine being and attributes. There is no "orthodox" doctrine of God, save what is declared with respect to the Trinity in the Nicene-Constantinopolitan Creed — and what I have said here is completely compatible with that creed, and with the Chalcedon Formula as well. To be sure, what I have set forth does collide with the views of "Fathers" who in some churches have the status of ecclesial "authorities." But from my perspective, as a Reformed Christian, individual theologians do not and cannot possess the authority of ecumenical councils. And, in any event, it is Holy Scripture which must finally decide all issues — even those previously addressed by councils.

I say all of this for the following reason. There was a time, not so long ago, when divine mutability and passibility threatened to become a new "orthodoxy," using the sheer force of the numbers of those thinking in this way to effectively silence those who would raise questions in opposition.

---

part of the divine essence, and therefore necessary, to become and be the God of man, Himself man. That He wills to be and becomes and is this God, and as such man, takes place in His freedom. It is His own decree and act. . . . [I]t is indeed a part of the divine essence to be free for this decree and its execution, to be able to elect and determine itself in this form." See above, note 65. What is set forth in this concept is an understanding of the divine essence as having a certain built-in plasticity, an openness to self-determination, since freedom lies at the very heart of the concept. One might be tempted to conclude from this that it is not the case that God gives to himself his essence in his eternal self-determination in election; he merely gives to an essence which is already his a "direction." On this basis, one might then also be tempted to say that the eternal act of self-determination is in no way constitutive of the being of God; it is *merely* determinative; that the act in which God constitutes himself as triune and the act in which he turns towards the human race in the covenant of grace are two acts that need to be kept separate. As appealing as this might seem (because it is, after all, "classical"), I would say that it runs aground on Barth's claim that humility and obedience are as *essential* to God as are majesty and command. An act of self-determination which is directed to the *essence* of God, a decision which makes *essential* all that follows from it, is a self-constituting act by any other name.

Bruce L. McCormack

Now, in many quarters, it would appear that the pendulum is swinging in the opposite direction. Theologians fed up with the tactics of intimidation employed by those committed to mutability and passibility are now tempted, as their numbers grow, to respond in kind. My plea, then, is that you will not respond in kind. It is important to understand that Karl Barth was neither an impassibilist nor a passibilist. His position would take us beyond that rather unfortunate set of alternatives. So reckoning with him is going to take time — and patience.

Impassibility in St. Hilary of Poitiers's *De Trinitate*

Trent Pomplun

Οἱ πεποιθότες ἐπὶ κύριον ὡς ὄρος Σιων
οὐ σαλευθήσεται εἰς τὸν αἰῶνα ὁ κατοικῶν Ιερουσαλημ.

PSALM 124:1

Et uideamus cuius corporis homo Christus sit,
ut carnem dolor manserit.

ST. HILARY OF POITIERS

Impassibility has played an important role in theology from Clement of Alexandria to the Roman Catholic manuals of the twentieth century. It may come as a surprise to contemporary theologians, however, that our predecessors largely ignored the question of God's impassibility. Satisfied that God was immutable (Mal. 3:6) and invariable (James 1:17), theologians took it for granted that the Most High was impervious to any *pathos* external to his own nature.[1] When they discussed *impassibilitas* (or *apatheia*), ancient and medieval theologians were primarily concerned with the life of prayer. Impassibility, while still possessed by God in his very nature, was more commonly considered one of the many fruits of as-

---

1. A concise dogmatic statement of God's impassibility is Cyril of Alexandria's letter to John of Antioch, which is included in the Council of Ephesus. Cf. G. Alberigo et al., *Conciliorum Oecumenicorum Decreta* [= COD], third edition (Bologna: Istituto per le Scienze Religiose, 1973), p. 72. An expansive and better-known example is Cyril's Second Letter to Nestorius, COD, pp. 40-44.

cetic practice and a necessary precursor to the pure prayer of trinitarian contemplation. It was an important aspect of any complete Christology, to be sure, but its part in any christological synthesis was concerned less with the nature of God himself than with the human nature he assumed. If, the ancients reasoned, "all treasures of wisdom and knowledge" were hidden in the incarnate Word (Col. 2:3) — if indeed in him "all the fullness of the Godhead dwells bodily" (Col. 2:9) — then Jesus Christ must have possessed perfect impassibility of body and soul. After all, the one mediator between God and man (1 Tim. 2:5) cannot be lacking in virtue or power of prayer. A perfect impassibility is a necessary aspect of Christ's perfect humanity, which is the wellspring of grace that allows the saints to fulfill his most daunting commandment: "Be perfect, as your Father in Heaven is perfect" (Matt. 5:48).

Such impassibility seems to fly in the face of Scripture, which everywhere maintains "Christ suffered for us in the flesh" (1 Pet. 4:1), and one might sympathize — if only for a second — with those who imagine that the Fathers allowed metaphysical speculations to overwhelm the common-sense meaning of Scripture. But, truth be told, such criticisms of traditional claims about impassibility simply have not attended to what the Fathers have said about it, especially with regard to Christ's body and soul. Hilary of Poitiers is a perfect test case in this regard. Arguably the strongest statement of Christ's human impassibility among the Fathers is found in the tenth book of his *De Trinitate*. Its twenty-third chapter is worth quoting in full:

> The man Jesus Christ, the only-begotten God, who through the flesh and the Word is the Son of Man as well as the Son of God, has assumed true humanity according to the likeness of our humanity, without ceasing to be God. But when struck by blows, or inflicted with wounds, or bound by ropes, or raised into the air, He felt the force of the suffering without its sorrow. When a javelin passes through water, pierces a flame, or wounds the air, each of these elements suffers according to its nature. The javelin penetrates, pierces, and wounds them, but no suffering lingers in them, because it is not in the nature of water to be penetrated, or fire to be pierced, or for the air to be wounded, although the javelin naturally penetrates, pierces, and wounds them.
>
> Our Lord Jesus Christ suffers when He is struck, when He is lifted up, when He is crucified, and when He dies, but the suffering that

rushed upon the body was not suffering, nor did it show the nature of suffering. The suffering inflicted punishment but the body's power received the violence of the punishment, without feeling the punishment itself. The Lord's body could have felt pain like ours, if our bodies possessed a nature that could walk on water, and tread upon the waves without sinking, or with the water holding firm under our footsteps. The Lord's body could have felt pain like ours, if our bodies passed through solid matter, or if barred doors posed no obstacle to us.

But the Lord's body alone of its nature and its power could be borne by His soul across the water, could tread upon the waves, and could pass through walls; how then can we judge the flesh conceived of the Holy Spirit in comparison to the nature of our own bodies? That flesh is the Bread of Heaven; that humanity is of God. He had a body that could suffer, and did suffer, but He did not possess a nature that felt pain. His body possessed a unique nature. It was transfigured with glory on the mountain; its touch put fevers to flight; its spittle gave sight to the blind.[2]

---

2. *Sancti Hilarii Pictaviensis Episcopi de Trinitate Libri VIII-XII* [= *Trin.*], *Corpus Christianorum Series Latina*, vol. 62A, ed. P. Smulders (Turnhout: Brepols, 1980), bk. 10, ch. 23, pp. 477-78: "Homo itaque Christus Iesus unigenitus Deus, per carnem et uerbum ut hominis filius ita et Dei Filius, hominem uerum secundum similitudinem nostri hominis, non deficiens a se Deo, sumpsit. In quo, quamuis aut ictus incideret, aut uulnus descenderet, aut nodi concurrerent, aut suspensio eleuaret, adferrent quidem haec inpetum passionis, non tamen dolorem passionis inferrent: ut telum aliquod aut aquam perforans aut ignem conpungens aut aera uulnerans, omnes quidem has passiones naturae suae infert, ut foret, ut conpungat, ut uulneret, sed naturam suam in haec passio inlata non retinet, dum in natura non est, uel aquam forari, uel pungi ignem, uel aerem uulnerari, quamuis naturae teli sit et uulnerare et conpungere et forare.

Passus quidem Dominus Iesus Christus, dum caeditur, dum suspenditur, dum crucifigitur, dum moritur; sed in corpus inruens passio nec non fuit passio, nec tamen naturam passionis exseruit: dum et poenali ministerio desaeuit, et uirtus corporis sine sensu poenae uim poenae in se desaeuientis excepit. Habuerit sane illud Domini corpus doloris nostri naturam, si corpus nostrum id naturae habet, ut calcet undas, et super fluctus eat, et non degrauetur ingressu, neque aquae insistentis uestigiis cedant, penetret etiam solida, nec clausae domus obstaculis arceatur.

Aduero si dominici corporis sola ista natura sit, ut sua uirtute, sua anima feratur in humidis, et insistat in liquidis, et extructa transcurrat, quid per naturam humani corporis conceptam ex Spiritu carnem iudicamus? Caro illa, id est panis ille, de caelis est, et homo ille de Deo est: habens ad patiendum quidem corpus, et passus est, sed naturam non habens ad dolendum. Naturae enim propriae ac suae corpus illud est, quod in caelestem gloriam conformatur in monte, quod adtactu suo fugat febres, quod de sputu suo format oculos."

All translations from the Latin are my own, although I have availed myself of existing

Theologians have had a devil of a time interpreting this passage. Despite being commonly considered a pillar of orthodoxy against Arianism in the West, Hilary does seem in danger of "sailing somewhat close to the cliffs of Docetism" as Förster famously remarked.[3] Presumably Hilary's teachings have been affected to some extent by his mannered and monumental style. But Augustine saw no need to censure him, nor did Ambrose or Jerome. Among the ancients, only Claudianus Mamertus criticized Hilary's teaching, despite its family resemblance to later *aphthartodocetae* such as Julian of Halicarnassus.[4] Among medieval theologians, Peter Lombard devoted a section of his *Sententiae* to "some rather obscure chapters of Hilary *(quibusdam Hilarii capitulis valde obscuris),*" in which he quoted several passages from the tenth book of *De Trinitate,* including all but the last sentence of the three paragraphs above; but the Lombard believed them to accord with the common teaching of the Fathers.[5] In fact, the medieval theologians who commented on these passages judged them quite kindly, as we shall see below.

This unanimity was broken only with Erasmus, who produced an edition of Hilary's works in 1523. Erasmus treated Hilary with great re-

---

translations when necessary. I have not standardized the various Latin spellings among the texts I've studied, but have rather respected each editor's choices. For a discussion of Smulder's "fastidious orthography," see the review by J. C. M. van Winden, *Vigiliae Christianae* 36 (1982): 80-84.

3. T. Förster, "Zur Theologie des Hilarius," *Theologische Studien und Kritiken* 61 (1888), p. 662. Others have issued surer condemnations. A. von Harnack, *Lehrbuch der Dogmengeschichte,* 4th edition (Tübingen, 1909), vol. 2, p. 316; R. P. C. Hanson, *The Search for the Christian Doctrine of God* (Edinburgh: T. & T. Clark, 1988), p. 501; and Kevin Madigan, "On the High-Medieval Reception of Hilary of Poitiers's Anti-'Arian' Opinion: A Case Study of Discontinuity in Christian Thought," *Journal of Religion* 78 (1998): 213-29. Compare M. Niccoli, "Docetismo e soteriologia nel *De Trinitate* di Ilario," *Richerche Religiose* 1 (1925): 262-74.

4. *De Statu Animae* 2.9: "Inter complura praecelsarum disputationum suarum, quiddam secius sentientem, duo haec veris adversa disseruisse: Unum, quod nihil incorporeum creatum dixit: Aliud nihil doloris Christum in passione sensisse. Cujus si passio vera non fuit, redemptio quoque nostra vera esse non potuit. Sed quando beatus Hilarius opinionis hujusce vitium virtute confessionis abolevit, sic sustinet reprehensionis stylum, quod non patitur detrimenta meritorum." On Claudianus, see E. L. Fortin, A.A., *Christianisme et Culture Philosophique au Cinquième Siècle: La Querelle de l'Âme Humaine en Occident* (Paris: Études Augustiniennes, 1959).

5. *Sententiae in IV libros distinctae,* ed. Ignatius C. Brady, 3rd revised edition (Grottaferrata: Collegium S. Bonaventurae ad Claras Aquas, 1971-1981), vol. 2, bk. III, d. 15.

spect, both as a theologian and a stylist, but he was among the first in the late medieval world to doubt the orthodoxy of Hilary's expressions, at least when judged by the standards of later doctrinal developments.[6] No less of an authority on the Fathers than Petavius judged Hilary's passages to be in error, but the great Jesuit also felt that Hilary corrected his mistakes in the *Tractatus super Psalmos.*[7] Hilary's reception has been similarly varied in modern theology. Although most Roman Catholic dogmatic theologians have been content to follow the lead of the high medieval theologians, those who have offered more expansive treatments of Hilary, such as Janssens or Stentrup, have not come to any agreement about his meaning.[8] Much the same can be said of nineteenth- and twentieth-century historians.[9] Some interpret Hilary to say that Christ simply did

6. *Opus Epistolarvm Des. Erasmi Roterdami,* ed. P. S. Allen and H. M. Allen (Oxford: Clarendon Press, 1906-1958), vol. 5, pp. 173-74: "Iam vero quoties incidebant loca quae videbantur ab opinionibus inter orthodoxos receptis dissidere, plus quam viginti locis pharmacum admiscuerant, maxime quoties disputat de doloribus aut cruciatibus, quibus affectum fuit corpus et anima Domini nostri Iesu Christi. Id facit, quum aliis aliquot locis, tum praecipue libro De Trinitate decimo; sed ita perplexe vt aliquoties plane videatur Christo tribuere corpus et animam nullis obnoxiam molestis affectionibus." Erasmus was no mere bystander in similar debates of his own day, and it is enlightening to read the preface of his edition of Hilary in light of his own *Disputatiuncula de Taedio, Pavore, Tristitia Iesu,* an epistolary debate with his friend John Colet that was often published in Erasmus's *Lucubratiunculae* with the more famous *Enchiridion militis christiani.* On this debate, see Daniel T. Lochman, "Colet and Erasmus: The *Disputatiuncula* and the Controversy of Letter and Spirit," *Sixteenth Century Journal* 20 (1989): 77-88.

7. Dionysius Petavius, *Dogmata Theologica,* ed. F. A. Zacharia, 8 vols. (Paris: Vivès, 1868), tom. 6, d. 10, ch. 5, p. 374: "Mea haec suspicio est, commentarium in *Psalmos* esse; in quo ad *Psalmum* sexagesimum octavum multa dicit superiori illi opinioni contraria, ut merito retractasse priora videri potuerit." There are a fair number of other early modern authors who wrote significant theological assessments of Hilary. Cf. Francisco Suárez, *Opera Omnia,* ed. Carolus Berton (Paris: Vivès, 1860), vol. 18, q. 15, a. 5, pp. 204-6; Juan de Lugo, *Disputationes Scholasticae et Morales,* ed. J. B. Fournials (Paris: Vivès, 1868), vol. 2, disp. 22, sect. 2, pp. 670-76; Louis Thomassin, *Dogmata Theologica,* ed. P. F. Ecalle (Paris: Vivès, 1864), tom. 3, lib. 4, ch. 13, pp. 497-505. A stroll through the local seminary library also uncovered an interesting discussion in Augustino Cabadés-Magi, *Institutiones Theologicae* (Valencia: Benedict Monfort, 1790), tom. 4, lib. 11, ch. 6, pp. 26-37.

8. Lawrence Janssens, O.S.B., *Tractatus de Deo-Homine sive de Verbo Incarnato,* 2 vols. (Fribourg: Herder, 1901), vol. 1, sect. 2, mem. 3, ch. 2, q. 15, pp. 542-55; Ferdinand Stentrup, S.J., *Praelectiones Dogmaticae de Verbo Incarnato* (Oeniponte [Innsbruck]: Feliciani Rauch, 1882), th. 56, pp. 896-911.

9. For summaries of Hilary's teaching on the suffering of Christ, see G. Giamberardini,

not suffer pain at all.[10] Others like to think that Hilary taught that Christ suffered pain in his humanity but not in his divinity.[11] A third group believe that Hilary taught that Christ could indeed suffer pain, but that his suffering did not admit of any necessity, but rather that every time that Christ suffered, it was an act of condescension.[12] This breadth of opinion is noteworthy, as is its general trajectory. Hilary's reputation, at least in these passages, seems to have suffered a steady decline from antiquity to our own day. Why did the ancient and medieval theologians serenely accept a teaching that so scandalizes modern theologians and historians? Did Jerome or Augustine fail to pay close attention to the words of Scripture? Were Peter Lombard and Thomas Aquinas misled by a slavish desire to maintain the integrity of tradition? I am not inclined to think so; in fact, I am inclined to think that these theologians understood Hilary quite well, despite the frequent corruption of his texts.[13] The summary of Hilary and his interpreters that follows should demonstrate that Bonaventure, Thomas Aquinas, and Duns Scotus instinctively understood the importance of maintaining Christ's impassibility. While tracing their interpretations of Hilary, I hope to show that much of the confusion that

O.F.M., "De Incarnatione Verbi secundum S. Hilarium Pictaviensem," *Divus Thomas* 50 (1947): 35-36, 194-205; 51 (1948): 3-18; C. F. A. Borchardt, *Hilary of Poitiers' Role in the Arian Struggle* (The Hague: Martinus Nijhoff, 1966), pp. 117-30; and Luis F. Ladaria, S.J., *La Cristología de Hilario de Poitiers* (Rome: Gregorian University, 1989), pp. 161-213.

10. J. P. Baltzer, *Die Christologie des hl. Hilarius von Poitiers* (Rottweil, 1889); G. Rauschen, "Die Lehre des hl. Hilarius von Poitiers über die Leidensfähigkeit Christi," *Theologische Quartalschrift* 87 (1905): 424-39; and P. Galtier, S.J., *Saint Hilaire de Poitiers le premier docteur de l'église latine* (Paris, 1960). Smulders holds the view that Christ's body suffered but that it did not affect his soul. Cf. P. Smulders, S.J., *La doctrine trinitaire de S. Hilaire de Poitiers* (Rome: Gregorian University, 1944).

11. Giamberardini, O.F.M., "De Incarnatione Verbi secundum," p. 12: "Potuit pati, quin doluerit, quia praeter verum hominem, verus quoque Deus est." Not surprisingly, the majority of Catholic theologians working in speculative or dogmatic theology followed this line of interpretation, which is rarer among historians because of its anachronistic use of later notions of Christ's two natures.

12. J. A. Dorner, *Entwicklungsgeschichte der Lehre von der Person Christi* (Berlin, 1851), vol. 1, pp. 1037-57; Förster, "Zur Theologie des Hilarius," pp. 645-86; A. Beck, *Kirchliche Studien und Quellen* (Amberg, 1903), pp. 82-102; J. N. D. Kelly, *Early Christian Doctrines* (London, 1958), pp. 334-36; Alois Grillmeier, S.J., *Christ in the Christian Tradition*, trans. John Bowden (Atlanta: John Knox Press, 1975), vol. 1, pp. 395-400.

13. P. Smulders, S.J., "Remarks on the Manuscript Tradition of the *De Trinitate* of Saint Hilary of Poitiers," *Studia Patristica* 3 (1961): 129-38.

surrounds the tenth book of *De Trinitate* results from the loss of the spiritual context that rendered it intelligible.

I. Pain and Passibility in St. Hilary

At first glance, the claim that Christ is impassible seems preposterous. If by "passibility," we mean a person's susceptibility to external forces that weaken the body or affect the soul, then we cannot deny that Christ was passible. Scripture makes it abundantly clear that Jesus Christ suffered the same corporeal and psychological privations that every other human being suffers. He was like us in every way except sin (Heb. 2:17; 4:15): he became hungry after his fast in the desert (Matt. 4:2) and thirsty on the cross (John 19:28); he became weary near Jacob's well (John 4:6) and fell asleep while crossing the Sea of Galilee (Matt. 8:24); he looked tenderly upon the young man who had followed the commandments (Mark 10:21) and was consumed by zeal for his Father's house as he drove the moneychangers from the temple (John 2:17). He rejoiced for his disciples' sake that they should see him raise Lazarus (John 11:15), but he was deeply moved, even troubled, as he approached his friend's tomb (John 11:33) and eventually wept before it (John 11:35). He became distressed and sorrowful at Gethsemane (Matt. 26:38) and, in a passage well represented in our collection of essays, cried out in abandonment from the cross (Matt. 27:46). It only seems natural that the "man of sorrows" (Isa. 53:3) and the slain Lamb (Rev. 5:6) feared his own death or felt the pain inflicted upon him during his passion.

None of these passages was unknown to Hilary, and yet he confidently asserted that Christ neither feared his own death nor felt pain. Before laying Hilary aside as yet another victim of Greek metaphysical incursions into sacrosanct Jewish territory, it is important that we not lose sight of the general context in which Hilary offered his reflections on Christ's impassibility.[14] Hilary is primarily concerned with battling the *ariomanitae* who would deny the Son's divinity. And so he says,

14. An article essential for understanding Hilary's role in the transformation of classical metaphysics is John M. McDermott, "Hilary of Poitiers: The Infinite Nature of God," *Vigiliae Christianae* 27 (1973): 172-202. For general studies of Hilary's anti-Arianism, see J. F. McHugh, *The Exaltation of Christ in the Arian Controversy: The Teaching of St. Hilary* (Shrewsbury: Gregorian University, 1959); C. F. A. Borchardt, *Hilary of Poitiers' Role;*

> Most do not wish Him to have the nature of the impassible God because of His fear during the passion and the weakness He suffered. They argue that He Who feared and felt pain could not enjoy the confidence of power that does not fear, or the incorruption of spirit that does not feel pain, but being of a nature lower than the Father, He was disturbed by the fear of human suffering and groaned before the cruelty of bodily punishment.[15]

In his desire to combat those who would relegate the Son to a nature lower than the Father, Hilary confronts the passages most commonly used by modern exegetes to establish God's passibility, most notably Christ's "sorrow unto death" (Matt. 26:38) and his cry of dereliction (Matt. 27:46). Given his anti-Arian commitments, Hilary has little patience with those who would interpret the cry of dereliction as a "bitter complaint" *(maxima quaerella):* "The violent presumption of an impious intelligence! How repugnant to the general meaning of all our Lord's words!"[16] Hilary's chief arguments against such interpretations, interestingly enough, are taken from the text of Matthew itself. How, Hilary asks his readers, could we suppose that Christ feared his own death, when he exhorted his disciples to martyrdom (Matt. 10:38-39)? Or after he told his disciples, "Do not fear those who kill the body" (Matt. 10:28)? Or after prophetically announcing

---

J. Doignon, *Hilaire de Poitiers avant l'exil. Recherches sur la naissance, l'enseignement et l'épreuve d'une foi épiscopale en Gaule au milieu du IVe siècle* (Paris: Études Augustiniennes, 1971); Ilona Opelt, "Hilarius von Poitiers als Polemiker," *Vigiliae Christianae* 27 (1973): 203-17; M. Simonetti, "Ilario di Poitiers e la crisi ariana storia dell'esegesi patristica," in *Patrologia* III, ed. A. di Berardino (Turin, 1978), pp. 33-58; and Daniel H. Williams, "The Anti-Arian Campaigns of Hilary of Poitiers and the *'Liber Contra Auxentium,'*" *Church History* 61 (1992): 7-22. Although Williams and R. P. C. Hanson have criticized the use of "Arian" as a description of the theological controversies of the fourth century, it is sufficient for the purposes of this study — and sufficient for Hilary's teaching — that Arius be a figurehead, whether he held the views ascribed to him or whether he exerted the influence usually attributed to him.

15. *Trin.* 10.9, pp. 465-66: "Volunt enim plerique eorum ex passionis metu et ex infirmitate patiendi non in natura eum inpassibilis Dei fuisse: ut qui timuit et doluit, non fuerit uel in ea potestatis securitate quae non timet, uel in ea Spiritus incorruptione quae non dolet; sed inferioris a Deo Patre naturae, et humanae passionis trepidauerit metu, et ad corporalis poenae congemuerit atrocitatem."

16. *Trin.* 10.49, p. 503: "Quae maximae quaerellae esse intellegitur protestatio, derelictum se esse conquaeri infirmitatique permissum. Verum haec inpiae intelligentiae uiolenta praesumptio, quam sibi in omni dictorum dominicorum genere conpugnat."

his own resurrection, "Hereafter you will see the Son of Man seated at the right hand of Power and coming on the clouds of heaven (Matt. 26:64)? Indeed, had Christ feared his death, his well-known rebuke of Peter would be arbitrary or unjust (Matt. 16:23).[17] Christ certainly knew that his Father would "not allow His holy one to see corruption" (Ps. 15:10). Hilary also turns to the passages one might expect from the other Gospels, notably the prediction that the temple of his body would be rebuilt in three days (John 2:19) and the assurance that Lazarus was rejoicing in Abraham's bosom (Luke 16:23).[18] For Hilary it is simply impossible that the incarnate Word could be overcome by fear when the Hebrew children sang songs among the flames or when Daniel walked with lions. How could the Resurrection and the Life tremble in the face of death? As one might expect, Hilary has a deep store of such passages, and the sheer number that he deploys during the course of his argument does make one wonder why modern theologians expect the cry of dereliction to bear such a heavy exegetical burden. Be that as it may, the passages that teach Christ's passibility are no mere jots and tittles, and a modern theologian may justifiably wonder whether Hilary seeks shelter in paradox. For all intents and purposes, Hilary does seem to say that Christ is both passible and impassible, not merely in his humanity and his divinity respectively, but in his humanity itself.

The solution to this difficulty is to be had in a closer analysis of Hilary's christological and psychological vocabulary. One of the most difficult aspects of Hilary's theology, for example, is the bewildering variety of uses to which he puts the term *natura*. Take the following text, for example: Christ, Hilary maintains, *habens ad patiendum quidem corpus et passus est, sed naturam non habens ad dolendum*. In the preface to his edition of Hilary's work, Erasmus complained that one manuscript solved the problem by inserting a qualification at this point in the argument, noting that Hilary denies that Christ has a nature "weakened by sin like our own."[19] I

---

17. I find it interesting, given Hilary's desire to maintain the general narrative structure of Matthew, that he does not explain the cry of dereliction as the singing of the opening lines of the twenty-second Psalm. He quotes later verses of the psalm elsewhere in *De Trinitate* (*Trin.* 11.15, p. 543; 12.14, p. 588). It seems doubly strange that he would not resort to this common argument since he turns to the Psalms immediately after exhausting the Matthean texts.

18. *Trin.* 10.12, p. 468.

19. Erasmus, *Disputatiuncula*, 5, p. 174: "Ac paulo inferius, quum diuus Hilarius scripsisset, 'Et homo ille de Deo est, habens ad patiendum quidem corpus, et passus est, sed

think this is fair enough — it explains Hilary's sense — but I am inclined to think that Hilary uses the term *natura* in the sense of St. Cyril of Alexandria's later slogan *una natura Verbi incarnata*. First, Hilary rarely speaks of human nature considered in itself when he speaks of Christ. In fact, he often criticizes those who think it possible. Hilary prefers to speak of the human "element" *(elementa)* of the divine Word, and his general usage is *hominem sumpsit* rather than *naturam sumpsit*.[20] In other words, Hilary attaches a meaning to *natura* that is different than the one it acquired after the later councils. His *natura* stands at a great remove from the medieval Aristotelian resonances of the term, although in rare instances Hilary even anticipates these later uses.[21] Secondly, Hilary does not limit the title "Christ" to the incarnate Word, but applies it to the Word in his relationship to the world. So in speaking of Christ, Hilary always means the Word.[22] Finally, the great majority of Hilary's passages simply imply the more Cyrillian meaning.

Consider the following passages:

> The chaos of hell and the terrors of death cannot lay hold of the nature that rules the world, boundless in the freedom of its spiritual power, and for whom the delights of paradise cannot be lacking. . . . Hew from his indivisible nature, a part that could fear punishment.[23]

---

naturam non habens ad dolendum'; sic erat correctus, hoc est deprauatus, locus, 'Et passus est, sed (imbecillem, vt nostra, ex peccato) naturam non habens ad dolendum.'"

20. For notes on Hilary's perplexing vocabulary, see P. Smulders, S.J., *La doctrine trinitaire*, p. 196; J. Doignon, "*Adsumo* et *adsumptio* comme expressions du mystère de l'Incarnation chez Hilaire de Poitiers," *Archivum Latinitatis Medii Aevi* 23 (1956), pp. 123-35; P. Galtier, *Saint Hilaire de Poitiers*, p. 128; Grillmeier, *Christ in the Christian Tradition*, p. 396; and W. G. Rausch, "Some Observations on Hilary of Poitiers' Christological Language in *De Trinitate*," *Studia Patristica* 12 (1975): 261-64.

21. *Trin.* 9.54, pp. 431-32: "Si enim natiuitas hominis naturam nouam intulit et humilitas formam demutauit sub adsumptione seruili, nunc donatio nominis formae reddit aequalitatem." *Trin.* 11.40, pp. 567-68: "Et quidem ab apostolo seruatus hic modus est, ut magistratibus et potestatibus euacuatio, inimicis uero subiectio deputaretur. Quibus subiectis, subicietur subicienti sibi omnia, Deo scilicet, *ut sit Deus omnia in omnibus*, naturae adsumpti corporis nostri natura paternae diuinitatis inuecta."

22. *Trin.* 2.6, pp. 42-43; 12.4, pp. 581-82.

23. *Trin.* 10.34, p. 487: "Et naturam hanc mundi dominam ac libertate spiritalis uirtutis inmensam, non sibi terrore mortis gehennae chaos uindicat, qua paradisi deliciae carere non possunt. . . . Deseca ad metum poenae naturae indesecabilis portionem."

The Only-begotten God suffered in Himself the attacks of all the weaknesses that we suffer, but He suffered in the power of His own nature, just as He was born in the power of His own nature. Nor at His birth did He lose His omnipotent nature by being born. . . . He suffered in His body after the manner of our weak bodies, yet bore the sufferings of our bodies in the power of His own body.[24]

There was no place for the anxiety of human trepidation in that nature, which was above man.[25]

In these passages, *natura* denotes both the person of the Word, who does not suffer according to his divinity, and the assumed humanity borne in the power of the Spirit. If one must force a later vocabulary upon Hilary, he really says no more than that natures, considered abstractly, do not suffer. Once we avoid the red herring of a human nature abstractly considered, Hilary's alleged Docetism disappears.[26] Like Clement of Alexandria, who uses similarly strong language, Hilary assumes that impassibility accords perfectly with having a normal human body and soul.[27] The charge of aphthartodocetism is more serious, but we can dismiss this without much ado as well.[28] When Hilary speaks of the incorruption of Christ, he

24. *Trin.* 10.47, p. 500: "Passus igitur vnigenitus Deus est omnes incurrentes in se passionum nostrarum infirmitates. Sed passus uirtute naturae suae, ut et uirtute naturae suae natus est. Neque enim cum natus sit, non tenuit omnipotentiae suae in natiuitate naturam. . . . Secundum quod ita ex infirmitate corporis nostri nostri passus in corpore est, ut passiones corporis nostri corporis sui uirtute susciperet."

25. *Trin.* 10.44, p. 497: "Non est itaque in ea natura, quae supra hominem est, humanae trepidationis anxietas."

26. Hilary does explicitly condemn the heresy after all. *Trin.* 10.41, pp. 494-95: "Sudorem uero nemo infirmitati audebit deputare: quia et contra naturam est sudare sanguinem, nec infirmitas est, quod potestas non secundum naturae consuetudinem gessit. Neque ad heresim infirmitatis pertinere ullo modo poterit, quod aduersum heresim fantasma mentientem proficiat per sudorem sanguinis ad corporis ueritatem."

27. *Strom.* 6, 9, 71: "Christ ate not for the sake of His body, which was sustained by a holy power, but that the false notion might not creep into the minds of His disciples, which others have lately conceived, that He had been manifested only in appearance. For He was altogether impassible, and no movement of the passions, whether of pleasure or pain, entered into Him from without." Cf. *Trin.* 10.24, p. 479: "Neque enim tum cum sitiuit aut esuriuit aut fleuit, bibisse Dominus et manducasse aut doluisse monstratus est: sed ad demonstrandam corporis ueritatem corporis consuetudo suscepta est, ita ut naturae nostrae consuetudine consuetudini sit corporis satisfactum."

28. Lawrence Janssens, O.S.B., *Tractatus de Deo-Homine sive de Verbo Incarnato*, p. 552:

refers not to his body, but to his spirit. There is no sense in which Hilary taught that Christ's body was incorruptible before the resurrection. Hilary *does* believe that Christ's body is borne by the power of his divine *natura* and so enjoys special privileges.[29] Christ is the "man from heaven" (John 3:13; 1 Cor. 15:47), and he possesses a "heavenly body" *(corpus coeleste)*.[30] He was not conceived through bodily passions but through his own self-fashioning, and freed thereby from "the sinful weakness of man."[31] In *De Trinitate* 10.23, Christ's body shows its "natural" condition when he walks on water, when his spittle heals the blind, and when he is transfigured before his disciples. The hand that was to be pierced shows the power that bears it when it restores the ear of the high priest's slave.

Commentators have long noted these Alexandrian aspects of Hilary's teachings — Suárez and Petavius are cases in point — but none grant the obvious importance of the eastern spirituality of *apatheia* in understanding Christ's "impassible nature."[32] Of course, there is no simple agreement among the Fathers about the passions and so none about impassibility itself. Many, seeing the passions as weak, reactive emotions, regarded *apatheia* as their uprooting, which was both a necessary precursor to true prayer and a continued practice in monastic communities. Others judged passions to be fundamentally good and thus believed *apatheia* to be a state

---

"Mentem S. Hilarii ab Aphthartodoketarum excessu non tantopere distare." As long as I am covering all possible charges against Hilary, I should add that his emphasis on the single *natura* of Christ is also open to accusations of Monophysitism — as St. Cyril's is — but such accusations depend on an anachronistic understanding of the term *natura*. Enough said.

29. On Hilary's anthropology, see P. Galtier, "La *forma Dei* et la *forma servi* (Phil 2:6s) selon S. Hilaire de Poitiers," *Recherches de Science Religieuse* 48 (1960): 101-18; M.-J. Rondeau, "Remarques sur l'anthropologie de S. Hilaire," *Studia Patristica* 6 (1962): 197-210; and E. Cavalcanti, "Filip. 2:6-11 nel *De Trinitate* di Ilario (De Trin. VIII, 45-47; X, 23-26)," *Pléroma. Salus carnis. Homanaje a Antonio Orbe*, ed. E. Romero Pose, J. Ruis-Camps, and J. Montserrat Torrents (Santiago Compostela: Compestellanum, 1990), pp. 421-41.

30. *Trin.* 10.18, p. 473: "Ut per hoc quod descendens de caelis panis est, non ex humana conceptione origo esse corporis existimaretur, dum caeleste esse corpus ostenditur." Cf. J. Doignon, "Sur la descente du Christ en ce monde chez Hilaire de Poitiers," *Revue d'Histoire des Religions* 207 (1990): 65-75; and J. Doignon, "La chair du Christ comme dépouille triomphale. Une lecture de Col. ii,15 par Hilaire de Poitiers," *Revue des Sciences Religieuses* 68 (1994): 447-52.

31. *Trin.* 10.25, p. 481: "Nec est in uitiosa hominis infirmitate qui Christus est."

32. Suárez, *Opera Omnia*, p. 206; Petavius, *Dogmata Theologica*, p. 376. Hilary should be read as a Latin counterpart to the Greek tradition discussed in David Bentley Hart, "No Shadow of Turning: On Divine Impassibility," *Pro Ecclesia* 11 (2002): 184-206.

in which the soul's natural dispositions and energies functioned with a maximal, Edenic integrity. In truth, the difference between such views is largely verbal. Whether one takes a stricter view of the passions or not, the ancient Fathers generally agreed that *apatheia* restores the integration squandered by sin. In other words, it does not prevent the soul from acting; it allows it to act. In this case, *apatheia* is not merely an attribute of God — although it is that, too — it is a virtue enjoyed by the saints and martyrs. For Clement of Alexandria, Christian *apatheia* consists in the love that surpasses all understanding, an imperturbable "gnostic" love, which is had only in radical conformity to Christ.[33] It is, for the tradition that follows Evagrius Ponticus, the fruit of ascetical practices *(praktike)* and the contemplation of the world through Christ *(theoria physike)* that leads to the pure prayer of trinitarian contemplation *(theologia)*. As such, it does not involve a suppression of vital or wholesome energies of the soul, but rather the demonic ones, especially *acedia*. "The state of prayer," Evagrius says, "is one of dispassion, which by virtue of the most intense *eros*, transports the intellect that longs for wisdom to the noetic realm."[34] It "enables the intellect to activate its own energy."[35] Nor is *apatheia* a natural state obtainable through our own effort; strictly speaking, it is a supernatural gift that restores the soul's true rhythms.[36] Nor should we exaggerate the differences between Greek and Latin theologians. Both traditions agree that impassibility, far from being a condition of mute stasis, is the condition for the possibility of illumination, achieved only (at least with us) in the purgation that begins the mystical life. Impassibility, in this sense, is a spiritual poise, whereby the mirror of the soul is steadied to better reflect God's glory. For this reason Jerome says Christ knew no passions but only *propassiones*.[37] He really says

33. *Stromata* 6.9.

34. *The Philokalia*, ed. and trans. G. E. H. Palmer, Philip Sherrard, Kallistos Ware (London: Faber & Faber, 1979), vol. 1, p. 62.

35. *The Philokalia*, vol. 1, p. 65.

36. Among the *scholia* of Maximus the Confessor's *Ad Thalassium*, one can find the love of the heavenly blessed as one of the four species of *apatheia*. Cf. *The Philokalia*, vol. 2 (London and Boston: Faber and Faber, 1982), p. 221.

37. *In Matt.* 5:28 (PL 26), col. 39: "Inter πάθος et προπάθειαν, id est, inter *passionem* et *propassionem*, hoc interest, quod passio reputatatur in vitium: propassio licet initii culpam habeat, tamen non tenetur in crimine. Ergo qui viderit mulierem, et anima ejus fuerit titillata, hic propassione percussus est. Si vero consenserit, et de cogitatione affectum fecerit, sicut scriptum est in David: *Transierunt in affectum cordis* (Ps 72:7), de propassione transivit ad passionem, et huic non voluntas peccandi deest, sed occasio. Quicunque igitur viderit

no more than that the divine Word incarnate could not be caught off guard or thrown off track by some wicked spirit. He rather met demons calmly and cast them out with the perfect theandric *apatheia*. Neither Clement nor Jerome deny that Christ felt emotion or pain on that account, but rather deny that he experienced any spiritual and corporeal movements that resulted from sin. To say that Christ suffered passions in this sense is tantamount to claiming that he was mastered by demons.

When we restore this spiritual dimension of Hilary's thought, it is much easier to untangle his complex vocabulary of pain and to understand the exact sense in which he denied that the Word suffered pain and punishment. Upon closer analysis, Hilary clearly distinguishes between *passio, tristitia, dolor,* and *poena.* While he admits that Christ suffers and is sorrowful even unto death, Hilary excludes *dolor* and *poena* from Christ in order to maintain his spiritual integrity. In other words, Hilary does not exclude pain in the normal sense that we give the word at all, but rather as a violent and unendurable passion that overwhelms the soul and — most importantly — prevents it from acting. Similarly, he does not exclude fear from Christ's mind, inasmuch as we understand that to be a "natural" aversion to the separation of body and soul, but rather *trepidatio,* an agitating or disturbing fear that would prevent him from accepting his death freely and thus carrying out his mission. The majority of passages in which Hilary denies pain and punishment to Christ add similar qualifications. When Hilary asks "What can we see in Him to fear, that the terror of an unendurable pain should take hold of Him?," he excludes the terror or dread *(formido)* that makes pain intolerable.[38] So, too, Hilary does not deny that Christ suffered the same punishment meted out to the thieves, but simply that he did not groan loudly *(congemuerit)* when faced with crucifixion.

There is a clear Stoic ring to these passages, but it would be wrong to assume that Hilary understood impassibility simply as the Stoics did.[39] For

---

mulierem ad concupiscendum, id est, si aspexerit ut concupiscat ut facere disponat, iste recte dicitur eam moechari in corde suo." Cf. *In Matt.* 26:39 (PL 26), col. 205: "Illud quod supra diximus de passione et propassione, etiam in praesenti capitulo ostenditur, quod Dominus, ut veritatem probaret assumpti hominis, vere quidem contristatus sit, sed ne passio in animo illius dominaretur, per propassionem coepit contristari."

38. *Trin.* 10.10, p. 466: "Quidnam uideatur timere potuisse, ut in eum formido intolerandi doloris inciderit."

39. Bernard Lonergan, S.J., *De Verbo Incarnato* (Rome: Gregorian University, 1961), p. 178: "Sententia Hilarii esse videtur ad mentem Stoicorum qui 'sapientem' laudabant quia

Hilary, Christ's freedom from *trepidatio, formido, dolor,* and *poena* is per-fectly compatible with the emotion that Christ feels when confronted with evil, loss, and suffering. Such intensity of feeling is compatible with and expressive of an active, indeed the supremely active, instance of divine love. And so Hilary can say, "How great a mystery of word and act, that Christ wept, that His eyes filled with tears from the anguish of His soul, but where is the defect in His soul that sorrow should bring tears from His body?"[40] Hilary understands tears to result, at least in normal human cir-cumstances, from a defect in the soul *(animae uitia),* a phrase that could hardly be stronger, implying as it does defilement and destructive viola-tion. That Christ weeps for Lazarus, without such defects, demonstrates the sovereign freedom of his love.

The exclusion of *animae uitiae* from Christ leads us to another, psy-chological aspect of this older spiritual tradition. For these theologians, impassibility is really a power of the soul, not of the body. This is why mar-tyrs and, indeed, even regular people in extraordinary circumstances, can sometimes be indifferent to pain and suffering:

> Thus the soul, in the blessed warmth of its own heavenly faith and hope, soars above its origin in an earthly body and raises the sorrowful body in sense and spirit, so that it neither feels nor suffers that which it un-dergoes. What do we say about the Lord's body, the body of the Son of Man who came down from heaven? Even earthly bodies can sometimes be made insensitive to pain and fear when they must face those things that cause them pain and fear.[41]

True to this ancient psychology, Hilary thus does not believe that the body "feels" pain as a sensation of which the mind is conscious. Rather, the body

---

ita animi motus dominabatur ut doloribus afflictus doloribus tamen non vinceretur. Quibus negari non videtur ipsa naturalis sensibilitas, sed potius affirmari possibilitas psychologica cuiusdam dominii partis superioris super ipsam sensibilitatem."

40. *Trin.* 10.55, p. 510: "Iamuero quantum illud est dictorum et gestorum sacramentum, flere Christum et per animi angorem lacrimas oculis effluere? Vnde eius animae haec uitia, ut fletum corpori tristitiae maeror eliceat."

41. *Trin.* 10.44, pp. 497-98: "Quae ubi caelestis spei ac fidei suae beato calore terrenae in corpore suo originis despexit exordium, sui quoque sensus ac spiritus corpus efficitur in dolore, ut pati se desinat sentire quod patitur; — etquid nobis de natura dominici corporis et descendentis de caelo fili hominis adhuc sermo sit? Ipsa terrena corpora timere ac dolere interdum nesciunt quod et doleri necesse est et timeri."

suffers the privations that the soul, which pervades and enlivens the body, feels as pain; otherwise, an anesthetized body could feel pain.[42] *Dolor,* then, is not pain in the normal sense of our word at all, either psychologically or physiologically; it is a spiritual state that results from the imbalance or discord between an imperfect body and an imperfect soul.[43] Jesus Christ lives continually, by virtue of being perfect man, in the ecstasy only occasionally granted to Moses or Paul, and the spiritual elation that accompanies such raptures naturally makes him impervious to *dolor,* understood in the technical sense with which Hilary endows the word. Not being subject to the imbalances caused by sin, neither is Christ subject to concomitant moral privations. Here, too, *poena* bears a technical meaning; it is sin itself, both the privation and the just punishment that accompanies it. To say that Christ suffers *poena* in this sense is a denial of Hebrews 4:15. For all that Christ truly suffers, he simply does not experience the same just punishment or dread of hell that accompanies our own sins. His body and soul, being perfect and in perfect accord, suffer from no moral imbalance whatsoever, even when bearing the sins of the entire world.

II. The High Medieval Development of Christ's Impassibility

The ambiguities of Hilary's *De Trinitate* did not escape the notice of medieval commentators. Peter Lombard devoted two sections of his third book of *Sententiae* to the interpretation of its tenth book, and his selections of Hilary's text largely determined the contours of high medieval

---

42. *Trin.* 10.14, p. 469. Paul Gondreau has made much — perhaps too much — of this passage, arguing that Hilary gives the notion of Christ's impassibility "a glorified twist by refusing to acknowledge the psychical impact of suffering. For Hilary, Christ suffered in a purely physical or somatic manner, without even the psychical perception of the pain his body was enduring, as if Christ's body were entirely anesthetized — he endured the physical injury but felt nothing." Cf. Paul Gondreau, *The Passions of Christ's Soul in the Theology of Thomas Aquinas,* Beiträge zur Geschichte der Philosophie und Theologie des Mittelalters, n.f., 61 (Münster: Aschendorff, 2002), p. 49. This interpretation, which was first advanced by Smulders, *supra,* unfortunately ignores the emotional-charged language that Hilary adopts elsewhere.

43. It is for this reason that Hilary, despite his reticence to attribute *dolor* to Christ, does not shy away from describing the very union of Christ's human soul with the Word in passionate terms, as a violence wrought upon the soul by the ravishing fire of divine love. Cf. *Tractatus super Psalmos* 68:4.

discussions on Christ's impassibility. A noted scholar of Franciscan history has recently argued that the high medieval theologians after Lombard willfully distorted the meaning of Hilary's texts in their desire to preserve his orthodoxy.[44] He charges that Bonaventure and Thomas Aquinas took the clear words of Hilary and made them more ambiguous than they actually were. This interpretive act, he claims, is evidence of a radical discontinuity between Hilary and the high medieval theologians, evidence that stands in stark opposition to the continuity of tradition that they sought so desperately to preserve. I will not answer this charge directly; that Lombard, Bonaventure, and Aquinas interpreted Hilary at all implies continuity — however one might construe it — and weighing such metaphysical categories as continuity and discontinuity on the scales of history seems to me a dreadfully boring enterprise. That being said, a closer analysis of these theologians will show that they sought to clarify the same ambiguities in Hilary's thought that have bedeviled modern historians. In doing so, however, they did not forget the spiritual meaning of impassibility, and together they provide an impressive analysis of Hilary's thought on this topic. The role of the particularly medieval preoccupation with the beatific vision in this synthesis is especially instructive. In fact, this preoccupation largely occasions the treatments of Hilary found among the commentators, because the Lombard placed his discussion on the "obscure chapters" of Hilary immediately after a distinction concerning Christ's earthly possession of the beatific vision. Because all agreed that the beatific vision entails perfect impassibility, and all likewise agreed that the incarnate Word possessed the beatific vision during his earthly life, high medieval theologians were forced to explain how Christ suffered at all. And yet all agreed that this impassible Christ suffered. In fact, Bonaventure, Thomas Aquinas, and John Duns Scotus, by "maximalizing" the patristic problem of impassibility in this fashion,

---

44. Kevin Madigan, "On the High-Medieval Reception of Hilary of Poitiers's Anti-'Arian' Opinion," p. 225: "The attempt to improve Hilary, to explain his words away, and to remove him from suspicion of error consumed enormous dogmatic and scholarly energy long after the close of the Middle Ages. Between the seventeenth and twentieth centuries, many scholars tortured themselves to show that Hilary did not in fact say what he clearly did and emphatically meant to say." "Tortured" is a strong word. Suárez treated Hilary more extensively than most, and he devoted two and a half pages of his estimated total output of 21 million words to the problem. Cf. Joseph Fichter, *Man of Spain: Francis Suárez* (New York: Macmillan, 1949), p. 327.

offer a christological solution that strikingly anticipates a number of the usual objections to God's impassibility.

The Lombard's discussion of Hilary's *De Trinitate* comes only at the end of his investigation of the normal limitations that the Word assumed in becoming man. His authorities, which include Augustine, Ambrose, and Pope Leo, allow Lombard to assert that Christ truly experienced suffering *secundum hominem*. Following Augustine, he also confirms the ancient psychological emphasis that we have already seen in Hilary, namely, that it is not the body that feels pain, but the soul that feels through the body.[45] Accordingly, the Lombard reasons, Christ assumed certain defects, but not all, taking punishment upon himself, but without blame, and assuming only those limitations that were fitting and did not insult his dignity.[46] Where one might expect the Lombard to privilege the strand of the tradition that emphasizes Christ's human suffering, he introduces Jerome's distinction between *passiones* and *propassiones* and, finally, a small *florilegium* of texts from the tenth book of *De Trinitate,* under the heading, "Of some rather obscure chapters of Hilary, which are seen to concur with the common pronouncements."[47] For all the hubbub that surrounds the interpretation of Hilary on this issue, the Lombard actually says very little.[48] Following Hilary's own explanations, he curtly concludes that Christ was not sad on his own account, but rather prayed that his death would not be scandal to the disciples.

---

45. *De Genesi ad litteram,* bk. 12, ch. 24: "*Non corpus sentit, sed anima per corpus: quo velut nuntio utitur ad formandum in seipsa, quod extrinsecus nuntiatur.*"

46. III. *Sent.,* d. 15. ch. 3: "Sentit ergo anima dolores; sed quosdam per instrumentum corporis, quosdam vero non. Suscepit autem Christus sicut veram naturam hominis, ita et veros defectus hominis, sed non omnes. Assumpsit enim defectus poenae, sed non culpae: nec tamen omnes defectus poenae, sed eos omnes quos eum assumere homini expediebat, et suae dignitati non derogabat." Later theologians would term these natural limitations, the *passiones universales sive irreprehensibiles,* and adventitious limitations, the *passiones particulares sive reprehensibiles.* Cf. Thomas Aquinas, *ST,* III, q. 14, a. 4.

47. III *Sent.,* d. 15, ch. 3: "De quibusdam Hilarii capitulis valde obscuris, quae videntur communi sententiae obviare." The Lombard adds small quotations from chapters 26–28 and 35–36 to the large quotation from chapter 23 that began this essay.

48. Here, it must be said that the words Madigan chose as an epigram for his own study (*Intende, lector, his verbis pia diligentia, ne sint tibi vasa mortis*) do not concern Christ's impassibility at all. They come later, when the Lombard is discussing the problem of how Hilary's emphasis on the single *natura* of Christ seems to imply Monophysitism. Cf. III *Sent.,* d. 17, ch. 3.

Bonaventure explicitly connects the question of Christ's passibility with the Lombard's previous question on the beatific vision — an insight that Duns Scotus will exploit to great effect later — asking how the humanity of Christ can enjoy the fullness of grace and knowledge while still being passible.[49] Bonaventure's solution to this theological dilemma takes the form of a dialectic between infinite power and finite fragility in the metaphysical order, which is mirrored by a dialectic between the highest justice and the fault of sin in the moral order. He divides the question of Christ's passibility into two articles: one on the general limitations that the Word assumes and a second on particular limitations, such as sadness and wrath.[50] In his first question, whether such defects are found to be fitting in Christ, Hebrews 2:17 or 4:15 forms the body of the *quod sic videtur* the Seraphic Doctor counters; the defect of fault *(defectus culpae)* is repugnant to the highest justice, just as the defect of fragility or impotence *(defectus fragilitatis et impotentiae)* is repugnant to the highest power. But since God has the defect of fault neither in his own nature nor in the nature he assumed, it follows that Christ cannot suffer defects of punishment or powerlessness *(defectus poenalitatis et impotentiae)*.[51] Bonaventure thus understands Christ's passibility in three ways, according to which Christ assumed defects in order to serve as a ransom for our salvation; in order to offer an example of virtue; and in order to be a pillar for own weaknesses. Bonaventure surprisingly takes as his text, "You know that you were ransomed from the futile ways inherited from your fathers, not with perishable things such as silver or gold, but with the precious blood of Christ" (1 Pet. 1:18-19), letting the accent fall on *non corruptibilibus auro et argento.* That which serves as our ransom cannot be perishable; Christ serves as our ransom; therefore Christ, in body and soul, must be imperishable. For the Seraphic Doctor, the incorruptibility of

49. III *Sent.,* d. 15, *divisio textus* [= *Opera Theologica Selecta,* ed. Leonardi M. Bello (Quarrachi: Collegium S. Bonaventurae, 1941), vol. 3, p. 321]: "Supra egit Magister de plenitudine gratiae et cognitionis in Christo ex parte humanitatis; in hac vero parte intendit agere de defectu passibilitatis."

50. There is occasional whimsy in Bonaventure's balancing of arguments *pro* and *contra,* as when he ponders whether *scientia inflat* (1 Cor. 8:1) ought to serve as an argument for Christ's ignorance. Cf. III *Sent.,* d. 15, a. 2, q. 1, n. 4, p. 330.

51. III *Sent.,* d. 15, a. 1, q. 1, sed contra 1, p. 323: "Sicut summae iustitiae repugnat defectus culpae, sic summae potentiae repugnat defectus fragilitatis et impotentiae; sed Deum summe iustum non decuit habere defectum culpae, nec in se nec in natura assumpta: ergo pari ratione nec defectum poenalitatis et impotentiae."

Christ's human soul — even his blood itself — spans the divide between the infinite and the finite, and Christ's weakness is joined to an interior power of his soul according to his status as the Redeemer.[52] Although this first move appears to add little to our discussion, it actually returns us to the spiritual use of the terms such as impassibility and incorruption and sets the stage for an approach not unlike Hilary's own when Bonaventure goes on to address Christ's possession of the "passion of sadness" *(passio tristitiae)*. Here, Matthew 26:38 serves as the first prooftext for the *quod sic videtur* that Bonaventure will later counter with Isaiah 42:4, which in the Vulgate reads *non erit tristis neque turbulentis*.[53] In order to treat both of these texts fairly, Bonaventure concludes that Christ is truly sad, but not in all the ways in which we are.[54] His spirit is saddened and troubled (John 11:33), quite simply, but not in a way that his reason is overcome. Similarly, Isaiah 42:4 does not exclude sadness *(tristitia)*, but simply the sadness that perturbs or overcomes the reason *(tristitia perturbans)*.

Bonaventure does not explicitly address Hilary until the *quaestiones* and *dubia* of the sixteenth distinction. He is most concerned with Hilary's statement that the power of Christ's body experienced the violence of the punishment without feeling the punishment itself. Although Bonaventure entertains the idea that Hilary retracted his teaching at a later date — as does Thomas Aquinas — he is more concerned to place Hilary in his anti-Arian context, noting that Hilary clearly intends only to exclude suffering from the divine nature.[55] Ultimately, Bonaventure thinks that Hilary did not maintain that Christ did not truly suffer *(non habuisse verum dolorem)*, but only that he did not have the cause of suffering *(non habuisse causa doloris)*, that is, he did not suffer the disordering privations of sin itself. This distinction, which parallels the distinction between *tristitia* and *tristitia perturbans*, highlights Christ's freedom from sin and its effects upon our

---

52. III *Sent.*, d. 15, a. 1, q. 1, ad 1, p. 324: "Infirmitas vero reddit magis laudabile, quando coniuncta est interiori virtuti animi secundum statum meriti."

53. III *Sent.*, d. 15, a. 2, q. 2, sed contra and resp., p. 332.

54. III *Sent.*, d. 15, a. 2, q. 2, resp., p. 332: "Textus etiam evangelicus confirmat, in Christo fuit vera tristitia, non tamen omni modo quo in nobis est."

55. III *Sent.*, d. 16, a. 1, q. 1, ad 1, pp. 339-340. Cf. *Collegii Salmanticensis Cursus Theologicus* (Paris: Victor Palmé, 1880), vol. 15, tract. 21, disp. 24, dub. 1, p. 420: "Probabile etiam est D. Hilarium errorem illum retractasse, ut tradit D. Thom. in 3, dist. 15. . . . Et hoc supposito, frustra laboramus in exponendo sententiam, quam Hilarius postea recognovit falsam, atque Catholice expunxit."

souls. Such distinctions might give one the impression that Bonaventure strains to make Hilary orthodox. After all, Bonaventure does say that Hilary's words appear "false, doubtful and erroneous" *(falsa, et dubia et erronea).*[56] But this misunderstanding is quickly dispelled when we see that in Bonaventure this judgment is the first *dubium* of the distinction, in which one would normally place objections to one's own position. And so Bonaventure immediately says Hilary's teachings, while appearing to be *contra fidem,* are in fact *pro fide.*[57] Returning to Hilary's understanding of the Holy Spirit's role in the conception of Christ, Bonaventure argues that Christ, being truly man, can suffer, but he does not have a nature capable of pain *(non habens ad dolendum).* This sentence, Bonaventure notes, shows the true meaning of Hilary's controversial statements. That holy flesh is passible, not *contra voluntatem,* but *ex voluntate.* Otherwise, Hilary himself would not have said that Christ *habens corpus ad patiendum, passus est.*[58] The entire life of our Lord, from his conception in the womb of the Blessed Virgin to his becoming all in all in order to return creation to the Father, is an act of condescension. Every pain that he endures, both during his earthly ministry and in his mystical body, has been chosen.

Thomas Aquinas provides a characteristically effortless summary of Hilary's position in his own commentary on Lombard's *Sententiae.* First, Christ cannot be overwhelmed by sin in any way. In this regard, he does not suffer *passiones* as such, but *propassiones.* Second, Christ was not obliged to suffer in any way; he voluntarily accepted his suffering and death in the same way that he voluntarily became incarnate. Third, Christ's suffering did not partake of the nature of punishment.[59] According to the

56. III *Sent.,* d. 16, dub. 1, pp. 353-54.

57. III *Sent.,* d. 16, dub. 1, resp., p. 354: "Dicendum quod ista verba Hilarii, etsi videantur esse contra fidem, tamen pro fide sunt."

58. III *Sent.,* d. 16, dub. 1, resp., p. 354: "Quia enim caro illa concepta fuit de Spiritu Sancto, ideo passibilitatem habuit, non contra voluntatem, sed ex voluntate; et hoc est quod dicit: 'habens corpus ad patiendum, passus est,' scilicet ex voluntate; 'sed naturam non habens ad dolendum,' id est ad patiendum contra dissensum voluntatis."

59. III *Sent.,* d. 15: "Solutio Magistri consistit in hoc, quod simpliciter noluit removere a Christo dolorem, sed tria quae sunt circa dolorem. Primo dominium doloris; quod patet ex hoc quod dicit: 'Quam igitur infirmitatem dominatam hujus corporis credis, cujus tantam habuit natura virtutem?' Secundo meritum doloris, quod patet ex hoc quod dicit: 'Non tamen vitiosa infirmitatis nostrae forma erat in corpore.' Tertio necessitatem doloris; quod patet ex hoc quod dicit: 'Videamus an ille ordo passionis infirmitatem in Domino doloris permittat intelligi.' Et secundum hoc solvuntur tria difficilia, quae in verbis eius videntur esse."

Angelic Doctor, Hilary's problematic phrase *non habens naturam ad dolendum* does not mean the nature of the body considered in itself, but only insofar as it is joined to divinity. So far, so good. The Angelic Doctor's genius is more apparent in the related questions of the *Summa theologiae*. Not surprisingly, the text of *De Trinitate* 10.23 is part of the first objection to the question whether there was sensible pain in Christ. Appealing to Isaiah 53:4 for his *sed contra*, Aquinas interprets Hilary "in all these and similar words" to exclude not the reality of pain, but its necessity. Although Aquinas notes that Christ was subject to the full range of passions, both sensible and psychological, he is also quick to point out, like Bonaventure, that Christ experienced such passions differently than we do. His passions in no way tend to unlawful things, for example, nor do his passions have their source anywhere except "from the disposition of His reason." The incarnate Word possesses his human soul in a total and integral fashion, Aquinas argues, because Augustine has written — in phrasing that echoes Hilary's own — "Christ assumed these movements in His human soul by an unfailing dispensation when He willed, even as He became man when He willed."[60] Nor, Aquinas maintains, do such passions "deflect" the reason. And so Aquinas appeals to Jerome's distinction between passions and propassions: "Our Lord, in order to prove the reality of the humanity He assumed, was in fact sorrowful, yet lest a passion should hold sway over His soul, it is by a *propassion* that He is said to have begun to grow sorrowful and to be sad."[61] In a final note to this question, Aquinas mentions that God prevented, by divine dispensation, the beatitude of contemplation from overflowing into Christ's sensitive powers and body, lest his passibility and mortality be taken away.

In an admittedly more shocking move, the Angelic Doctor actually appeals to the tenth book of Hilary's *De Trinitate* to establish the position that Christ endured *all* human suffering. It would seem that he did, Aquinas argues, since Hilary says, "God's only-begotten Son testifies that He endured all suffering in order to accomplish the sacrament of His death, when He bowed His head and gave up the spirit."[62] Aquinas believes that Hilary's

---

60. *De Civitate Dei* 14.9.

61. *In Matt.* 26:39, PL 26, col. 205.

62. *ST* III, q. 46, a. 5, obj. 1. Cf. *Trin.* 10.11, p. 467: "Vnigenitus autem Deus, ita potestatem habens ponendae animae ut resumendae, ad peragendum in se mortis sacramentum, cum poto aceto consummasse se omne humanarum passionum opus testatus esset, inclinato capite Spiritum tradidit."

words are to be understood as referring to all general classes of suffering (on the part of men, on the part of sufferings a man can endure, and with regard to bodily members), rather than every individual suffering (his bones were not broken, for example), but the fact that Aquinas chose this text, even as the first objection, implies that he did not seriously question Hilary's position on Christ's impassibility. Building upon Lamentations 1:12, "See if there is any sorrow like my sorrow" *(Videte si est dolor, sicut dolor meus),* Aquinas argues further that the pain of Christ's passion was greater than any other pain. In so doing, the Angelic Doctor masterfully incorporates Hilary's claim that Christ endured all suffering — a text, incidentally, that many interpreters ignore — by developing Hilary's understanding of the divine origin of Christ's body. For Aquinas, Christ's pain is greater than all others on account of his perfect constitution, which he owed to the conception of the Holy Spirit, and on account of his voluntary acceptance of suffering. For these reasons, Christ can apprehend all causes of sadness "most vehemently" in his soul, and his pain is proportionate to the magnitude of redemption that was purchased on the cross.[63]

Duns Scotus largely follows the high medieval consensus on questions about Christ's limitations, and so he begins his *scholia* on the fifteenth distinction of the *Sententiae* not by asking whether Christ assumed a human nature with normal limitations, but by asking whether Christ experienced a true sorrow in the highest part of his soul.[64] This emphasis allows Scotus to maximize the question about impassibility and the beatific vision implicitly created by Peter Lombard and explicitly raised by his Franciscan confrere. Apart from the claim that Christ knows all things actually and not merely habitually in the beatific vision — a disputed question among Scotists — and his typical insistence on treating the relationship of necessity and fittingness *(convenientia)* in terms of the divine will, the Marian Doctor differs very little from Bonaventure and Thomas Aquinas in the body of this question.[65] Scotus's contribution to our understanding of Hil-

---

63. *ST* III, q, 46, a. 6, resp.

64. *Ordinatio* III, d. 15, qu. unica [= *Opera Omnia,* ed. Luke Wadding (Hildesheim: Georg Olms, 1968), vol. 7.1, pp. 326-61]. Scotus skips ahead to the question Bonaventure will only address in III *Sent.,* d. 16, a. 2, q. 2, pp. 349-51. He treats Christ's limitations in *Ordinatio* III, d. 7, q. 3; d. 16, q. 2; and d. 19.

65. On Scotus's teaching on actual and habitual knowledge in the beatific vision, see Hieronymus de Montefortino, *Ven. Ioannis Duns Scoti Summa Theologica* (Rome: Typographia Sallustiana, 1903), vol. 5, par. 3, q. 10, a. 2, pp. 136-38. The treatment of *convenientia* in

ary is his well-known account of the beatific vision.[66] By presenting the beatific vision as the supremely free act of will, in which natural necessity and perfect spontaneity coincide, Duns Scotus provides a final note necessary for a properly theological understanding of Christ's impassibility.

The Marian Doctor's *scholia* begins in a fairly typical way. It would appear, he reasons, that Christ could not have enjoyed a true sorrow in the highest part of his soul, since joy and sadness are "maximally opposed," and contraries cannot exist in the same thing. Although Scotus does not quote him, Hilary is marshaled among the initial authorities for the *quod non*, because he "expressly removes true sadness and pain from Christ."[67] But this is merely an opening gambit: Scotus will quickly dismantle the idea, so beloved of many modern theologians, that such ontic oppositions can explain Christ's sufferings, and so restore Hilary's intentions just as his contemporaries did.[68] Taking Isaiah 53:4, "truly He has borne our pains" *(vere dolores nostros ipse portauit)*, Lamentations 1:12, "See if there is any sorrow like my sorrow" *(Videte si est dolor, sicut dolor meus)*, and Psalm 88:3, "My soul is full of sorrows" *(repleta est malis anima mea)* as his texts, Scotus establishes that Christ does feel sorrow even as he experiences the beatific vision.[69] In this, as in his arguments, Scotus largely follows his pre-

---

ibid., vol. 5., par. 3, q. 14, a. 2 and q. 46, a. 1 can profitably be compared to the related questions in Aquinas's *Summa theologiae.*

66. *Ordinatio* IV, d. 49, q. 4-q. ex latere [= *Opera Omnia*, vol. 10, pp. 379-422].

67. *Ordinatio* III, d. 15, q. unica, p. 327: "Praeterea, Hilarius in litera videtur expresse remouere tristitiam veram et dolorem a Christo."

68. The editors of the Nicene and Post-Nicene Fathers edition of Hilary are typical in this regard. Hilary, they say, "balances with scrupulous reverence mystery against mystery, never forgetting that he is dealing with infinites. In this case the one is made to overwhelm the other; the infinite glory excludes the infinite sorrow from his view" (p. lxxvii).

69. Scotus appeals to Augustine's *De Civitate Dei* 14.15: "Dolor carnis tantummodo offensio est animae ex carne, et quaedam ab eius passione dissensio, sicut animi dolor, *quae* tristitia nuncupatur, dissensio *est* ab his rebus, quae nobis nolentibus acciderunt." The point of this passage, as Augustine says, is that it is really the man who suffers when the flesh is said to suffer pain. It is also worth noting that Augustine glosses the eighty-eighth Psalm with *non vitiis, sed poenis*, to which Scotus also appeals. Of course, neither Jerome nor Augustine felt a need to excise *dolor* and *poena* from their christological vocabularies. Boyd Taylor Coolman has some wonderful passages on the patristic and medieval vocabulary of suffering in his recent article on Alexander of Hales, which can also be read fruitfully as the larger background to the meditations of Bonaventure, Scotus, and to a lesser degree Aquinas. Cf. Boyd Taylor Coolman, "The Salvific Affectivity of Christ According to Alexander of Hales," *The Thomist* 71 (2007): 1-38.

decessors: Christ's sorrow overwhelms neither his reason nor his will; he does not suffer passions, strictly speaking, but *propassions;* Hilary does not exclude *dolor* from Christ so much as he excludes the sinful causes of sorrow. Christ, Scotus concludes, possesses both greater sorrow — and experiences greater pain — in the sensitive part of his soul while he possesses maximum joy in the will and intellect.[70] Christ's maximal impassibility allows him to suffer greater passibility, and it is by dint of an unceasing miracle that the glory Christ experiences in his soul does not overflow into his body.

So far Scotus has simply followed the path laid out by Lombard, Bonaventure, and Aquinas. What he adds to their contributions is a strong account of the compatibility of necessity and spontaneity in the beatific vision. It is well known that Scotus believes that the will takes pride of place in man's perfection. Unfortunately, this argument all too often serves as a defense of modern voluntarism, since Scotus argues that the will is a self-moving and self-determining power. In truth, it is a decisive theological argument against such modern notions, for the Marian Doctor is quick to point out that the perfection of the will is had only in the one instance in which it cannot offer the usual half-hearted refusals, in the immediately compelling vision of God's ravishing and perfecting love. The beatific vision is thus the sole instance in which an act of the will is wholly free and wholly subject to its own natural necessity. Plunging into the abyss of trinitarian love is akin, Scotus says, to a man who dives into the sea from a high cliff. He cannot stop in mid-flight — gravity carries him downward with natural necessity — but he can still desire and indeed delight in the desire to plunge into the water below. That he can still will, even though he cannot arrest his fall, proves the will to be a spontaneous power. But in stark contrast to modern voluntarism — this cannot be pointed out nearly enough — the soul enjoys such delightful spontaneity only because she has been created with a natural desire for supernatural fulfillment.

This conception of the beatific vision is an important bulwark against the misleading objection that Hilary's teaching implies that the Word did not suffer "naturally" or "spontaneously."[71] On such an interpretation, a

---

70. Scotus is reluctant to say that Christ felt maximum sorrow, because he believes that to be the inconsolable sorrow of damnation, which is not applicable to Christ Himself. Cf. *Ordinatio* III, d. 15, q. unica, n. 37, p. 360.

71. Joseph Pohle, *Dogmatic Theology* (St. Louis: Herder, 1941), vol. 4, pp. 80-81: "This

miraculous and/or supernatural impassibility must somehow make Christ "less" human. One might here note the parallel between this objection and common objections to Christ's possession of the beatific vision.[72] But this is a falsely conceived dichotomy. The beatific act that perfects human nature cannot make us less human. One may as well argue that possessing perfect redness prevents an apple from being red, and Bonaventure and Thomas Aquinas have already given us good reasons for supposing that Christ's impassibility — the unique integrity of his body and soul — is precisely what allows him to experience pain more vehemently and so identify with those who suffer in a way that we cannot. Some theologians also imagine — curiously — that Christ's impassibility must make him somehow "less" free.[73] But we must reject this as a perverse suggestion. Christ's freedom from pain's tyranny cannot make him less free. To imagine that freedom is realized only in the mute acceptance of one's own violation is a morbid Romantic fantasy. If the only flame that kindles one's imagination is the dim bulb of personal resignation, one is left, like Prometheus, chained to the rock, awaiting the bird. Freedom without fire, and some freedom!

In any event, Scotus's understanding of the beatific vision allows us to overcome both of these objections. Just as perfect impassibility ensures that Christ feels suffering and sorrow all the more vehemently, the perfect love of the beatific vision enables Christ to accept that suffering and sorrow with a perfectly natural spontaneity. Christ's possession of the beatific vision not only guarantees that his humanity is a perfect instrument (in the properly Thomist sense of the phrase), it also ensures that his sacred body suffers in the mystical proportion necessary to reconcile the world to

---

sublime conception of Christ led St. Hilary to lose sight of the soteriological character of His mission. The Incarnation of the Son of God was dictated for practical reasons and required for its consummation a painful atonement which involved His death on the Cross. The passibility of Christ must, therefore, be held to be wholly natural and spontaneous. A supernatural or artificial passibility, based on an unbroken chain of miracles, could not have accomplished the purposes of the Redemption."

72. For the main sources for this debate, I direct readers to articles of two of our contributors: Thomas G. Weinandy, "Jesus' Filial Vision of the Father," *Pro Ecclesia* 13 (2004): 189-201; and Thomas Joseph White, "The Voluntary Action of the Earthly Christ and the Necessity of the Beatific Vision," *The Thomist* 69 (2005): 497-534.

73. Dorner, *Entwicklungsgeschichte der Lehre von der Person Christi*, p. 320. Those who have followed contemporary debates about Christ's earthly possession of the beatific vision will note that this is also a common objection to the traditional teaching.

himself.[74] His saving atonement, the consummation of love and spontaneity, requires nothing less than perfect impassibility. More importantly, the two are theologically inseparable: The suffering that Christ obediently undertook as a necessary component of his mission — "He learned obedience from what He suffered" (Heb. 5:8) — becomes *true* passion by dint of the perfect and total cooperation afforded by the beatific vision that Christ possessed from the moment of his conception — "For this I was born, and for this I have come into the world" (John 18:37).

And so it remains that Christ felt the force of his suffering without its sorrow, for his suffering was made all the greater by the impassible nature he had from the Father, coursing into the soul that bore his body across the waters, that shook his sacred body with tears for his friend Lazarus, that blazed in his transfiguration like fire flashing in an alabaster jar. That Hilary saw no need to trisect Christ into deity, soul, and body is his strength. But if we must import the later categories of divine and human nature, considered abstractly, into his meditations, we can see that the medieval and early modern treatments of Hilary largely make more sense than most of our contemporary historical treatments. Knowing full well the difficulties that surrounded Hilary's peculiar vocabulary, these theologians confronted the difficult passages of *De Trinitate* with the same ardor, but without the same perplexity, as many of their modern successors. Having never forgotten the spiritual importance of impassibility, they applied the necessary distinctions in the serenity afforded by their common tradition. They maximalized the Patristic tradition, to be sure, but they also humanized Christ, and their joint contribution to Christology shows us that impassibility — properly understood — allows Christ to suffer more, not less; allows him to do so with greater freedom, not less; allows him to embody the maximal love (John 15:12) and nothing less. It allows, in sum, God's power to be made perfect in weakness (2 Cor. 12:9), and so overcome weakness once and for all.

---

74. Some readers may note that I am offering a brief Scotist variant on an argument for Christ's earthly possession of the beatific vision already provided by Thomas Joseph White, "The Voluntary Action of the Earthly Christ."

St. Thomas Aquinas, the Communication of Idioms, and the Suffering of Christ in the Garden of Gethsemane

Paul Gondreau

The purpose of this essay is to pursue the manner in which a christological line of inquiry sheds light on the question of suffering or passibility in God. More specifically, I wish to complement Bruce Marshall's treatment (from the present volume) of Christ's cry of dereliction on the cross. This I will do with my own reflection, following the lead of St. Thomas Aquinas, on Jesus' darkest hour of internal suffering which occurred the night before this cry was issued, during his agony in the garden of Gethsemane. Profoundly indebted to the celebrated patristic principle known as the communication of idioms *(communicatio idiomatum),* or "exchange of predicates" in the incarnate Word, and always with an eye on the Chalcedonian definition of Christ, Aquinas holds that the Word, the second person of the Holy Trinity, becomes the subject of human attributes, including human passibility, human suffering, especially in the garden of Gethsemane. This allows us to affirm unequivocally, if still qualifiedly, that God does indeed suffer.

I. The Communication of Idioms and the Fathers

We begin by taking a cursory look at the communication of idioms and its rich patristic legacy. The communication of idioms attempts to reconcile problematic statements in Scripture that *prima facie* seem in conflict with each other. For we find, on the one hand, scriptural statements that apply specifically human attributes to God in the person of Christ, as when St. Paul affirms "the Lord of Glory was crucified" (1 Cor. 2:8). On the other, we also find statements that apply specifically divine attributes to the human Jesus. The hymn to the Philippians, for instance, speaks of the man Jesus as deserving of adoration proper to God alone, proclaiming that "at the name of Jesus every knee should bow, in heaven and on earth and under the earth" (Phil. 2:10). Formulated in light of later patristic christological developments, the communication of idioms affirms the veracity of both types of predication by holding that the attributes (or "idioms") which belong properly to either of Christ's distinct natures, his human nature or his divine nature, can be predicated of or credited to the other on account of their union in the one divine person of the Word (or Son).[1]

The list of towering Church Fathers, from both east and west, who favored and employed the communication of idioms to great end is impressive: among the Greek Fathers are Ignatius of Antioch (who offers a beginning attempt at this tenet c. 110), Origen (†254), Athanasius (†373), Cyril of Jerusalem (†386), Gregory of Nazianzus (†389), Gregory of Nyssa (†395), Epiphanius (†403), Cyril of Alexandria (†444), Pseudo-Dionysius (c. 500), and John Damascene (†749); among the Latin Fathers we find Tertullian (†225), Hilary of Poitiers (†367), Ambrose (†397), Augustine (†430), and Leo the Great (†461).[2] There are more, but these are the ones read by Aquinas, the chief focus of this essay.

1. Cf. A. Michel, "Idiomes (communication des)," in *Dictionnaire de théologie catholique*, vol. 7, 1 (Paris: Librairie Letouzey et Ane, 1927), cols. 595-602, at 595. Cf. as well "Communicatio Idiomatum," in *The Oxford Dictionary of the Christian Church*, 2nd edition, ed. F. L. Cross and E. A. Livingstone (Oxford: Oxford University Press, 1988), pp. 321-22; Peter Parente et al., "'Communicatio Idiomatum' (Communication of Idioms)," in *Dictionary of Dogmatic Theology*, trans. Emmanuel Doronzo (Milwaukee: Bruce Publishing, 1951), pp. 51-52.

2. References to the use of the communication of idioms in all these Fathers (save in Ignatius of Antioch, which comes in his *Letter to Trallians*, ch. 10, in his *Letter to the Smyrnaens*, chs. 1–5, and in his *Letter to the Ephesians*, ch. 7, and in Pseudo-Dionysius, which comes in *Ecclesiastical Hierarchy*, III, 11) can be found in: J. N. D. Kelly, *Early Christian Doctrines*, 2nd edition (New York: Harper & Row, 1960); A. Michel, "Idiomes (communication des)," cols. 596-601; and Johannes Quasten, *Patrology. Vol. II: The Ante-Nicene Literature After Irenaeus* (Westminster, Md.: Newman Press, 1953), and *Vol. III: The Golden Age of Greek Patristic Literature. From the Council of Nicaea to the Council of Chalcedon* (Westminster, Md.: Newman Press, 1960). For a closer examination of Augustine's use of this tenet, cf. Joseph Torchia, "The Significance of the *Communicatio Idiomatum* in St. Augustine's Christology, with Special Reference to His Rebuttal of Later Arianism," in *Studia Patristica, Vol. 38: Papers Presented at the Thirteenth International Conference on Patristic Studies Held in Oxford 1999. St. Augustine and His Opponents. Other Latin Writers*, ed. M. F. Wiles and E. J. Yarnold (Leuven: Peeters, 2001),

Paul Gondreau

Even if formulated before the Council of Chalcedon in 451, the communication of idioms correlates with this council's definition of the hypostatic union.[3] Chalcedon of course confesses, on the one hand, a unity of person in Christ (as owing to the profession of the Council of Ephesus twenty years earlier), and, on the other, a distinction in natures with their respective properties or predicates. As many know, the key phrase of Chalcedon reads: "one and the same Christ, Son, Lord, only-begotten, acknowledged in two natures which undergo no confusion (ἀσιγχύτως), no change (ἀτρέπτως), no division (ἀδιαιρέτως), no separation (ἀχωρίστως)."[4] Pope Leo the Great's *Tome to Flavian*, solemnly endorsed at Chalcedon ("it is in agreement with Peter's confession"), famously formulates this delicate balance between unity of person and distinction of respective natural properties: "Each form accomplishes in concert with the other what is appropriate to it, the Word performing what belongs to the Word, and the flesh [or the human nature] carrying out what belongs to the flesh."[5]

Put simply, in Christ there is one subject of predication or attribution, the person of the Word, who is joined to two natures, human and divine, along with their respective properties. Christ is ontologically one and constituted by one unique hypostasis, the hypostasis of the Word, in two na-

---

pp. 306-23. For more on the communication of idioms in some of the early patristic authors, cf. M. Slusser, *Theopaschite Expressions in Second-Century Christianity as Reflected in the Writings of Justin, Melito, Celsus and Irenaeus* (Oxford: D.Phil. dissertation, 1975). Cf. as well J. J. O'Keefe, "Impassible Suffering? Divine Passion and Fifth-Century Christology," *Theological Studies* 58 (1997): 39-59.

3. Thomas G. Weinandy (*Does God Suffer?* [Notre Dame: University of Notre Dame Press, 2000], p. 175) even goes so far as to assert "the whole of orthodox patristic Christology, including the conciliar affirmations, can be seen as an attempt to defend the practice and to clarify the use of the communication of idioms." Weinandy's treatment of the communication of idioms comes amidst his reflections on the christological side of the question of suffering in God in his chapter entitled, "The Incarnation — The Impassible Suffers," pp. 172-213.

4. For Chalcedon's decree, cf. Norman Tanner, ed., *Decrees of the Ecumenical Councils*, vol. 1 (Washington, D.C.: Georgetown University Press, 1990), p. 86.

5. Leo the Great, *Tomus ad Flavianum* (DS 294): "Agit enim utraque forma cum alterius communione quod proprium est. Verbo scilicet operante quod Verbi est et carne exsequente quod carnis est." John Damascene, who was clearly influenced by Leo's *Tome*, reproduces the equivalent of this axiom all throughout his *De fide orthodoxa*, Bk. III, chs. 19–20 (in *De fide orthodoxa. Versions of Burgundio and Cerbanus*, ed. E. M. Buytaert [St. Bonaventure, N.Y.: Franciscan Institute, 1955], pp. 256-60).

Aquinas, the Communication of Idioms, and the Suffering of Christ

tures. And because this one subject (God the Word) possesses two natures, we can predicate of that one subject idioms or attributes of both natures. Cyril of Alexandria rightly perceived that the Nestorian view (which posits two subjects of predication in Christ: namely, Christ the man and the Son or the Word) rules out any mutual exchange in attributes. In contrast to this view he writes: "We must therefore confess that the Word has imparted the glory of the divine operation to His own flesh, while at the same time taking to Himself what belongs to the flesh."[6]

The God of Glory Is Said to Have Died

It is the foregoing logic that led the early Church Fathers, echoing St. Paul's assertion in 1 Corinthians 2:8 that "the Lord of Glory was crucified," to proclaim nearly from the outset the great paradoxical, and seemingly oxymoronic, truth relative to the theme of the present volume: God has suffered and died in Jesus Christ. The Fathers speak as one voice on this as from a resounding chorus: Ignatius of Antioch holds "God the Word . . . was crucified in reality, and not in appearance, not in imagination, not in deceit, and he truly died"; Melito of Sardis (†190) writes "God has been murdered" and "the impassible suffers . . . [and] the immortal dies"; Origen asserts "the Son of God is said to have died"; Athanasius affirms "the Word undergoes death"; Gregory of Nazianzus speaks of "God crucified"; Cyril of Alexandria proclaims "the Word of God suffered in flesh"; Ambrose professes "the Lord of majesty is said to have been crucified"; and John Damascene, writing against the Aphthartodocetic denial of Christ's corruptibility and passibility, asserts "the God of glory was crucified."[7] Indeed, the Nicene-Constantinopolitan creed has itself formally

---

6. Cyril of Alexandria, *De incarn. unigen.* (PG 75, col. 1241); cited in J. N. D. Kelly, *Early Christian Doctrines*, p. 322. For an overview of the communication of idioms in Cyril of Alexandria, cf. Thomas Weinandy, *Does God Suffer?*, pp. 182-206. Cf. as well Peter Parente et al., "'Communicatio Idiomatum' (Communication of Idioms)," pp. 51-52.

7. Ignatius of Antioch, *Letter to Trallians*, ch. 10; Melito of Sardis, *Peri Pascha*, 96.711-15, and frag. 13.14-19; Origen, *De princ.* 2.6.3 (cited in Johannes Quasten, *Patrolog. Vol. II*, p. 81); Athanasius, *Or. Arian.* 1.42 (cited in Johannes Quasten, *Patrology. Vol. III*, 75); Gregory of Nazianzus, *Or.* 45.29; Cyril of Alexandria, *Anath.* 12; Ambrose, *De fide*, 2.58 (these last three are cited, respectively, in J. N. D. Kelly, *Early Christian Doctrines*, pp. 298, 322, and 336); John Damascene, *De fide orth.*, Bk. III, ch. 4 (ed. Buytaert, p. 182), cited by Aquinas in *Summa*

canonized this particular formulation of the communication of idioms when it professes belief "in the only Son of God, eternally begotten of the Father, God from God, light from light, true God from true God," the true God who "became incarnate, became man" and who "suffered, died, and was buried."[8] In short, it is *de fide* to profess God as having suffered and died.

Yet the careful wording of the Fathers alerts us to the *qualified* manner of expressing this truth: God *the Word* has suffered and died, that is, God the Word *as incarnate* has undergone in his humanity what God cannot undergo in his divine nature, as Cyril of Alexandria observes.[9] So, yes, God has suffered and died, but *not* in his impassible divine nature.[10] We predicate suffering (passibility) and death of God but only in virtue of the humanity he, in the person of the Word, joins to himself in a union of hypostasis. We predicate suffering and death of God as the subject, the hypostasis, of an assumed humanity. God the Word communicates to his divine nature attributes of his assumed humanity (such as suffering and death) because he is the subject of that human nature (just as God the Word communicates to his assumed humanity attributes of his divine nature, such as being worthy of adoration).[11]

But let us be clear: there is no *direct* exchange of attributes from one nature to the other; rather, the exchange occurs in virtue of the hypostasis, that is, insofar as each nature subsists in the same hypostasis or subject.

---

theologiae (hereafter cited as *ST*) III, q. 16, a. 4, *sed contra*. It is strange that in his survey of patristic literature on the christological side of the question of divine suffering, Joseph M. Hallman (*The Descent of God: Divine Suffering in History and Theology* [Minneapolis: Fortress Press, 1991]) never once refers to the communication of idioms. For an exegetical treatment of the notion of "God crucified," cf. Richard Bauckham, *God Crucified: Monotheism and Christology in the New Testament* (Grand Rapids: Eerdmans, 1998), esp. pp. 69-77.

8. Thomas makes this observation already in his commentary on Peter Lombard's *Sentences,* Bk. III (hereafter cited as III *Sent.*), d. 7, q. 2, a. 1, *sed contra*.

9. Cyril of Alexandria, *Ep.* 4; 45 (PG 77, cols. 48 and 236); cited in Kelly, *Early Christian Doctrines,* p. 322.

10. Some trends in modern theology wish to argue that Christ's suffering does indeed imply passibility in the divine nature itself. For a good and influential example of this, cf. Jürgen Moltmann, *The Crucified God,* trans. R. A. Wilson and John Bowden (New York: Harper & Row, 1974); Moltmann (pp. 228-31) does not conceal his misgivings concerning Chalcedonian language, specifically the doctrine of Christ's two natures, and, as Bruce Marshall's essay shows, Moltmann insists that Christ's cry of dereliction from the cross belongs to Christ's divine nature itself.

11. Michel, "Idiomes (communication des)," col. 595.

While it remains entirely true, then, to speak of a "passible God," of a "crucified God," we must understand this to mean "but only in the person of the Word *qua* incarnate": "in the mystery of the Incarnation," Aquinas observes, "we say that the Son of God suffered, yet we do not say that the divine nature suffered."[12] God enters into the mystery of human suffering *only* on account of his becoming the subject of human predication, that is, only on account of his assuming a passible human nature and having it subsist in the divine person of the Son.

With this segue to Aquinas, we turn to consideration of the thought of this thirteenth-century Master and of his appropriation of the communication of idioms, understood in light of his view on Christ's unique mode or manner of being, and of the impact this bears on his theology of Christ's agony in the garden of Gethsemane.

The Communication of Idioms in Aquinas

Of the Fathers listed above in whom we find christological use of the communication of idioms — Ignatius of Antioch, Tertullian, Origen, Hilary of Poitiers, Athanasius, Cyril of Jerusalem, Gregory of Nazianzus, Gregory of Nyssa, Ambrose, Epiphanius, Augustine, Cyril of Alexandria, Leo the Great, Pseudo-Dionysius, and John Damascene — all were known to Aquinas and influenced the shaping of his Christology. (Damascene is his preferred *auctoritas* when treating the communication of idioms, but he also cites Athanasius, Gregory of Nazianzus, Cyril of Alexandria, Ambrose, Augustine, Leo the Great, and Pseudo-Dionysius.)[13]

St. Thomas is remembered, after all, for having the custom of going from Dominican priory to priory digesting different works, especially those of the Fathers, and of procuring the best possible texts and translations for himself.[14] He is also remembered for enjoying singular thirteenth-century

---

12. *ST* III, q. 16, a. 5, ad 1.

13. These patristic citations come in Thomas's treatment of the communication of idioms in *ST* III, q. 16, and q. 46, a. 12. In Aquinas's writing on the communication of idioms at the beginning of his career in III *Sent.*, d. 7, qq. 1-2, he cites only Augustine, Pseudo-Dionysius, and Damascene, testifying to the patristic amplification of the post-Orvieto writings, as shall be explained immediately below.

14. This is noted by Jean-Pierre Torrell, *Saint Thomas Aquinas: The Person and His Work*, trans. R. Royal (Washington, D.C.: Catholic University Press of America, 1996), p. 140,

access to patristic writings and to the decrees of the early christological councils while serving at the papal court in Orvieto from 1261 to 1265. Scholars have observed how the fruits of this firsthand unique access to patristic and conciliar texts appear in his post-Orvieto writings, notably in the *Catena aurea* (written between 1264 and 1268) and in the *Tertia Pars* of the *Summa theologiae* (penned between 1272 and 1273).[15] In this latter work a veritable burgeoning of patristic references, which is not seen in his earlier works, appears in Aquinas's writings — including references to certain Greek Fathers cited for the first time in the Latin West.[16] Little wonder con-

---

and M.-D. Chenu, *Toward Understanding Saint Thomas,* trans. A.-M. Landry and D. Hughes (Chicago: Henry Regnery Co., 1964), pp. 47-48. Cf. as well Thomas F. O'Meara, *Thomas Aquinas, Theologian* (Notre Dame: University of Notre Dame Press, 1997), pp. 22-24. For the role of the patristic voice in Aquinas's theology, cf. C. G. Geenen, "The Place of Tradition in the Theology of St. Thomas," *Thomist* 15 (1952): 110-35; C. G. Geenen, "Saint Thomas et les Pères," in "Thomas d'Aquin (saint)," *Dictionnaire de théologie catholique* 15, 1 (1946), cols. 738-62; C. G. Geenen, "Le fonti patristiche come 'autorità' nella teologia di San Tommaso," *Sacra Doctrina* 20, no. 77 (1975): 7-17; Hermann Diepen, "La critique du baslisme selon saint Thomas d'Aquin," *Revue Thomiste* 50 (1950): 82-118 and 290-329; Ignaz Backes, *Die Christologie des hl. Thomas von Aquin und die griechischen Kirchenväter* (Paderborn: Ferdinand Schöningh Verlag, 1931); and Leo J. Elders, "Thomas Aquinas and the Fathers of the Church," in *The Reception of the Church Fathers in the West: From the Carolingians to the Maurists,* vol. 1, ed. I. Backes (Leiden: Brill, 1997), pp. 337-66.

15. The key study on this is Louis Bataillon, "Saint Thomas et les Pères: De la *Catena* à la *Tertia Pars,*" in *Ordo sapientiae et amoris.* Image et message de saint Thomas d'Aquin à travers les récentes études historiques, herméneutiques et doctrinales. Hommage au Professeur Jean-Pierre Torrell O.P. à l'occasion de son 65ᵉ anniversaire, ed. C.-J. Pinto de Oliveira (Fribourg: Editions Universitaires, 1993), pp. 15-36. According to Ignatius T. Eschmann ("A Catalogue of St. Thomas' Works: Bibliographical Notes," in Etienne Gilson, *The Christian Philosophy of St. Thomas Aquinas,* trans. L. K. Shook [New York: Random House, 1956], pp. 381-430, at 397), the *Catena aurea* "marks a turning point in the development of Aquinas's theology." Jean-Pierre Torrell (*Saint Thomas Aquinas: The Person and His Work,* p. 139) agrees. This is borne out in Thomas's handling of the communication of idioms in *ST* III, q. 16 (and q. 46, a. 12), where he cites five additional patristic sources from the three he cites in III *Sent.,* d. 7, qq. 1-2, as already observed. For the dating of the *Catena aurea* and the *Tertia Pars,* cf. Torrell, *Saint Thomas Aquinas,* pp. 333-38. For an enlightening study on the conciliar impact of the Orvieto years on Aquinas's theology, cf. C. G. Geenen, "The Council of Chalcedon in the Theology of St. Thomas," in *From an Abundant Spring: The Walter Farrell Memorial Volume of 'The Thomist,'* ed. Staff of *The Thomist* (New York: P. J. Kenedy, 1952), pp. 172-217.

16. Louis Bataillon ("Saint Thomas et les Pères," p. 16) notes, for instance, that Victor of Antioch (fifth century) and the Byzantine exegete Theophylact (†1108) are among the various authorities cited in the *Catena aurea* who were unknown in the Latin West before the publication of this work.

temporary scholars of Aquinas like Jean-Pierre Torrell have labored to recover the deep patristic (and biblical) undercurrents that run throughout St. Thomas's entire theology.[17]

In the comprehensive Christology he forges in the *Tertia Pars* of the *Summa,* Aquinas treats the communication of idioms amidst a series of questions devoted to what he terms the *consequentia unionis* (qq. 16-26), that is, the logical and necessary consequences of the Word's assumption of a true and integral human nature. The first such consequence he lists is the communication of idioms (treated in q. 16). Almost immediately thereafter Thomas examines other such *consequentia unionis* as Christ's unity of will and Christ's prayer, treated in qq. 18 and 21 respectively, wherein we find his reflections on Jesus' agony in the garden of Gethsemane.

In point of fact, these latter treatments of Christ's unity of will and of his prayer are not to be seen as simple additions to a list of consequences of the incarnation beginning with the communication of idioms. Rather, in the organic, cohesive study of Christ to which most of the *Tertia Pars* is devoted, q. 16 sets the stage for qq. 18 and 21. The upshot is that Christ's agony in the garden is to be examined *in light of* the communication of idioms. Also setting the stage for qq. 18 and 21, as indeed for the entire treatment of the *consequentia unionis* itself, is Thomas's study on Christ's unique mode or manner of being which appears in the opening queries of the *Tertia Pars.* Aquinas's treatment of Christ's agony in the garden, in other words, is meant to be understood not only in light of the communication of idioms, but in light of his theology of Christ's unique mode of being as well.

That Thomas expects his reader to understand this is almost certainly beyond doubt. Yet such an expectation is often lost on contemporary readers of Aquinas who read the *Summa* as if it were a modern work, namely, from one argument to the next or one article to the next without any thought of a common thread uniting the various *quaestiones* together, let alone uniting the whole in a marvelous *ordo disciplinae,* that is, in a grand, organically orchestrated masterpiece.

---

17. As for the biblical current, Thomas himself writes in *ST* I, q. 36, a. 2, ad 1: "we should not say anything about God that is not found in sacred Scripture, either explicitly or implicitly." On this point, Etienne Gilson (*Les tribulations de Sophie* [Paris: J. Vrin, 1967], p. 47) observes how "the entire theology of St. Thomas is a commentary on the Bible; he advances no conclusion without basing it somehow on the word of sacred Scripture, which is the Word of God" (translation mine).

For, if it is true that Aquinas intends his treatment of Christ's agony in Gethsemane to be understood in light of his theology of the communication of idioms and of Christ's unique mode of being — both of which exhibit a profound debt to the patristic witness as well as an originality and synthesis that characterize so markedly Thomas's thought — he does not make this explicit. The purpose of the remainder of this essay, then, is to make explicit the way in which this most poignant moment in the life of Jesus, via Aquinas's theology of the communication of idioms and of Christ's hypostatic mode of being, helps us place a wholly concrete, existential face on the doctrine of God's suffering, of God's passibility.

II. Jesus' Agony in the Garden

Seared into the imagination of all readers of the Gospels is the scene of Jesus' anguish in Gethsemane. As Mark 14:32-36 (RSV) recounts for us:

> And they went to a place which was called Gethsemane; and he said to his disciples, "Sit here, while I pray." And he took with him Peter and James and John, and began to be greatly distressed and troubled. And he said to them, "My soul is very sorrowful, even to death; remain here, and watch." And going a little farther, he fell on the ground and prayed that, if it were possible, the hour might pass from him. And he said, "Abba, Father, all things are possible to thee; remove this cup from me; yet not what I will, but what thou wilt."

At the risk of understatement, this scene has perplexed commentators throughout the ages. The perplexity arises not only from its presentation of an apparent clash of wills between Jesus and the Father, but also from the shocking display of acute human weakness exhibited by Jesus, namely, the undergoing of real "fear" or "distress" (ἐκθαμβεῖσθαι, or *pavere* in the Vulgate), "anguish" (ἀδημονεῖν, *taedere*) and "sorrow" (περγιλυπός, *tristis*), which not only Mark but all the Evangelists do not hesitate to depict (cf. Matt. 26:36-39; Luke 12:20; John 13:21). In point of fact, the display of emotional turmoil seems to introduce moral discord within Jesus' human soul, which links it with the clash of wills between Jesus and the Father, since this turmoil appears to act as the very source of this clash of wills.

On the issue of Jesus' display of intense human emotion, Arianism provides a convenient escape. Arianism takes this scene, and, indeed, Jesus' passibility as a whole, as sufficient proof that the Son is not equal to the Father (i.e., Jesus is not divine), since God cannot be subject to passibility (which implies mutability).[18] As Thomas Weinandy has noted, however, Arius's error consists in his conceiving of the person of the Word as having united himself *not* to a human body and a human soul *together* (i.e., to an integral human nature) but to a human body *alone,* in such wise that the Word *takes the place of* a human soul and thus joins himself to a body *after the manner of* the soul's union with the body: "in conceiving the union in such a manner," Weinandy concludes, "the experiences of the flesh were placed within the very nature of the Son. Arius rightly perceived that this would entail that the Son of God changed his nature in becoming man and so was passible within his new fleshly existence."[19]

Monothelitism supplies a way out of the dilemma of a clash of wills between Jesus and the Father by simply denying the presence of a human will in Christ. Yet, in countering the monothelite view (which the Third Council of Constantinople would officially condemn in 680-81), Maximus the Confessor (†662) offers a distinction between various types of willing in order to show (1) that Jesus' very surrender to the will of the Father gives evidence of his possession of a human will, and (2) that Jesus at the same time and without contradiction suffers an instinctive desire to forgo the Father's cup.[20] This distinction passes to John Damascene, who in turn be-

---

18. Cf. Eustathius of Antioch, in Michel Spanneut, *Recherches sur les écrits d'Eustache d'Antioche* (Lille: Facultés Catholiques, 1948), frag. 18 (101), 23 (102), 24 (102-3), 25 (103), 27 (103); and Joseph Torchia, "The Significance of the *Communicatio Idiomatum* in St. Augustine's Christology, with Special Reference to His Rebuttal of Later Arianism," pp. 308-9.

19. Weinandy, *Does God Suffer?*, p. 175, n. 5. Cf. as well Aloys Grillmeier, *Christ in Christian Tradition: From the Apostolic Age to Chalcedon (451)*, vol. 1, trans. John Bowden (2nd ed., Atlanta: John Knox Press, 1975), pp. 219-32.

20. Maximus the Confessor, *Opusc. I ad Marinum* (PG 91, cols. 12-28); *Disput. cum Pyrrho* (PG 91, col. 309). For more on Maximus's theology of the agony in the garden, as well as on monothelitism and how this heresy is condemned by the Third Council of Constantinople, cf. F.-M. Léthel, "La prière de Jésus à Gethsémani dans la controverse monothélite," in *Maximus Confesseur*. Actes du Symposium sur Maxime le Confesseur, ed. F. Heinzer and C. Schönborn (Fribourg: St.-Paul, 1982), pp. 207-14; F.-M. Léthel, *Théologie de l'agonie du Christ*. La liberté humaine du Fils de Dieu et son importance sotériologique mises en lumière par Saint Maxime le Confesseur (Paris: Editions du Cerf, 1979).

queaths it to the twelfth- and thirteenth-century scholastics, including Aquinas.[21] To this distinction we now turn our close attention.

Θέλησις and Βούλησις in the Garden

Maximus the Confessor's analysis is in fact based upon a distinction found within the Greek text of the New Testament itself. Whereas the English language does not distinguish between different types of willing, Koine Greek does, such as we see employed by Luke in his depiction of Jesus' prayer in Gethsemane: "Father, if you will (βούλει) it, remove this cup from me; nevertheless not my will (θέλημά), but yours be done" (Luke 22:42).[22] Luke's language in other words suggests two types of appetitive movements in Jesus, the one, θέλησις, a more spontaneous and naturally instinctive type of desire, and the other, βούλησις, a more reflective or deliberated type of willing.[23]

With Maximus the Confessor's exposition in hand, John Damascene reproduces the distinction in his highly influential *De fide orthodoxa*.[24]

---

21. Cf. Damascene, *De fide orth.*, Bk. III, chs. 14–19 (ed. Buytaert, pp. 213-59). P. Bonifatius Kotter (*Die Schriften des Johannes von Damaskos*, vol. 2 [Berlin and New York: Walter de Gruyter, 1973], p. xxix) has identified seventy passages in Damascene's *De fide orthodoxa* in which remarks on Christ's wills and energies can be traced to Maximus; cf. as well Aloys Grillmeier, *Christ in Christian Tradition: From Chalcedon to Justinian I*, vol. 2, pt. 1, trans. P. Allen and J. Cawte (Atlanta: John Knox Press, 1987), p. 76. For more on the influence of Maximus the Confessor on Damascene's Christology, cf. Keetje Rozemond, *La christologie de saint Jean Damascène* (Ettal: Buch-Kunstverlag Ettal, 1959), pp. 37-40; and M. Jugie, "Jean Damascène (saint)," *Dictionnaire de théologie catholique* 8, 1 (1947), cols. 693-751, at 698. Damascene's appropriation of this distinction is also somewhat reliant upon Nemesius of Emesa (c. 400), who had intimated the distinction in an anthropological study on the act of choice ("De electione") in his work *De natura hominis*, ch. 32, in *Némésius d'Émèse De natura hominis. Traduction de Burgundio de Pise*, ed. G. Verbeke and J. R. Moncho (Leiden: Brill, 1975), p. 127.

22. Matthew and Mark merely intimate this distinction, as Mark 14:36 reads, "not what I will (θέλω), but what thou wilt (ἀλλὰ τί σύ)," with Matthew 26:39 doing the same.

23. The classic exegetical study on this distinction is Paul Joüon, "Les verbes βούλομαι et θελω dans le Nouveau Testament," *Revue des Sciences Religieuses* 30 (1940): 227-38.

24. In *De fide orth.*, Bk. III, ch. 23 (ed. Buytaert, pp. 265-66), Damascene affirms "natural fear" *(timor naturalis)* in Jesus, while ruling out "reflective fear" *(timor cogitationis)*. Also, in Bk. II, ch. 22 (ed. Buytaert, pp. 135-40), Damascene explains, "θέλησις and βούλησις are two different things. . . . θέλησις is the natural and vital appetite of nature, [while] βούλησις,

Most late twelfth- and early thirteenth-century scholastics, beginning with Peter Lombard and encompassing Hugh of St. Victor, Alexander of Hales, Albert the Great, and Bonaventure, appropriate to varying degrees Damascene's use of the distinction.[25] But it is Aquinas who gives its classic scholastic expression, penned already in his commentary on the *Sentences:* "In Christ there was both a *voluntas ut natura* [an instinctive type of willing], which equates with θέλησις, and a *voluntas ut ratio* [a deliberative type of willing], which corresponds to βούλησις."[26]

Aquinas's theology of Christ's agony in the garden of Gethsemane follows, then, in the tradition, especially, of John Damascene and Maximus the Confessor. What is new with him is the specifically Aristotelian resonance he gives to this notion of willing *ut natura* and willing *ut ratio* (even if the distinction in both Maximus and Damascene bears the influence of the Stagirite's thought), particularly as it relates to Jesus. What also is new are the implications that Aquinas's theology of the communication of idioms, understood in light of Christ's unique mode of being, bear on this twofold distinction in willing. We shall now examine these two novel developments.

---

which is a kind of θέλησις, is the rational appetite for some thing." I quote the terms of Burgundio of Pisa's Latin translation of Damascene's work, since this is the one known to Aquinas. (Though Cerbanus had completed a Latin translation of the *De fide orthodoxa* in 1145, widespread Latin familiarity with Damascene's work would not come until Burgundio's translation in 1153-54.)

25. For Peter Lombard (III *Sent.*, d. 17, ch. 2, in *Magistri Petri Lombardi Sententiae in IV libris distinctae*, ed. Collegii S. Bonaventurae ad Claras Aquas [Grottaferrata: Editiones Collegii S. Bonaventurae ad Claras Aquas, 1971-81], vol. 2, pp. 106-7], Christ's "fear of his suffering and death" issued from his sensitive affect rather than his rational affect. Here Lombard grounds his thought somewhat in the anonymous *Summa sententiarum* (produced by the school of St. Victor shortly after 1137), ch. 17 (PL 176, col. 76). Hugh of St. Victor (*De quatuor voluntatibus in Christo* [PL 176, col. 841]) speaks of a "will of pity" *(voluntas pietatis)* in Christ, which Aquinas (III *Sent.*, d. 17, a. 1, sol. 3, ad 6; a. 3, sol. 4, ad 2; and *ST* III, q. 18, a. 3, ad 3) takes as equating with *voluntas ut natura.* Alexander of Hales reproduces Damascene's "natural fear" and "reflective fear" distinction in his *Quaestiones disputatae 'antequam esset frater,'* q. 16, *De passibilitate animae Christi et Adae*, disp. 2, mem. 4, n. 50 (Quaracchi, Florence: Collegium S. Bonaventurae, 1960, vol. 19), p. 247; cf. as well his *Summa theologiae (Summa halensis)*, Bk. III, inq. 1, tr. 5, q. 1, mem. 2, ch. 1, a. 2 (ed. Quaracchi, vol. 4), pp. 200-201. Albert affirms that Jesus' prayer in Gethsemane concerns his *oratio ut est natura* in III *Sent.*, d. 17, a. 7. Bonaventure is the first to appropriate directly Damascene's θέλησις/βούλησις distinction and render it as *voluntas naturalis/voluntas deliberationis* in his III *Sent.*, d. 17, a. 1, q. 1, *sed contra* 3 (ed. Quaracchi, p. 366).

26. III *Sent*, d. 17, a. 1, sol. 3, ad 1.

Christ's Twofold Appetitive Ordering

When he comes to the question of Christ's unity of will in *Tertia,* q. 18, Aquinas launches immediately into a discussion on the different types of willing in Jesus' human nature. Armed with an anti-docetic adherence to the integrity of Christ's full humanity and with an appreciation of the objective goodness of God's entire created order, Aquinas affirms the presence, "as together with whatever belongs to animal nature," of a sensitive appetite in Christ, that is, of an internal animal-like ordering to bodily goods or evils perceived by the senses.[27] This appetite acts as the seat of human passibility, that is, the seat of human emotion, human affectivity, as Aquinas defines the emotions (or the passions) as movements of this lower animal-like inclination to sense goods or evils.[28] In short, by virtue of his

---

27. *ST* III, q. 18, a. 2 (cf. III *Sent.,* d. 17, a. 1, sol. 2); Thomas begins this *corpus* with the remark: "the Son of God assumed human nature together with everything pertaining to the perfection of human nature. Now in human nature is included animal nature." Whereas modern rationalism has implanted in the modern mindset a disdain for what is inferior and animal-like in us, since this is seen to constitute the "less than human," such disdain is foreign to Aquinas. The term "sensitive appetite" goes back to Aristotle (*De anima,* Bk. II, ch. 3 [414b1-2]) and Nemesius of Emesa (*De nat. homin.,* ch. 15 [ed. Verbeke-Moncho, p. 93]), but is also found in Damascene (*De fide orth.,* Bk. II, ch. 22 [ed. Buytaert, p. 132]) and Albert the Great (*De homine,* q. 68, a. 1). For an extensive treatment of Christ's full human affectivity in Aquinas, cf. my own *The Passions of Christ's Soul in the Theology of St. Thomas Aquinas,* "Beiträge zur Geschichte der Philosophie und Theologie des Mittelalters. Neue Folge, 61" (Münster: Aschendorff, 2002); and in Alexander of Hales, cf. Boyd Taylor Coolman, "The Salvific Affectivity of Christ," *Thomist* 71 (2007): 1-38. For more on Aquinas's theology of Christ's full humanity, cf. my own "The Humanity of Christ, the Incarnate Word," in *The Theology of Thomas Aquinas,* ed. J. Wawrykow and R. van Nieuwenhove (Notre Dame: University of Notre Dame Press, 2005), pp. 252-76, and "Anti-Docetism in Aquinas's *Super Ioannem:* St. Thomas as Defender of the Full Humanity of Christ," in *Reading John with St. Thomas Aquinas: Theological Exegesis and Speculative Theology,* ed. M. Dauphinais and M. Levering (Washington, D.C.: Catholic University of America Press, 2005), pp. 254-76. Among those Thomist scholars who have underscored Aquinas's anti-docetism, Jean-Pierre Torrell merits singular mention for his *Le Christ en ses mystères. La vie et l'oeuvre de Jésus selon saint Thomas d'Aquin,* 2 vols. (Paris: Desclée, 1999). Cf. as well Ghislain Lafont, *Structures et méthode dans la "Somme théologique" de saint Thomas d'Aquin* (Paris: Les Editions du Cerf, 1996), p. 349.

28. In *ST* I-II, q. 22, a. 3, *sed contra,* Thomas cites John Damascene's definition of passion (found in *De fide orth.,* Bk. II, ch. 22 [ed. Buytaert, p. 132]; cf. as well Nemesius of Emesa, *De nat. homin.,* ch. 15 [ed. Verbeke-Moncho, p. 93]) as "a movement of the sensitive appetitive faculty in response to the perception of something good or bad." Contrary to its

sensitive appetite, Jesus was subject to an affective type of willing, a type of willing connected to the desire for bodily goods.

Like all humans, Jesus enjoyed not merely an affective animal-like type of willing, but a higher rational one as well. His humanity was endowed with the higher internal appetitive ordering of the will to the universal good, to the *summum bonum*.[29] This twofold appetitive ordering in the human being, the one sensitive and the other rational, results in an interplay between the two that casts a whole new dynamic on the human experience of emotion, since "in man," John of St. Thomas notes (†1644), "[the passions are] governable by reason."[30] Following Aristotle, in fact, Aquinas

---

usage in modern parlance, where it often connotes fits of affective vehemence, the term passion *(passio),* for Aquinas, means simple sensate (or lower animal-like) movements of the soul. Thomas also notes in *De veritate,* q. 26, a. 3, that in a broad sense passion simply means that which is acted upon, or that which occurs when something is received and something else is taken away, yet "strictly speaking, passion is only in the sense appetitive part." Nonetheless, it is on account of the broad sense of passion that Thomas holds that passion in its most proper sense implies a "change from a natural state to a contrary one" *(De veritate,* q. 26, a. 8), or when "a thing recedes from what is suitable to it. . . . Hence, sorrow is more properly a passion than joy" *(ST* I-II, q. 22, a. 1). In this sense, suffering and passion are nearly equivalent. Aquinas also teaches that a passion necessarily involves a bodily change or transmutation; cf. *ST* I-II, q. 17, a. 7; q. 22, a. 3.

29. "Now the will pertains to the perfection of human nature, being one of its natural powers, along with the intellect. Hence we must say that the Son of God assumed a human will, together with human nature." Aquinas, *ST* III, q. 18, a. 1. Earlier when considering the incarnated *assumpta* (the Word's assumption of the essential elements of human nature) in q. 5, aa. 1 and 4, Thomas explains: "[I]t pertains to the essence of human nature to have a true body. . . . (Christ) must consequently have assumed a real body. . . . [Further] since the body is proportioned to the soul as matter to its proper form, it is not true human flesh if it is not completed by a human, i.e., rational, soul."

30. John of St. Thomas (John Poinsot), *Introduction to the* Summa Theologiae *of Thomas Aquinas. Isagogue of John of St. Thomas,* Bk. II, Pt. I-II, trans. Ralph McInerny (South Bend, Ind.: St. Augustine's Press, 2004), p. 65. Aquinas himself writes in *ST* I-II, q. 24, a. 1, ad 1: "Considered in themselves the passions are common to both man and animal, but as commanded by reason *(a ratione imperantur),* they are proper to man." As Servais Pinckaers ("Reappropriating Aquinas's Account of the Passions," in *The Pinckaers Reader: Renewing Thomistic Moral Theology,* ed. John Berkman and C. S. Titus [Washington, D.C.: Catholic University of America Press, 2005], pp. 273-87, at 276) observes: "the problem of the moral quality of the emotions situates them in relation to reason and will, and attributes to them a dimension they do not have among the animals. St. Thomas considers them as human emotions, integrated in the human composite." For more on this, cf. Stephen Loughlin, "Similarities and Differences Between Human and Animal Emotion in Aquinas's Thought," *Thomist* 65 (2001): 45-65.

insists that excellence in the moral life requires, through the work of moral virtue, the integration of our lower affective movements into the higher life of reason. Moral virtue owns the task of "humanizing" the emotions.[31]

Finally, unlike all humans, Jesus, as Son of God, also possessed a divine will in virtue of his divine nature: "by the assumption of human nature," explains Thomas, "the Son of God suffered no diminution of what pertains to his divine nature, to which it belongs to have a will."[32] This is the one identical divine will shared by all three persons of the Holy Trinity. Consistent with the teaching of Constantinople III, Aquinas affirms that, because he was sinless and because the subject of his human willing was a divine person, there was always perfect accord between Jesus' higher rational will and his divine will.[33]

"Rational by Participation"

We return to the twofold appetitive ordering in the human being. Thomas maintains that when moral virtue succeeds in humanizing the emotions, that is, when our lower affective movements speak the same voice as reason, our emotions or passions become, in a phrase borrowed from Aristotle, "rational by participation."[34] This holds true especially for Christ,

31. For Aristotle (*Nic. Ethics*, Bk. II, ch. 6 [1106b15-16]), moral virtue "is concerned with passions and actions," and for Aquinas (*ST* I-II, q. 59, aa. 4-5; and q. 60, a. 3), the passions constitute the proper "matter" of the moral virtues. For similar positions, cf. Nemesius of Emesa, *De nat. homin.*, ch. 31 (ed. Verbeke-Moncho, p. 126); and Albert the Great, *De bono*, tr. 1, q. 5, a. 1, ad 4 (ed. Coloniensis, p. 74).

32. *ST* III, q. 18, a. 1.

33. *ST* III, q. 18, a. 5: "In his will as reason *(voluntas ut ratio)* he always willed the same as God. . . . For he willed in his reason that the divine will should be fulfilled." According to Constantinople III (680-81), "the two natural wills were not in opposition, as the impious heretics say, far from it, since his human will followed, and did not resist or struggle against, but was in fact subject to his divine and all-powerful will." DS 556; *Decrees of the Ecumenical Councils*, ed. Tanner, vol. 1, p. 128.

34. Aquinas, *In Ethic.*, Bk. I, lect. 13 (n. 242), and Aristotle, *Nic. Ethics*, Bk. I, ch. 13 (1102b13-14), where the Stagirite also affirms that in the fully virtuous person, "every act [of the lower sensitive appetite] harmonizes (*homophonia* [literally 'is of one voice']) with reason." Thomas outlines this position in much greater depth in three principal *loci*: *ST* I-II, q. 56, a. 4; *Quaestiones disputatae de virtutibus in communi*, a. 4 ("Whether the irascible and concupiscible appetites can be the subject of virtue"), which was written just after the completion of the *Prima Secundae Pars* of the *Summa;* and III *Sent.*, d. 33, q. 2, a. 4, qla. 2. The

since Jesus enjoyed perfect moral harmony between his two appetitive orderings, the one to lower created bodily goods and the other to the universal good, the good of reason. And Aquinas, bolstered by the affirmation of the Second Council of Constantinople (553) that Jesus was "not troubled by the passions of the soul nor the desires of the flesh," does not hesitate in introducing this notion of rational by participation into his opening remarks on Christ's possession of a sensitive appetite in *Tertia,* q. 18.[35]

In the backdrop of this view on the sensitive appetite becoming rational by participation stands the Aristotelian notion of *principatus politicus.*[36] By this term Aristotle (and Thomas after him) liken the type of relationship that exists between our highest faculties, reason and will, and our lower sensitive appetite to an association of governance. Although reason and will retain a natural "power to command" *(imperium)* our lower animal-like ordering to bodily goods, this power is not absolute. The sensitive appetite retains its own quasi-autonomy, as it were. For the emotions can "talk back" to our highest faculties, they can obey (or disobey) on their own reason and will's *imperium.* This situation contrasts with that of our bodily limbs, which always carry out the commands of reason and will, as the hand, the foot, the arm, the neck will always observe what the mind commands of them and would never, on their own, resist the commands of reason and will. The relationship between our bodily limbs and reason and will better approximates the political model of a despotic association.

Principatus politicus means, then, that the lower appetite and the emo-

<hr>

classic study of this issue is M.-D. Chenu, "Les passions vertueuses. L'anthropologie de saint Thomas," *Revue Philosophique de Louvain* 72 (1974): 11-18; and M.-D. Chenu, "Body and Body Politic in the Creation Spirituality of Thomas Aquinas," *Listening* 13 (1974): 214-32. For another excellent study on this issue, cf. William Mattison, "Virtuous Anger? From Questions of *Vindicatio* to the Habituation of Emotion," *Journal of the Society of Christian Ethics* 24 (2004): 159-79; and Bonnie Kent, *The Virtues of the Will: The Transformation of Ethics in the Late Thirteenth Century* (Washington, D.C.: Catholic University of America Press, 1995). This issue is also the subject of my own "The Passions and the Moral Life: Appreciating the Originality of Aquinas," in *The Thomist* (July 2007): 419-50.

35. Constantinople II, twelfth anathema (DS 434; *Decrees of the Ecumenical Councils,* ed. Tanner, vol. 1, p. 119). For Aquinas's profound knowledge of the teaching of the Second Council of Constantinople, cf. Martin Morard, "Une source de saint Thomas d'Aquin: Le Deuxième Concile de Constantinople (553)," *Revue des Sciences philosophiques et théologiques* 81 (1977): 21-56.

36. The classic text from Aquinas affirming this comes in *ST* I, q. 81, a. 3, ad 2; and from Aristotle in *Politics,* Bk. I, ch. 5 (1254b2-5).

tions which arise from it can be likened to free subjects who participate in limited ways, namely, through their free consent, in the governance of a sovereign, the sovereign in this case being reason and will. Today we would say constitutional monarchy best corresponds to the type of political model to which Aquinas wishes to compare the "power to command" *(imperium)* exercised by reason and will over the sensitive appetite.

In likening the sensitive appetite to a free subject under a sovereign, Thomas does not mean to suggest that the lower appetite is "free" in the same univocal sense as the rational appetite (the will), our power of free choice, is free. At the same time, it is not merely a metaphorical use of the term *free* either. Aquinas truly believes that the dynamic interplay between our higher faculties and our lower ones is such that, through the work of moral virtue, reason and will penetrate into the very sensitive appetite and endow it with a real, albeit derived and partial, sharing in rationality and freedom. For Thomas, the lower appetite, our animal-like inclination to bodily goods, has the capability of becoming rational (and thus free) by participation.

Now, based on the fact that the sensitive appetite must give its consent (again, by participation) to the will's command that it carry out a judgment of right reason on the appropriateness (or inappropriateness) of a given movement of emotion (it is in this that an act of moral virtue consists), Aquinas concludes that the lower sensitive appetite can act as an *active principle,* as a *source,* of virtuous behavior.[37] Moral virtue, in other

---

37. This judgment of right reason on the appropriateness or inappropriateness of a given movement of passion is made in light of the truth of the human person and of how the sensible good in question is ordered to our highest good. For this the virtue of prudence is indispensable, since prudence allows right reason to know when a particular inclination to some sensed good falls in line with our ordering to the First Good. For an excellent study on right reason as the rule and measure of human acts, cf. Laurent Sentis, "La lumière dont nous faisons usage. La règle de la raison et la loi divine selon Thomas d'Aquin," *Revue des Sciences philosophiques et théologiques* 79 (1995): 49-69. Also, it is through moral virtue that such consent on the part of the lower appetite occurs. Thomas, with Aristotle, knows full well that it is possible to do the virtuous good, yet without the consent of the sensitive appetite. This defines the continent person, i.e., the person who acts virtuously but only after waging a struggle against disordered bodily desires. Cf. Aristotle, *Nic. Ethics,* Bk. I, ch. 13 (1102b17-19), and Bk. III, ch. 2 (1111b15); and Aquinas, *In Ethic.,* Bk. VII, lect. 9 (n. 1443) (trans. C. I. Litzinger [Notre Dame: Dumb Ox Books, 1993]). There is also the case of the incontinent person, i.e., the person who succumbs to his disordered bodily desires, and thus acts contrary to his principles, contrary to what he knows he ought to do. In short, it is only

words, succeeds in converting the very emotions themselves into virtue-oriented movements. This especially explains what Aquinas means by the sensitive appetite becoming, in its very act, "rational by participation." Not rational *per se,* the passions become rational by active, co-opted collaboration with reason and will; in this way Thomas considers them rational by participation.

Willing Ut Natura *and Willing* Ut Ratio *in Christ*

While the foregoing excursus on the moral quality of our lower animal-like ordering to bodily goods may seem to have taken us afield, this material forms the necessary preamble to Aquinas's treatment of Christ's agony in the garden.

In his exegesis on this Gospel scene, St. Thomas, in a conceptual move unique to him, carefully distinguishes between the fear Jesus experiences and his express will not to follow through with his impending death ("Father, if you will it, remove this cup from me"). While the first is confined to Christ's lower sensitive appetite (since fear properly speaking is a passion), the second encroaches, he says, upon both his sensitive appetite and his rational will. On Aquinas's account, in other words, there are two movements of soul in Christ (actually, three) in the garden, the one relating to fear and the other to his desire to forgo the Father's cup, and this latter desire is expressive of both his lower sense appetite and his will (thus comprising in itself two movements of soul). By doing this, the Dominican Master affirms the totality of Christ's internal (psychological) suffering, inasmuch as his suffering comprises both affective and spiritual dimensions.

To affirm *both* Christ's express desire, via his human will, not to die *and* the perfect conformity always uniting Christ's human and divine wills, Thomas appeals to the *voluntas ut natura* (θέλησις) and *voluntas ut ratio* (βούλησις) distinction. The former signifies not simply, as one might think, the animal-like sensitive appetite, but also the will (i.e., a spiritual faculty) as acting by natural instinct. *Voluntas ut natura* concerns "the pure and simple willing of the good before any kind of qualification," to

---

in the fully virtuous individual where the sensitive appetite can be said to be rational by participation; cf. Aquinas, *In Ethic.,* Bk. I, lect. 13 (n. 239), and Bk. VII, lect. 9 (n. 1453-4). For more on this, cf. my own "The Passions and the Moral Life," pp. 438-42.

quote Jean-Pierre Torrell, that is, the will's desire of its proper object — the good in itself — prior to any specification of the good.[38] *Voluntas ut ratio,* on the other hand, relates to the choice of the will as following upon the reflected deliberation of reason. It pertains to the will's choice of a particular good which reason, guided by prudence (and charity in Jesus' case) in its (reason's) comparison of the particular goods presented to it, has determined is best to favor.

What Jesus, therefore, spontaneously, naturally, and instinctively wills or desires is to spare his life — "Father, remove this cup from me" — yet what he actually *chooses* deliberatively, that is, what he wills "deep down" as based upon the judgment of right reason, is to fulfill the Father's will — "not my will, but yours be done." By willing *ut natura,* that is, by desiring the good in the form of the preservation of his life previous to any reasoned consideration, Jesus suffers internally (i.e., spiritually) and prays to have the cup removed from him. By willing *ut ratio,* that is, by choosing something in view of procuring a certain end (in this case, the redemption of the human race), Jesus at length embraces the Father's cup. There occurs, then, a clash of wills between Jesus and the Father (or between Christ's human and divine wills) at the level *not* of willing *ut ratio* but of willing *ut natura.* The perfect harmony between Christ's human and divine wills, this distinction suggests, requires unity between Christ's divine will (or the Father's will) and his human will *ut ratio,* not his human will *ut natura.* As Aquinas observes, "strictly speaking the human will is the will of reason [i.e., *voluntas ut ratio*], as we will absolutely what accords with reason's deliberation."[39] Or as Thomas writes elsewhere, in what represents his most significant passage on the matter:

> Christ allowed all the powers of the soul to be moved according to the order of their nature. It is clear that the will of sensuality [i.e., the sensitive appetite] naturally recoils from physical pain and bodily injury. In like manner, the will as nature [i.e., *voluntas ut natura*] rejects what is contrary to nature and what is evil in itself, such as death and the like. However, the will of reason [i.e., *voluntas ut ratio*] may at times choose these things [i.e., evil things] in relation to an end [i.e., in view of a cer-

---

38. J.-P. Torrell, *Le Christ en ses mystères. La vie et l'oeuvre de Jésus selon saint Thomas d'Aquin,* vol. 2, p. 360 (trans. mine). Cf. as well Colman O'Neill's translation of *ST* III, q. 18, a. 3 in *Summa theologiae,* vol. 50, *The One Mediator* (London: Blackfriars, 1965), p. 73.

39. *ST* III, q. 21, a. 4.

tain good], as when a man's will of sensuality, considered absolutely, re-coils from being burned, but which the will of reason may choose for the sake of health. . . . Hence, Christ clearly could will something other than what God willed by his will of sensuality and by his will *ut natura;* but by his will *ut ratio,* Christ always willed the same as God, which appears from what he says in Matt. 26:39: "Not as I will, but as you will." . . . Christ willed to fulfill the divine will, yet not by his will of sensuality, nor by his will *ut natura,* which responds to objects considered absolutely rather than to objects considered in relation to the divine will.[40]

As this passage makes plain, and as already highlighted, Aquinas does not make Jesus' express will to forgo his impending death a moment of purely spiritual anguish, but an affective one as well. Here, in fact, Thomas presupposes his view of the human being (which he ascribes here to Christ) as an integrated, participated whole, by which the various powers of the soul retain an intimate synergistic union with each other. Jesus' entire internal ordering to the good, both sensitive or animal-like *and* rational, gives rise to an instinctive recoiling from approaching violent death. His sensitive appetite, too, shrinks from a perceived evil, in this case, his bodily torture and death. In his treatment of Christ's prayer, Aquinas explicates well the affective dimension of Jesus' desire not to die:

> In saying, "Remove this cup from me," Christ indicates the natural movement of his lower appetite, whereby all naturally recoil from death and desire to preserve their life. In saying, "not my will, but yours be done," he expresses the movement of his higher reason, which considers all things in relation to the ordinances of divine wisdom. . . . Since prayer manifests desire . . . [when] Christ prayed that the Father's will might be done, he was expressing his absolute desire, whereas in praying that the cup might be removed from him, he expressed not what he desired absolutely, but what he desired in his lower part.[41]

---

40. *ST* III, q. 18, a. 5. Thomas offers essentially the same argument in III *Sent.,* d. 15, q. 2, a. 3, sol. 2. Cf. as well *De veritate,* q. 26, a. 9, ad 7; and *Lectura super Mattheum,* ch. 26, lect. 5.

41. Though this passage is from *Compendium theologiae,* ch. 233, it corresponds to Thomas's teaching on Christ's prayer as outlined in *ST* III, q. 21, a. 4.

Discord or Harmony of Soul in Christ?

With Aquinas having safeguarded the perfect conformity between Christ's divine and human wills by appeal to the *voluntas ut natura/voluntas ut ratio* distinction, the problem remains of a seeming clash, or even of a moral discord, between Jesus' lower sensitive powers, or his emotions, and his reason and will. As already seen, Aquinas sees Christ as the highest, even infallible, embodiment of what it means for the passions, via the work of moral virtue, to become rational by participation. In Christ we see the *summum exemplar perfectionis,* "the supreme model of perfection," as Thomas says in his commentary on John's Gospel, or the *exemplum virtutis,* "the model of virtue," to quote *Tertia,* q. 15, a. 1.[42] And where the passions are rational by participation, they speak the same voice as reason rather than speak back to reason.

Yet, by Aquinas's own admission, we seem to have a case here in the garden where Jesus' sensitive appetite speaks back to his reason, as it were. We appear, in other words, to have an example of the struggle of the flesh against the spirit in Jesus, the succumbing to which Peter, James, and John, at the moment of Jesus' return from his period of agony, appear to be guilty of: "And he came and found them sleeping, and he said to Peter, 'Simon, are you asleep? Could you not watch one hour? . . . [T]he spirit indeed is willing, but the flesh is weak'" (Mark 14:37).

The Christian theological tradition has employed the term "concupiscence," as a consequence of original sin, to refer to this contest of appetitive pulls in the human person, the one to bodily goods (the lower sensitive pull) and the other to our highest good, the good of reason (the superior intellectual pull). St. Paul poignantly describes this internal strife

---

42. *In Ioannem,* ch. 12, lect. 1 (n. 1604). A bit later in the same commentary (ch. 13, lect. 3 [n. 1781]), Thomas writes: "the example of a mere human being would not be an adequate model for the entire human race to imitate. . . . And so we were given the example of the Son of God, which cannot err *(quod est infallibile)* and which meets the needs of all human beings." Thomas writes the same in *Summa contra gentiles,* Bk. IV, ch. 54: "it was not possible to be infallibly certain of a mere man's goodness, since even the most holy men have at times been found wanting. So that man might be strengthened in virtue, it was therefore necessary for him to be taught virtue by the word and example of God incarnate." Here Aquinas points toward the position Vatican II will take in its Pastoral Constitution on the Church in the Modern World, *Gaudium et spes,* §22: "It is only in the mystery of the Incarnate Word that the mystery of man truly becomes clear. . . . Christ, the new Adam, fully discloses man to himself."

as a "war among his members" making him "not do the good he wants" (Rom. 7:14-24).[43] Do we have the same internal strife on display in Jesus' express desire to forgo the Father's cup? If so, how can such a desire give witness to Christ as the *summum exemplar perfectionis*? Put in other terms, when Aquinas elsewhere rules out the presence of concupiscence (as well as what the medieval schoolmen identify as the source of concupiscence, the *fomes peccati*) in the sinless Christ, is he simply laying aside this Gospel scene?[44]

To respond, we should bear in mind that, on Aquinas's account, Jesus' repulsion from death corresponds to the natural, instinctive, affective aversion to death that all animals (as with all creatures) possess; his aversion to death does not pertain to a fully elicited appetitive movement as such.[45]

---

43. In Aquinas the term *concupiscence* connotes a state of general disorder in the human condition, whereby the sensitive appetite remains inordinately inclined to lower, mutable goods. Cf. *ST* I-II, q. 82, a. 3 and a. 4, ad 1; q. 91, a. 6; *De malo*, qq. 3-4; and *De veritate*, q. 25, aa. 6-7. For a detailed analysis of this point, cf. M.-M. Labourdette, "Aux origines du péché de l'homme d'après saint Thomas d'Aquin," *Revue Thomiste* 85 (1985): 357-98, at 371-85; and my *The Passions of Christ's Soul in the Theology of St. Thomas Aquinas*, pp. 294-300.

44. "There was no conflict of appetites in Christ, or rebellion of the flesh against the spirit." Aquinas, *Comp. theol.*, ch. 232; cf. *ST* III, q. 19, a. 2. Jean-Hervé Nicolas (*Synthèse dogmatique. De la Trinité à la Trinité* [Fribourg: Editions Universitaires, 1985], p. 411) explains that "'concupiscence' presupposes peccability, [as it is marked by] a pronounced positive propensity to sin." Cf. *De veritate*, q. 24, aa. 12-13. For Christ's immunity to the *fomes peccati*, which signifies the affective spark to sin, or the inherent proclivity of the sensitive appetite to illicit goods, to be always ready to be prodded at an instant's notice to lunge after some object of sense desire irrespective of the commands of reason, cf. *ST* III, q. 15, a. 2; *Comp. theol.*, ch. 224; and III *Sent.*, d. 17, a. 1, sol. 2, ad 4. The term *fomes peccati* originates with the *Liber pancrisis* of William of Champeaux (†1121), if not earlier, and, beginning with Peter Lombard, the notion bears the influence of John Damascene's remark that "law of sin" in the human being signifies "the concupiscence and the sudden unforeseen movements of the body and of the irrational part of the soul." *De fide orth.*, Bk. IV, ch. 22 (ed. Buytaert, p. 359). For an overview of the twelfth-century development of the term *fomes peccati*, cf. Odon Lottin, *Psychologie et morale aux XIIe et XIIIe siècles*. Problèmes de morale: Pt. 3, vol. 4 (Gembloux, Belgium: J. Duculot, 1954), pp. 22-74. Those who, previous to Aquinas, exclude the *fomes peccati* from Christ include the unidentified Magister Willermus (from the early thirteenth century; cf. Walter Principe, "*Quaestiones* Concerning Christ from the First Half of the Thirteenth Century: II: *Quaestiones* from Douai Ms. 434: The Need of the Incarnation; The Defects Assumed by Christ," *Mediaeval Studies* 42 [1980]: 1-40, at 33, n. 3), Alexander of Hales (*Qu. disp. 'ant. esset frater,'* q. 16, disp. 3, mem. 3, n. 73 [ed. Quaracchi, p. 259]), Albert the Great (III *Sent.*, d. 17, a. 4), and Bonaventure (III *Sent.*, d. 15, a. 1, q. 2, *sed contra* 3 [ed. Quaracchi, p. 332]).

45. Cf. *ST* III, q. 14, a. 2, ad 1; q. 15, a. 7; and q. 21, a. 2.

Jesus' agony in the garden does not, strictly speaking, confront us with a movement of passion that resists the *imperium* of reason and will. Christ undergoes an instinctive aversion to death rather than a fully elicited affective desire not to follow through with his death. If his lower animal-like ordering to bodily goods experiences such a natural aversion to death, it is because the situation of *principatus politicus,* even in the case where moral virtue enjoys total reign, leaves room for instinctive impulses of affectivity. Such instinctive affective impulses are expressive of the sensitive appetite's quasi-autonomy. But even here such impulses, in Christ, are finalized by reason, that is, they are fully integrated into Christ's perfection in moral virtue before they reach the stage of a fully elicited movement of the lower appetite.

Before proceeding to the larger issue of suffering in God, we must give brief consideration to the final element of Thomas's exegesis on Christ's agony in the garden, namely, the *other* movement of soul Jesus experiences there: fear.

Fear, Agony, Dread in the Garden

"[T]here was an agony in Christ as regards the sensitive part, inasmuch as it implied a dread of coming trial," writes Aquinas, alluding to the passion of fear Jesus undergoes.[46] Later he affirms that Christ endured all suffering "in his soul, as from sorrow, weariness and fear, and in his body, from wounds and scourgings."[47] The reason Thomas insists upon delineating both fear of coming trial and desire to forgo the Father's cup is because fear and desire are distinct movements of the soul and are distinguished by their formal objects: desire responds to some good — in Jesus' case, the preservation of his life (or, ultimately, the salvation of the human race) — whereas fear regards an impending bodily evil perceived or imagined as difficult to avoid — namely, his violent bodily torture and death.[48]

---

46. *ST* III, q. 18, a. 6, ad 3; here Thomas refers to Damascene, *De fide orth.,* Bk. III, ch. 18 (ed. Buytaert, pp. 253-54). Aquinas's remarks on Christ's fear in the *Summa* presuppose the earlier treatment of the passion of fear he offers in I-II, qq. 41-44, which, in fact, appears amongst his much larger and nearly exhaustive treatise on the passions in I-II, qq. 22-48.

47. *ST* III, q. 46, a. 5.

48. "A passion of the soul is determined in type by its object. . . . [T]he object of fear is a future evil, which is difficult yet seemingly impossible to avoid." *ST* I-II, q. 41, a. 2.

In his treatise on Christ's passions in *Tertia,* q. 15, Aquinas devotes explicit attention to the passion of fear in Jesus (a. 7). Here the main thrust of his position centers on the fact that fear arises only when the possibility of escaping the impending evil exists. Since Jesus retains a glimmer of hope that his awaited fate may yet be avoided, he naturally experiences fear.[49] And since fear regards a future evil, this passion issues from the *imagined* reality of the future evil, which in Jesus' case concerns extreme bodily pain and death.[50] Aquinas also sees the timing of Jesus' agony in the garden, namely, a few short hours before the onset of bodily torment, as a result of the fact that fear becomes more acute and intense when the imminent evil appears "near at hand" *(malum propinquum)* rather than far removed.[51] Jesus suffers greatly on account of his fear, his dread, his sorrow, movements which, as Aquinas tells us, chiefly have the character of passion on account of the unsuitable or disagreeable state they induce.[52] At the same time, later in the *Summa* Thomas does not confine Christ's anguish merely to his affective side, but acknowledges a spiritual dimension to his anguish: "The cause of [Christ's] interior pain was, first of all, the sins of the human race . . . [as well as] the loss of his bodily life, which is naturally horrible to human nature."[53]

Further, whereas Thomas affirms that Christ's express desire to forgo the Father's cup issues from his sensitive appetite (as well as from his human will *ut natura*) as by natural instinct, the fear of bodily pain and death denotes something more. If Jesus' desire to have his life spared pertains to an instinctive and spontaneous *impulse* of affectivity, his fear over his impending death concerns a *fully elicited* movement of the sensitive appetite. That is, it concerns a passion in the proper sense of the term, since his fear does not involve a *direct* clash with the Father's will. For this reason, Thomas does not see the need to apply the *voluntas ut natura/voluntas ut*

---

49. "[T]he sensitive appetite naturally shrinks from bodily harm . . . through fear if it is yet to come. In this way, Christ experienced fear." *ST* III, q. 15, a. 7.

50. "[F]ear is a passion that arises from the imagination of an imminent evil. . . . [Hence] whatever removes the imagination of the future evil removes the fear also." *ST* I-II, q. 42, aa. 2 and 4. Cf. Aristotle, *Rhetoric,* Bk. II, ch. 5 (1382a21), cited in q. 42, a. 2: "Fear may be defined as a pain or disturbance due to the imagining of some destructive or painful future evil."

51. *ST* I-II, q. 43, a. 1; cf. as well q. 42, a. 5.

52. Cf. *ST* I-II, q. 22, a. 1; q. 41, a. 1; and *De veritate,* q. 26, a. 8.

53. *ST* III, q. 46, a. 6. Here Thomas also affirms that "(Christ's) soul, from its internal powers, apprehended most vehemently all the causes of sadness."

ratio distinction to Christ's experience of fear (here he departs from John Damascene, who for his part does affirm "natural fear" *(timor naturalis)* in Jesus but not "reflective fear" *(timor cogitationis)*.[54] At the same time, Aquinas is careful to point out that, whereas fear can often disrupt reason and will's *imperium* over the sensitive appetite, in no sense did this occur to Jesus the man of consummate moral virtue.[55]

The Soteriological Stakes

While Aquinas's exegesis of Christ's agony in the garden may leave itself open to further scrutiny, we need to stress that (1) Thomas takes the Gospel scene of Jesus' agony seriously and does not attempt to tone it down, explain it away, or otherwise anesthetize Jesus (as we find, say, in Hilary of Poitiers) from the experience of extreme anguish in the very depths of his soul, but (2) allows this agony the full weight that a consciously delineated Aristotelian psychology can bear on it.[56] This Aristotelian psychology, grafted onto a firm adherence to the Gospel and patristic witnesses, allows Aquinas to affirm meaningfully both the real horror Jesus feels in the face of his impending death, the profound depths of suffering into which Jesus' dreadful agony in the garden plunges him, and his simultaneous willingness to accomplish the Father's will.

---

54. Damascene, *De fide orth.*, Bk. III, ch. 23 (ed. Buytaert, pp. 265-66).

55. *ST* III, q. 15, a. 7, ad 1. Bonaventure offers the same view in III *Sent.*, d. 15, a. 2, dub. 3 (ed. Quaracchi, p. 342). Earlier in *ST* I-II, q. 44, a. 2, ad 2, and a. 4, Thomas explains: "The stronger the passion, the greater a hindrance it is to the man affected by it. Consequently, when fear is intense . . . and increases to the point that it disquiets the reason, it impedes action even on the part of the soul."

56. In his polemic with Arianism, which took Jesus' passibility as sufficient grounds for denying Christ's divinity, Hilary of Poitiers goes too far by acknowledging a purely physical or somatic suffering in Christ with no corresponding psychical or affective perception of such suffering: "He [the Lord] felt the force of passion," Hilary writes, "but without its pain. . . . He had a body that could undergo passion, and it did undergo passion, but he had not a nature that could feel pain." *De Trinitate*, Bk. X, chs. 23–27 (CCSL 62A, pp. 477-501). Not surprisingly, Hilary explicitly rules out fear in Christ in Bk. X, ch. 10 (pp. 466-67). In my *The Passions of Christ's Soul in the Theology of St. Thomas Aquinas*, pp. 48-51, I argue that this position of Hilary's would act as the principal source and focal point of the entire medieval debate over Christ's passibility. As for Aquinas, who proposes a *benigna interpretatio* of Hilary's view, we see him touch on the matter in *ST* III, q. 15, a. 5, ad 1; q. 46, a. 5, ad 1; *De veritate*, q. 26, a. 8, ad 7; and III *Sent.*, d. 15, q. 2, a. 3, sol. 1.

If not all readers find his exegesis entirely adequate, we need to see behind it Aquinas's concern to balance delicately two sides of the one soteriological coin. On the one hand, we have the hard reality of Christ's suffering in both body and soul, by which redemption of the human race is accomplished, as "all Christ's actions and passions [or sufferings]," Thomas insists, "operate instrumentally in virtue of his divinity for the salvation of men."[57] And on the other side of the soteriological coin is the fact that only a sinless savior, that is, a savior of consummate virtue whose passions submit perfectly to reason and will's *imperium,* can adequately atone for the sins of the human race.[58]

III. Christ's Unique Mode of Being, the Communication of Idioms, and the Suffering of God

To see how Jesus' agony in the garden of Gethsemane, at least on Aquinas's account, bears on the question of suffering or passibility in God, we need first to consider Thomas's view on Christ's unique mode or manner of being and from there proceed to the communication of idioms. When coupled with the communication of idioms, Aquinas's doctrine on Christ's unique mode of being yields a refined theology of divine suffering and one that puts a less abstract and more concrete or existential face on the mystery of the God who suffers.

Christ's Unique Mode of Being

Thomas Joseph White has recently shown that Aquinas's adherence to the Chalcedonian definition of Christ leads the Dominican Master to affirm

---

57. *ST* III, q. 48, a. 6; cf. as well q. 49, a. 1.

58. The principal passage affirming this in as much as it relates to Christ's affectivity or passibility comes in *ST* III, q. 15, a. 1, as well as in q. 14, a. 1, ad 1, where Aquinas writes: "It was necessary for Christ's soul to possess perfect virtue, so that he would have the power of satisfying." Also, in *Compendium theologiae,* ch. 226, we read: "no one offers satisfaction to God by his soul being in a state of [moral] disorder." Here Thomas follows in the tradition of Peter Lombard, III *Sent.,* d. 15, a. 1 (ed. Coll. Bonaventure, pp. 93-94), of Albert the Great, III *Sent.,* d. 15, a. 1, *sed contra* 1, and aa. 5-6, and of Bonaventure, III *Sent.,* d. 15, a. 1, q. 2 (ed. Quaracchi, pp. 332-33). Cf. Lafont, *Structures et méthode dans la "Somme théologique" de saint Thomas d'Aquin,* p. 358.

human actions in Christ that are not only fully human "in their nature" (in keeping with Chalcedon's distinction of natures), but also expressive of Christ's divine personhood "in their mode" (with respect to Chalcedon's unity in hypostasis or in person).[59] The distinction in natures implies, for instance, that the Son of God knows in a truly human way with his human mind and that this human knowledge is in no way confused or somehow intermingled with what he knows in his divine mind. But the unity in person means the one who acts humanly, the one who knows humanly, is none other than the person of God the Word. The divine person of the Word is always the acting subject of all Christ's human actions, as his assumed human nature, John of St. Thomas observes, is that *whereby (quo)* God the Word exists and acts humanly.[60]

In other words, it is one thing to speak of Christ's human nature and of the attributes of that nature, another to speak of the hypostatic mode or manner in which this human nature subsists — and acts. Because it subsists not in a human person (as with all other human beings) but in a divine person, Christ's human nature possesses a unique mode of being, and thus enjoys a unique mode of acting.[61] In terms of nature, Christ's human actions are identical to ours. But in terms of the subject of those actions, in terms of the person whose actions they are, Christ's human actions are

59. Thomas Joseph White, "The Voluntary Action of the Earthly Christ and the Necessity of the Beatific Vision," *The Thomist* 69 (2005): 497-534. White additionally shows that Aquinas's distinction in nature and mode in Christ follows in the line of Damascene (*De fide orth.*, Bk. III, ch. 14) and, through Damascene, of Maximus the Confessor (*Disp. Cum Pyrrho* [PG 91, col. 293A]). White takes his inspiration from Jean-Miguel Garrigues, "La conscience de soi telle qu'elle était exercé par le Fils de Dieu fait homme," *Nova et vetera* (French edition) 79 (2004): 39-51; Garrigues, "L'instrumentalité rédemptrice du libre arbitre du Christ chez saint Maxime le Confesseur," *Revue Thomiste* 104 (2004): 531-50; and Hermann Diepen, "La psychologie humaine du Christ selon saint Thomas d'Aquin," *Revue Thomiste* 50 (1950): 515-62. Cf. as well Weinandy, *Does God Suffer?*, pp. 206-11.

60. John of St. Thomas, *Introduction to the* Summa Theologiae *of Thomas Aquinas*, Bk. II, Pt. III (trans. R. McInerny, p. 161).

61. As Aquinas writes in *ST* III, q. 2, a. 2, ad 3: "we must bear in mind that not every individual in the genus, even in rational nature, is a person, but that alone which exists by itself. . . . Therefore, although (Christ's) human nature is a kind of individual in the genus of substance, it has not its own personality, because it does not exist separately, but in something more perfect, namely, in the person of the Word." Lafont (*Structures et méthode*, pp. 355-59) notes that it "is truly unique to St. Thomas" always to look upon Christ's human nature as subsisting in a divine person. For more on Aquinas's conception of the hypostatic union, cf. Nicolas, *Synthèse dogmatique*, pp. 301-58.

unique — they have their own mode. The actions of Christ's humanity are the personal actions not of a human person but of the Son of God: "to the hypostasis alone," Aquinas writes, "are attributed the operations and the natural properties, and whatever belongs to the [human] nature [of Christ] in the concrete."[62] Qualifying this understanding is the claim, derived from John Damascene, that Christ's humanity is the "instrument" *(organum)* of his divinity. Christ's divine person acts through his humanity in the way a principal agent acts through a conjoined or assumed (not separated) instrument, since the Word is the acting subject of this humanity.[63] Among his scholastic contemporaries, only Aquinas teaches that Christ's humanity acts as the conjoined "instrument" *(organum)* of his divinity, and this only later in his career (the *De veritate* marks the decisive turning point).[64]

---

62. *ST* III, q. 2, a. 3.

63. Later when discussing the sacraments in *ST* III, q. 62, a. 5, Thomas holds that the sacraments, too, act as instruments of Christ's divinity, but after the manner of a separated instrument, "like a stick," not of a conjoined instrument, "like a hand." Still, in the case of the sacraments, "the separate instrument is moved by means of the conjoined instrument, as a stick by the hand. Now the principal efficient cause of grace is God himself, to whom Christ's humanity is conjoined as an instrument, whereas the sacraments are separate instruments."

64. For Aquinas's definitive position on Christ's humanity as the *organum* of his divinity, cf. *ST* III, q. 19, a. 1, *corpus* and ad 2; and *In Ioan.*, ch. 6, lect. 6 (n. 959) (the definition of instrumental causality comes in *ST* I, q. 45, a. 5); for Damascene's remarks, the source of this teaching, cf. *De fide orth.*, Bk. III, chs. 15 and 19 (ed. Buytaert, pp. 239 and 258). Other scholars who have treated this element of Thomas's thought, including its development and the reasons thereof, include: Jean-Pierre Torrell, "La causalité salvifique de la résurrection du Christ selon saint Thomas," in *Recherches Thomasiennes.* Études revues et augmentées (Paris: J. Vrin, 2000), pp. 214-41 (originally published in *Revue Thomiste* 96 [1996]: 179-208); White, "The Voluntary Action of the Earthly Christ," pp. 510-13; and Theophil Tschipke, *Die Menschheit Christi als Heilsorgan der Gottheit unter besonderer Berücksichtigung der Lehre des heiligen Thomas von Aquin* (Freiburg im Breisgau: Herder, 1940), pp. 116-45 (recently published in French as *L'humanité du Christ comme instrument de salut de la divinité* [Fribourg: Editions Universitaires, 2003]). For the position of Thomas's contemporaries on the matter (take note that all were familiar with Damascene), cf. Albert the Great, *De resurrectione*, tr. 2, q. 1, sol. (ed. Coloniensis, vol. 26, p. 259); and Bonaventure, IV *Sent.*, d. 43, a. 1, q. 6, *corpus* and ad 4 (ed. Quaracchi, p. 895) (Torrell ["La causalité salvifique," p. 220, n. 3] observes that Bonaventure "sees [in Christ's humanity] no proper causality" with respect to the accomplishments proper to his divinity).

The Unique Mode of Christ's Fear and Anguish

If all the logical and necessary consequences of the Word's assumption of a true and integral human nature take on a unique mode of being and acting, as the foregoing implies, this would include both the Word's possession of a sensitive appetite and the subsequent movements of this appetite (the emotions).[65] The fear and anguish that torment Jesus' soul in Gethsemane are the emotions of no mere human being, as neither is the spiritual anguish he experiences. *Who*, after all, is the one who suffers such horrifying fears and *who* is the one who chooses to embrace the Father's cup despite such fears but God the Son? God the Word, as principal agent cause, embraces the will of the Father by means of his human will (as by means of a conjoined instrument). God the Word, as principal efficient cause, experiences the depths of affective fear, distress, and sorrow by means of the conjoined instrument of his sensitive appetite. The Son of God suffers unspeakable fear and anguish at the thought of his violent death, as these emotions arise from the assumed humanity that subsists in the person of the Word.

So while Christ's fear and anguish are identical in type to the fear and anguish that any human being can experience relative to our common human nature, his fear and anguish are wholly unique inasmuch as they are emotions not of a human person but of a divine person, the person of the Son.

Christ's Affective and Spiritual Suffering and the Communication of Idioms

When we link the communication of idioms to the doctrine of Christ's unique mode of being and acting, we can go further than to say simply that Jesus' affective and spiritual sufferings are personal acts of the Son of God himself. Given the exchange of predicates between the natures, we can

---

65. While not addressing the unique mode of the movements of Christ's sensitive appetite *per se*, Thomas does say the following about the unique mode of Christ's acts of will: "When we say to will in a certain way, we signify a determinate mode of willing. . . . Hence the human will of Christ had a determinate mode from the fact of being in a divine hypostasis, i.e., it was always moved in accordance with the bidding of the divine will." *ST* III, q. 18, a. 1, ad 4.

predicate Jesus' sufferings of the divine nature itself, and thereby come one step closer to attributing passibility to the impassible God. At the same time, one predicates Christ's sufferings of the divine nature with the important proviso that this only be done in consideration of the two natures of Christ *qua* concretely joined in the same hypostasis: "what belongs to one nature cannot be predicated of the other," Aquinas writes, "if they are taken in the abstract. . . . [But] of concrete terms [which signify the hypostasis] we may predicate indifferently what belongs to either nature."[66] We cannot predicate suffering of the divine nature in abstraction from the hypostasis, in abstraction from the personal subject of that suffering. Thomas is no crypto-Nestorian, nor is he a passibilist: "Christ's Passion belongs to the supposit [or hypostasis] of the divine nature by reason of the passible nature assumed, but not on account of the impassible divine nature."[67]

In other words, what the sharing of predicates between Christ's two natures ultimately signifies is the hypostasis, not the natures *per se:* "of [Christ's] manhood may be said what belongs to the divine nature, as of a hypostasis of the divine nature," Thomas again explains, "and of God may be said what belongs to the human nature, as of a hypostasis of human nature."[68] Commenting on this passage from Aquinas and echoing the Chalcedonian language of distinction in natures and union in hypostasis or person, John of St. Thomas observes (using the term *supposit* for *hypostasis*):

> [A]ll the predicates ["idioms"] which are said of the supposit [i.e., of the hypostasis, or of the Person of the Word] by reason of nature [whether of the human nature or of the divine nature] can be predicated of both natures taken concretely, because to be taken concretely is to be taken for the supposit [i.e., the Person of the Word], and thus is verified the truth that God has died and suffered, etc., and that man is creator and God. But if the nature [whether human or divine] is taken abstractly, such sharing [of predicates or idioms by the two natures] does not take place, because they are not taken for the supposit, but for the nature, and this [i.e., the two natures] remains unconfused.[69]

66. *ST* III, q. 16, a. 5.
67. *ST* III, q. 46, a. 12.
68. *ST* III, q. 16, a. 4.
69. John of St. Thomas, *Introduction to the* Summa Theologiae *of Thomas Aquinas,* Bk. II, Pt. III (trans. R. McInerny, p. 161).

Following Aquinas, then, we can affirm that the spiritual and affective anguish Jesus experiences in the garden of Gethsemane can be predicated of God. Since God, in the person of the Word, is the hypostasis of his human nature, he is the personal Subject of this anguish. We can attribute any emotion Jesus experiences, whether fear or anguish, sorrow or pity, to God himself, just as we can attribute to God the spiritual suffering Jesus undergoes when he desires *ut natura* to forgo the Father's cup. By affirming the experience of real fear in Jesus and real *ut natura* recoiling from his impending death, we can affirm (predicate) real fear and *ut natura* anguish of God (the Word), and even of the divine nature itself (*qua* concretely joined by hypostatic union to his assumed humanity).[70]

IV. Conclusion

In conclusion, then, I think we stand on firm ground when we say that St. Thomas's theology of Christ's agony in the garden of Gethsemane yields the following. God enters into the mystery of human suffering in the "only" way he in his impassible divine nature can: by being the subject of human predication, that is, by assuming a possible human nature and having it subsist in one of his persons (the person of the Son).[71] In this way he

70. We should distinguish here Aquinas's position from that of Lutheran or Reformed theologians who opine that the incarnation allows us to ascribe divine attributes (such as omnipotence) directly and fully to Christ's humanity, as well as human attributes (such as suffering) directly to the divine nature. Examples would include: Wolfhart Pannenberg (*Jesus — God and Man,* trans. Lewis Wilkins and Duane Priebe [Philadelphia: Westminster Press, 1968], pp. 297-304), who succinctly explicates the traditional Lutheran position; and, from a Barthian perspective, Bruce L. McCormack, "Karl Barth's Christology as a Resource for a Reformed Version of Kenoticism," *International Journal of Systematic Theology* 8 (2006): 244-51. For Aquinas, one ascribes passibility to the divine nature *only* inasmuch as this nature is hypostasized by a person who undergoes passibility through his assumed human nature.

71. We should note that such accomplished twentieth-century Thomists as Jacques Maritain and Charles Journet did attempt to "go a step further on the road opened up by St. Thomas" and affirm a "quasi-suffering" in God (i.e., in his divine nature as such) as "a divine perfection that for us remains nameless and unnamable" and which relates to "an *excess* of love and joy" in God. See Charles Journet, "La Rédemption, drame de l'amour de Dieu," part 1, *Nova et Vetera* (French edition) 48 (1973): 46-75, at 55-58; Journet, "De l'espérance," *Nova et Vetera* (French edition) 45 (1970): 161-222, at 206; Jacques Maritain, "Quelques réflexions sur le savoir théologique," *Revue Thomiste* 69 (1969): 5-27, at 14-27. These passages

makes the suffering he undergoes in his humanity truly his own as a divine person, as God. Only the incarnation, that is, only a confession of Jesus Christ as true God and true man, allows one to affirm the doctrine of divine passibility. As Thomas Weinandy writes: "Who is it who truly experiences the authentic, genuine, and undiminished reality of human suffering? None other than the divine Son of God! . . . What is the manner in which he experiences the whole reality of human suffering? As man!"[72] God, in the person of the Word, knows our suffering from the inside, since, as the Letter to the Hebrews attests, "he himself partook of the same nature [as the children of flesh and blood] . . . [and] because he himself has suffered and been tempted, he is able to help those who are tempted" (Heb. 2:14, 18).

God could do no more to prove he is anything but cold or indifferent to our suffering than to take on a nature capable of suffering and in that nature undergo the worst imaginable type of suffering, whether physical, affective, or spiritual, which no mere human experience of suffering could equal. Let no one look at Christ and accuse God of *apatheia* if this is to mean a remaining distant from or unmoved by our suffering. Let no one look at Christ and assert that God does not suffer. God places upon himself, that is, upon the human nature he weds to himself in the person of the Son, what he would place upon no one else: the sins of all of humanity of all epochs, whether they be the unspeakable evils of the Auschwitz gas chambers, or of the Cambodian killing fields, or of the myriads of torturous devices borne of human malice, including Roman crucifixion, or of any human atrocity. All such evils distressed Jesus' soul in Gethsemane: "Christ grieved not only over the loss of his own bodily life," Aquinas observes, "but also over the sins of all others. And this grief in Christ surpassed all grief . . . since he grieved at the one time for all sins."[73] This is God himself who grieves for the sins of the world.

---

are cited in Gilles Emery, "The Question of Evil and the Mystery of God in Charles Journet," *Nova et Vetera* (English edition) 4 (2006): 529-55, at 546-51.

72. Weinandy, *Does God Suffer?*, p. 201.

73. *ST* III, q. 46, a. 6 ad 4.

The Dereliction of Christ and
the Impassibility of God

Bruce D. Marshall

I

Christians have long found their attention arrested by Jesus' cry on the cross, "My God, my God, why have you forsaken me?" (Matt. 27:46; Mark 15:34). This cry of dereliction or abandonment has its home in the quite similar passion narratives of St. Matthew and St. Mark, where these words are, indeed, the only ones Jesus speaks from the cross. This desolate utterance could hardly have a place in the passion as told by St. Luke or St. John, where Jesus carries on encouraging dialogues from the cross, and dies not desolate or forsaken, but profoundly confident in the God who sent him. Yet Christian faith and devotion have not generally tried to overlook or play down Jesus' cry of dereliction in favor of the more positive Lucan and Johannine renderings of Jesus' passion. Along with its companions from Luke and John, "My God, my God, why have you forsaken me?" belongs among the traditional seven last words of Jesus, and as such has been the subject of countless Lenten meditations. Hymns both Catholic and Protestant allude to this cry, and it has elicited reflection from theologians, spiritual writers, and exegetes since the early Church.

It would not, in fact, have been difficult to understand if Christians had wanted to pass over these words in silence. After all, Jesus apparently here attributes God-forsakenness to himself. The common assumption that he is quoting the opening words of Psalm 22 fails to mitigate this self-attribution. To be sure, that psalm ends as a hymn of confidence and praise to the God of Israel. But even if Jesus begins the psalm precisely in order to utter its confident conclusion (a suggestion for which the texts of Matthew and Mark themselves offer no support, and which seems in fact at odds with the desolate scene they depict), he has presumably passed through the God-forsakenness of which the opening verses of the psalm speak. Otherwise there would be no purpose in praising Israel's God from the cross with just this psalm, rather than one of the many that give praise from the outset.

Why should there be a problem with the thought that Jesus suffered abandonment by God, or even that he merely felt abandoned, though he was mistaken and God in fact remained close to him? We may be inclined to suppose that the difficulty lies in the thought that actually God abandons anyone, under any circumstances, though we can fail to perceive God's continuing presence. Whatever the merits of that suggestion, the problem with the divine abandonment of Jesus is of a different order. Christians, after all, believe that the human being Jesus is himself God. Mary's only begotten is the eternal Father's only begotten; her Son is his Son. The one born of a woman in time is the same — the same hypostasis and person, according to Chalcedon's definition of ecumenical dogma — as the one born of the Father eternally. So if Jesus is abandoned by God, then apparently God is abandoned by God, the eternal Son by the eternal Father.

Just because Jesus is God incarnate, it will be difficult to chalk up his cry of dereliction to a loss of faith, a temporary failure to perceive God's presence. In our own case we can do that, indeed we may take refuge in it, but in Jesus' case this recourse seems unpromising. One person of the Trinity presumably knows when another is near at hand, and cannot be mistaken on this score. "My God, my God, why have you forsaken me?" seems to pose a problem, therefore, for the Christian doctrine of God, that is, for the doctrine of the Trinity. Intelligibility is part of the problem. How shall we understand the idea that God is forsaken by God, even — indeed precisely — in trinitarian terms? Moreover, to the extent that we understand this idea, it seems a deeply disturbing one. If God himself is abandoned by God, if one person of the Trinity suffers genuine God-forsakenness at the hands of another, then the abyss of hell seems to open up in God himself. What is hell, save where God unmistakably is not, and what is it to be in hell, if not to be unmistakably forsaken by God? How, though, can God be anyone's redeemer from the abyss of hell if he has somehow consigned himself there, if hell has entered into who God is?

II

A stream of recent theology has been undeterred by the worries for Christian faith and theology to which Jesus' cry of dereliction apparently gives rise. In fact these worries stem, a good many theologians have lately argued, not from Jesus' scripturally attested words themselves, but from the traditional attempt to read them so that they square with belief in God's impassibility. The solution to this problem is to get rid of the idea of divine impassibility. Indeed theologians in this stream regularly take Jesus' cry from the cross as the ultimate refutation of the claim that God is impassible, for here God himself experiences the uttermost extreme of suffering.

Jürgen Moltmann's book *The Crucified God* offers an especially clearcut and influential example of this approach to the cry of dereliction. In fact it might not be too much to say that for Moltmann, at least in this book, the cry from the cross is the key to the whole enterprise of theology; it has to guide our understanding of the incarnation, the Trinity, and the saving work of God. Part of the reason for this is that Moltmann assumes, in fairly standard fashion, that the identity of Jesus has to provide the main warrants for what we say about incarnation, Trinity, and salvation. But he also assumes that we can only get a fix on the identity of Jesus through historical criticism of the Gospels, rather than through a synoptic reading of the canonical scriptures as a whole. This leads him to suppose that Mark's passion narrative, and in particular the cry of God-forsakenness in Mark 15:34, must be as close as we can get to "the historical reality" of Jesus' crucifixion, and thus to the most decisive aspect of his human identity.[1] The Lukan and Johannine accounts are not only theological elaborations on the death of Jesus without historical foundation; they are deliberate attempts to weaken the scandal of Jesus' dereliction. Christology, therefore, may and should ignore them.

---

1. Jürgen Moltmann, *Der gekreuzigte Gott,* 4th edition (Munich: Chr. Kaiser Verlag, 1981), p. 140, in English (= ET) as *The Crucified God,* trans. R. A. Wilson and John Bowden (New York: Harper & Row, 1974), p. 147; I have sometimes modified this translation in light of the German original. Mark's depiction of Jesus' "profound abandonment by God" *(tiefer Gottesverlassenheit),* Moltmann argues, "seems to be as near as possible to the historical reality of the death of Jesus." In the rest of the book "we start," he emphasizes, from this assumption. This sort of assurance about the competence of historical criticism to deliver theologically basic results is taken for granted less today than it was when Moltmann wrote this book, but it remains widespread.

Moltmann, however, has larger theological reasons for placing such great weight on Jesus' abandonment by God. From an early point, he holds, Christian faith and theology have been kept from a proper appreciation of Jesus' words from the cross by the doctrine of the two natures. First articulated in a doctrinally normative way at the Council of Chalcedon, and often reaffirmed, this is the teaching that in Jesus Christ are united two complete natures, divine and human, so that the one person Jesus Christ is both true God and true man. Recourse to talk of distinct divine and human "natures" was driven, Moltmann argues, by a misguided desire to maintain God's immutability and impassibility, the essentially pagan philosophical convictions that God is incapable of change and suffering.[2] Jesus' human nature can and does suffer the torment embodied in his dereliction. But since the divine nature by definition cannot suffer, Jesus' divinity, what makes him God, must always remain untouched by his human suffering, and above all by his dereliction, his God-forsakenness.

In Moltmann's view this outlook governs the whole two-nature tradition, which is to say, the entire tradition for which the first seven ecumenical councils are doctrinally normative. As a result, even those theologians in the two-natures tradition who had the strongest views of Christ's personal unity, like Cyril of Alexandria and above all (for Moltmann) Martin Luther, are unable to see what really happens in Christ's dereliction. They can and do say that "God" suffers and dies on the cross, but they inevitably deprive these statements of their real force by holding the divine nature aloof from suffering and death. In manifest contradiction to the total anguish of Jesus' cry, they allow that only part of his person was actually involved in his suffering. They cannot say "of the whole divine and human person of Christ that he suffered and died forsaken by God."[3]

2. Thus, e.g., *Der gekreuzigte Gott*, p. 215 (ET, p. 228): "If one considers the event on the cross between Jesus and his God in the framework of the doctrine of the two natures, then the Platonic axiom of the essential *apatheia* of God sets up an intellectual barrier against the recognition of the suffering of Christ, for a God who is subject to suffering like all other creatures cannot be 'God.'"

3. *Der gekreuzigte Gott*, p. 219 (ET, p. 231). That Jesus Christ "crucified in the flesh" (or better, "with respect to the flesh") is "true God, the Lord of glory, and one of the Holy Trinity" is, it should be recalled, not simply the opinion of various theologians in the two-natures tradition, but ecumenical dogma; see Canon 10 of Constantinople II, DH 432 (= *Enchiridion symbolorum definitionum et declarationem de rebus fidei et morum,* ed. Heinrich Denzinger and Peter Hünermann, 40th edition [Freiburg: Herder, 2005]). Moltmann curiously says this teaching "was rejected" (p. 215; ET, p. 228). But even if he had his history

If divine dereliction is that element in the gospel story which divine impassibility most makes unintelligible, then "My God, my God, why have you forsaken me?" will be the best place to start in developing a doctrine of God that is truly shaped by the gospel. Rather than trying to fit the profound forsakenness of the crucified into an alien philosophical outlook that can hardly make sense of it, we will take Jesus' abandonment as clear and work out our doctrine of God around it. We can do this by understanding the dereliction of Christ in trinitarian terms, which in Moltmann's view is not a complement to, but rather the opposite of, understanding of the cross by way of the two-natures doctrine.

The thought that the trinitarian Father abandons his righteous but suffering Son on the cross suggests a division and conflict within God himself. As Moltmann sees it, we cannot shrink from recognizing that the dereliction of Jesus presents us with "God against God," even an enmity or hostility *(Feindschaft)* between one divine person and another: "The cross of the Son separates God from God to the utmost degree of enmity and difference."[4] Initially the idea that the cross confronts us with a conflict of "God against God" may seem to pose a serious problem, but the difficulty is only apparent. It arises from taking "God" as a covering term for both the Father and the Son, and thereby failing to appreciate the depth of their distinction from one another. The Son suffers the Father's abandonment unto death, but the Father suffers the grief of handing over the Son to death; in a way the Father's suffering is greater, since the suffering of Jesus ends in death, but the Father must undergo the death of his Son. Moltmann writes:

> The Son suffers in dying, the Father suffers the death of the Son. The hurt *(Schmerz)* of the Father here is just as important as the death of the Son. To the Fatherlessness of the Son corresponds the Sonlessness of the Father, and if God has constituted himself as the Father of Jesus Christ, then in the death of the Son he also suffers the death of his own being as Father *(Vaterseins)*.[5]

---

straight the two-natures tradition would still be a failure in Moltmann's view, since even when crucifixion is explicitly attributed to "one of the Holy Trinity," the qualification "in the flesh" introduces all the problems he associates with that tradition.

4. *Der gekreuzigte Gott*, pp. 144-45: "Das Kreuz des Sohnes trennt Gott von Gott bis zur völligen Feindschaft und Differenz" (ET, p. 152).

5. *Der gekreuzigte Gott*, p. 230 (ET, p. 243).

To be sure, the resurrection of Jesus, and even more the outpouring of the Holy Spirit, sets things right.[6] But for our purposes the chief point is that we now have a doctrine of the Trinity where God, far from being impassible, suffers all the way down. In fact in the suffering of Golgotha between the Son and the Father, God admits "*all* disaster, forsakenness by God, absolute death, the infinite curse of damnation and sinking into nothingness" into his own reality.[7] In just this, God's love consists. The Son and the Father not only suffer as we do, they have already undergone all our actual sufferings, the worst that we have suffered or can suffer. "God's being is in suffering and the suffering is in God's being itself, because God is love."[8] Thus in the dereliction of Christ God proves himself worthy of the worship and love of his creatures, who must themselves suffer every kind of disaster, abandonment, and death. Only in sharing the life of this suffering God can there be "eternal salvation" and "infinite joy."[9]

Moltmann, to be sure, interprets the theological consequences of Jesus' dereliction in a highly revisionist way. Other recent theologians have shared the view that in the passion and cross of Jesus death enters intimately and permanently into God's own reality, but have not reached this assertion in the same way as Moltmann, or drawn exactly the same conclusions from it. Eberhard Jüngel, for example, holds that God "defines himself *as* God in the death of Jesus, so that death has *ontological relevance* for the being of God," and "God's being as God has to be understood on the basis of the event of this death."[10] For Jüngel the cross is God's way of joining death forever to himself, so that death can no longer be "loosed" from God. "*In just this way* God kills death — not by putting and leaving death behind himself, but by taking death with himself into the life which is God

6. Cf. *Der gekreuzigte Gott*, p. 234 (ET, p. 247), there also the suggestion that "God" names not a single personal reality, nor even three persons singly subsisting, but an event *(Geschehen)*, namely "the event of Golgotha." "God" is not a person, but "there are persons in God," that is, in this all-encompassing event. Cf. also p. 192 (ET, p. 207): "it is advisable to abandon the concept of God. . . ."

7. *Der gekreuzigte Gott*, p. 233, my emphasis (ET, p. 246).

8. *Der gekreuzigte Gott*, p. 214 (ET, p. 227).

9. *Der gekreuzigte Gott*, p. 233 (ET, p. 246).

10. See Jüngel, "Vom Tod des lebendigen Gottes. Ein Plakat," in *Unterwegs zur Sache* (Munich: Chr. Kaiser, 1972), pp. 105-25. The quoted passages are from p. 119, with the emphasis in the original. Cf. p. 122: "Gott definiert sich an einem Toten, indem er den Toten als Gottes Sohn definiert," consequently "der Tod [wird] zu einem das Sein Gottes bestimmenden Prädikat"; also a similar formulation on p. 118.

himself," so that from here on out, wherever death comes, God comes with it.[11] Jüngel thus shares with Moltmann the idea that the cross is saving because it in some way makes death — that which is utterly foreign to God and opposed to God — constitutive of God himself, or of what it is to be God. Because of the cross, death apparently enters into what the tradition thinks of as the divine nature: "Death's essential act is essential to God himself."[12] But Jüngel develops this view of God, at least in this paper, without specific attention to the cry of dereliction, and perhaps for this reason without any suggestion that the trinitarian Father suffers, or actually ceases to be the Father, when the Son dies.

The reflections of Hans Urs von Balthasar on the dereliction of Christ are extensive, complex, and much debated; I will not try to enter into them in detail here. We may simply recall that for Balthasar, the passion of Jesus Christ and especially his descent into hell are a true suffering of "the second death," the biblical death not of nothingness, but worse, of the active and radical divine rejection, curse, and abandonment due to sin.[13] But Balthasar too declines to extend this suffering to the Father, and seems not to think that his view of Jesus' dereliction requires rejecting the immutability (and thus impassibility) of God, still less that it requires rejecting the two-natures doctrine.[14] These theologians and others genuinely differ on

---

11. "Vom Tod des lebendigen Gottes," p. 123, Jüngel's emphasis; there also the reference to death not loosing itself from God, so that "Wo der Tod nun auch hinkommt, da kommt Gott selbst."

12. "Vom Tod des lebendigen Gottes," p. 120: "Der Wesensakt des Todes ist Gott selbst wesentlich eigen." By thus ceasing to be "foreign" to God, Jüngel argues, death itself is changed, and robbed of its power; it is no longer "der Fremde, weil von Gott Entfremdende" (p. 119).

13. See, *inter alia*, Balthasar, "Mysterium Paschale," originally in Johannes Feiner and Magnus Löhrer, eds., *Mysterium Salutis: Grundriss heilsgeschichtlicher Dogmatik*, vol. III/2 (Einsiedeln: Benziger Verlag, 1969), pp. 133-326, later published separately as *Theologie der Drei Tage* (Einsiedeln: Benziger Verlag, 1970); in English as *Mysterium Paschale*, trans. Aidan Nichols (Edinburgh: T. & T. Clark, 1990). Note, e.g., the section "The Hiatus" (referring to Holy Saturday), which begins Balthasar's chapter on "The Death of God as the Wellspring of Salvation, Revelation, and Theology" ("Mysterium Paschale," pp. 159-61; ET, pp. 49-52). In his "going to the dead," his realization of the "second death," Jesus Christ descends "außerhalb der von Gott im Anfang geordneten Welt. . . . Somit ist es wirklich Gott, der das auf jeden Fall Widergöttliche, von Gott ewig Verworfene in der Weise des letzten Gehorsams des Sohnes an den Vater auf sich nimmt" ("Mysterium Paschale," pp. 160-61; ET, pp. 51-52).

14. The paschal mystery, he suggests, requires an alternative to standard conceptions of both "divine immutability" and "divine mutability." See "Mysterium Paschale," pp. 152-54 and (drawn mostly from Barth's *Kirchliche Dogmatik* IV/1), pp. 182-84 (ET, pp. 34-36, 79-83).

the theological implications of Jesus' God-forsakenness. But two common threads apparently run through the differing views of Moltmann, Jüngel, and Balthasar. First, on the cross the human being Jesus experiences God-forsakenness in its most radical form, the greatest possible distance or alienation from God, and thus a condition in some way akin to the lot of the lost, of those finally rejected by God. Second, this God-forsakenness belongs, because of the unity of his person, to God the Son himself. We need to look more closely at these two propositions.

III

For theologians who embrace these two claims, to deny that God himself undergoes God-forsakenness on the cross is either to miss the clear import of the passion narrative in Matthew and Mark, or to exhibit a radically defective view of the incarnation (or perhaps, of course, both). In a brief discussion of the Christology of the early Church, Moltmann, for example, finds fault with St. Cyril of Alexandria's account of Christ's dereliction. According to Moltmann, Cyril's reading of Christ's cry from the cross "is a last retreat before the axiom of *apatheia*."[15] Here Cyril lacks (uncharacteristically, it would seem) the courage of his christological convictions. His high claims about the incarnation of the Logos ought to make him ascribe Jesus' human God-forsakenness "to the complete, divine and human person of the Son."[16] But here the great doctor of the unity of Christ in the ancient Church shrinks back, and insists that when it comes to dereliction, any suggestion "that Christ is overcome with fear and weakness" is incompatible with the belief that he is true God.[17] Thomas Aquinas, Moltmann briefly adds, has the same problem. A defective theology of incarnation keeps both from properly ascribing Jesus' human dereliction to the person of God the Son. Indeed on this reading both Cyril and Aquinas have what amounts to a crypto-Nestorian outlook, though Moltmann does not put it this way.

15. *Der gekreuzigte Gott*, p. 216 (ET, p. 229).
16. *Der gekreuzigte Gott*, p. 215 (ET, p. 229).
17. *Der gekreuzigte Gott*, p. 216 (ET, p. 229); the quoted phrase is from Werner Elert's (posthumous) *Der Ausgang der altkirchlichen Christologie* (Berlin: Lutherisches Verlagshaus, 1957), upon which Moltmann depends for his account of St. Cyril's Christology (cf. Elert, p. 95).

The curious suggestion that St. Cyril, or for that matter St. Thomas, was really a Nestorian at heart may prompt us to wonder what each of them actually thought about Christ's dereliction. Each, in fact, makes for an instructive contrast with Moltmann and other contemporary theologians bound by the two "common threads" I have just mentioned. Moltmann is right, I think, to sense that there is between him and both Cyril and Thomas a deep disagreement about the dereliction of Christ, but wrong about where the disagreement lies. It is not, as Moltmann supposes, a disagreement about whether we should try to keep some portion of Christ's person out of his dereliction, but rather about what *sort* of dereliction this person could possibly undergo, and so a disagreement about how to interpret the cry of dereliction in the first place.

Cyril is quite clear, as Moltmann indicates, that there is only one subject, one hypostasis or person, of all that Jesus Christ does and suffers. That subject or hypostasis is the Father's eternal Logos, to whom fully belongs not only Jesus' divine actions and attributes, but also his human ones. Thus Cyril insists that everything Scripture says of Jesus Christ, whether it is the sort of thing that belongs to God alone or the sort of thing that belongs to frail human creatures, is true of the one enfleshed Logos, and cannot be split up between two subjects, one divine and one human. This teaching, often repeated by Cyril, finds particularly pointed formulation in his fourth anathema against Nestorius, where Cyril rejects any distribution of the scriptural terms "applied to Christ . . . to two persons or subjects"; we cannot attach "some to the man considered separately from the Word of God, some as divine to the Word of God the Father alone."[18] This teaching becomes ecumenical dogma at the Council of Chalcedon, with its repeated Cyrillian insistence that "the same one" is truly God and truly man, the Father's Son in eternity and Mary's Son in time.[19]

Cyril does not hesitate to acknowledge that we must, if we accept this teaching, attribute weakness, ignorance, suffering, and death — whatever belongs to the fleshly form of a servant in Jesus Christ — to God the Logos himself (or as Cyril puts it, "to the one incarnate subject [hypostasis] of the Word"). We should not be "ashamed" of this, retreating before

---

18. *Letter* 17 (3rd Letter to Nestorius), in Lionel Wickham, ed. and trans., *Cyril of Alexandria: Select Letters* (Oxford: Clarendon Press, 1983), p. 31; for the same teaching in the body of the letter, cf. §8 (pp. 23-25).

19. See DH 301.

Nestorian objections that we are speaking and thinking of God in an unworthy manner. "Why should one who condescends to voluntary abasement for us refuse the conditions appropriate to that abasement?"[20]

We need to distinguish, however, between what God the Son becomes in order to transform it, and what he becomes in order to destroy it. Some elements of the human condition after Adam the Logos takes to himself in order to cleanse and perfect them, but other aspects he takes to himself in order to do away with them. Cyril is attentive to those scriptural passages, understandably central to contemporary dereliction theology, which speak of Christ becoming "sin" for us (2 Cor. 5:21) and becoming "a curse for us" (Gal. 3:13). But "it is foolishness," he bluntly observes, "to think or affirm that the Word became flesh in just the same way as he became curse and sin."[21] Sin is destroyed when the Logos becomes flesh subject to sin, the divine curse against transgressors of the law is lifted when the enfleshed Logos comes to be cursed by the penalty against transgression, death is trampled down when the Logos tastes death in his flesh. But our mortal and corruptible flesh itself is of course not destroyed or done away with when the Logos of God assumes it. Rather our whole flesh, our human body and soul, is rendered immortal and incorruptible, indeed deified, when the Logos becomes it. "If," Cyril argues, "it is true that the Word became flesh in exactly the same way that he became curse and sin . . . then surely he must have become flesh for the suppression of flesh," since that is the way he became curse and sin. But the opposite is the case. He became flesh in order to "exhibit the incorruptibility and imperishability of flesh which he achieved, first of all in his own body."[22]

This distinction between what the Logos perfects, and what he destroys, by becoming flesh underlies Cyril's interpretation of the cry of dereliction. Jesus' words from the cross should not be understood as an assertion that he, and therefore the Logos, is undergoing God-forsakenness, the anguish of the damned, or anything of the sort. Like Jesus' prayers, tears,

20. The quoted phrases are from *Letter* 17, §8 (Wickham, p. 25).

21. St. Cyril of Alexandria, *On the Unity of Christ*, trans. John Anthony McGuckin (Crestwood, N.Y.: St. Vladimir's Seminary Press, 1995), p. 56. Greek text of this treatise (generally known by its Latin title, *Quod Unus sit Christus*) in Cyrille d'Alexandrie, *Deux dialogues christologiques* (*Sources Chrétiennes* [= SC] 97), ed. G. M. de Durand (Paris: Editions du Cerf, 1964), p. 322 (p. 720a in the 1638 Aubert edition of Cyril's works; this pagination is also retained in the edition of the text in PG 75, 1253-1362).

22. *The Unity of Christ*, p. 57 (SC 97, p. 322; Aubert 720b).

and obedience in Hebrews 5:7-9, his cry on the cross should be understood as an action that the Logos made flesh undertakes for our benefit, so we may see how his passion destroys our sin and all its consequences.

One of the consequences of sin, in fact its ultimate consequence, is dereliction, abandonment by God. By his obedience unto death, Cyril reasons, the incarnate Word does not undergo our abandonment, but "undoes" it. He destroys in our flesh the cause for which God abandons human flesh, namely the sin of disobedience. So because of what the Word incarnate has done, our flesh is no longer abandoned by God — first in the case of Jesus' own flesh, the very flesh of the Logos, and then in the case of those who, by their Eucharistic share in his life-giving flesh, belong to him.[23] When Jesus says "My God, my God, why have you forsaken me?" he is, in effect, addressing to the Father a rhetorical question, using his own first language, that of Israel's worship. Speaking "as one of us and on behalf of all our nature," in whom "the nature of man was made rich in all blamelessness and innocence," the incarnate Word asks his Father what cause there could now be for abandoning those who possess that nature. In asking that question precisely from the cross, when the work of obedience and submission was done, he "call[s] down the heavenly graciousness of the Father" upon our flesh, not upon his own flesh, which has no need of it, but upon us who share his flesh. And he announces to the rest of us, who have had a taste of divine abandonment — who have uttered the opening lines of Psalm 22 in earnest — that he has bound the strong man and cast him out, the one who held us captive in God-forsakenness.[24]

Cyril evidently declines to attribute God-forsakenness to the Logos, but not because of a defective theology of the incarnation, or of the unity of Christ's person. "My God, my God, why have you forsaken me?" is as much an utterance of the Logos himself as everything else Jesus says; it cannot be attached to any "person or subject" besides the Logos himself. Cyril differs from Moltmann and other contemporary theologians of dereliction not because he separates the words and deeds of Jesus from the words and deeds of God the Son, but because he interprets this particular word quite differently from them. For Cyril, Jesus on the cross does not at-

---

23. See *Letter* 17, §7: in the Eucharist we receive "the personal, truly life-giving (ζωοποιοῦν) flesh of God the Word himself" (Wickham, p. 23, translation altered).

24. See *The Unity of Christ*, p. 105, from which the quoted phrases are taken (SC 97, pp. 442-44; Aubert 756e-757a).

tribute God-forsakenness to himself, however plain this attribution may seem to us. He attributes to himself rather the destruction of God-forsakenness, its permanent undoing.

Cyril's unwillingness to suppose that Jesus personally experiences God-forsakenness does not stem from any squeamishness about attributing suffering and even death to God. As he holds in the twelfth anathema against Nestorius, "Whoever does not acknowledge God's Word as having suffered in flesh, been crucified in flesh, tasted death in flesh [Heb. 2:9]" is anathema, outside the faith.[25] The Logos, Cyril is careful to stress, suffered and died "impassibly." This should not be taken as an implicit denial that the Logos "really" suffered and died, but rather indicates the unique mode in which not only suffering and death, but anything creaturely and human, can belong to a divine person. The impassible suffering of the Logos in the flesh strains, to be sure, the limits of our understanding, though Cyril sometimes takes the soul's experience of the body's wounds as a remote analogy. But that the Logos so suffers is basic to scriptural faith. "We confess that the very Son begotten of God the Father, the only-begotten God, impassible though he is in his own nature, has (as the Bible says) suffered in the flesh for our sake and that he was in the crucified body claiming the sufferings of his flesh as his own impassibly."[26]

Why, if Cyril is quite willing to say that the Logos suffers and dies, though impassibly, is he unwilling to say that the Logos suffers God-forsakenness, though in a mysterious impassible mode? Cyril's argument here, while perhaps familiar, is no less telling for that. The economy of God the Word made flesh, his self-emptying completed on the cross, "brought help to the nature of man."[27] But what help would there be in a God-forsaken God?

When the Word of God assumes our flesh he accepts with it our suffering and death, in order to destroy death forever, to trample down death by death and so liberate our flesh for life in God. He can do this just because he is, as God, impassible. The suffering and death he accepts in our flesh are creaturely realities that cannot, as such, disturb his impassibility. On the contrary, just because he is impassible he destroys death by "tast-

25. *Letter* 17, in Wickham, p. 33. Cf. Cyril's defense of this proposition in *The Unity of Christ*, pp. 115-18 (SC 97, pp. 468-76; Aubert 765a-767b).

26. *Letter* 17, §6 (Wickham, p. 21).

27. *The Unity of Christ*, p. 115 (SC 97, p. 468; Aubert 764e).

ing" it — destroys death, as it were, on contact. The death of the Logos does not contradict his impassibility. Rather God the Logos can taste death, but not be taken captive by it, or forsaken in it, just because he is impassible. Just because death in no way enters into his constitution as God, into the nature which makes him God, death is abolished by its contact with the impassible Logos.[28]

But tasting God-forsakenness would be quite another matter. A genuine abandonment of the Son by the Father would, it seems, have to enter into the very relationship between the two as persons. If God were really forsaken by God on the cross, it would seem that forsakenness would have to affect or characterize what makes the Son and the Father the divine person each is. And with that, forsakenness would become an element in what constitutes each, Father and Son, as God. One can sense why Moltmann, taking the cry of dereliction as a real abandonment of the Son by the Father, insists that forsakenness must belong to the divine nature, and not only to the person of the Son. If there is to be a genuine God-forsakenness of one divine person by another, it must finally belong to what makes each person God, and could not be limited — like death — simply to the temporal economy of the Son.

Thus Cyril's rhetorical question, his objection. How, despite Moltmann's assurances, can there be "eternal salvation" in a forsaken God, even — indeed precisely — a risen one? For Cyril the resurrection of Jesus is God's total destruction of death. It is the definitive entry of our common flesh, but precisely not of its death, into the life of God. The resurrection of a forsaken Son would, by contrast, only serve to eternalize his God-forsakenness, and so forever to fix the darkness of death at the heart of God, never to be loosed from God's own being. Such a God would bring no help, and the help the economy of the incarnate Word brings us shows that he is no such God.

---

28. Cf. *The Unity of Christ*, p. 115: The Father "caused him who knew not death (since the Word is life and life-giver) to suffer in the flesh. But insofar as he is considered as God he remained outside suffering in order that we might live through him and in him" (SC 97, p. 468; Aubert 764c-d).

IV

In its chief aims St. Thomas's treatment of the cry of dereliction is similar to Cyril's, though it stems not directly from Cyril himself, but from John of Damascus and, by way of Augustine, from Tyconius. For reasons I will look at momentarily, Thomas considers Jesus' cry from the cross in connection with the standard scholastic question whether there was sin in Christ.[29] In characteristic fashion he gets at the issue by making a distinction, in this case one drawn from Damascene's *De Fide Orthodoxa,* III, 25. In Scripture some of what is said of Jesus, and by Jesus, is said of him as a particular human being, as the divine hypostasis or subject of an individuated human nature. Such things are said, as Thomas puts it, "with regard to a natural and hypostatic property." Other scriptural statements about Jesus, and by him, do not apply to Jesus as an individual human being, but rather are said on account of some relationship he has with us. These statements are made, as Aquinas puts it, "with regard to a personal and relational *(habitudinalem)* property." They are statements which, while true of him, do not apply to him "in and of himself" *(secundum se),* but in a different way, in virtue of relations with others.[30]

The distinction Thomas has in mind seems to be like that between the statement "Bruce Marshall is six feet tall" and the statement "Bruce Marshall is taller than his brother-in-law Doug." That I am of some height or other is a natural property. It goes with being the possessor of a human nature, as all subjects of human nature have height. That I am six feet tall is a hypostatic property; it is the particular height I possess as an individual human being. That I have Doug as a brother-in-law is, by contrast, a product of my personal history, of a decision I made about whom to marry. That I am taller than Doug is a relation I bear to him. Thus, that I am taller than my brother-in-law is a personal and relational property.

Now an important difference between natural and hypostatic properties, on the one hand, and personal and relational properties on the other, is that properties of the second kind can come and go without changing or affecting properties of the first kind. Natural and hypostatic properties are fixed features of my makeup, which I have in virtue of the kind to which I belong and my individual constitution. Personal and relational properties

---

29. See *Summa theologiae* III, q. 15, a. 1, ad 1.

30. The quoted passages are from *ST* III, q. 15, a. 1, ad 1; for the text, see the next note.

change depending on events in the world and choices I make; they belong to my condition *(habitudo)*, not to my constitution. This, I take it, is the point with which Aquinas is mainly concerned here. Being six feet tall and being taller than my brother-in-law Doug are both properties that I have. But I would still be six feet tall if Doug were not my brother-in-law (because, for example, I had chosen not to marry), if I were shorter instead of taller than he (as I am shorter than his twin brother Don), or if Doug did not exist at all, and I had no relation to him, heightwise or otherwise. In this sense, the statement "Marshall is six feet tall" is true of me "in and of" myself, while the statement "Marshall is taller than his brother-in-law Doug" is not, but is true of me in virtue of a relation I have to another.

Under the first heading, of utterances that attribute natural and hypostatic properties, falls not only the statement that Christ "has been made man," but also, as with Cyril, the statement that "he suffered for us." Such statements would be true of Jesus even apart from his relationship with us — even if we did not exist, as it were (crucifixion would have brought suffering in any case, though if we were not, he would naturally not have suffered "for us"). The cry of dereliction, Thomas here argues, falls into the second class. It belongs among those utterances that attribute personal and relational properties to their subject. These are true statements about Jesus which are not, however, true of him "in and of himself" *(secundum se)*, but rather are true of him in virtue of a particular sort of relation he has to us. It is right to say "Jesus was forsaken on the cross," as it is right to say "Jesus suffered on the cross." But the grammar of the two statements is different. Jesus suffered "in and of himself," or in his own person, but he was God-forsaken not in his own person, but "in our person," *in persona nostra*. Here Thomas's position seems to coincide with Cyril's. It may seem obvious to us that Jesus utters the cry from the cross in his own person (that is, naturally and hypostatically), just as he suffers in his own person. But as Thomas sees it, Jesus here speaks not for himself, as one forsaken, but for us, who have known, and merited, God-forsakenness.[31]

---

31. All quotations from *ST* III, q. 15, a. 1, ad 1: "[S]icut Damascenus dicit, dicitur aliquid de Christo, uno modo, secundum proprietatem naturalem et hypostaticam, sicut dicitur quod factus est homo, et quod pro nobis passus est; alio modo, secundum proprietatem personalem et habitudinalem, prout scilicet aliqua dicuntur de ipso in persona nostra quae sibi secundum se nullo modo conveniunt."

Aquinas evidently treats this sort of distinction between what belongs to Christ *in persona nostra* and *secundum se*, traceable to Augustine, as familiar and uncontested. Its use will

Or so one can infer from what Thomas says here. What actually concerns him about the cry from the cross in the passage we have been looking at is not, however, "Why have you forsaken me?" (Vulg.: *ut quid dereliquisti*), but the further words of Psalm 21(22):1, which Thomas and his objector both assume must be words of Christ, like the whole psalm (a reading required, as Thomas sees it, by Jesus' use of the psalm's opening words from the cross).[32] The Vulgate rendering of Psalm 21(22):1, based on the Septuagint by way of Origen's Hexapola, has a quite different sense from the Hebrew, and thus from any modern translation. In the Vulgate the speaker (David) does not ask, as we might expect, "Why are you so far from the words of my groaning?" but says "The outcry of my sins puts me far from my salvation" (literally, "the words of my sin . . .": *longe a salute mea verba delictorum meorum*). In the text which had authority for Thomas, therefore, Psalm 21(22) is not a cry for justice from an innocent man baffled by God's absence, but a plea for mercy from one who recognizes the consequences of his sin.[33]

---

continue. The proximity, for example, between what St. Thomas says here and Luther's teaching that Christ is "a sinner" in our person rather than in his own person cannot be overlooked. Commenting on Galatians 3:13, Luther observes that Paul "[n]on enim dicit Christum factum Maledictum pro se, sed 'pro nobis.' . . . Nam Christus, quod ad suam personam attinet, est innocens. Ergo non debebat suspendi in lingo." Yet "Christus ipse etiam secundum legem Mosi suspendi debuit, Quia gessit personam peccatoris et latronis" (WA 40/I, p. 433.15-21). In a related vein Luther argues that "[E]x te et [Christo] fiat quasi una persona quae non possit segregari sed perpetuo adhaerescat ei et dicat: Ego sum ut Christus, et vicissim Christus dicat: Ego sum ut ille peccator, quia adhaeret mihi, et ego illi" (p. 285.25-27; compare Aquinas's language at notes 36 and 40, below). This raises intriguing (and so far as I know, largely unstudied) questions about what the precise relationship between the two might be. But here I will not enter into the difficult task of sorting that out.

32. For Aquinas this is the first of the passion psalms (of which there are five, matching the five wounds of Christ), that is, of those "which speak at length *(prolixe)* of Christ's passion." Psalm 21(22) in particular "treats in a special way the passion of Christ," hence "it was precisely this Psalm which he uttered in the passion when he cried out, 'My God, My God. . . .'" The literal meaning of this psalm must therefore be precisely the sense it has on the lips of the crucified Christ, while the sufferings of the Old Testament author himself constitute the figurative meaning of the passage; they are a figure, that is, of Christ's passion yet to be. *Super Psalmos* 21, 1: "Et inter alia specialiter iste Psalmus agit de passione Christi. Et ideo hic est eius sensus litteralis. Unde specialiter hunc Psalmum in passione dixit cum clamavit. . . . Et ideo licet figuraliter hic Psalmus dicatur de David, tamen specialiter ad litteram refertur ad Christum" (Parma edition, vol. 14, p. 217a).

33. Though the Latin Psalter translated from the Septuagint (viz., the "Gallican Psalter,"

Since this psalm is first of all the utterance of Jesus in his passion, it is Jesus himself who here speaks of "my sins," and who attributes to himself not only dereliction, but sin. This is what most concerns Thomas, since he takes it as a matter quite basic to scriptural faith in Christ and his saving work that Christ is, in fact, sinless. Establishing this is the burden of the present article (*ST* III, q. 15, q. 1), and the reason the cry of dereliction comes up in connection with the more basic problem, as Thomas sees it, of Jesus' attribution of sin to himself.[34] When Jesus speaks of "my sins," he is of course telling us the truth. But he cannot be God incarnate, or offer his human flesh for the life of the world, unless he is sinless in his own hypostasis and human nature, wholly without actual and original sin *secundum se.* This is the reason we must take Jesus to be speaking here not for himself, but for us who are sinners, not "in his own person," but "in our person." When Jesus says "my sins," in other words, we must apply the first rule of Tyconius, as reported by Augustine (in *De Doctrina Christiana* III.xxxi.44), namely that "Christ and the Church are reckoned *(aestimatur)* as one person." When we look at the matter in this way, Thomas comments, we see that "Christ speaking in the person of his members says 'the outcry of my sins'; it does not mean that there was sin in the head himself."[35] The same goes *a fortiori* when Jesus says he is forsaken by God. No sin, no dereliction, since abandonment by God is a consequence of sin.

---

upon which Thomas bases his exegesis) had been the normal Vulgate version of the Psalms since the Carolingian era, Aquinas recognizes that Jerome had also translated the passage in a different way (in fact from the Hebrew, the version of Jerome's Psalter widely used in Spain and Italy in the early Middle Ages): "littera Hieronymi habet, 'longe a salute mea verba gemitus mei'" (*Super Psalmos* 21, 1; Parma edition, vol. 14, p. 218b). This is the reading familiar to us: "Why are you, my salvation, so far from the words of my sighing?" Thomas accepts Jerome's authority on the matter, and admits this as a legitimate reading, but does not think it changes the basic sense of the cry from the cross, giving us license to take Jesus as an innocent sufferer agonized by God's absence. He attributes Jesus' sigh *(gemitus)* to the natural weakness of his perishing flesh (about which more in section VI, below), rather than to any bafflement about God's purposes.

34. Cf. *ST* III, q. 15, a. 1, c: One who is a sinner himself cannot save sinners (in particular, Aquinas here observes, cannot make satisfaction to the Father for sinners), he cannot embody human nature as God created it and intends it to be, and he cannot be the paradigm of a life of virtue for sinners. See also, e.g., *ST* III, q. 14, a. 3; q. 31, a. 7.

35. "'Christi et Ecclesiae una persona aestimatur.' Et secundum hoc, Christus ex persona membrorum suorum loquens dicit, 'verba delictorum meorum'; non quod in ipso capite delicta fuerint" (*ST* III, q. 15, a. 1, ad 1).

So Jesus must be derelict in the same sense in which he is a sinner, namely not in his own person, but in ours, not speaking for himself, but for us.

V

What, though, is Thomas getting at when he says that Jesus is derelict, and a sinner, not in his own person but in ours, that he cries out from the cross not speaking for himself, but for us? Here Thomas does not, so far as I can see, go exactly Cyril's route and suggest that Jesus is asking what amounts to a rhetorical question when he says, "My God, my God, why have you forsaken me?" Instead he thinks about the issue by reflecting further on Christ as the head of the Church, that is, on the baptismal unity of the Church with Christ to form one subject, a single mystical person.

Evidently not everyone can speak for others the way Jesus does on the cross. In order for one person to speak for another, or for many others, there has to be some sort of bond among them, a unity more or less closely analogous to the organic bond among the parts or members of a body. A characteristic of this sort of bond is that what is done or suffered by one member of the body *secundum se* is rightly counted as done or suffered by all the members, because of the unity of the body. Thus when my foot hurts, I hurt (or my body hurts), when my right hand makes a good catch, I make a good catch (or my body does). Or, to use Thomas's more theologically freighted example, "a man may compensate for a wrong done with his feet by a good work he does with his hands."[36] If I kick a hole in my neighbor's door, and have the needed carpentry skills, I can compensate for my misdeed, set it right, by using my hands to repair or replace the door. If someone else's hands have to do it, hands that are not organically related to my feet, then I have not made good my foot's misdeed, and will have to do so in some other way. So the capacity to speak for others, as Jesus does here, is basically the capacity of one person to take responsibility for others in some way, on account of a bond similar to that among the members of a body. Thus the hand can take responsibility for the foot, because they are united as members of one physical body, and parents can take responsibility for their children, because they are united as members of one family.

---

36. *ST* III, q. 49, a. 1, c: "[S]icut si homo per aliquod opus meritorium quod manu exerceret redimeret se a peccato quod pedibus commisisset."

Jesus is of course an individual person distinct from us, who as such speaks for himself, just as we do. However: "in the same way as a natural body consisting of many members is only one body, so also the whole Church, which is the mystical body of Christ, is counted as *(computatur)* a single person, in a way, with its head, who is Christ."[37] The human being Jesus unites the Church to himself by the outpouring *(effluxus)* of grace which comes from him alone, and by his direction and governance of the whole body as its principal agent.[38] Since he is in this way one person with his Church, Jesus can speak for all his members, and not only for himself. He can accept responsibility for our sin and dereliction.

So Jesus does when he speaks of himself as a sinner, and as abandoned by God. Human beings can speak for each other in many ways, but the responsibility for others that Jesus accepts in Gethsemane and on Golgotha,

---

37. "Sicut enim naturale corpus est unum ex membrorum diversitate consistens, ita tota Ecclesia, quae est mysticum corpus Christi, computatur quasi una persona cum suo capite, quod est Christus" (*ST* III, q. 49, a. 1, c). Aquinas says "quasi" here because the Church and Christ are not literally a natural body with its head, but are like one in a range of pertinent ways. "[S]icut tota Ecclesia dicitur unum corpus mysticum per similitudenem ad naturale corpus hominis . . . ita Christus dicitur caput Ecclesiae secundum similitudinem humani capitis" (*ST* III, q. 8, a. 1, c; cf. ad 2).

38. *ST* III, q. 8, a. 6, c: "Interior autem effluxus gratiae non est ab aliquo nisi a solo Christo, cuius humanitas, ex hoc quod est divinitati adiuncta, habet virtutem iustificandi. Sed influxus in membra Ecclesiae quantum ad exteriorem gubernationem potest aliis convenire," but "[d]ifferenter tamen a Christo," especially because "Christus est caput Ecclesiae propria virtute et auctoritate; alii vero dicuntur capita inquantum vicem gerunt Christi."

Aquinas often says that Christ is the head of the Church militant and triumphant (e.g., *ST* III, q. 8, a. 1, obj. 1-2; q. 8, a. 4, ad 2), and indeed of the angels themselves (cf. *ST* III, q. 8, a. 4, c), as a human being *(secundum quod homo)*, and not only as God. Thus, e.g., regarding the Church: "[C]apiti comparatur Christus, secundum visibilem naturam, qua homo hominibus praefertur" (*ST* III, q. 8, a. 1, ad 3). When Aquinas asserts that Christ alone *(solo)* is the source of grace, and thus alone head of the Church, he means (1) that among human beings only he has the inherent power to justify sinners by the outpouring of grace which joins others to himself, and (2) that among the three divine persons, who together pour out grace as a single divine act, Jesus Christ is the source of this act in a distinctive way; it is "appropriated" to him. Compare Aquinas's account of Christ's power to judge human beings and angels, which also (*ST* III, q. 59, a. 2, c; a. 6, c) belongs to him *secundum quod homo:* "iudicaria potestas sit communis toti Trinitati. . . . Sed tamen per quamdam appropriationem iudicaria potestas attribuitur Filio" (*ST* III, q. 59, a. 1, ad 1; cf. c). Regarding the theology of trinitarian appropriations, particularly in Aquinas, see Bruce D. Marshall, *Trinity and Truth* (Cambridge: Cambridge University Press, 2000), pp. 251-56.

the prerogative to speak for all of us when it comes to sin and God-forsakenness, belongs uniquely to him. For Jesus is the head not only of the Church, but of all human beings, who are at least potentially his members through baptism and faith, and for whose sins he has made good by an offering that immeasurably exceeds all their need.[39] "Why are you so far from saving me?" Jesus calls out to God from the cross, not because the Father has rejected him as an individual person, but because the sinners for whom Jesus speaks face this rejection. God dwells with the holy, not with sinners. Jesus speaks of God as far off not because the Father is far from *him* (cf. John 16:32), but because the sinners for whom he speaks and takes responsibility are far from the Father.[40]

While Jesus Christ is the head of all human beings insofar as they have at least the possibility of belonging to his body, he is head of the Church in a different and more intimate way. Only those who are actually his members through baptism are joined to him so as to be *quasi una persona* with him. Although Jesus has no sin *secundum se,* as an individual person, he can rightly speak of the sins and forsakenness of his members as his own, since they form one corporate person with him. When he cried out on the cross,

> Christ spoke in the person of the sinner, or of the Church. . . . [T]hose things which belong to his members Christ says of himself, because Christ and the Church are like one mystical body. Therefore they speak like one person, Christ transforming himself into the Church, and the Church into Christ, as Romans 12:[5] says: "we who are many are one body in Christ."[41]

---

39. Cf. *ST* III, q. 8, a. 3, sc, with reference to 1 Timothy 4:10 and 1 John 2:2: "Salvare autem homines aut propitiatorem esse pro peccatis eorum competit Christo secundum quod est caput. Ergo Christus est caput omnium hominum." Those are most fully Christ's members "qui actu uniuntur sibi per gloriam," but as long as human beings are at least potentially his members, he remains their head (q. 8, a. 3, c).

40. Cf. *Super Psalmos* 21, 3 "[L]oquatur Christus in persona peccatoris; quasi dicat, Ideo es longe a salute mea, quia non habitat in peccatoribus; sed in sancto" (Parma edition, vol. 14, p. 219a).

41. "Unde haec verba dixit Christus in persona peccatoris, sive Ecclesiae. . . . [E]a quae pertinent ad membra, dicit Christus de se, propter hoc, quod sunt sicut unum corpus mysticum Christus et Ecclesia; et ideo loquuntur sicut una persona, et Christus transformat se in Ecclesiam, et Ecclesia in Christum: Rom. 12[:5]: 'Multi unum corpus sumus in Christo.'" When Christ speaks from the cross "in persona peccatorum," he takes responsibil-

Since he forms the Church as, in a sense, a single person or subject with himself, Jesus is able to speak, and take responsibility, for the whole body, for the single corporate person of which he is the head. Conversely the members of the body, all those for whom he speaks and takes responsibility on account of their union with him, are radically different because he speaks for them, more different than they could ever be *secundum se,* in and of themselves.

By uttering the psalmist's cry, "My God, my God, why have you forsaken me?" from the depths of his passion, Jesus is inviting us sinners to see and believe that here, at the most extreme moment of his suffering, he speaks for us. We who truly stand to suffer God-forsakenness, who face divine rejection in our own persons, can here be sure that he takes responsibility for us and for our sin. We can be sure of this just because we may be certain that precisely here, in his deepest agony, he cannot be speaking for himself, or in his own person.

More than that: by speaking for us Jesus is here inviting us to be joined to him, to become his members by the influx of his own plenitude of grace, and so to find our own life and suffering transformed into a share in his passion.[42] He is inviting us, in other words, to be baptized into his death (cf. Rom. 6:3).[43] As his members we can rightly speak of his superabundant satisfaction and sacrifice for sin as our own, even though *secundum se,* as individual persons considered apart from our baptismal membership in his body, we can make no satisfaction for our sins.

> In baptism a person is incorporated into the passion and death of Christ. . . . From this it is clear that the passion of Christ is shared with

---

ity precisely for those are abandoned by God because of their sins, "qui quandoque propter peccata derelinquuntur a Deo." *Super Psalmos* 21, 1 (Parma edition, vol. 14, p. 218b).

42. The grace by which Jesus joins us to himself is simply that complete fullness of grace (cf. John 1:16) which belongs to him as an individual human being (*singularis homo; ST* III, q. 7, prooem.), now shared with us. "[E]x eminentia gratiae quam accepit, competit sibi quod gratia illa ad alios derivetur; quod pertinet ad rationem capitis" (*ST* III, q. 8, a. 5, c). This gift of his own deiform humanity (cf. *ST* III, q. 7, a. 1, obj. 1 & ad 1) to us takes place, Thomas emphasizes, "per solam personalem actionem ipsius Christi" and not simply in virtue of our shared human nature (*ST* III, q. 8, a. 5, ad 1).

43. "[H]omo per baptismum incorporatur ipsi morti Christi" (*ST* III, q. 68, a. 5, c). This baptismal membership in Christ's death comes to pass, as we have just observed, by the gift of Christ's own grace. As Augustine says, "'[B]aptizati Christo incorporentur ut membra eius.' A capite autem Christo in omnia membra eius gratiae et virtutis plenitudo derivatur" (*ST* III, q. 69, a. 4, c).

every baptized person as the remedy [for sin], as if he himself had suffered and died. But the passion of Christ . . . is the sufficient satisfaction for all the sins of all people. Therefore a person who is baptized is freed from liability to every penalty which is owed to him on account of his sins, as if he himself had sufficiently made satisfaction for all his sins.[44]

The baptized can say, "We have made sufficient satisfaction for our sins" in just the same way that Christ can say, "I am a sinner," or "Why have you forsaken me?" The baptized do not make satisfaction for sin in their own persons, but in the person of Christ, to whom they are joined; the body can speak of having made satisfaction, because the head has. Just so, Jesus Christ is not a sinner, and thus God-forsaken, in his own person, but in the person of his members, who are joined to him. The head can speak of being a sinner, because the members are.

Christ speaks of himself as a sinner and one forsaken, we can say by way of summary, not because he, as an individual person, has sins or is forsaken. Rather by calling himself a sinner he announces to his members, from Abel and Abraham to the end of time, that in his passion he has consumed their sins, and with that their God-forsakenness — that he is the great high priest who has forever devoured their sins by the offering of himself.

Here the idea that in his passion Jesus is both priest and victim has important work to do.[45] He makes satisfaction for sin before God as the vic-

---

44. *ST* III, q. 69, a. 2, c: "[P]er baptismum aliquis incorporatur passioni et morti Christi. . . . Ex quo patet quod omni baptizato communicatur passio Christi ad remedium ac si ipse passus et mortuus esset. Passio autem Christi . . . est sufficiens satisfactio pro omnibus peccatis omnium hominum. Et ideo ille qui baptizatur liberatur a reatu omnis poenae sibi debitae pro peccatis, ac si ipse sufficienter satisfecisset pro omnibus peccatis suis." Cf. *ST* III, q. 48, a. 2, ad 1: "[C]aput et membra sunt quasi una persona mystica. Et ideo satisfactio Christi ad omnes fideles pertinet sicut ad sua membra." This capacity to count Christ's satisfaction for sin as one's own depends on being configured to Christ in baptism, on being *quasi una persona* with him: "[A]d hoc quod consequamur effectum passionis Christi oportet nos ei configurari. Configuramur autem ei in baptismo sacramentaliter" (*ST* III, q. 49, a. 3, ad 2; to be sure, a person may be configured to Christ by the faith that desires baptism into him, even if she does not receive the sacrament itself; cf. q. 68, a. 2, c).

On the question of what Aquinas means when he speaks of Christ's passion as "satisfaction" for sin, which there is no room to explore here, see Emmanuel Perrier, "L'enjeu christologique de la satisfaction," *Revue Thomiste* 103 (2003): 105-36, 203-47.

45. See *ST* III, q. 22, a. 2, c: "[I]pse Christus, inquantum homo, non solum fuit sacerdos, sed etiam hostia perfecta."

tim upon whom the totality of sin is laid, as, by way of anticipation, it was laid on the victims of the Old Testament sacrifices. He is the perfect offering for sin, who more than makes good all the wrong done by sin. In just this sense, Aquinas argues, Paul says that God "made Christ to be sin" (2 Cor. 5:21). "Not that he had sin in himself, but that [God] made him to be the victim for sin."[46]

At the same time Jesus is the priest who offers the perfect sacrifice for sin, by offering himself. As not only victim but priest Jesus consumes the sins of those for whom the offering is made, namely his members, as the Levitical priests consumed, by way of anticipation, the sacrifices they offered for sin. The priests "eat the sins of my people," says Hosea (4:8). Aquinas takes this not, as the context suggests, to be a prophetic denunciation of the Levitical priests for encouraging the sins of the Israelites, but rather as a reference to their ritually prescribed consumption of a portion of the Temple sacrifices. "Hosea says, 'they eat the sins of my people,' that is, the priests, who according to the law consumed the victims offered for sin."[47] And so, in a way, Jesus does here. He consumes the sins laid upon him, the sins for which he is the victim. More precisely, he not only accepts the responsibility for our sin — has our sin laid upon him — by offering, as victim, the fullest possible satisfaction and most perfect sacrifice to the Father. As priest, he also accepts responsibility for our sins by consuming them, by taking them into himself. So Aquinas observes, commenting on John 1:29 ("Behold the Lamb of God, who takes away the sin of the world"): "'he takes away,' that is, he accepts into himself, the sins of the whole world, because 'he bore our sins in his own body' (1 Pet. 2:14), and 'he has borne our sufferings, and carried our

---

46. "Non quidem ut in se peccatum haberet, sed quia fecit eum hostiam pro peccato." This is, equally, the sense of Isaiah 53:6 ("The Lord has laid on him the iniquities of us all."). "[Q]uia scilicet [Dominus] eum tradidit ut esset hostia pro peccatis omnium hominum" (*ST* III, q. 15, a. 1, ad 4).

47. "Sicut Osee dicitur, 'Peccata populi mei comedent,' scilicet sacerdotes, qui secundum legem comedebant hostias pro peccato oblatas" (*ST* III, q. 15, a. 1, ad 4). The presenting question here is why texts like 2 Corinthians 5:21 say that Christ not only has, but is, "sin." Aquinas introduces the Hosea passage in order to show that Scripture sometimes refers to the victim offered in sacrifice for sin as itself "sin." Cf. *In Rom.* 8, 1 (no. 609: Christ "factus est hostia pro peccato, quae in sacra Scriptura dicitur peccatum") and *In II Cor.* 5, 5 (no. 201). But the more suggestive thought here lies in the parallel (or more exactly, the figurative relation), which Aquinas often draws, between the Levitical priesthood and the priesthood of Christ.

griefs (Isa. 53:4).'"[48] Jesus does not bear our sins, take them into himself, by somehow being the one who commits the sins of his members, or being regarded by God as the one who has committed them. He takes them in by consuming them, incinerating them in the fire of his passion.[49] The sins of the members — of those who actually did commit them — are devoured by their baptismal contact with Christ's passion, by the sacramental gift which makes them *quasi una persona* with him. And so "Christ by his cross has destroyed sin," and with that the abandonment by God which sin brings with it.[50]

VI

Although Aquinas evidently regards the idea that Jesus speaks *in persona nostra* as indispensable to an adequate understanding of the cry of dereliction, he grants that there is also an important sense in which Jesus is, as an individual person, forsaken by God. Rightly understood the two are compatible, and Thomas maintains, characteristically, that both should be taken as legitimate interpretations of the cry from the cross. "These words of Christ in prayer can be explained in two different ways."[51]

One meaning of "forsake" or "abandon" is "hand over," in the sense of

48. "'[T]ollit,' idest in se accipit, 'peccata' totius 'mundi'; quia, ut dicitur I Pet. 2:14, 'Qui peccata nostra pertulit in corpore suo.' Is. 53:4: 'Dolores nostros ipse tulit, et languores nostros ipse portavit.'" Following an established gloss, Thomas goes on to note that the evangelist says "sin" here, rather than "sins," in order to make clear that what Christ accepts into himself, and so takes away, is not simply some sins, but sin across the board, "the whole genus of sin." "Dicit autem, secundum Glossam, 'Peccatum,' et non 'peccata,' ut ostendat in universali, quod abstulit totum genus peccati." *Super Ioannem* 1, 13 (no. 259).

49. Without his humanity the eternal Son would not be a priest, but the high priestly act he undertakes on the cross is one which only God incarnate can accomplish. "[L]icit Christus non fuerit sacerdos secundum quod Deus, sed secundum quod homo, unus tamen et idem fuit sacerdos et Deus. . . . Et ideo, inquantum eius humanitas operabatur in virtute divinitatis, illud sacrificium erat efficacissimum ad delenda peccata" (*ST* III, q. 22, a. 3, ad 1).

50. *In Col.* 1, 5 (no. 53): "Christus per crucem destruxit peccatum. . . ."

51. *Super Psalmos* 21, 1: "Sed haec verba Christi orantis possunt dupliciter exponi" (Parma edition, vol. 14, p. 218b). Thomas is speaking here of Christ's prayer in the garden of Gethsemane, but he interprets "let this cup pass from me" (Matt. 26:39) in the same twofold way as the cry on the cross. Both conform to the same exegetical pattern: Christ speaks here both "quasi gerens infirmorum personam, qui sunt in Ecclesia," and at the same time "Alio modo . . . protulit hanc petitionem gerens officium carnis infirmae in Christo" (p. 218b).

failing or declining to protect another from suffering. As traditional interpretation of the Gospels had long held, the Father himself is among those
who hand Jesus over to suffering and death, in his own way. There is thus a
clear sense in which the Father forsakes Jesus, namely that he does not protect Jesus from his passion. "God the Father hands Christ over to his passion . . . by not protecting him from the passion, but instead exposing him
to his persecutors. For this reason Christ, hanging on the cross, said 'My
God, why have you forsaken me?' as we read in Mt. 27:46."[52] God, as St.
Paul teaches, "did not spare his only Son, but gave him up for us all" (Rom.
8:32), abandoning Jesus to suffering and death at the hands of men.[53]

So understood, Jesus' abandonment, like the suffering that follows
upon it, is his own, and not that of his members. When Jesus cries out
from the cross he speaks not only in our person, but in his own person,
not only for us, but for himself (or *secundum se*). The same utterance has
both senses, but it is important to keep them distinct. We can and should
take Jesus to attribute sin to himself here, and the God-forsakenness
which sin brings with it — the lot of the damned. But taken this way he
speaks, as we have seen, for us, and not for himself.[54] We should also take
him as speaking for himself, and not only for us. But taken this way he attributes to himself not sin, but suffering, and not damnation, but the per-

52. "Deus Pater tradidit Christum passioni . . . non protegendo eum a passione, sed
exponendo persequentibus. Unde, ut legitur Matt. 27:46, pendens in cruce Christus dicebat:
'Deus meus, ut quid dereliquisti me?'" (*ST* III, q. 47, a. 3, c). In fact this is the last of three
senses in which Aquinas holds that the Father "hands over" the Son to suffering; beyond
this, he gives Jesus the grace to accept the passion in love *(caritas)*, and wills eternally that Jesus' passion be the way humanity shall be freed from sin. On the latter, see below, note 61.

53. See *Super Psalmos* 21, 1: "Est autem sciendum, quod aliquis dicitur derelictus a Deo
quando non adest ei Deus, sicut videtur adesse quando protegit eum, et implet eius
petitionem. . . . Et quia Christus non est liberatus a passione corporali cum esset in passione,
secundum hoc dicitur ad horam derelictus, idest passioni expositus: Rom. 8: 'Proprio filio
suo non perpercit'" (Parma edition, vol. 14, p. 218a).

54. That Jesus does not experience the sufferings of hell in his own person follows from
his sinlessness, which would make it unjust for God to subject him to this, and also from his
possession of the full vision of God even in his passion, which would make it metaphysically
impossible for him to suffer in this way (I will not pursue the complexities of these two issues here). But in any case Thomas is explicit about the point. "[C]um Christus non
assumpserit nisi dolorem viatoris, dolor damnati . . . est maior quam fuerit dolor Christi;
quia ille dolor facit damnatum miserum: quod absit ut de Christo dicatur." *In* III *Sent.* d. 15,
q. 2, a. 3, qla. iii, ad 5 (= *Scriptum super libros Sententiarum*, vol. 3, ed. M. F. Moos [Paris:
Lethielleux, 1933], p. 502, §154).

mission of his suffering by the Father, without which it could never take place.

That Jesus does not, "in his own person," actually suffer the lot of the damned on the cross is not to say that his abandonment and suffering are superficial or without distress. On the contrary, "His cry makes plain the magnitude of his human feeling."[55] The dereliction Jesus accepts *secundum se* naturally brings with it great bodily or physical pain. Jesus suffers even this bodily pain, of course, in a distinctively human way. It penetrates to the depths of his soul, as he confronts "the loss of bodily life, which is naturally horrible to human nature."[56] So Jesus cries out to the Father who has handed him over to death, remaining silent in the face of his prayer (Matt. 26:39) that he be spared this cup of suffering. Jesus accepts this lot voluntarily out of love for the Father and for us, despite the natural and profound human resistance that his question to the Father attests.[57]

Jesus suffers more, however, than the imminent and exceptionally agonizing loss of his bodily life. The sins of the world, all the sins of every human being, afflict him. Aquinas is certainly willing to say that Jesus suffers for our sins in the sense that he accepts the punishment or penalty due to sin, in manifold ways (such as hunger, thirst, and death).[58] But more than

---

55. "[I]deo ingeminat, ut magnitudinem affectus humani designet." *Super Matthaeum* 27, 2 (no. 2383).

56. "[A]missio vitae corporalis, quae naturaliter est horribilis humanae naturae" (*ST* III, q. 46, a. 6, c); cf. *Super Psalmos* 21, 1: the flesh in its weakness "in Christo . . . naturaliter timet et fugit mortem" (Parma edition, vol. 14, p. 218b). On Christ's passion affecting his entire soul, and reaching all the way down, cf. *ST* III, q. 46, a. 7, c: "[C]orpore patiente et disposito ad separationem ab anima, tota anima patiebatur . . . omnes enim potentiae animae radicantur in essentia eius, ad quam pervenit passio, passo corpore, cuius est actus." Thus the "flesh" which recoils from death is not simply Jesus' body, but includes his human will. "Christus habuit naturalem hominis voluntatem; hoc autem est quod mortem refugiat" (*Super Matthaeum* 26, 4 [no. 2232]).

57. One way to interpret the cry from the cross, Thomas observes, is precisely to take it with reference to the prayer in the garden, which is also twofold: not only that the cup of suffering might pass from him, but that he will do the Father's will come what may. "Vel dicit se derelictum quantum ad illam orationem, qua dixerat 'Pater, si fieri potest, transeat a me calix iste,' ut Augustinus dicit" (*ST* III, q. 50, a. 2, ad 1; cf. obj. 1). On the agony in the garden see Paul Gondreau's paper in this volume.

58. Thus *ST* III, q. 14, a. 1, c: "Filius Dei, carne assumpta, venit in mundum, ut pro peccato humani generis satisfaceret. Unus autem pro peccato alterius satisfacit dum poenam peccato alterius debitam in seipsum suscipit. Huiusmodi autem defectus corporales, scilicet mors, fames et sitis, et huiusmodi, sunt poena peccati." Note that Thomas links satisfaction

that: out of love for the Father and for sinners, Jesus accepts responsibility for all the sorrow human beings owe to God for the total reality of sin, for all the sins of every sinner. "Christ not only suffered on account of the loss of his own bodily life, but also for the sins of everyone else." In his passion Jesus undertakes one great act of contrition for the sins of the world, an act of the deepest possible human sorrow for sin, rooted in the greatest possible *caritas.* "Christ's suffering exceeded all the anguish of any penitent, because it came from greater wisdom and love, which intensifies the suffering in contrition, and because he suffered for all sins at the same time." Jesus does not lament any sins of his own, but the sins of others, of all those who are at least potentially his members (that is, of every human being). This does not diminish, but increases, his suffering. As every penitent knows, contrition is always painful, and the peculiar suffering it brings — voluntary self-humiliation out of sorrow for sin — in fact increases the more the sorrow springs from love for God, freely given. (The saints, who among the redeemed love God the most in this life, are also the most acutely aware of their sins.) Jesus' sorrow for sin is purely voluntary (since he has no sins of which he needs to repent), supremely rooted in love, and extends to every single sin. He alone "truly bears our griefs" (Isa. 53:4), and this is one way in which his suffering is like no other (cf. Lam. 1:12).[59]

---

for sin in part to the suffering of sin's penalty (see also ad 1 & 3 here), rather than, like St. Anselm, taking *satisfactio* and *poena* as opposites. Cf. Anselm, *Cur Deus homo* I, 15: "Ipsa namque perversitatis spontanea satisfactio *vel* a *non* satisfaciente poenae exactio — excepto hoc quia deus de malis multis modis bona facit — in eadem universitate suum tenent locum et ordinis pulchritudinem . . . necesse est ut omne peccatum satisfactio *aut* poena sequatur" (Schmitt edition, vol. 2, pp. 73.19-22, 74.1-2; my emphasis); cf. I, 12 (Schmitt, vol. 2. p. 69.25) and I, 13 (p. 71.24-25). In Thomas, see also *In Gal.* 3, 5 (no. 149), on Galatians 3:13 ("Christus . . . factus pro nobis maledictum"): "Christus liberavit nos a poena, sustinendo poenam et mortem nostram: quae quidem in nos provenit ex ipsa maledictione peccati."

59. The quoted sentences are from *ST* III, q. 46, a. 6, ad 4: "Christus non solum doluit pro amissione vitae corporalis propriae, sed etiam pro peccatis omnium aliorum, qui dolor in Christo excessit omnem dolorem cuiuscumque contriti: tum quia ex maiori sapientia et caritate processit, ex quibus dolor contritionis augetur; tum etiam quia pro omnibus peccatis simul doluit, secundum illud Is. [53:4], 'Vere dolores nostros ipse tulit.'" Aquinas takes Lamentations 1:12 — "Look and see if there is any suffering like my suffering" — as spoken "ex persona Christi" (*ST* III, q. 46, a. 6, c), and so as warrant for saying that Christ's passion exceeds all other suffering when taken as a whole, though not in every particular respect (he does not, e.g., suffer the specific misery of the lost; cf. note 54). For a full treatment of Aquinas on Christ's suffering, see Paul Gondreau, *The Passions of Christ's Soul in the Theology of St. Thomas Aquinas* (Münster: Aschendorff, 2002).

Here the link between what Jesus does in his own person and what he does for us, or in our person, is especially clear. What Jesus suffers in his own person, in particular the contrition he offers for our sin, is part and parcel of his sacrifice, of his perfect offering of himself to the Father in love. The sins Jesus mourns in his passion, and for which he offers himself to the Father in Gethsemane and on Calvary, are not his own. He mourns over sin *in persona nostra.* But his sorrow over all the sins of the world brings with it a suffering in body and soul which is his own, and which has no parallel in our suffering — we who do not mourn our own sin, let alone the sins of others, as Jesus does. Without this suffering *secundum se,* Jesus could not be the head of his earthly body, at least not a body sinners could be invited to join. By deciding to speak for sinners, to have members in whose person he can speak, Jesus accepts in love a suffering that is uniquely his own.

For Thomas there is, then, a soteriologically significant sense in which Jesus suffers the Father's abandonment, not only when he speaks for us, but when he speaks for himself. None of this is to say, though, that "in his own person" Jesus suffers, or could suffer, the total loss of God. To say that the Father abandons Jesus to a voluntary passion for our salvation, Thomas stresses, is quite a different matter from saying that the divine Logos abandons the human being Jesus on the cross, as ancient heresy held (prompted in part by the cry of dereliction).[60] The Father "exposes" or hands Jesus over to his passion, but he does not consign him to a condition where God is utterly and irrevocably absent — to damnation. This would mean, *per impossibile,* that the human being Jesus had ceased to be united to God the Word.

So far as I can tell, Thomas never entertains the thought that God the Word *himself* is abandoned by the Father, that the eternal Father deserts or departs from his own eternal Word on the cross. To be sure, the Father sends his Son into the world so that the Son, become our flesh, can accept

60. Whether openly or by implication, Aquinas argues, both Arian and Nestorian Christologies embrace this conclusion. Interpreting the cry of dereliction, the Arians "[d]icunt quod hoc dicebat Verbum Dei, et vocat eum Deum, quia creatura sua est," while for the Nestorians Jesus "conqueritur, quod hoc Verbum fecit sibi uniri, et post dereliquit eum." But in either case "haec est expositio impia, quia semper cum eo est; unde divinitas non dimisit carnem, nec animam" (*Super Matthaeum* 27, 2 [no. 2383]). Cf. *ST* III, q. 50, a. 2, ad 1: "[D]erelictio illa non est referenda ad solutionem unionis personalis, sed ad hoc quod Deus Pater eum exposuit passioni."

his passion for our salvation.[61] But for some recent theologians, as we have seen, this familiar way of taking the scriptural indications that the Father hands his own Son over to suffering and death fails to go far enough, and so misses what really happens on the cross. The cross can only be saving, they suggest, if Jesus — the incarnate Word himself — undergoes the most extreme possible form of human abandonment by God. Our salvation requires, on views of this sort, that the Word on the cross experiences the complete withdrawal of God, rightly perceiving the real and hopeless absence of the Father who sent him.

Unwilling to regard the Gospel of John as a secondary (let alone distorting) theological gloss on "the historical reality" of Jesus' passion, Aquinas would surely regard this idea as manifestly unbiblical. On the eve of his passion Jesus tells his disciples that they will all forsake him and leave him alone, "but nevertheless," he adds, "I am not alone, because the Father is with me" (John 16:32). "In other words," Thomas comments, "I have not come forth from the Father in such a way that I have departed from him."[62] If we read the cry of dereliction in the context of the scriptural canon, or simply in the context of the Gospel quartet, we cannot take it to mean that one divine person vanishes, as it were, from the sight of another.

Moreover, it is difficult to see how the thought that the incarnate Word himself suffers a real (and not merely apparent) Fatherlessness on the cross is compatible with even a minimally coherent Trinitarian theology. Moltmann and others suggest that some such radical absence of the Father from the crucified Son, whether it be thought of as "Fatherlessness" or in some cognate way, is necessary for an adequately robust understanding of the Trinity. If this thought means anything, though, it presumably means — *maxime per impossibile* — that the Father has somehow ceased

---

61. "Deus Pater tradidit Christum passioni. Uno quidem modo secundum quod sua aeterna voluntate praeordinavit passionem Christi ad humani generis liberationem, secundum illud quod dicitur Is. [53:6]: 'Dominus posuit in eo iniquitatem omnium nostrum,' et iterum, 'Dominus voluit conterere eum in infirmitate'" (willed, we may perhaps say here, to receive from him in his passion perfect contrition for our sins); *ST* III, q. 47, a. 3, c. When Jesus characterizes himself as "sent" by another, he "insinuat Patrem auctorem incarnationis" (*Super Ioannem* 7, 3 [no. 1065]). But the Father already has the cross in view when he "authorizes" or wills the Son's visible mission, as also does the Son when, in the unity of the one divine will, he accepts it.

62. "[Q]uasi diceret: Etsi sum unum cum Patre per unitatem essentiae, non sum solus per distinctionem personalem: unde non sic a Patre exivi ut ab eo recederem" (*Super Ioannem* 16, 8 [no. 2172]).

the eternal act of origination by which he brings forth the Son in the unity of the divine nature.

To explain a bit. God the Son can be truly Fatherless only if God the Father has genuinely given up whatever is necessary for his paternal relationship with the Son. In the created world this does, unfortunately, sometimes happen. Fathers and mothers bring forth children, and then abandon them, which can happen because the creaturely act of generation is not by itself sufficient for what is involved in created fatherhood or motherhood (and indeed, as adoptive parents know, is not even necessary for it). Among creatures fathers, mothers, and children all remain persons even when the parents have failed to accept the relations to their children involved in full fatherhood or motherhood. In God, however, the person of the Father is inseparable from the act of generation by which he eternally brings forth the Son. Without this act of generation there would simply be no person of the Father *in divinis*. The act of generation is, in other words, a necessary condition for the Father's own existence.[63] So if *God* gives up his Fatherhood, there will be no act of generation in God. There will be no act of origination by which the Father (eternally) brings the Son to be. Were God the Father to renounce his paternity in the passion of his incarnate Son, therefore, the Son would at that moment cease to be brought forth from the Father. If *this* Son came to be Fatherless he would himself instantly cease to be. At the same time he would naturally cease to suffer the Father's dereliction, since what is not cannot suffer.

Of course if God the Father gives up his Fatherhood, not only the Son ceases to be, but the Father himself. Moltmann, to his credit, is candid about this. If the Son's cry of dereliction attests the real absence of the Father all the way down, then a "Sonlessness" of the Father must match the Fatherlessness of the Son. And with that, the Father "suffers the death of his own being as Father."[64] At this point, of course, the Father cannot really suffer over his dead Son, since the Father has also ceased to be; nor can he rescue his derelict Son from death, since what is not cannot raise the dead. Perhaps there would still be a God, who was neither eternal Father nor eternal Son (nor, *a fortiori*, Holy Spirit), but this would, in the strictest

---

63. This holds good whether we take the relation that results from the act of generation (viz., *paternitas*) to constitute the Father as a distinct divine person (following Thomas and others), or whether we take the act of generation itself, as a unique mode of production *in divinis*, to be person-constituting for the Father (following Scotus and others).

64. See above, note 5.

Bruce D. Marshall

sense, be an unknown God, and not the Trinity who lets us know him intimately in the temporal economy of salvation.[65]

Whatever it means to say that on the cross God himself is abandoned to suffering and death (about which more in the next section), it cannot mean this. Rather than opening the way to a full appreciation of the Son's dereliction, a Trinitarian theology of this sort turns out to be self-refuting. Taken in earnest, it would mean not that we had rightly heard Jesus' cry as the utterance of God incarnate, forsaken for a suffering world, but that the Son and the Father had alike ceased to be, and with that any dereliction of the one by the other. Like David of Dinant's suggestion that God is actually prime matter, this way of taking the Son's dereliction evidently seems, at least for Thomas, too wildly off base to require comment.

Aquinas does suggest, though, that a problem this serious stems from hearing the cry of dereliction in precisely the wrong way — not, in fact, as the utterance of God incarnate, but as though the one who spoke it were not true God. He cites, with obvious approval, Origen's interpretation of the cry from the cross: "You should not suppose that the Savior said this in a human way, on account of the calamity which had overtaken him on the cross. If you took it that way, you would not hear the power in his voice, which shows that something great is hidden here."[66] The "powerful voice" (magnam vocem) to which the passage refers is that of Matthew 27:46, the voice in which Jesus calls out to the Father. Rather than indicating that Jesus has now become "Fatherless," the power in his voice attests that Jesus here speaks as true God. Even here, where the fact lies most hidden, he speaks as the Father's only-begotten Son, who exists as God because of the Father's unalterable act of origination. On the cross itself the incarnate Son is God from God, and the Father the God from whom he is, just as each would be if the cross, and the world, were not.

65. We will pursue this point in more detail in section VIII below.
66. *Catena Aurea in Matt.*, 27, 9: "Non autem aestimes humano more Salvatorem ista dixisse, propter calamitatem quae comprehenderat eum in cruce: si enim ita acceperis, non audies magnam vocem eius, quae ostendit aliquid esse magnum absconditum" (*S. Thomae Aquinatis Catena Aurea in Quatuor Evangelia*, ed. Angelicus Guarienti [Turin: Marietti, 1953], vol. 1, p. 412a-b). The passage is from Origen's homilies on Matthew, which survive for the later chapters of the Gospel only in an early Latin translation. Cf. PG 13, 1787A (where the last portion of the text is different from what Thomas gives: ". . . magnam vocem in qua ista locutus est, nec digna voce divina requires").

VII

Like Cyril, Aquinas insists that the passion of Jesus is the suffering and death of God himself, in the person of the Son. In fact he invokes Cyril's authority to make this point.

> If there were some other subject in Christ beyond the hypostasis of the Word, it would follow that what belongs to him as a human being would be true of someone other than the Word — for example, to be born of the Virgin, to suffer, to be crucified, and to be buried. But this view has been condemned, with the approval of the Council of Ephesus, in these words: "If anyone divides between two persons or subjects those things which are said of Christ in the evangelical and apostolic scriptures . . . and applies some to a human being understood precisely as distinct from the Word of God, and others to the Word of God the Father alone, because only these are fitting of God, *anathema sit.*"[67]

Any denial that God the Word himself has suffered, been crucified, and lain dead in the tomb is condemned, in other words, by Cyril's fourth anathema against Nestorius.[68] Thomas has no trouble saying this in his own voice as well. The proclamation of the cross is foolishness to those who are perishing (1 Cor. 1:18), he observes, because it includes "what human wisdom regards as impossible, namely that God dies, and that the omnipotent falls prey to the hands of violent men."[69] But for Christ's faith-

---

67. *ST* III, q. 2, a. 3, c: "Si ergo sit alia hypostasis in Christo praeter hypostasim Verbi, sequetur quod de aliquo alio quam de Verbo verificentur ea quae sunt hominis, puta esse natum de Virgine, passum, crucifixum et sepultum. Et hoc etiam damnatum est, approbante Concilio Ephesino, sub his verbis, 'Si quis personis duabus vel subsistentiis eas quae sunt in evangelicis et apostolicis Scripturis impartitur voces, aut de Christo a Sanctis dictas, aut ab ipso de se; et quasdam quidem velut homini praeter illud ex Deo Verbum specialiter intellecto applicat, quasdam vero, velut Deo decibiles, soli ex Deo Patre Verbo: anathema sit.'"

68. Cf. above, note 18. Earlier in this article Thomas explicitly attributes to Cyril the anathemas approved (he assumes) at Ephesus, in a discussion of the third anathema (*ST* III, q. 2, a. 3, c, though Thomas does not number them), and he ascribes the fourth anathema itself to Cyril in *ST* III, q. 16, a. 4, c and *Summa Contra Gentiles* (= *SCG*) IV, 38 (no. 3767).

69. *In I Cor.* 1, 3 (no. 47): "[P]raedicatio crucis Christi aliquid continet, quod secundum humanam sapientiam impossibile videtur, puta quod Deus moriatur, quod omnipotens violentorum manibus subiiciatur." The cross is "foolishness to the Gentiles" (1 Cor. 1:23) because "contra rationem humanae sapientiae videtur quod Deus moriatur et quod homo iustus et sapiens se voluntarie turpissimae morti exponat" (no. 58). Cf. *SCG* IV, 34, where

ful this gospel is the saving power of God, precisely because "they recognize in the cross of Christ the death of God, by which he conquers the devil and the world. As the Apocalypse [5:5] teaches: 'Behold the lion of the tribe of Judah has conquered.'"[70] Indeed the Old Testament already makes it plain, if we pay attention, that God will conquer death by his own passion and death. "If we put together the words of the prophet [Zech. 12:10], it is obvious that Christ crucified is God. For what the prophet says in God's own person, the evangelist [John] attributes to Christ."[71]

At the same time, Aquinas also insists that God the Son suffers because he is a human being, and not because he is God. That is: God suffers in Gethsemane and dies on Golgotha on account of his human nature, and not on account of his divine nature. Here again Aquinas follows Cyril. All that it is to be God, and all that the human being Jesus is, does, and suffers, belongs to one and the same irreducible subject or "supposit," the Father's eternal Word. But some things belong to the Logos in virtue of his eternal divinity, and others in virtue of the flesh he assumed — or as Aquinas typically puts it, what is true of the incarnate Word belongs to him either in virtue of his divine nature or in virtue of his human nature. The suffering of Christ, he argues,

> must be attributed to a subject *(supposito)* of divine nature, though not by reason of the divine nature — which is impassible — but rather by reason of the human nature. Thus Cyril says, "If anyone does not confess that the Word of God has suffered in the flesh, and been crucified in the flesh, let him be anathema." Therefore the suffering of Christ belongs to a subject of divine nature, by reason of the passible nature he has assumed, but not by reason of the impassible divine nature.[72]

Thomas reads a number of other Pauline texts in the same way: "Manifestum est igitur recte dici 'Deum, Dei Verbum, esse passum et mortuum'" (no. 3705; cf. 3707); "Vere igitur dici potest quod 'Deus sit crucifixus'" (no. 3706).

70. "[I]psi [fideles] in cruce Christi mortem Dei cognoscunt, qua diabolum vicit et mundum. Apoc. V, 5: 'Ecce vicit leo de tribu Iuda.'" *In I Cor.* 1, 3 (no. 47).

71. *Super Ioannem* 19, 5 (no. 2462): "Unde si nos coniungimus verbum Prophetae, manifestum est quod Christus crucifixus est Deus. Nam quod Propheta dicit in persona Dei, Evangelista attribuit Christo." On the passion of Christ as conquering death by death, cf. *ST* III, q. 46, a. 12, ad 2: "'[M]ors Christi tanquam facta mors Dei,' scilicet per unionem in persona, 'destruxit mortem.'" The quotation is from the acts of the Council of Ephesus known to Thomas, and traceable to a sermon there by Theodotus of Ancyra. See also *ST* III, q. 16, a. 4, ad 2.

72. "[S]upposito divinae naturae attribuenda est passio, non ratione divinae naturae,

With respect to his divine nature God the Son remains impassible precisely in his human suffering and death, which exceeds the suffering of any other creature. Thus it is true to say, as the Church has held from an early point, "The impassible God suffers and dies."[73]

Aquinas, we should briefly note, sees no daunting logical problem here. Impassibility and exposure to suffering — passibility — are opposites, which naturally prompts the thought that they cannot be predicated of the same subject or person. But since we do not predicate them of the incarnate Word in the same respect, the appearance of contradiction is easily disposed of. "It is impossible for opposites to be predicated of the same thing in the same respect, but nothing prohibits predicating them of the same thing in different respects. It is in this way that opposites are predicated of Christ: not in the same respect, but with respect to different natures."[74] In its utter uniqueness, the union of divine and human natures in the person of the Word — the state of affairs that must obtain if an ut-

---

quae est impassibilis, sed ratione humanae naturae. Unde Cyrillus dicit, 'Si quis non confitetur Dei Verbum passum carne, et crucifixum carne, anathema sit.' Pertinet ergo passio Christi ad suppositum divinae naturae, ratione naturae passibilis assumptae, non autem ratione divinae naturae impassibilis" (*ST* III, q. 46, a. 12, c). The quoted passage is from Cyril's twelfth anathema against Nestorius; cf. above, note 25.

73. "[I]mpassibilis Deus patiatur et moriatur" (*In I Cor.* 15, 1 [no. 896]). Aquinas here numbers this among the articles of faith, which begin where reason fails: "[I]bi incipit articulus fidei, ubi deficit ratio" (*In I Cor.* 15, 1 [no. 896]). He is stating the views of an objector, but the point in dispute is whether to number the burial of Christ as a separate article of faith, not whether the suffering of the impassible God belongs among the articles. Cf. *SCG* IV, 55 (no. 3947): "Sic enim facta est unio in persona ut proprietas utriusque naturae maneret, divinae scilicet et humanae. . . . Et ideo, patiente Christo etiam mortem et alia quae humanitatis sunt, divinitas impassibilis mansit, quamvis, propter unitatem personae, dicamus Deum passum et mortuum."

Language of this kind is already attested in the second century, perhaps most strikingly by Melito of Sardis. "Et horruit creatura, stupescens ac dicens: '. . . impassibilis patitur, neque ulciscitur; immortalis moritur, neque respondet verbum; coelestis sepelitur, et (id) fert.' . . . At quum dominus noster surrexit e mortuis, et pede deculcavit mortem, et vinxit potentem, et solvit hominem: tunc intellexit omnis creatura propter hominem . . . impassibilem passum esse, et immortalem mortuum esse, et coelestem sepultum esse" (Fragment XIII). Méliton de Sardes, *Sur la Pâque et fragments* (*Sources Chrétiennes* 123), ed. Othmar Perler (Paris: Editions du Cerf, 1966), p. 238. Karl Barth quotes some of these phrases to his own ends in *Kirchliche Dogmatik* IV/1, p. 193 (ET, pp. 176-77).

74. "[O]pposita praedicari de eodem secundum idem est impossibile: sed secundum diversa, nihil prohibet. Et hoc modo opposita praedicantur de Christo: non secundum idem, sed secundum diversas naturas" (*ST* III, q. 16, a. 4, ad 1).

Bruce D. Marshall

terance like "The impassible God suffers and dies" is true — poses difficult metaphysical questions, to the point of being metaphysically unfathomable by human beings, at least in this life. In the incarnation God is united to a created reality "in a more sublime way" than the human mind can grasp, united "in a certain incomprehensible and unutterable way."[75] But logically, "The impassible God suffers and dies" is no more puzzling than "Corruptible man is incorruptible" — corruptible with respect to his flesh, incorruptible with respect to his soul, as all of us are.[76] The logic of the matter can be illustrated, in fact, by the most metaphysically prosaic cases. "That man is curly" (in virtue of his hair, not in virtue of what makes him a human being), we say without logical strain, or "The Ethiopian is white" (with respect to his teeth, but black with respect to his skin).[77] The rule is: opposites can be predicated of the very same thing, and yield true statements, as long as we can make a distinction between that in virtue of which, or the respect in which *(id secundum quod)*, each is predicated.[78]

75. *De rationibus fidei* 6 (ed. Leonine, vol. 40B, p. 63.89-96): "[S]ublimiori modo potest Deus creaturae uniri quam intellectus humanus capere possit. Quodam ergo incomprehensibili et ineffabili modo dicimus Deum fuisse unitum humanae naturae in Christo non solum per inhabitationem sicut ceteris sanctis, sed quodam singulari modo, ita quod humana natura esset quaedam filii Dei natura." Therefore even the most apt creaturely parallels to the hypostatic union (especially the unity of soul and body, for Aquinas) "multum a praedictae unionis repraesentatione deficiunt, sicut et cetera exampla humana a rebus divinis" (pp. 63-64.115-17).

76. Cf. *De unione Verbi incarnati* 3, ad 13: "[N]ihil prohibet contrarias et incompossibiles differentias inesse eidem secundum diversa: sicut homo secundum animam est incorruptibilis, et secundum corpus corruptibilis. Et ita etiam in Christo opposita quaedam conveniunt secundum humanam et divinam naturam."

77. Regarding the christological usefulness of these examples see III *Sent.* d. 11, q. 1, a. 3, c & ad 5 (ed. Moos, pp. 367-68, §§50-51; 56-57); also *SCG* IV, 48 (no. 3835).

78. *SCG* IV, 39 (no. 3772), in the midst of a detailed explanation of the point: "[N]ecesse est quod secundum aliud et aliud divina et humana praedicentur de Christo. Sic igitur quantum ad id *de quo* utraque praedicantur, non est distinctio facienda, sed invenitur unitas. Quantum autem ad id secundum *quod* praedicantur, distinctio est facienda." On the logic of expressions that specify, by the use of qualifiers like "secundum quod," the respect in which a particular predicate (like "suffers") applies to a particular subject (like "God"), see also *ST* III, q. 16, a. 10, c & ad 2-3; a. 11, c; a. 12, c, and *De rationibus fidei* 6, p. 65.233-68 (in medieval semantics an expression of this kind was called a "reduplication," e.g., "Deus, secundum quod homo, est passus, mortuus, et sepultus," which Thomas holds to be true [cf. above, notes 70 and 71]).

A distinction between what the incarnate Son does and suffers "as God" and "as man" is already noticed by Melito. For him Jesus Christ is at once "cibo, in quantum homo erat,

This works for the metaphysically trivial case of the curly man, and for the metaphysically unparalleled case of the incarnate God.

It must, then, be possible for a subject (a supposit or hypostasis) of divine nature to suffer, since one actually does. But he suffers only by reason of his human nature, that is, only because of the passible flesh he has freely accepted. In St. Gregory of Nyssa's exact formulation, God is not limited by that which is contrary to his nature.[79] God can become incarnate, but the suffering that is one of the present circumstances of human nature remains contrary to God's nature, and belongs to God the Son only on account of his assumption of our flesh. Were there no incarnation, there would be no suffering of God.

Nowadays this argument is commonly assumed to be a deliberate evasion, a convoluted way of saying that God the Word is not "really" the subject of Jesus' human actions and passions. For Aquinas (or Cyril), so this standard rebuttal goes, God does not really suffer and die, even though we talk about him as though he did. The human nature in Christ assuredly suffers, but God cannot truly accept suffering, since the divine nature in Christ — what makes him God — is entirely withheld from all change and passion. Or, in Moltmann's version of this objection, while the human nature's torment means that the one person in Christ genuinely suffers, the traditional view cannot say that "the *whole* divine and human person of Christ" undergoes the agony of his cross and dereliction, since a large part of that person — his divine nature — must remain aloof from all suffering.[80] Thus the common objection that the two-natures doctrine, combined with the claim that the divine nature includes impassibility among its properties, radically fails to do justice to the reality of Christ's passion.

Though widespread, this objection exhibits a basic confusion. Natures

---

indigens, et non desinens mundum alere, in quantum deus erat" (Fragment XIV; *Sur la Pâque et fragments*, p. 240).

79. *Catechetical Discourse*, 24: Ἡ δὲ πρὸς τὸ ταπεινὸν κάθοδος περιουσία τίς ἐστι τῆς δυνάνεως οὐδὲν ἐν τοῖς παρὰ φύσιν κωλυομένος ("The descent [of God] to what is lowly belongs to his superabundant power, which is not limited by that which is contrary to its nature"). Grégoire de Nysse, *Discours catéchétique* (*Sources Chrétiennes* 453), Greek text of E. Mühlenberg, ed. and trans. R. Winling (Paris: Editions du Cerf, 2000), p. 254.14-16. From this follows the reason, as Thomas sees it, why we must recognize that God is personally united to human nature in Christ in a more sublime way than we can grasp — that is, "cum efficacia divinae virtutis humano intellectu comprehendi non possit" (*De rationibus fidei* 6, p. 63.87-91; cf. above, note 75).

80. My emphasis; see above, note 3.

do not suffer or act. Persons do, because they have a nature that allows them to suffer, and to act. More generally, only the subject (in Thomas's lexicon, the *suppositum* or *hypostasis*) of a nature acts or suffers, if it has a nature that includes some capacity for action or passion. If a subject or supposit has a rational nature, that subject will be a person; if the rational nature includes flesh and bone — embodiment — the subject will be a human person. In any case it is always the person or supposit who acts, not the nature. "Actus sunt suppositorum": actions belong to individual subjects, not to the nature they share with others.[81] More precisely, "action is attributed to that which acts: not the nature, but the person."[82] The same goes for being acted upon, that is, for passions.[83]

The reason for this is not hard to see. Human nature did not prove Fermat's Last Theorem, Andrew Wiles did, though he was able to do so because he has a nature that includes the needed capacities for thought, action, perception, and so forth. If the act of proving Fermat's Last Theorem were an ingredient in human nature, then since the nature is common to Andrew Wiles and me, it would be true of both of us that we had proved the Theorem, as it would, of course, be true of every human being. Likewise human nature did not bleed copiously and feel faint when my neighbor John laid open his right hand with a sword during a martial arts exercise gone awry. If it had, we would all have felt it, since we all share his human nature.

81. The quoted phrase is from *ST* I, q. 39, a. 5, ad 1; cf. q. 40, a. 1, ad 3.

82. *ST* III, q. 20, a. 1, ad 2: "Agere autem non attribuitur naturae sicut agenti, sed personae: 'actus enim suppositorum sunt et singularium,' secundum Philosophum." The locus in Aristotle is *Metaphysics* I, 1, 981a16; see Aquinas's commentary, *In Met.* 1, 1 (nos. 20-21), also *ST* I, q. 29, a. 1, c. As Aquinas knows, this same principle might be invoked against the teaching that in Christ there are two distinct modes or types of action *(operationes),* in virtue of his two distinct natures. "[O]peratio pertinet ad hypostasim vel personam, nihil enim operatur nisi suppositum subsistens," an objector argues, "Ergo in Christo est una et eadem operatio divinitatis et humanitatis" (*ST* III, q. 19, a. 1, obj. 3). In reply Aquinas grants the principle, but observes that the range of actions available to an agent, the type or species of action it can undertake, depends on its nature. "[O]perari est hypostasis subsistentis, sed secundum formam et naturam, a qua operatio speciem recipit" (ad 3). We count actions by counting agents, and we count species or types of action by counting natures. So both are true: there is in Christ only one person, and therefore a single agent and a single action, but there are two natures, and therefore two distinct but always interrelated ways of acting, divine and human.

83. Applied to the christological case, this means that "communicatio idiomatum fit ratione unionis in supposito. Et quia suppositum non importatur nomine naturae, sicut hoc nomine Deus vel filius; ideo non potest dici natura passa, sicut Deus passus." III *Sent.* d. 5, q. 2, a. 2, ad 4 (ed. Moos, p. 202, §86).

Of course if John did not have this nature, he could not have suffered in this way. We act and suffer as we do in virtue of the sort of nature we have, but it is we who do the acting and suffering, not our nature.

Thus Christ's human *nature* did not suffer in his passion, any more than his divine nature did. He, the person of the Word become flesh, suffered, because he had assumed a nature that exposes its possessors to suffering. To say that the divine nature is impassible is not arbitrarily to exempt God's nature from a lot to which created natures are subject, but to observe that the divine nature, among its transcendent perfections, does not expose the Three who have it to suffering. It is therefore bootless to suggest that if the divine nature fails to suffer, Christ himself, or his whole person, does not truly suffer. As much suffers as can: the whole person, on account of his human, not his divine, nature.

VIII

The worry, then, about whether both natures suffer or only one is not so much a question as a category error. Granted this, though, a real question does remain. Ecumenical dogma holds that God ("one of the Holy Trinity") suffered in the flesh.[84] This plainly implies, as Robert Jenson observes at the outset of his contribution to this volume, that God is passible. Cyril and Thomas clearly embrace this conclusion, with the proviso that God incarnate is passible only on account of his flesh, or his human nature, and not on account of his divine nature.

This is the point that remains in dispute. Once we straighten out the logic of "nature" and "person," many recent theologians evidently still want to insist that God incarnate is passible, and suffers, in virtue of his divine nature, and not only in virtue of his human nature. Only if God the Son has suffered for us in his divinity or Godhead, and not just "in the flesh," can we truly claim that God has accepted our human lot even "unto death, death on a cross" (Phil. 2:8). Cyril and Thomas deny that the truth of this basic Christian claim depends on taking passibility as a property of the divine nature. For the tradition they exemplify, we can and should say that God himself dies for our salvation, without saying that passibility in any way enters into the divine nature itself. But if, as we have seen, the

84. See above, note 3.

point of this reservation is not to render homage to the pagan idea of divine *apatheia* by exempting God from real suffering, why hold onto it at all? Why not simply say that God is passible, that one of the features of divinity itself is passibility?

According to Moltmann, God the Father loses his own being as Father when Jesus dies, though perhaps he recovers it later. In a similar vein Jüngel holds that God "defines himself as God" in the death of Jesus.[85] In his contribution to this volume Bruce McCormack attributes a cognate claim to Karl Barth. "[I]t is precisely the Father's command which posits the Son — and which thereby makes the Father to be *Father*," the very command, I take it, which is obeyed in the historical "self-emptying and self-humiliation of Jesus Christ" in Gethsemane and on Calvary.[86] What these claims have in common is not the suggestion that the Father himself ceases to be, or that death becomes a feature of the divine essence, but the more basic and important assertion that the identity of a divine person depends on temporal events, actions, or states of affairs. Cyril and Thomas make their characteristic reservation — God the Son is passible and suffers with respect to his human nature, but not his divine nature — in order to avoid this utterly undesirable result.

In order to see how this traditional reservation bears on the identity of the divine persons, and with that why it is undesirable to make the identity of a person of the Trinity depend on anything temporal, it will help to look more closely at the idea McCormack ascribes to Barth. On this reading, Barth apparently holds that the Father is constituted as a divine person (Barth would say "mode of being," but we can leave that aside) by a command that a particular act take place in time, namely the humble obedience of the man Jesus. Presumably this command also constitutes the man Jesus as the Son of God, "positing" him as a divine person distinct from the Father (or perhaps Jesus' actual obedience to the command does this). A command whose content is the performance of a historical action is, we could say, an identity-constituting property of God the Father: without this command, he would not be the Father, but someone or something else. Similarly, being commanded to undertake this historical action is, it

---

85. See above, notes 5 and 10.

86. See above, pp. 172 and 171, the latter quoting Barth, *Kirchliche Dogmatik* IV/1, p. 211 (ET, p. 193). Whether or not this view is actually Barth's own, or results (as McCormack suggests) when one makes Barth a bit more consistent with himself, I will not try to decide. But McCormack surely makes a provocative and plausible case.

seems, an identity-constituting property of the man Jesus, and just so of God the Son, as a divine person (or perhaps Jesus' actual execution of what is commanded has the identity-constituting function).

Cyril and Aquinas represent a long tradition for which it is basic that the identity of the persons of the Trinity is not contingent. And, since the three divine persons just are the one God (whether taken one by one or together, disjunctively or conjunctively), the identity of God is also not contingent. All temporal actions, events, and states of affairs are, by contrast, contingent. Time belongs to creation, and creation in its totality is contingent. The triune God freely creates all that is not God, so it is possible for creation as a whole, and in all of its parts, not to be. The triune God is the creator of the world, and the redeemer of his creation. But neither "creator" nor "redeemer" can belong to the identity of a divine person, or (therefore) of the one God, because the identity of the divine persons is not contingent, while being creator and redeemer of the world is. For this tradition, then, it is impossible for the identity of a divine person or of the one God to include or depend on anything temporal, including any temporal event or state of affairs brought about by divine action.

The non-contingency and contingency in play here are both propositional and ontological. That is, the proposition "God is the Father" is non-contingently (or necessarily) true; there are no circumstances under which this proposition could possibly be false. And God is non-contingently (or necessarily) the Father; it is impossible that God not be the Father, or that the state of affairs such that there is a person who is God and is the Father could fail to obtain. The same goes for the proposition "God is the Son" and the state of affairs such that God is the Son, and equally for the proposition "God is the Holy Spirit" and the state of affairs such that God is the Holy Spirit. In each case it is impossible that the proposition be false, and it is impossible that God not be the Son, and also that God not be the Holy Spirit.

By contrast the proposition "God (or 'the Father,' or 'the Son,' or 'the Holy Spirit,' or 'the Trinity') is the creator of the world" is true, but only contingently so; there are circumstances under which it could be (or could have been) false — if, for example, the triune God had not freely willed to create this world, or any world at all. And God (or the Father, or the Son, or the Holy Spirit, or the Trinity) is contingently the creator of the world; it is possible that the triune God not be the creator of a world (or: for the triune God not to have created a world). *If* there is a created world, the triune

God must be its creator, but this is a different matter. It is contingent that the triune God create a world, but non-contingent that any real world be created by the triune God; creating a world is contingent for God, but being created by God is non-contingent for a world. The same goes for the proposition "(The triune) God is the redeemer of the world," and the state of affairs such that God redeems the world. The proposition is true, but contingently so, and it is possible (or would have been possible) that the triune God not redeem the world.[87]

By holding that the identity of the divine persons, and so of the one God, is constituted by particular actions and passions the persons undertake in the created world, and in time, Barth (as presented by McCormack) breaks in a deep-going way with the tradition embodied by Cyril and Thomas. So, it seems, do Moltmann, Jüngel, and perhaps Balthasar, each in his own fashion. The motives for this innovation are multiple, but almost always involve an insistence on avoiding any separation or distance between God "in himself" and God "for us," between God as he is eternally and God as he acts in time, between the "immanent Trinity" and the "economic Trinity." Otherwise, so these theologians worry, the latter member in each pair fails to give us access to the former member — to God as he really is, God in his inmost reality. This requires, among other things, that God be passible by (divine) nature, inherently and eternally passible, since God is evidently passible in time.

Making the identity of the divine persons, and thus of the one God, depend on temporal actions, events, or states of affairs evidently requires accepting one of two alternatives.

(1) The identity of each divine person is itself contingent, since it includes or depends on that which is contingent — so that, for example, "God is the Father" is only contingently true, and God is only contingently the Father.

(2) The temporal actions, events, or states of affairs on which the identity of each divine person depends are themselves necessary, since the identities of these divine persons are not contingent — so that, for ex-

---

87. These observations distinguishing necessity from contingency I take to be commonplace, and sufficient for present purposes. The nature of necessity and contingency, including what to make of *de dicto* (or propositional) necessity and *de re* (or ontological) necessity is, to be sure, a complex and debated philosophical problem.

ample, "God the Father commands Jesus to suffer and die" is true necessarily, and it is impossible for God the Father not to command (or to have commanded) Jesus to die.

This is a genuine dilemma, which we would surely rather not have. Accepting either alternative brings with it quite unwelcome consequences.

(1) This is perhaps the more natural way of taking the thought that the identity of a divine person depends on, or is constituted by, temporal actions like commanding and being commanded (or obeying). We are familiar with such actions, and readily regard them as the contingent decisions of free agents, whose decisions depend on their own will, and who could have done otherwise than issue, or follow, a particular command. If a free decision on God's part makes him to be the Father, then God is the Father only contingently. By depending on a decision that might not have been made, the very existence of the Father, and with that his personal identity, will no more be necessary than the decision itself. It will be contingent that there is a divine person who has the Father's unique person-constituting property (or properties), and possible that God not be (or not have been) the Father. If the Son's personal identity also depends on this action, on being the recipient of the Father's command, then it is likewise contingent that God has a Son. When we take this alternative, the Son comes forth from God not by nature, but by will (as the Arians once held, for their own reasons), indeed by the same free act in which God contingently constitutes himself as Father. If we take our lead from the contingency of a free agent's acts, it is just as contingent that God is the Father, the Son, and the Holy Spirit as that God creates, or redeems, a world. Each depends alike, or they all depend together, on a free decision of God, which could have been otherwise.

Among the drawbacks of seizing this alternative is that it fails to address the issue which often motivates theologians to think of temporal acts as constitutive of God's identity in the first place. In fact it guarantees that the relationship between God "in himself" and God "for us," instead of becoming transparent, will become a completely insoluble problem. By temporal acts like commanding Jesus to suffer and die, God has, on this alternative, freely decided to be the Father, the Son, and the Holy Spirit, and *eo ipso* to be these three for us. God may be this way eternally, because he has so decided, or his being this way may be coincident with the temporal enactment of his decision (or perhaps both, somehow). In any case, God's being this way is contingent, dependent on his free decision so to be.

If so, then who, or what, *makes* this decision? "God," presumably, but not God the Father, God the Son, or God the Holy Spirit. These three are the contingent outcome of God's decision about who he will be (of God's "self-determination," as Barth and others sometimes put it), and so cannot, individually or jointly, be the ones who make it. "For us," God is the Trinity, and what we know of God always depends on the way God is for us in his temporal actions. As a result, who or what it is that makes the decision to be the Trinity for us is truly the unknown God. On this scenario, who or what God is "in himself," what the proto-God who decides to present himself to us as the Trinity is really like, we cannot begin to say, at least as long as our knowledge of God depends on what God does for us in time.[88] Someone or something unknown has decided to be God for us in this way; we can go no further. Making the identity of the divine persons depend on contingent temporal actions does not, as its advocates hope, usher us into the deep things of God, but ensures that the depths of God will be forever closed to us.[89]

(2) Perhaps troubled by these evidently self-defeating consequences, some theologians in the grip of this dilemma more or less clearly hold that the identity of the divine persons and of the one God is genuinely non-contingent, while insisting that the identity of the triune God depends on temporal actions and events. This means, to recall the case of the Father's command and the Son's obedience, that the Father must necessarily com-

---

88. And so it will depend forever, assuming — as theologians who link God's identity to the temporal usually do, whether they follow option (1) or option (2) — that our knowledge of God "in himself" inherently or necessarily relies on how God is "for us."

89. Holding that the identity of the three divine persons and of the one God is not contingent, while all the temporal acts of the triune God are, the traditional view sees here not so much a soluble problem, as no real problem at all. What seems like a hopeless difficulty arises just because one accepts the (more or less Hegelian) assumption that God's identity is constituted by temporal actions, while also (rightly enough) wanting to maintain that God undertakes these actions freely. For theologians like Cyril and Aquinas, the contingent temporal missions of the Son and the Spirit from the Father in incarnation and sanctifying grace unmistakably exhibit the non-contingent relations of origin which obtain among them, and with that their non-contingent person-constituting properties. Christmas, Good Friday, Easter, and Pentecost are not who the triune God is, but what the triune God does, and nobody else could do. I cannot spell this out here; see my essays, "*Ex Occidente Lux?* Aquinas and Eastern Orthodox Theology," *Modern Theology* 20, no. 1 (2004): 23-50, "The Trinity," *The Blackwell Companion to Modern Theology*, ed. Gareth Jones (Oxford: Blackwell, 2004), pp. 183-203, and "The Filioque as Theology and Doctrine," *Kerygma und Dogma* 50, no. 4 (2004): 271-88.

mand Jesus in Gethsemane to die on Calvary, and Jesus must accept and carry out this command. If this command is genuinely constitutive of the Father's identity, and if God is the Father non-contingently, then this command will be no less necessary than the Father himself. It will be impossible that the Father not command his Son to die at a particular place and time, just as it is impossible that God not be the Father. Similarly, if Jesus' obedience to the Father in the garden and on the cross makes him to be God the Son, then his obedience is just as necessary as his own non-contingent identity. It will be impossible for Jesus not to obey the Father's command, to decide otherwise; his human obedience and suffering can no more fail to occur than God can fail to be the Son. When we take this alternative, it seems that not only the Son, but the cross, comes forth from God by nature, and not by will (Hegel's revenge, we might call this). If we take our lead from the non-contingency of the divine persons and their identities, it is just as necessary that God send his Son to the cross for our salvation, and pour out the Holy Spirit at Pentecost, as that God is the Father, the Son, and the Holy Spirit. The former, no less than the latter, belong to the identity of God, which could not have been otherwise.

Going this route in a consistent way surely avoids the problem posed by (1): God "in himself" is just the same as God "for us." Perhaps the most obvious drawback of seizing this alternative, however, is that the Father ceases to be a free agent, as do the Son, the Holy Spirit, and the one God. Or more precisely, neither the Father nor the Son is the free subject of those saving temporal actions or passions in which his identity consists, like commanding to die and accepting this command, but each can be the free subject only of those temporal acts (if there be any such) that are adventitious to his own non-contingent identity (the same goes, one assumes, for the identity of the Holy Spirit).

If so, then the saving temporal acts of God, so far as they belong to his identity, cannot be grace and gift. Neither the divine acts themselves nor their created effects — the Father's command, the Son's obedience, the Spirit's outpouring for our sanctification, and the rest — can be free, since it is impossible for them not to occur. But if these saving acts were not free, then "grace would no longer be grace" (cf. Rom. 11:6, cited in this connection at least since Augustine). Unless they are freely accomplished, God's saving works are not gifts freely given, a wholly unexacted outpouring of generosity, but the payment of a debt (cf. Rom. 4:4). Here, however, the debt that excludes grace would not, as Pelagians old and new maintain, be owed by God to creatures, exacting in justice a payment due to their merits. It would be a primordial debt God owed himself, exacting payment in time simply because of who God is, because of his unalterable identity. So if the salvation worked by the triune God can only be free grace and gift, then God's identity cannot be constituted by any saving act in time — assuming, with (2), that God's identity is itself not contingent.

If we take "God the Father commands Jesus to die on Calvary" to be true necessarily, so that it is impossible for the Father not to issue this command, we cannot stop there. This command can only take place in a particular world, with a particular history. Since God's non-contingent identity requires that the Father give this command and Jesus obey it, the propositions "God creates a world in which he commands Jesus to die on Calvary" and "God creates a world in which Jesus obeys his command to die on Calvary" are, presumably, also true necessarily. In fact we need to go further. If the Father commands and the Son obeys because the identity of each requires that he act in this way, then it will be true necessarily not only that God creates a world, but that he creates *this* world, or one very much like it.

More than that. God will not only create this world necessarily, as the place in which alone he can give and obey this particular command. He will create this world *in order to* give the command obeyed on Calvary. The triune God needs this world, logically and ontologically, so that he can undertake the non-contingent actions in which his identity consists. The very existence of this created world will not, therefore, be an act of pure generosity on God's part, a free sharing of his goodness unexacted by anything in God, let alone by the not-yet-existent creature. It will be an act of self-preservation on God's part, an act undertaken in his own interests, not the creature's.

Finally, the temporal acts in which the triune God has his non-contingent identity are those by which God conquers sin and evil. The defeat of sin and evil belongs to the specific character of these acts, of what happens in Gethsemane and on Calvary. Otherwise they would simply not be the acts that they in fact are. Differently put: a world in which even one innocent person is crucified is a fallen world, one marked by sin. According to (2), a crucified innocent belongs non-contingently to God's identity, to the Son as the innocent one who undergoes the cross, and to the Father as the one who commands it. This means, though, that God needs more than this created world in order to be himself. In order to carry out the temporal acts that make him who he is, God needs this world's *sin*. He needs his creation to be overcome by evil, so that he can conquer evil by his own incarnation and cross. On this scenario, in other words, God must will evil and sin for the sake of redemption in Christ. He must will evil, moreover, for his own sake, not the creature's, not so that he can save the creature (though he does, as a kind of by-product), but so that he can avoid losing himself. Or perhaps better, God does not will to have an identity constituted by the garden and the cross; for (2) his identity is not contingent, and could not be otherwise. As a result God does not really will this created world either, or its sin. They just occur, inexorably, given who God is. Creation and sin are not so much personal acts as inevitable events. God can be said to will them, at best, in that he assents to what he himself must, in any case, bring to pass.

This is not an attractive picture, and theologians who opt for (2) generally shrink from it before they reach this dismal point. Of course God undertakes the history of salvation freely, they tend to reply, and would be (the same) God without us, and without any creation at all. But if we would abide by revelation and Scripture, we can say nothing about what this God would be (not even, perhaps, that God would be the Trinity) apart from the creation and salvation on which he has decided. This reply, of course, does not solve the problems posed by (2). It simply returns to (1), and the problems posed by it. So theologians typically proceed who take the fatal first step of making God's identity depend on the temporal: they lean toward (1) or, more often, toward (2), but when confronted by the problems one of these options poses, they take refuge in the other, oscillating between two mutually exclusive, and equally undesirable, alternatives.

The upshot of this argument for the question with which we began is not hard to see. Against the traditional reservation that the impassible God truly suffers, but only on account of the human nature he has assumed, Moltmann and others now maintain that God cannot really be subject to suffering in Christ unless the possibility of suffering belongs to him by nature. On this view passibility is an ingredient in the divine nature, and not only in human nature. As such it belongs to what makes the Father, the Son, and the Holy Spirit to be God, and is common to the three, rather than being a property of the incarnate Son alone.

To be passible, I have suggested, is to be exposed to real suffering, even if one does not actually suffer. Suffering, like any passion or "undergoing," is a kind of change, so having the attribute of passibility entails having the attribute of mutability, of being subject to change (even if one is not actually changing). Change takes time, so having the attribute of mutability entails, in turn, having the attribute of temporality, of being subject to time. Thus a being by nature passible must also be by nature mutable and temporal. If God is passible by nature — if Jesus suffers not only in virtue of his human nature, but also of his divine nature — then God must also be mutable and temporal by nature.

Should the triune God be temporal by nature, the identity of each divine person, and of the one God, will depend on actions, events, or states of affairs that are themselves temporal. This will be the case even if we suppose that God's time is different from created time (as Barth and others suggest), and even if the triune God were to create no world, so that the only existents were the Father, the Son, and the Holy Spirit. That the identity of the divine persons must in some sense be constituted temporally, given a divine nature with the attribute of temporality, assumes, of course, that whatever belongs to God's nature must characterize each of the three persons. Otherwise they would lack some attribute necessary for each of them to be God. So if God is temporal by nature, the three persons will be temporal by nature, and their identities constituted by temporal actions, events, or states of affairs.

Now the temporal actions, events, or states of affairs on which the identity of each divine person depends will either be contingent, or they will not be contingent. As we have seen, however, linking the identity of the persons of the Trinity and the one God either to (1) contingent or to (2) non-contingent temporal acts, events, or states of affairs creates serious, indeed unacceptable, difficulties. In order to avoid these difficulties, we need to drop the idea that God is temporal by nature. But if God is not temporal by nature, then he cannot be mutable by nature, and if he is not mutable by nature he cannot be passible by nature. Passibility is not, therefore, an attribute that belongs to the triune God in virtue of the divine nature, but one that belongs only to the incarnate Son, in virtue of the passible created nature he has assumed.

This may seem more obvious in the case of (1) than of (2). Holding (1) means supposing that the temporal acts or events that belong to each divine person's identity are contingent, even if these are purely intra-divine temporal acts or events, rather than occurrences in the created world (which was the form in which we initially considered both [1] and [2]). In that case we quickly find ourselves mired in the difficulties confronting (1), compelled to ask a question we cannot hope to answer: since God's triune identity is contingent, who or what decided that God would look this way?

Surely, though, it remains possible to hold, with (2), that the identity of the divine persons is constituted temporally, but that the divine persons and their identities are not contingent. As long as we stick with intra-divine temporal acts or events, and avoid the mistake, common enough among followers of (2), of supposing that *created* temporal acts or events can give a divine person his identity, we should be able to avoid the problems we have located in (2). That is, we can grant that the temporal acts or events that are person- or identity-constituting in God (for example, the processions of the Son from the Father, and of the Holy Spirit from the Father and the Son) are genuinely not contingent, without having to concede that creation, and even redemption, are necessary for God. This, it seems, would give us a relatively problem-free way of saying that temporality, and therefore passibility, belong to God's nature as well as ours, without having to say that the triune God's identity is contingent, or that God creates and redeems by necessity.

It is not clear, however, that the thought of God's identity being temporally constituted in this way, yet non-contingent, is coherent. Created temporal individuals (supposits or hypostases) find their identity given at least partially by causal factors outside their control (to be born at a certain place and time, to be male or female, and so forth). The identity of created persons, as distinguished from agents who are not persons (like cows) and impersonal objects (like split-level houses), is also partially within their voluntary control. God, by contrast, is a personal agent whose identity cannot be given or shaped by anything outside himself, since he freely creates everything that is not himself. If God is by nature temporal, and thus inherently subject to change, this makes it seem as though a deliberate act of will on his part will be required in order for God to have, or maintain, an identity. Nothing else could keep his identity from changing. And this is to say that God's identity is contingent. So it seems as though the notion of a natural divine passibility, since it presupposes a natural temporality, requires that God's identity (whether as the Trinity or something else) be contingent; on this assumption (2) apparently reduces to (1).

We can perhaps avoid this result, and eliminate any trace of contingency from God's identity as Father, Son, and Holy Spirit, by holding that the temporal happenings that constitute the identity of each person (now not created but intra-divine events) are themselves simply not contingent. They cannot fail to occur, so the argument might go, and to occur always.

It is difficult, however, to think of genuinely temporal events as lacking

293

contingency unless they are causally necessitated by some other, if not prior, event or state of affairs.[90] As a result, it is difficult to think of God's triune identity as constituted temporally, yet not contingent. Were that the case, Father, Son, and Spirit would each be the unique divine person he is by some kind of causal necessity. But this means they would not be persons, since temporal individuals whose identity is wholly a result of causal necessity are at best involuntary agents, if not impersonal objects. To take the most obvious trinitarian case, the Father, assuming that his personal identity is bound up with bringing forth the Son, would generate the Son, and so have his own identity, by a causal necessity imposed upon him from without (perhaps by his own divine nature, constantly acting as an external cause, compelling him to emit the Son). Were the Father a temporal reality of this sort, he would not be a voluntary agent, a person, but a sub-personal, if not impersonal, entity. Of course the point is not that the Father brings forth the Son by an act of will, which would make both the Son and the Father contingent. The lesson, rather, is that we should not think of the identity of the divine persons as constituted by anything temporal in the first place, whether a voluntary act or an involuntary event.[91]

90. In fact it is difficult to think of any temporal occurrence as lacking all ontological contingency, as taking place in all possible worlds (to use one idiom for making the point). Temporal events are necessary under certain conditions, or given some antecedent situation. In scholastic terms, a temporal event can be non-contingent *secundum quid* or *ex suppositione,* but not *simpliciter:* in a particular respect or given a particular assumption, but not without any qualification. If God's identity as Father, Son, and Holy Spirit is without contingency *simpliciter* — as it surely must be — then it is impossible from the start for the identity of a divine person to depend on, or be constituted by, any temporal event, created or intra-divine. For the purpose of the present argument, though, we can leave this aside.

91. When he considers whether the Father generates the Son by a free act or by causal necessity, Aquinas tellingly argues that neither can be right. The Father brings forth the Son by nature (as the ancient Church had already maintained, e.g., the *Fides Damasi;* cf. DH 71), which is to say in a uniquely divine way that cannot be assimilated to any sort of temporal action or causality: it is the doing of a supremely voluntary agent, but wholly lacks the contingency that goes with the voluntary acts of temporal creatures. "Deus Pater non genuit Filium voluntate, sed voluntate produxit creaturam" (*ST* I, q. 41, a. 2, c). At the same time "Deus non est propter finem neque coactio cadit in ipsum"; neither type of necessity can apply to a divine person (ad 5). The necessity of the act by which the Father generates the Son must simply be its non-contingency, the impossibility that it not be; this is all we can mean when we say that the Father generates "by nature." "Per se autem dicitur aliquid necessarium quod non potest non esse. Et sic Deum esse est necessarium et hoc modo Patrem generare Filium est necessarium" (ad 5). Thomas's unwillingness to make the processions in God fit

For the sake of argument, though, let us grant that we can make sense of the thought that the triune God's identity is temporally constituted, yet not contingent. Would this give us a coherent account of the claim that God is passible by nature, that is, an account that avoided the difficulties to which (2) is liable?

Passibility, I have suggested, is real exposure or vulnerability to suffering. Or, more broadly, passibility is real exposure to involuntary change, to an alteration that comes upon an agent rather than being within the agent's control. An agent that is passible in this sense need not actually suffer, but has to exist in circumstances where suffering could actually occur (as opposed to being merely conceivable, were the circumstances different). But surely God could not be naturally or inherently passible in this sense. Suppose that God had created no world. If the triune God were nonetheless passible, some constituent feature of at least one divine person, or of the divine nature, would have to threaten at least one divine person, and perhaps all three, with real suffering. One wonders what this could be. The trinitarian Father, for example, does not need to worry, as earthly fathers do, how his Son will turn out. But assuming that we could identify some feature of a divine person or the divine nature that offered the real possibility of suffering, the triune God could not enjoy beatitude. Even if the divine persons succeeded eternally in staving off actual suffering, they could not enjoy perfect blessedness, since they would always face the real possibility of losing it. Otherwise they would not be inherently passible. Lacking beatitude themselves, they could not give it to us, should they decide to create a world. If, on the contrary, they enjoy perfect beatitude, then they cannot be passible by nature.

Suppose, to take a different tack, we say that there is nothing about a divine person or the divine nature that really exposes God to suffering, but God is nonetheless inherently passible, as his actual suffering in Christ attests. What, though, could present the real possibility of suffering to God if

---

with created and temporal modes of action is of a piece with his radical understanding of God's difference from creatures, that is, of God's transcendence — in this case, of God's supra-temporal eternity, which can be equated neither with created time nor its negation.

These observations naturally raise questions that I cannot go into here. For a highly informative account of the debates over volition and necessity in later medieval trinitarian theology, see Russell L. Friedman, "The Voluntary Emanation of the Holy Spirit: Views of Natural Necessity and Voluntary Freedom at the Turn of the Thirteenth Century," in *Trinitarian Theology in the Medieval West*, ed. Pekka Kärkkäinen (Helsinki: Luther-Agricola Society, 2008), pp. 124-48.

nothing about God did so? It would, presumably, have to be something other than God. Creation, in other words, or some part of it, would have to expose God to suffering. On this scenario, therefore, God would have to create a world in order to expose himself to suffering, to meet the demand his own nature imposes upon him, but does not supply. A world, however, in which some creatures suffer by the deliberate design of others — the sort of suffering God undergoes in his flesh — is not simply a created world, but a fallen world, a world with sin. Should we need an inherent divine possibility in order to account for God's exposure to the suffering he actually accepts by becoming incarnate, then God will not only have to create a world, but a fallen world. These are just the consequences of (2) that we hoped to avoid.

To sum up: we evidently have no way to maintain that God is passible, and *a fortiori* temporal, by nature, without incurring the most serious difficulties. Either God is only contingently the Trinity, and thus unknowable in himself, or God is not free, and thus neither creation nor salvation is grace, and sin is necessary. Better then to drop the idea that God is inherently temporal, and with that the idea that God is by nature passible.

IX

Writing early in the last century, the English Congregationalist theologian P. T. Forsyth colorfully claims that in order properly to appreciate the cross of Christ, we have to see that "[t]here was a Calvary above which was the mother of it all."[92] Much subsequent theology has taken this to heart, if not usually by way of Forsyth. Whatever the incarnate God does and suffers in time, or at least what is most decisive for our salvation, must be grounded or based on an act or state that already belongs to God inherently, whether in virtue of the divine nature or the identity of the divine persons. The sav-

---

92. P. T. Forsyth, *The Person and Place of Jesus Christ* (London: Independent Press, 1909), p. 271. Forsyth continues, in a vein that has since become familiar: "His obedience, however impressive, does not take divine magnitude if it first rose upon earth, nor has it the due compelling power upon ours. His obedience as man was but the detail of the supreme obedience which made him man." Balthasar quotes this passage approvingly in "Mysterium Paschale," p. 153 (ET, p. 36), with "the mother of it all" rendered in a more straightforwardly causal manner than the English might suggest: "von dem alles ausgeganen ist" ("from which everything originated").

ing work of Jesus Christ in the temporal economy must, in one way or another, be the repetition, duplication, realization, or extension — the temporal twin, as it were — of a prior reality that belongs to God's very being or identity. Otherwise we cannot really believe that the temporal events belong to God at all. If they do not, they are not saving. So for the Calvary below there must be a Calvary above, for the kenosis below a kenosis above, for the dereliction below a possibility, if not quite yet a dereliction, above. For some theologians this still seems to put too much distance between God as he is "for us" and God as he is "in himself," and they suggest that God's suffering below just *is* an inherent divine suffering above; God's death below just *is* a death above, a death that simply belongs to him as God.[93]

Saints Cyril and Thomas Aquinas represent a tradition for which this pattern of thought is, as we have argued, out of the question. The Calvary below is our salvation only if it is *not* the repetition of, let alone identical with, a Calvary above. Yet this tradition certainly embraces the conviction that God himself has suffered in the flesh for our salvation, and thereby acknowledges that God is passible. If this passibility does not belong to God by nature, if it is not inherent in being God, then what is it about God that accounts for the fact that God actually suffers?

We have already touched on the answer to this question, which theologians in this tradition evidently do not consider especially daunting. God suffers on account of the flesh he assumes, and not on account of what makes him God, or his divine nature. So whatever it is about God that explains the possibility of his becoming incarnate will explain the possibility of his suffering. The possibility of God's incarnation, however, depends not on an inherently divine passibility — an exposure to real suffering which God has by nature — but, quite the contrary, on God's inherent power. The capacity for action God has by nature, rather than any inherent susceptibility to passion, accounts for the possibility of God's becoming flesh, and so for the exposure to suffering which belongs to God in the flesh. Gregory of Nyssa already isolates the basic point. Unlike creatures, whose power is limited to what comports with their nature, God's unlimited power is precisely his capacity fully to embrace (that is, to become the subject of) that which is contrary to his own nature — to become finite,

---

93. Both Moltmann and Jüngel, it seems, incline to this identification of the above with the below.

mortal, and passible flesh.[94] God's capacity to become incarnate is not the ability to realize or fulfill himself or his nature, to replicate, extend, or enact what he already is or has decided to be, but just the opposite: the capacity — the power — to accept as his own what is contrary to his nature and does not belong to him as God.

For Cyril and Aquinas alike, God, by becoming flesh, freely belongs to a kind that is not naturally his own. The members of this kind are inherently exposed to the possibility of change, suffering, and death — and all, in the present fallen condition of that kind, actually do suffer and die. Since he willingly accepts being one of our perishing kind, God actually suffers our death. But even in his dying Jesus remains God. His divine nature — what makes him God (and which forms no kind, or genus) — is wholly unchanged by his human suffering and death. The death of God in no way enters, let alone is it necessarily a part of, what makes him God. His human agony introduces no new property or characteristic into either his divine nature or his personal identity, and causes them to lose none. What it is to be God, and what it is for *the Son* to be God, in distinction from the Father and the Holy Spirit, is just the same as it would be had he not become flesh, and had there been no created world and no flesh to become. Nothing about what makes him God exposes him to change, or, therefore, to suffering. Still less does his divine nature require change and suffering, or bring it about that he actually suffers. The temporal economy of salvation, including the suffering and death of the incarnate Son, is what the triune God does, not who the triune God is.

In the incarnate Son's passion and death he and his Father perfectly love one another in the unity of the Holy Spirit, as much as they would if the world were not. Just because the Father and the Son abide with one another in love even there, the Son's passion is our salvation. The Son's passion is the way the abiding in love of the Father and the Son becomes salvation for us, for sinners who have opposed that love. His passion is our way into the love which infinitely and unalterably goes with being God, into the perfect blessedness and rest of God's own life. God the Son, in other words, remains impassible in his own human suffering and death, since he there — above all, there — remains God.

---

94. See above, note 79, for both Nyssa and Aquinas on God's power as the locus of his capacity to become flesh; in Aquinas, see also *ST* III, q. 3, a. 5, c: "Principium autem actus [assumptionis] est virtus divina: terminus autem est persona."

Impassibility as Transcendence:
On the Infinite Innocence of God

David Bentley Hart

So kann, wo alles Anwesende sich im Lichte des Ursache-Wirkung-Zusammenhangs darstellt, sogar Gott für das Vorstellen alles Heilige und Hohe, das Geheimnisvolle seiner Ferne verlieren. Gott kann im Lichte der Kausalität zu einer Ursache, zur causa efficiens, herabsinken. Er wird dann sogar innerhalb der Theologie zum Gott der Philosophen, jener nämlich, die das Unverborgene und Verborgene nach der Kausalität des Machens bestimmen, ohne dabei jemals die Wesensherkunft dieser Kausalität zu bedenken.

HEIDEGGER[1]

I

Perhaps the most difficult discipline the Christian metaphysical tradition requires of its students is the preservation of a consistent and adequate sense of the difference between primary and secondary causality: between, that is, the transcendent and the contingent, or between — to abuse

1. Martin Heidegger, "Die Frage nach der Technik," in *Die Technik und die Kehre*, 7th edition (Stuttgart: Verlag Günther Neske, 1988), p. 26. [Thus, when all that comes to presence presents itself in the light of the connection between cause and effect, even God — as far as representation is concerned — can lose all that is high and holy, the very mysteriousness of his distance. God, seen in the light of causality, can sink to the level of a cause, to the level of the *causa efficiens*. Even in theology, then, he is thus transformed into the God of the philosophers, which is to say, of those who define the unhidden and the hidden according to the causality of making, without ever also considering the essential origin of this causality.]

299

Heidegger's idiom — the ontological and the ontic. It is a distinction so elementary to any metaphysics of creation that no philosophical theologian consciously ignores it; and yet its full implications often elude even the most scrupulous among us. This is no small matter; for the theological consequences of failing to observe the proper logic of divine transcendence are invariably unhappy, and in some cases even disastrous.

Consider, for instance, Reginald Garrigou-Lagrange's most cherished axiom: "God determining or determined: there is no other alternative."[2] This is a logical error whose gravity it would be difficult to exaggerate. It is a venerable error, admittedly, adumbrated or explicit in the arguments of even some of the greatest theologians of the western church; but an error it remains. Applied to two terms within any shared frame of causal operation, between which some reciprocal real relation obtains, such a formula is perfectly cogent; but as soon as "God" is introduced as one of its terms, the formula is immediately rendered vacuous. If divine transcendence is an intelligible concept, it must be understood according to a rule enunciated by Maximus the Confessor: Whereas the being of finite things has non-being as its opposite, God's being is entirely beyond any such opposition.[3] God's being is necessary, that is, not simply because it is inextinguishable or eternally immune to nothingness, but because it transcends the dialectic of existence and non-existence altogether; it is simple and infinite actuality, utterly pure of ontic determination, the "is" both of the "it is" and of the "it is not." It transcends, that is to say, even the distinction between finite act and finite potency, since both exist by virtue of their participation in God's infinite actuality, in which all that might be always supereminently *is.* God is absolute, that is to say, in the most proper sense: He is eternally "absolved" of finite causality, so much so that he need not — in any simple univocal sense — determine in order to avoid being determined. His transcendence is not something achieved by the negation of its "opposite."

This logic should always govern our talk of divine *apatheia.* Though

2. This is far and away the most tiresome refrain in his "classic" work on predestination (a book that often seems to consist almost exclusively in tiresome refrains); in fact, it is the phrase with which the text closes — at least, if one reads through to the end of the appendices. See Reginald Garrigou-Lagrange, *Predestination: The Meaning of Predestination in Scripture and the Church,* trans. Dom Bede Rose (Rockford, Ill.: TAN Books and Publishers, Inc., 1998).

3. Maximus the Confessor, *Chapters on Love,* III.65.

the theologian certainly must affirm that God is by nature beyond every pathos — in the purely technical sense of a change or modification of his nature or essence, passively received *ab extra* — this is not merely to say that he is impervious to external shock. If it were, it would mean only that he enjoys to a perfect degree the same affective poverty as a granite escarpment. He would not really be *beyond* suffering at all, but simply incapable of it; to call him impassible would be then to say no more than that, in the order of the mutable, he is immutable;[4] or that, in the order of the contingent, he is rescued from contingency simply by virtue of being that force that is supreme among all other forces. This would, in a very real sense, place God in rivalry to finite things, though a rivalry that — through the sheer mathematics of omnipotence — he has always already won. But this is folly. Divine *apatheia* is not merely the opposite of passibility; it is God's transcendence of the very distinction between the responsive and the unresponsive, between receptivity and resistance. It is the Trinity's infinite fullness of perfected love, which gives all and receives all in a single movement, and which does not require the supplement of any external force in order to know and to love creation in its uttermost depths. Whereas we — finite, composite, and changing beings that we are — cannot know, love, or act save through a relation to that which affects us and which we affect, God's impassibility is the infinitely active and eternally prior love in which our experience of love — in both its active and its passive dimensions — lives, moves, and has its being. God's *apatheia* is his perfect liberty to be present in both our passions and our actions, but in either case as a free, creative, and pure act.

This is, after all, the great "discovery" of the Christian metaphysical tradition: the true nature of transcendence. When, in the fourth century, theology took its final leave of all subordinationist schemes of Trinitarian reflection, it thereby broke irrevocably with all those older metaphysical systems that had attempted to connect this world to its highest principle by populating the interval between them with various intermediate degrees of spiritual reality. In affirming that the Persons of the Trinity are coequal and of one essence, Christian thought was led also to the recognition that it is the transcendent God alone who gives being to creation; that he is able to be at once both *superior summo meo* and *interior intimo meo;* and that he is not merely the supreme being set atop the summit of beings, but is instead the one who is transcendently present in all beings, the ever

---

4. I am grateful to Andrew Peach for this formulation.

more inward act within each finite act. And it is precisely *because* God is not situated within any kind of ontic continuum with the creature that we can recognize him as the ontological cause of the creature, who freely gives being to beings. True divine transcendence, it turns out, is a transcendence of even the traditional metaphysical demarcations between the transcendent and the immanent. At the same time, the realization that the creature is not, simply by virtue of its finitude and mutability, alienated from God — at a tragic distance from God that the creature can traverse only to the degree that everything distinctively creaturely within it is negated — was also a realization of the true ontological liberty of created nature. If God himself is the immediate actuality of the creature's emergence from nothingness, and of both the essence and the existence of the creature, then it is precisely through becoming what it is — rather than through overcoming those finite *"idiomata"* that distinguish it from God — that the creature truly reflects the goodness and transcendent power of God.

Now, in all likelihood, very little of what I have said to this point would surprise or offend anyone sympathetically inclined towards the traditional Christian teaching of divine impassibility. And in the past, when I have written on these matters,[5] it has never occurred to me to defend this understanding of divine transcendence against any theologies but those that explicitly reject that teaching. I have come to believe, however, that in many cases it is those who adhere most fiercely to the traditional language of impassibility who often prove most oblivious to the true logic of transcendence, and that their maladroit devotion to a principle they only partially understand frequently leads them to conclusions that cannot help but bring that principle into disrepute. This may have been an especially prevalent tendency in the theology of the sixteenth and seventeenth centuries, a period when metaphysical subtlety seems to have been at its lowest ebb throughout the Christian world. It was certainly pronounced in the Baroque "commentary Thomism" of Domingo Bañez, Diego Alvarez, John of St. Thomas, and others, as it was in the theology of their disciples, such as — in the twentieth century — Garrigou-Lagrange and Jean-Hervé Nicolas, and as it is in the thought of a small number of marginal contemporary Thomists. And nowhere was this tendency more resplendently ob-

---

5. David Bentley Hart, "No Shadow of Turning: On Divine Impassibility," *Pro Ecclesia* (Spring 2002): 184-206; Hart, *The Beauty of the Infinite: The Aesthetics of Christian Truth* (Grand Rapids: Eerdmans, 2003), pp. 155-67, 354-60.

vious than in the "Bañezian" concept of the *praemotio physica:* an irresistible divine movement of the creature's will that in no way violates the creature's own freedom.

There is, of course, something inherently absurd in an Eastern Orthodox theologian presuming to weigh in on the *"de auxiliis"* controversy (especially since, from the Orthodox perspective, the principal issue of debate — the idea of predilective predestination to salvation — is an ancient exegetical error, abetted by an unfortunate Latin translation of the Epistle to the Romans, and so without any real theological legitimacy to begin with). Nor is there really an urgent need for anyone to address a school of thought that so obviously has no significant future within its own church. And arguments regarding which kind of Thomism is truest to Thomas do not much concern me.[6] My interest in this issue is bloodlessly clinical. To me, the *praemotio* is a perfect specimen of a deformation of theological reason that seems especially characteristic of the modern age, both early and late: not necessarily a conscious denial of any of classical Christianity's claims regarding God's nature, but rather a far more general and destructive forgetfulness of the true meaning of those claims — one that renders either their denial or their affirmation largely irrelevant.

II

The concept of physical premotion is not terribly difficult to grasp.[7] It is a device intended, in principle, to safeguard a proper understanding of di-

---

6. Being merely a selective reader of Thomas, whose interest in Thomas's thought begins and ends with his metaphysics of *esse* and of *actus,* I lack the authority necessary to pronounce upon the degree to which Bañez or the larger Baroque commentary tradition "got Thomas right" on this matter. I tend to think that it was a vanishingly small degree, however, and find the expositions of a number of scholars of Thomas entirely persuasive on this score. The now classic "refutation" of the older reading of Thomas on divine causality is, of course, Bernard Lonergan's *Grace and Freedom: Operative Grace in the Thought of St Thomas Aquinas* (Toronto: University of Toronto Press, 2000). See also Brian J. Shanley, "Divine Causation and Human Freedom in Aquinas," *American Catholic Philosophical Quarterly* 72, no. 1 (1998): 99-122. Lonergan's book is especially important for demonstrating that the "classical Thomist" understanding of causality can be applied only anachronistically to Thomas's own thought.

7. In fact, most of what one needs to know about the concept — if one is not interested in its precise history — can be extracted from certain recent attempts to rehabilitate the Ba-

vine transcendence and omnipotence (though, in fact, it accomplishes precisely the opposite). It is called "physical" in order to make clear that it is not merely a moral premotion, which would act only as a final cause upon the rational will; it is a work of real efficient agency on God's part.[8] As a *pre*-motion, its priority is one not of time, but only of causal order. As God is the primary cause of all causing — so the argument goes — he must be the first efficient cause of all actions, even those that are sinful;[9] and yet, as he operates in a mode radically transcendent of the mode of the creature's actions, he can do this without violating the creature's freedom. From eternity, God has infallibly decreed which actions will occur in time, and he brings them to pass either by directly willing them or by directly permitting them. Nor is divine permission in any way indeterminate, such that God would have to "wait upon" the creature's decisions, for then God's power would be susceptible of a moral or epistemic pathos;[10] rather, his is

roque Thomist position. Two articles that appeared in 2006, side by side in a single issue of the English-language version of *Nova et Vetera*, are particularly convenient in this regard: Thomas M. Osborne, Jr., "Thomist Premotion and Contemporary Philosophy of Religion," *Nova et Vetera* 4, no. 3 (2006): 607-31; Steven A. Long, "Providence, Freedom, and Natural Law," *Nova et Vetera* 4, no. 3 (2006): 557-605. Both essays are quite accurate as regards the fundamental ideas and concerns of the tradition they defend, as far as I can tell from my sporadic readings in classical Thomism, and most of the defects in their arguments are directly attributable to that tradition. Neither essay makes a convincing case for the Baroque position, admittedly, however scrupulously it is argued, or however precisely; but the apologetic urgency with which both have been written serves, if nothing else, to clarify the failings of that position. Bañez himself — for all his considerable limitations as a theologian or philosopher — was an exceedingly clear and careful writer and is, in that respect, preferable to many of his later expositors; but I — in my admittedly limited survey of his works — have failed to find a single comprehensive summary of his understanding of the *praemotio physica* that is easily extractable from its context. Perhaps the best treatment of the theme in the Dominican literature written during the early disputes with the Molinists is that of Diego Alvarez in his *De auxiliis gratiae et humani arbitrii viribus* (Rome, 1610); see especially disps. 28 and 83. The most thorough later defense of the position can be found in A. M. Dummermuth, *Defensio doctrinae S. Thomae Aq. de praemotione physica* (Paris, 1895) — a title that somewhat obscures the not insignificant point that Thomas himself never anywhere enunciates a doctrine of *praemotio physica*. See also Dummermuth's *S. Thomas et doctrina praemotionis physicae* (Paris, 1886).

8. See Thomas de Lemos, *Acta omnia congregationum et disputationum . . . de auxiliis divinae gratiae* (Louvain, 1702), p. 1065.

9. Domingo Bañez, *Commentaria in Summa Th. S. Thomae*, 1st part (Salamanca, 1584), I, q. 14, a. 13.

10. See Alvarez, *De auxiliis*, disp. 24: 15.

an eternal and irresistible "permissive decree," which predetermines even the evil actions of creatures.[11] God, however, is not the cause of evil; such is the natural defectibility — the inherent nothingness — of finite spirits that they cannot help but err if not upheld in the good by an extraordinary grace, and so if God withholds this grace they will, of their own nature, infallibly gravitate towards sin; and the will towards evil must, then, be ascribed entirely to the creature.[12] There is no injustice in this, moreover, inasmuch as God is not obliged to supply the creature with any grace at all; and so God remains innocent of any implication in the creature's sin, even though he has irresistibly predetermined in every instance that the creature will commit *this* sin.[13]

As for human freedom, the argument continues, it is in no wise abrogated by the *praemotio*. The proper definition of a free act is one that is not *contingently* determined, for an effect is deemed necessary or contingent only in regard to its proximate cause; hence, even if an act is determinately present in its primary cause, so long as it is contingent as regards its antecedent secondary causes, it is by definition free. Logically the creature could act otherwise, though in fact this possibility will never — can never — be realized; for though the creature's act is contingent in its own mode, it is necessary as eternally decreed by God. That is, it is not necessary in a "divided sense" (which would be the case only if the creature's potentiality for doing otherwise simply did not exist), but is necessary only in a "composed sense" (which is to say, necessary only in the sense that the creature cannot actually do otherwise than it is doing — which God has irresistibly predetermined).[14] It is not a physical necessity, therefore, but a necessity of "supposition"; for it lies within God's omnipotence irresistibly to predetermine an effect *as* a contingent effect. In the case of the rational creature, God infallibly causes him to act through his own intellect and will.[15] Nor are God and the creature competing causes within the act; so radically different are their proper modes of causality, and so radically distinct the orders to which they belong, that each can be said entirely to cause the act,

11. Alvarez, *De auxiliis,* disp. 83: 9.

12. Charles René Billuart, *Summa summae S. Thomae sive compendium theologiae* (Liège, 1754), *Tractatus de Deo et eius attributis,* dissertatio VIII, a. 5.

13. Alvarez, *De auxiliis,* disp. 19: 7. See Osborne, "Thomist Premotion," pp. 608-13; and Long, "Providence, Freedom, and Natural Law," pp. 569, 572, 584, 588, 594, 595, etc.

14. Billuart, *Summa summae: de Deo,* dissertatio VIII, a. 4.

15. See Alvarez, *De auxiliis,* disp. 22: 19.

though as superior and inferior agents.[16] Indeed, God does not even really *determine* the will; this he could do only by way of secondary causes, which would make the creature's act logically necessary; rather he directly and, so to speak, vertically *predetermines* the will, creating its power to choose and then efficiently causing the entire act he intends:[17] thus the will remains free.[18]

Thomists of this persuasion sometimes argue that one cannot deny the reality of the *praemotio* without simultaneously denying the omnipotence and primary causality of God. To suggest that human beings are free either to resist God's grace, or even to act at all without God directly "applying" them to their actions, is both morally and metaphysically incoherent. To suggest that God's "permissive will" might actually liberate the creature to an indeterminate diversity of possible free acts would be to imply that human liberty escapes divine providence and that the human will enjoys an absolute libertarian autonomy that places it beyond divine causality.[19] God then could know the creature only by way of a pathos, to which he would then reactively respond.[20] But, as Bañez says, "God knows sin by an intuitive cognition, insofar as the will of God is the cause of the entity of the sinful act *(causa entitatis actus peccati)*" — though, he adds, God *permits* free will to fail to observe the proper law of action, and thus to "concur with this act *(ad eundem actum concurrat)*."[21] Moreover, these Thomists contend, every act of the will is a movement from potency to act, a new actuality, which can be supplied only by the first cause of all being;[22] creatures are not able to bring about a new effect *ex nihilo*, but must be "applied" to action by a divine act; thus, in addition to his act of creation,

16. Alvarez, *De auxiliis,* disp. 22: 39.

17. See Alvarez, *De auxiliis,* disp. 28; see also Jean Baptiste Gonet, *Clypeus theologiae thomisticae contra novos eius impugnatores* (Bordeaux, 1659-1669), disp. 11: 5.

18. See Osborne, "Thomist Premotion," pp. 611-19, 623-29, 630; see especially 625: "If God physically predetermined the will through intermediate causes, then in Thomist language such motion would not be predetermination but determination, and consequently incompatible with free choice."

19. Alvarez, *De auxiliis,* disp. 122: 16. Long is especially — and especially crudely — insistent upon this point: "Providence, Freedom, and Natural Law," pp. 558, 559, 562, 564, 591, 601, 603, etc., etc. See also Osborne, "Thomist Premotion," pp. 611, 627.

20. John Paul Nazarius, *Commentaria et controversiae in Summa Th. S. Thomae,* 1st part (Bologna, 1620), I, q. 22, a. 4.

21. Bañez, *Commentaria in Summa Th.,* I, q. 23, a. 3, d. 2, c. 2.

22. See de Lemos, *Acta,* p. 1065.

God must always supply an additional movement of the will, directing it towards one end or another.[23]

That God elects to predetermine good acts in some and evil acts in others belongs, of course, to his predilective predestination of a few to salvation and his reprobation of the rest to damnation. As for the scriptural assurance that God wills that all men be saved, it would impugn God's causal omnipotence to suggest that what he "efficaciously" wills could possibly fail to occur;[24] thus his "universal will to salvation" applies only to the order of grace, where he supplies what is "sufficient" for the redemption of all; in the order of nature, however, he generally declines to provide the *praemotio* of the creature's will necessary to make that grace "efficacious." And God's purpose in infallibly permissively decreeing the evil that men do is to make both his mercy and his justice known: through the gratuitous rescue of the elect and the condign damnation of the derelict. After all, any world that God might create would still be composed of finite beings, inherently prone to defect, moved by competing and contrary goods, and every possible world falls infinitely short of the goodness of God; thus the permission of evil is intrinsic to the act of creation. But — by God's providence — evil will always serve a greater good: the final knowledge of God's goodness in the variety of its effects.[25]

III

The immediate and vulgar response of most Christians to this style of theology is to dismiss it as absurd and repellant. The more considered and sophisticated response, however — by one of those delightful coincidences that are all too rare — is usually the same. The difference is one of detail. One must concede, though, that the God of this obviously rather degenerate theology is indeed impassible — if only in a trivial sense. But he is certainly not truly transcendent.

It is one thing for a theologian simply to assert that God's "mode of causality" is utterly different from that of the creature, and that therefore

23. Gonet, *Clypeus,* disp. 9: 5; Osborne, "Thomist Premotion," pp. 612, 626; Long, "Providence, Freedom, and Natural Law," pp. 559, 562-63, 567, 569, 573, etc.

24. Alvarez, *De auxiliis,* disp. 92: 6.

25. See Long, "Providence, Freedom, and Natural Law," pp. 572-77.

God may act within the act of the creature without despoiling the latter of his liberty; but such an assertion is meaningful only if all the conclusions that follow from it genuinely obey the logic of transcendence. As primary cause of all things, after all, God is first and foremost their *ontological* cause. He imparts being to what, in itself, is nothing at all; out of the infinite plenitude of his actuality, he gives being to both potency and act; and yet what he creates, as the effect of a truly transcendent causality, possesses its own being, and truly exists as other than God (though God is not some "other thing" set alongside it). This donation of being is so utterly beyond any species of causality we can conceive that the very word "cause" has only the most remotely analogous value in regard to it. And, whatever warrant Thomists might find in Thomas for speaking of God as the first efficient cause of creation (which I believe to be in principle wrong), such language is misleading unless the analogical scope of the concept of efficiency has been extended almost to the point of apophasis.

Easily the weakest traditional argument in favor of the idea of the *praemotio* is that God must supply the "effect of being" for each movement of the will from potency to act. For one thing, this line of reasoning simply assumes the identity of ontological causation and efficient predetermination, which is the very issue in dispute. More to the point, it divides primary causality into two distinct moments: creation and an "additional" predetermining impulse of the will. This is simply banal. Obviously the act of creation is not simply the act of giving bare existence to static essences, which then must be further animated by some other kind of act. As the transcendent cause of being, God imparts to the creature its own dependent actuality, while also creating the potentialities to which that actuality is adequate; and, inasmuch as both act and potency are ontologically reducible to, and sustained by, their primary cause, and inasmuch as the will is always moved by its primordial inclination towards the good, it is absurd to speak of the need for something in addition to creation to "cause" the movement of the spiritual will. What God gives in creation is the entire actuality of the world, in all of its secondary causes; and, as those causes possess actual being, they are able to impart actuality to potentialities proportionate to their powers. It certainly, at any rate, makes no sense to say that every particular act is a unique creation *ex nihilo,* of which the distinction between act and potency in creation is a purely formal condition. This would be no better than a straightforward occasionalism — which is surely not what it means to say that all causes are reducible to the first cause.[26]

All of this, however, merely points to the more pervasive problem bedeviling physical premotion. Champions of the concept clearly believe that it serves to protect a proper understanding of the qualitative difference between divine and human action; and yet this is precisely what it can never do. For, if the *praemotio* works as its defenders say it does, as the direct and infallible efficient predetermination of *this* rather than *that* act, then God and the creature most definitely operate within the same order; and, though the neo-Bañezian may claim otherwise, God acts as a rival — indeed, even in a kind of "negative real relation" — to the creature (though this is, again, a rivalry God has always already won). The God of physical premotion is not fully transcendent, but merely supreme; he is not a fully primary cause, but merely a kind of "infinite" secondary cause; he is not fully the *causa in esse* of all things, but merely the *causa in fieri* that reigns over all other motive forces. Rather than causing all causes as causes, he is that absolute immanent power that all other immanent causes at once dissemble and express. Thus, when the "classical Thomist" attempts to explain how God can create dependent freedom, the best he seems able to manage is to talk of a direct and irresistible predetermination of the will, and then — to avoid the contradiction this entails — to attempt to reduce the question of freedom to one of mere logical contingency. But freedom lies not in an action's logical conditions, but in the action itself; and if an action is causally necessitated or infallibly predetermined, its indeterminacy with regard to its proximate cause in no way makes it free.

Of course, it may well have been that, in the late sixteenth century — due to certain drastic changes within the idea of causality — the very concept of a created freedom had become all but unintelligible. It is, at least, tempting to see the notion of physical premotion as a kind of invasion of theology by the mechanical philosophy. Certainly at this point in intellectual history, any concept of ontological causality could not help but seem rather vague and fabulous; and to speak of the infinite plenitude and transcendence of God's creative act somehow no longer seemed an adequate way of affirming his omnipotence. In the age of mechanism, the only fully

26. For an especially enlightening treatment of the issue of God's causation of freedom as occurring within the act of creation, see David B. Burrell, *Freedom and Creation in Three Traditions* (Notre Dame: University of Notre Dame Press, 1993); see especially pp. 95-139.

credible kind of causality — the cause *par excellence* — was efficient causality. Whereas once it might have sufficed to assert that, within the fourfold causality of finite reality, there dwelled another, mysterious, and transcendent cause, acting in an entirely different manner, it now became necessary to ground God's transcendence in a more respectable kind of causality: efficient supremacy. And even spiritual freedom was reduced to the physical effect of a prior external force.

One unavoidable result of this general impoverishment of metaphysics was that God had to be conceived as the author of evil — whether directly and explicitly, as with the Calvinists, or elliptically and self-deludingly, as with the Bañezians. And the "classical Thomist" evasion of this conclusion scarcely rises to the level of the risible. Neither the theologically dubious notion that the "natural" tendency of any defectible rational creature not upheld by extraordinary grace is towards sin, nor the related claim that when God permits evil he does no more than abandon the creature to its own inevitable operations, exculpates the creator of complicity in the creature's sins. To begin with, if God's relation to creation really is efficiently causal in the way Bañezian thought suggests, then the very distinction between nature and grace within God's creative act is largely specious; the question becomes simply at what stage of gratuitously imparted blessings — being, will, reason, adherence in the good — he elects to halt in his creative activity towards the creature. And if he has elected to relinquish his gracious "restraint" of the creature's "naturally defectible" will while yet sustaining the creature in being; and if he has eternally, infallibly, irresistibly, "permissively" decreed that the creature will commit *this* sin and suffer *this* damnation, not on account of any prevision of the creature's sins, but solely on account of his own predetermining act of reprobation; and if this irresistible "antecedent permissive decree" applies even to the creature's intention of evil (as logically it must); and if the creature is incapable of availing himself of "sufficient" grace — or indeed incapable of any motion of the will at all — without being applied to its act by God's physical premotion; then moral evil is as much God's work as is any other act of the will.[27] Only if providence is as transcendent as the ontological

---

27. See Jacques Maritain, *God and the Permission of Evil,* trans. Joseph W. Evans (Milwaukee: The Bruce Publishing Co., 1966), pp. 30-31: "In the theory of the antecedent permissive decrees, God, under the relation of efficiency, is not the cause, not even (that which I do not concede) the indirect cause, of moral evil. But he is the one primarily responsible for its

cause it manifests — if, that is, it is the way in which God, to whom all time is present, permits and fully "accounts for" and "answers" acts that he does not directly determine, but that also cannot determine him — is God's permission of evil indeed *permission*. But if instead it is an irresistible pre-determination of every action, then it neither preserves creaturely freedom nor wrests good from evil, but merely accomplishes the only action within creation that is truly undetermined: God's positive intention — for the purpose of a "greater good" — towards evil.

In fact, it can plausibly be argued that, in a very real sense, the Bañezian God does not create a world at all, and that this species of "classi-cal" Thomism amounts only to what the greatest Catholic philosopher of the twentieth century, Erich Przywara, called "theopanism."[28] After all, the *praemotio* is not a qualitatively different act on God's part within the crea-ture's act, but merely a quantitatively more coercive variety of the same kind of act. To speak of a superior and inferior agent within a single free operation is perfectly coherent, so long as the infinite analogical interval between ontological and ontic causality is observed; but to speak of a su-perior and inferior determining efficient cause within a single free opera-tion is gibberish. If there were such a physical premotion, all created ac-tions would be merely diverse modalities of God's will. And inasmuch as God is not some distinct object or physical force set over against the world, but is the supereminent source of all being, then — apart from some kind of *effective* divine indetermination of the creature's freedom in regard to specific goods — there is no ontological distinction between God and the world worth noting. It is true that *agere sequitur esse,* but also true that each essence *is* only insofar as it discloses itself in its act; and if all acts are expressions of the divine predetermination of *these* particular acts, then all essences are merely modes — or phenomenal masks — of the divine will.

What is, of course, absent from this picture of divine causality is that

---

presence here on earth. It is He who has invented it in the drama or novel of which He is the author. He refuses His efficacious grace to a creature because it has already failed culpably, but this culpable failure occurred only in virtue of the permissive decree which preceded it. God manages to be nowise the cause of evil, while seeing to it that evil occurs infallibly. The antecedent permissive decrees, be they presented by the most saintly of theologians — I can-not see in them, taken in themselves, anything but an insult to the *absolute innocence of God.*"

28. See Erich Przywara, *Analogia Entis: Metaphysik: Ur-Struktur und All-Rhythmus* (Einsiedeln: Johannes-Verlag, 1962), pp. 70-78, 128-35, 247-301.

ancient metaphysical vision that Przywara chose to call the *"analogia entis."* In this "analogical ontology," the infinite dependency of created being upon divine being is understood strictly in terms of the ever greater difference between them; and, under the rule of this ontology, it is possible to affirm the real participation of the creature's freedom in God's free creative act without asserting any ontic continuity of kind between created and divine acts. When, however, the rule of analogy declines — as it did at the threshold of modernity — then invariably the words we attempt to apply both to creatures and to God (goodness, justice, mercy, love, freedom) dissolve into equivocity, and theology can recover its coherence only by choosing a single "attribute" to treat as univocal, in order that God and world might be united again. In the early modern period, the attribute most generally preferred was "power" or "sovereignty" — or, more abstractly, "cause."

IV

Can God really create freedom? Is his so transcendent an act that he can — without suffering any pathos — create wills capable of resisting him? Certainly no answer can be provided in the terms of the early modern debates between Bañezians and Molinists. Anyway, the two positions are effectively the same. The logic of Molina's position, after all, was that God — in knowing all possible worlds and states of affairs — chooses one reality to make actual and thereby infallibly destines all real actions. This implied — oddly enough — that it is secondary causes that determine free choices, and consequently that God's election of one world out of an infinity of incompossible alternatives is an act of divine predetermination, however it may be portrayed as a divine "response" to the creature. Bañez, being more rigorous, denied that there was any such response; but for him, still, God's "vertical" predetermination of the creature's "free" act nevertheless aborts all other possible courses of action. In either case, God elects this world out of an infinity of possibilities and thereby infallibly decrees what shall be. Molina was perhaps the more amiable figure of the two, insofar as he hoped to preserve some sense of the innocence of God; but that was an impossible ambition given the narrowly mechanistic concepts available in his time. And, on either side of the debate, theologians were attempting to remedy the ontological deficiency of their theory by way of an ontic supplement: either *praemotio physica* (a solution conceived from the perspective of act) or *scientia media* (a solution conceived from the perspective of potency).

Of course, the very notion of God choosing among possible worlds — especially if, as the classical Thomist position holds, there is by definition no "best" world among them — is already haunted by the specter of a kind of divine voluntarism, an arbitrariness that would make God that much more complicit in each particular evil within creation. But, more importantly, it is a view of creation utterly uninformed by revelation. At the very least, one must start from the knowledge that this world — as the world that belongs to the event of Christ — is the world (fallen or unfallen) in which God most fully reveals himself; and, unless one thinks Christ was merely an avatar of God, and that his human identity was somehow accidental to his divine identity, one must then also grant that the world to which the human identity of Christ naturally belongs is one uniquely and eternally fitted to that revelation. Creation is not simply a multifarious demonstration of God's power and goodness, which might equally well be expressed by some other contingent cosmic order, but is the event within God's Logos of beings uniquely — and appropriately — called to union with him. And within this world — within God's manifestation of himself in the Son — freedom necessarily exists, as the way by which created being can be assumed into the eternal love of the Trinity.

To say, moreover, that this freedom is not causally predetermined by God does not imply that it is somehow "absolute" or that it occupies a region independent of God's power (as one strain of neo-Bañezian apologetics contends). It is in his power to create such autonomy that God's omnipotence is most abundantly revealed; for everything therein comes from him: the real being of agent, act, and potency, the primordial movement of the soul towards the good,[29] the natural law inscribed in the creature's intellect and will, the sustained permission of finite autonomy; even the indetermination of the creature's freedom is an utterly dependent and unmerited participation in the mystery of God's infinite freedom; and, in his eternal presence to all of time, God never ceases to exercise his providential care or to make all free acts the occasions of the greater good he intends in creating. The purpose of created autonomy is, as Maximus the Confessor says, its ultimate surrender in love to God, whereby alone

29. See Shanley, "Divine Causation," pp. 112-14.

rational nature finds its true fulfillment.[30] But, whereas in God perfect freedom and "theonomy" coincide in the infinite simplicity of his essence, in us the free movement of the will towards God is one that passes from potency to act, and as such is dynamic and synthetic in form. Thus God works within the participated autonomy of the creature as an act of boundless freedom, a sort of immanent transcendence, an echo within the soul of that divine abyss of love that calls all things to itself, ever setting the soul free to work out her salvation in fear and trembling.

In the end, it is no more contradictory to say that God can create — out of the infinite wellspring of his own freedom — dependent freedoms that he does not determine, than it is to say that he can create — out of the infinite wellspring of his being — dependent beings that are genuinely somehow other than God. In neither case, however, is it possible to describe the "mechanism" by which he does this. This aporia is simply inseparable from the doctrine of *creatio ex nihilo* — which, no matter how we may attempt to translate it into causal terms we can understand, remains forever imponderable. There is no process by which creation happens, no intermediate operation or *tertium quid* between God and what he calls into being. As for those who fear that, in knowing actions he does not predetermine, God proves susceptible of pathos, one can only exhort them always to consider the logic of transcendence. God knows in creating, which is an action simply *beyond* the realm of the determined and the determining. Nothing the creature does exceeds those potentialities God has created, or draws upon any actuality but that which God imparts, or escapes God's eternal knowledge of the world of Christ. Just as — according to Thomas — God can know evil by way of his positive act of the good, as a privation thereof,[31] even so can he know the free transgressions of his creatures by way of the good acts he positively wills through the freedom of the rational souls he creates. Just as the incarnate Logos really suffers torment and death not through a passive modification of his nature, imposed by some exterior force, but by a free act, so God can "suffer" the perfect knowledge of the free acts of his creatures not as a passive reaction to some objective force set over against himself, but as the free, transcendent act of giving being to the world of Christ — an act to whose sufficiency there need attach no mediating "premotion" to assure its omnipotence.

---

30. See Maximus, *Ambiguum* 7, PG 91:107B.
31. Thomas Aquinas, *Summa theologiae* I, q. 14, a. 10.

And that eternal act of knowledge is entirely convertible with God's free intention to reveal himself in Christ.

V

The issue of God's epistemic passibility, of course, is far less pressing if one does not presume real differentiations within God's intention towards his creatures. For, surely, Scripture is quite explicit on this point: God positively "wills" the salvation of "all human beings" (1 Timothy 2:4). Paul does not say that God merely generically desires that salvation, or that he simply formally allows it as a logical possibility, or that he wills it antecedently but not consequently, or that (most ridiculous of all) he enables it "sufficiently" but not "efficaciously." If God were really to supply saving grace sufficient for all, but to refuse to supply most persons with the *necessary* natural means of attaining that grace, it would mean that God does *not* will the salvation of all.

Certainly, a far better account of the relation of God to the free acts of his creatures would be that of, for instance, Maximus the Confessor. For Maximus, I think it fair to assert, one could never truly say that God causes some to rise while permitting others to fall; rather, one would have to say that he causes all to rise, and permits all to fall, and imparts to all — out of his own abyssal freedom — the ability to consent to or to resist the grace he extends, while providentially ordering all things according to his universal will to salvation. Or, rather, perhaps one should say that God causes all to rise, but the nature of that cause necessarily involves a permission of the will. God's good will and his permission of evil, then, are simply two aspects of a single creative act, one that does not differ in intention from soul to soul: God's one vocation of all rational creation to a free union in love with himself; his one gracious permission that spiritual freedom in some way determine itself in relation to the eternal good towards which it is irresistibly drawn; his one gift of sufficient aid, both in conferring saving grace on all and in sustaining human nature in its power to respond; his one refusal to coerce the will as some kind of determining cause; his one providence; his one upholding of all in being. Indeed, in this sense it almost makes sense to speak of God's infallible permissive decree for his creatures *ante praevisa merita:* in God's one act of self-outpouring love, he decrees that the creature will always be moved by its primordial impulse towards the good, and will always act under permission towards various ends; and that permission infallibly sets the creature free — within its irresistible natural impulse towards the good — to whatever end the creature elects. God and the creature do indeed act within utterly different orders.

This double movement of the will Maximus defines as the distinction between the "natural" and "gnomic" wills within us[32] (a distinction, incidentally, absolutely central to orthodox Christology, East and West). The former is that dynamic orientation towards the infinite goodness of God that is the source of all rational life and of all desire within us; the latter is that deliberative power by which we obey or defy the deep promptings of our nature and the rule of the final good beyond us. It is the movement of the natural will towards God, moreover, whose primordial motion allows the gnomic will its liberty and its power of assent to or rejection of God. In the interval between these two movements — both of which are rational — the rational soul becomes who God intends her to be or, through apostasy from her own nature, fabricates a distance between herself and God that is nothing less than the distance of dereliction. For, whatever we do, the desire of our natural will for God will be consummated; it will return to God, whether the gnomic will consents or not, and will be glorified with that glory the Son shares with the Father from eternity. And, if the gnomic will within us has not surrendered to its natural supernatural end, our own glorified nature becomes hell to us, that holy thing we cannot touch. Rejection of God becomes estrangement from ourselves, the kingdom of God within us becomes our exile, and the transfiguring glory of God within us — through our refusal to submit to love — becomes the unnatural experience of dereliction.[33] God fashions all rational natures for free union with himself, and all of creation as the deathless vessel of his eternal glory. To this end, he wills that the dependent freedom of the creature be joined to his absolute freedom; but an indispensable condition of what he wills is the real power of the creature's deliberative will to resist the irresistible work of grace. And God both wills the ultimate good of all things and accomplishes that good, and knows the good and evil acts of his creatures, and *reacts* to neither. This is the true sublimity of divine *apatheia:* an infinite innocence that wills to the last the glorification of the creature, in the

---

32. See, for instance, Maximus, *Opusculum* 14, PG 91:153A-B.
33. See Maximus, *Quaestiones ad Thalassium* 59, PG 90:609A-B.

depths of its nature, and that never ceases to sustain the rational will in its power to seek its end either in God or in itself.

VI

One reason, I would think, for preferring this vision of God's will for the creature to the Bañezian — quite apart from its closer conformity to revelation — is the not insignificant concern that the God described by the latter happens to be evil. This seems as if it should be a problem. I hasten to add, moreover, that I do not think I am guilty, in using this word, of the querulous vessel's impertinent reproaches of its maker. For one thing, the Bañezian God is a monstrous and depraved fantasy, who has no real being and whom consequently it is impossible to blaspheme; for another, the use of the word "evil" here is nothing more than an exercise in sober precision. In the "classical Thomist" understanding of God, the word "good" has been rendered utterly equivocal between creatures and God; it has become simply a metaphysical name for the divine essence, to which no moral analogy attaches, and so — as far as common usage is concerned — has been rendered vacuous. If, though, God acts as the Bañezian position claims, and if indeed his "justice" is expressed in his arbitrary decision to inflict eternal torment on creatures whom he has purposely crafted to be vessels of his eternal wrath, then it is possible to construct an *analogia mali* between human cruelty and God's magnificent "transcendence" of the difference between good and evil, without doing the least violence to language or reason. And, as for the ancient argument that such actions constitute no injustice on God's part, because the creature cannot *merit* grace, this should be dismissed as the fatuous *non sequitur* it has always been. The issue has never been one of merit — for, indeed, the creature "merits" nothing at all, not even its existence; the issue is, rather, the moral nature of God, as revealed in his acts towards those he creates. And the God of this theology is merely an infinite engine of pure, self-expressive, amoral power, who creates untold multitudes for everlasting misery, and whom — were he really to exist — it would be an act of supreme condescension on our parts to view with contempt. This sort of "Christianity" enjoys no conspicuous moral superiority over satanism — indeed, it makes the latter seem somehow morally pardonable.

No less distasteful — but even less intellectually respectable — is the equally ancient argument that God requires the dereliction of the reprobate in order to make his "goodness" more fully known, through a display of both his justice and his mercy.[34] If ever there were a purely *ad hoc* attempt to justify a morally incoherent position, this is it. For one thing, it is sheer nonsense to suggest that anything meaningfully called "goodness" could be revealed in God's willful, eternal, and predetermining reprobation of souls to endless suffering, simply as "demonstration cases," so to speak. For another, the full nature of God's justice was revealed on the cross, where God took the penalty of sin upon himself so that he might offer forgiveness freely to all. Moreover, the image this entire line of reasoning summons up is at best coarsely mythological. Nothing could be cruder than the notion that final knowledge of God is like knowledge of some external object set before the intellect, which needs to be grasped by an extrinsic, calculative cognition of its "attributes," and by an accumulation of "information" about the divine essence, and by edifying displays of God's power to torture and destroy. The beauty and variety of creation declares God's glory, but God, being infinite, could never be an extrinsic "object" for the finite mind. True knowledge of God comes, rather, through an immediate and deifying communication of divine goodness to the created intellect, by which the created soul is in some way admitted into a remote, created participation in God's knowledge of himself. And that goodness — since all real possibility is supereminently present in it — is sufficient to communicate itself without the "clarifying" supplement of evil; even if the finite mind cannot grasp God's goodness in its infinite simplicity, the infi-

34. The passage from Paul typically adduced to support this argument (Rom. 9:22-23) proves no support at all if it is read in the context of the argument that unfolds from chapter 9 through chapter 11. For one thing, the issue of election in these verses has no obvious or even logical connection to the idea of the predestination of souls to salvation or damnation; rather, it concerns solely the election of either Israel or the Church as the people of God within history, as bearers of the covenant before the nations. More importantly, when Paul reaches the conclusion of his argument, he proclaims that in fact the purpose behind the mystery of election is not an eschatological demonstration of divine power in the destruction of vessels of wrath and preservation of vessels of mercy; rather, it turns out, it is for the sake of a reconciliation between the two peoples, Church and Israel, whereby a blessing will be bestowed on all; for, as Paul says, God binds all in disobedience in order to show mercy towards all — and all of Israel shall be saved. This is, after all, the pattern of election as one finds it displayed in Hebrew Scripture, especially in Genesis. The tragic tradition of selective reading within, and misprision of, these chapters, is of course irreversible; but that does not make it somehow theologically legitimate. An error, however ancient, is still only an error.

nite diversity of goods of which the divine essence is capable nowhere requires the shadow of evil to make the lineaments of those goods more evident.[35] And created reason, if it is indeed naturally fitted to the good, would suffer no deficiency of knowledge in being "deprived" of the vision of damnation — which, as I have argued above, is nothing but an internal and utterly invisible absurdity, the "impossible" experience of exile in the very midst of an infinite glory.

Simply said, if God required evil to accomplish his good ends — the revelation of his nature to finite minds — then not only would evil possess a real existence over against the good, but God himself would be dependent upon evil: to the point of it constituting a dimension of his identity (even if only as a "contrast"). And one cannot circumvent this difficulty by saying that the necessity involved applies only to finite creatures and not to God in himself; for if God needs the supplement of evil to accomplish any good he intends — even a contingent good — then he is dependent upon evil in an absolute sense. There would be goods of which the good as such is impotent apart from evil's "contribution." And, if in any way evil is necessary to define or increase knowledge of the good, then the good is not ontological — is not, that is, convertible with real being itself — but is at most an evaluation.

What must be emphasized here, however, is that the defects within the Bañezian position are the result not of too strict a fidelity to the principle of divine impassibility, but of an absolute betrayal of that principle: one that robs it of its true meaning, and thereby reduces God to a being among lesser beings, a force among lesser forces, whose infinite greatness is rendered possible only by the absolute passivity of finite reality before his absolute supremacy. It is the failure to understand omnipotence as transcendence that renders every attempt to speak coherently of God's innocence futile. It is the failure to place divine causality altogether beyond the finite economy of created causes that produces a God who is merely beyond good and evil.

---

35. Thomas's notorious argument to the contrary, in *ST* I, q. 23, a. 5, ad 3, is unobjectionable in suggesting that it is through the variety of created goods that finite minds conceive some knowledge of the plenitude of God's goodness; but, in trying to integrate the theology of predilective predestination *ante praevisa merita* into this vision of things, he attempts to import an impossible alloy into his reasoning. Indeed, the entirety of I, q. 23, inasmuch as it merely attempts to justify a late Augustinian reading of Paul that is objectively wrong, can largely be ignored as a set of forced answers to false questions.

VII

The great irony of the enthusiasm that a few traditionalist Catholic scholars harbor for Bañezian or "classical" Thomism is their curious belief that such a theology offers a solution to the pathologies of modernity — voluntarism, antinomianism, atheism, disregard of natural law, nihilism. Nothing could be farther from the truth. Far from constituting an alternative to modernity, Baroque Thomism is the most quintessentially *modern* theology imaginable. To think that one could defeat the pathogens of human voluntarism by retreating to what is in effect a limitless divine voluntarism is rather like thinking one could cure tuberculosis with consumption. And the mere formal assertion by the Bañezian party that, in their system, God's will follows his intellect — which is the very opposite of the voluntarist view — simply bears no scrutiny. No less than in any of his other variants — Lutheran or Calvinist, for example — the modern God of the Bañezians is one whose will is defined by an ultimate spontaneity, and a quite insidious arbitrariness. A God whose predestining and reprobative determinations are both utterly pure of prevision and irresistible, who creates a world that bears no more proper relation to his nature than any among an infinite number of other possible worlds, who requires a justice of his creatures that he himself does not exhibit, who condemns whom he chooses to condemn, and who is himself an efficient cause of the sinful actions he punishes, is a God whose will is sheer power, not love, and certainly not governed by reason. This is the God of early modernity in his full majesty: the God who either determines or is determined, and who therefore must absolutely determine all things — a pure abyss of sovereignty justifying itself through its own exercise. He may be a God of eternal law, but behind his legislations lies a more original lawlessness. He is, in every way, the God of nihilism.

Voluntarism, after all, began as a doctrine regarding God, and only gradually (if inevitably) migrated to the human subject. The God of absolute will who was born in the late Middle Ages had by the late sixteenth century so successfully usurped the place of the true God that few theologians could recognize him for the imposter he was. And the piety he inspired was, in some measure, a kind of blasphemous piety: a servile and fatalistic adoration of boundless power masquerading as a love of righteousness. More importantly, this theology — through the miraculous technology of the printing press — entered into common Christian consciousness as the theology of previous ages never could, and in so doing provided western humanity at once both with a new model of freedom and with a God whom it would be necessary, in the fullness of time, to kill. It was from this God that we first learned to think of freedom as a perfect spontaneity of the will, and from him we learned the irreducible preroga-tives that accrue to all sovereign power, whether that of the absolute mon-arch, or that of the nation state, or that of the individual. But, if this is in-deed what freedom is, and God's is the supreme instance of such freedom, then he is not — as he was in ages past — the transcendent good who sets the created will free to realize its nature in its ultimate end, but is merely the one intolerable rival to every other freedom, who therefore invites creatures to rebel against him and to attempt to steal fire from heaven. If this is God, then Feuerbach and Nietzsche were both perfectly correct to see his exaltation as an impoverishment and abasement of the human at the hands of a celestial despot. For such freedom — such pure *arbitrium* — must always enter into a contest of wills; it could never exist within a peaceful order of analogical participation, in which one freedom could draw its being from a higher freedom. Freedom of this sort is one and indi-visible, and has no source but itself.

More importantly, perhaps, so terrible was the burden that this cruel predestining God laid upon the conscience of believers that it could not be borne indefinitely. It was this God who, having first deprived us of any true knowledge of the transcendent good, died for modern culture, and left us to believe that the true God had perished. The explicit nihilism of late mo-dernity is not even really a rejection of the modern God; it is merely the in-evitable result of his presence in history, and of the implicit nihilism of the theology that invented him. Indeed, worship of this god is the first and most inexcusable nihilism, for it can have no real motives other than cra-ven obsequiousness or sadistic delight. Modern atheism is merely the con-summation of the forgetfulness of the transcendent God that this theology made perfect. Moreover, it may be that, in an age in which the only choice available to human thought was between faith in the modern God of pure sovereignty and simple unbelief, the latter was the holier — indeed, the more Christian — path. For, at some level, faith in the God of absolute will always required a certain extirpation of conscience from the soul, or at least its pacification; and so perhaps it is better that the natural longing of each soul for God — even if only in the reduced form of moral alarm, or an inchoate impulse towards natural goodness, or of a longing for a *deus ignotus* — refuse to make obeisance before this idol. Perhaps it was the last living trace of Christian conscience in western man that moved him — like the Christian "atheists" of the first few centuries of the church — to reject any God but a God of infinite love. Late modernity might even be thought of as a time of purgatorial probation, a harsh but necessary hygiene of the spirit, by enduring which we might once again be made able to lift up our minds to the truly transcendent and impassible God, eternally absolved of all evil, in whom there is no darkness at all.

I began this essay with a quotation from Heidegger, and shall draw to a close with another. Speaking at one point of how God enters into philosophy — specifically, modern metaphysics, which understands "being" solely as the causal ground of beings — Heidegger writes:

> . . . [der] Grund selbst aus dem von ihm Begründeten her der ihm gemäßen Begründung, d.h. der Verursachung durch die ursprünglichste Sache bedarf. Dies ist die Ursache als die Causa sui. So lautet der sachgerechte Name für den Gott in der Philosophie. Zu diesem Gott kann der Mensch weder beten, noch kann er ihm opfern. Vor der Causa sui kann der Mensch weder aus Scheu ins Knie fallen, noch kann er vor diesem Gott musizieren und tanzen.
>
> Demgemäß ist das gott-lose Denken, das den Gott der Philosophie, den Gott als Causa sui preisgeben muß, dem göttlichen Gott vielleicht näher. Dies sagt hier: Es ist freier für ihn, als es die Onto-Theo-Logik wahrheben möchte.[36]

Such, at least, is Heidegger's verdict upon the god of "onto-theo-logy," the god of the metaphysics of the "double founding" — the grounding of beings in being and of being in a supreme being — which reduces all of reality (including divine reality) to a closed totality, an economy of causal power, from which the mystery of being has been fully exorcised.

---

36. Martin Heidegger, "Die Onto-Theo-Logische Verfassung der Metaphysik," in *Identität und Differenz*, 10th edition (Stuttgart: Verlag Günther Neske, 1996), pp. 64-65. [. . . (the) ground itself must in due measure be grounded: that is, must be caused by the most primordially causative thing. This is the cause understood as *causa sui*. This is how the name of God appropriate to philosophy is inscribed. To this god can man neither pray nor make offering. Neither can man fall to his knees in awe before the *causa sui*, nor before this god can he make music and dance. Perhaps, then, that god-less thinking that must abandon the god of philosophy — God, that is, understood as *causa sui* — is nearer to the divine God. That is to say, it is freer for him than onto-theo-logy would wish to grant.]

I confess that, in twenty years of reading Heidegger, I have never before allowed myself to feel the full force of these words: *freier für ihn. . . .* There are some things that I simply have not cared to be told by Heidegger — whereof I here repent. One need not accept Heidegger's monolithic history of metaphysics, or despair as he did of the possibility of speaking analogically of God, or embrace his ontology, to value his thought as a solvent of the decadent traditions of early modern metaphysics. When all that is high and holy in God has been forgotten, and God has been reduced to sheer irresistible causal power, the old names for God have lost their true meaning, and the death of God has already been accomplished, even if we have not yet consciously ceased to believe. When atheism becomes explicit, however, it also becomes possible to recognize the logic that informs it, to trace it back to its remoter origins, perhaps even to begin to reverse its effects. It may be that a certain grace operates through disbelief: perhaps we shall be ready again to receive the truly "divine God" (as Heidegger phrases it) only when certain gods of our own making have vanished. This is the moment (as Heidegger also says) of highest risk, a moment in which an absolute nihilism threatens; but it is also then a moment in which it may become possible once again to recall the God who is beyond every nihilism. It is certainly not a moment for lamentation or misguided nostalgias. Better to fix before our minds the piercing words of Meister Eckhart: "I pray that God deliver me from god."[37] It is principally the god of modernity — the god of pure sovereignty, the voluntarist god of "permissive decrees" and the *praemotio physica* — who has died for modern humanity, and perhaps theology has no nobler calling for now than to see that he remains dead, and that every attempt to revive him is thwarted: in the hope that, in becoming willing accomplices in his death, Christians may help to prepare their world for the return of the true God revealed in Christ, in all the mystery of his transcendent and impassible love.

37. Meister Eckhart, Sermon 52: "Beati pauperes spiritu."

Divine Providence and the Mystery of Human Suffering: Keynote Address, Providence College, May 30, 2006

Avery Cardinal Dulles, S.J.

The reality of evil is a matter of experience for anyone, but the problem becomes most acute in connection with major disasters such as the Holocaust, the Tsunami, or a hurricane like Katrina. At such junctures some become angry with God and others lose their faith, since faith requires us to believe that God is all-powerful and could therefore prevent any such calamity.

Every Sunday in our liturgy we confess our belief in one God, the Almighty, creator of heaven and earth. The creed simply reflects consistent biblical teaching. Speaking to Abraham, God said, "I am God almighty" (Gen. 17:1). He said the same to Jacob (Gen. 38:11). The same theme runs like a refrain through the Old Testament and the New, right up to the Book of Revelation, in which God several times asserts: "I am the Alpha and the Omega . . . who is and who was and who is to come, the Almighty" (Rev. 1:8; cf. 4:8; 15:3; 16:7, etc.).

The biblical authors were all too familiar with droughts and floods, famines and plagues, oppression and poverty, wars, deportations, and captivity. But they never showed the slightest inclination to doubt the existence, goodness, and power of God.

The psalmist confesses that he finds it hard to understand the prosperity of the wicked and the sufferings of the poor and innocent (e.g., Ps. 10 and Ps. 73). Jeremiah complains to God: "Why does the way of the wicked prosper? Why do all who are treacherous thrive?" (Jer. 12:1). Habakkuk protests to God, "Why are you silent when the wicked swallows up the man more righteous than he?" (Hab. 1:13). And Job observes in his dialogue with his accusers that the wicked seem to go unpunished to the end (Job 21:30-33).

Grappling with this immense problem, the prophets sought to discover some meaning in evil. They interpreted the afflictions of Israel as punishments inflicted to requite the nation's sins and lead it to repentance and reform. The prayer of Azariah in the Book of Daniel reflects this interpretation of the Babylonian captivity: "Thou hast executed true judgments in all that thou hast brought upon us and upon Jerusalem, the holy city of our fathers, for in truth and justice thou hast brought all this upon us because of our sins" (Dan. 3:27-28).[1]

As attention shifted increasingly from the fate of the nation to that of individuals, the idea of corporate guilt receded into the background. Later prophets such as Jeremiah and Ezekiel assured their audiences that no one would be punished for the sins of others. But this individualism made it still more difficult to explain the sufferings of persons who seemed, by human standards, to be innocent. The Book of Job poses that problem in starkest form. It tells the story (fictitious, no doubt) of a man who perfectly observes God's law, and yet suffers the loss of his family, fortunes, health, and good name. His friends, schooled in the moralistic teaching of the prophets, express their sympathy but try to persuade him that he has no cause for complaint against God, because God is utterly just. It follows, therefore, that Job must have committed some serious sin, even unknown to himself. His friends try to help him examine his conscience. In this case, however, they are wrong. Job's sufferings are not a punishment, as his friends suppose. In the end, God vindicates him.

Why, then, does Job suffer? According to the preface (Job 1:6-12), it is to demonstrate his fidelity. Even in the midst of ordeals that he knows to be undeserved, Job cannot be induced to curse God. He recognizes that suffering is a mystery that he as a creature cannot comprehend. Before the ineffable mystery of God's designs he can only bow his head in adoring silence.

The message of the book, as I read it, is that when God permits adversity he does so for good reasons, but these reasons may not be evident to the sufferer, who must therefore submit in faith. Job's suffering was permitted in order to test his fidelity and purify his love, so that his religion would not be a matter of *quid pro quo,* but of serving God because of God's own sovereign goodness. God trusted Job's readiness to suffer without suc-

1. The Prayer of Azariah is one of the additions to the Book of Daniel that are not found in the Hebrew and are absent in most Protestant editions of the Bible.

cumbing to bitterness and, when Job had proved himself, rewarded him richly.[2]

In terms of religious wisdom, Job represents a new high point, surpassing in some ways the prophets' interpretation of suffering as punishment. But toward the end of the Old Testament period, we get intimations of two further developments that anticipate the New Testament.

The first of these developments is the realization that life in this world is not final. It is a mere probation for a fullness that is to come after death. In books such as Daniel, Wisdom, and Second Maccabees, we are taught not to seek the totality of meaning within human history but only at its completion. On the last day God will appear in manifest glory to establish his kingdom, and the saints will enjoy a share in that glorious reign. According to Daniel, the archangel Michael will come at the end of time and summon the dead, some to everlasting life and others to everlasting shame and contempt (Dan. 12:2). The Maccabean martyrs go to their deaths in confidence that they will rise again to everlasting life because they have observed God's laws (2 Mac. 7:9, 11, 14, 23). The Wisdom of Solomon states explicitly that the souls of the just are in the hand of God (Wis. 3:1) and that the early death of the righteous, though it may look like a divine punishment, is in fact a passage to a blessed immortality (Wis. 3:2-9). Those who have suffered patiently on earth will receive ample compensation in the joys of heaven.

The second breakthrough is the idea of vicarious expiatory suffering. In the second part of Isaiah, we find the famous Servant Songs, in which a mysterious figure, the Suffering Servant, is chastised for the sins of the multitude, and goes meekly like a sheep to the slaughter, in order to make reparation for their offenses (Isa. 53:1-12). In the end the Servant is exalted and brings blessings on those for whom he intercedes.

These final insights of Old Testament theology bring us very close to the New Testament, which makes the extraordinary claim that God him-

---

2. For a long meditation on Job see John Paul II, Apostolic Letter *Salvifici doloris,* in *Origins* 13 (Feb. 23, 1984): 609-24. Not all scholars interpret Job in this way. R. C. Zaehner, for example, held that Job's friends were right, and that Job was guilty of presumptive self-esteem. See Zaehner, *Concordant Discord* (Oxford: Oxford University Press, 1970), pp. 349-54. This and Carl Jung's interpretations of Job are discussed by Michael Galligan, *God and Evil* (New York: Paulist, 1976), pp. 57-60. William J. O'Malley, in *Redemptive Suffering* (New York: Crossroad, 1997), examines the theme of Job in the writings of Archibald MacLeish and Jack Miles (pp. 78-83).

self plunges into human history in order to bear in his person the full weight of human guilt, thereby healing evil at its root. Like the Suffering Servant, by whom he is prefigured, Jesus takes on himself in some sense the infirmities and diseases of the whole human race and pays the price for every sin (cf. Matt. 8:17). Jesus in a sense becomes the new Job, suffering to the very limit, especially in his Passion. Everything providentially conspires to subject him to the most extreme humiliation, pain, and abandonment. On the cross, it would seem, he even experiences a sense of being forsaken by his Father, so that his desolation becomes total. But he continues to trust his Father and is vindicated by a glorious resurrection. As Newman explains in his famous sermon on "The Mental Sufferings of Our Lord in His Passion," Jesus suffered spiritual pains exceeding even his physical tribulations.[3] The passion and death of Jesus are the culmination of the history of evil, and at the same time the climax of the history of redemption. The greatest crime that was ever committed against God is, from another perspective, the supreme demonstration of divine love and forgiveness.

The New Testament authors, far from being embarrassed by the sufferings of Jesus, glory in them on various grounds. First of all, Jesus expiates all the sins of the world (1 John 2:2; 1 Pet. 1:18-19). Second, Jesus has left us an example of patient suffering that Christians are invited to follow (1 Pet. 2:21). Third, the Paschal mystery fills us with courage and with assurance that, as Paul writes to the Romans, "the sufferings of this time are not worth comparing with the glory that is to be revealed to us" (Rom. 8:18). Or as he tells the Corinthians, "This slight momentary affliction is preparing for us an eternal weight of glory beyond all comparison" (2 Cor. 4:17). Fourth, Christians are able to apply their sufferings for redemptive purposes, as Christ did. In a passage from Colossians not easy to interpret, Paul writes that he rejoices in his sufferings because they enable him to fill up for Christ's body what is wanting to the sufferings of the Head (Col. 1:24). From certain passages, such as the text from Colossians I have just discussed, we get the impression that Paul delights in the sufferings that come to him in the service of the gospel. They give him a closer resemblance to the crucified Lord, the object of his love. He is eager to suffer the loss of all things, to share in Christ's afflictions, and thereby become more

---

3. John Henry Newman, *Discourses to Mixed Congregations* (new edition, London: Longmans, Green & Co., 1893), pp. 323-41, especially pp. 336-39.

like him in his death, as a fitting preparation for sharing in the glory of his risen life (2 Cor. 4:16-18; Phil. 3:8, 10-11). Paul urges Christians to adopt the same attitude. "We rejoice in our hope of sharing the glory of God. More than that, we rejoice in our sufferings, knowing that suffering produces endurance, and endurance produces character, and character produces hope" (Rom. 5:2-4; 2 Cor. 1:4-7). The First Letter of Peter speaks in similar terms: "Rejoice insofar as you share Christ's sufferings, that you may also rejoice and be glad when his glory is revealed" (1 Pet. 4:13).

The Bible does not purport to give a speculative solution to the problem of evil, but it points out ways of coping with evil that may point the way to a better theory.

*   *   *

The problem of evil is practically as old as mankind. It was not unknown to Greek and Roman antiquity. Several centuries before the coming of Christ, the Stoics called attention to the beneficial effects of pain and adversity. Chrysippus argued that the individual blemishes actually contribute to the good of the whole, so that "there is really no evil when things are looked at *sub specie aeternitatis*."[4] The Roman Emperor Marcus Aurelius in his *Meditations* took the position that we should resign ourselves to the misfortunes that come our way, since they are part of a larger plan, in which God provides for the general good. Our protests, he held, come from looking at things from a narrowly selfish point of view rather than from the standpoint of universal reason.[5] But the Stoic theory of evil did not meet with universal satisfaction. Epicurus, in opposition, held that the evil in the world proves that the gods have no concern for human affairs.

In the Christian era, St. Augustine was so vexed by the problem of evil that he for some years joined the Manichaean sect, which held that the material world was created by an evil deity. But in his dialogue with Bishop Faustus, Augustine found that the Manichaean leaders were unable to answer his questions. Then, influenced in part by the neo-Platonists, he real-

---

4. Frederick Copleston, *A History of Philosophy* (Garden City, N.Y.: Doubleday Image, 1962), vol. 1, Part 2, summarizing the views of Chrysippus.

5. Marcus Aurelius, *Meditations,* especially Book IV, Everyman's Library (New York: E. P. Dutton & Co., 1906), pp. 27-41.

ized that nothing could be substantially evil. Evil, as a privation, cannot exist except in a subject that is good. God the Supreme Good is incorruptible, but all earthly goods may be diminished or increased. The will is good, but when it rebels against God its acts are evil. Insofar as they are evil they violate the will of God and are attributable to the creature alone. By evil acts the will corrupts itself and deprives itself of goods that it ought to have. Diminishment is an evil, but even a diminished being is good to the extent that it still exists.[6] In his work *Of True Religion,* Augustine contends that all evil is either sin or the consequence of sin.[7]

Thomas Aquinas essentially follows Augustine, but he analyzes the various causes and kinds of evil more systematically, both in the *Summa theologiae*[8] and in his long work that bears the title *De Malo.*[9] He distinguishes between moral and physical evil and shows how God relates himself to each. Some evils God directly causes for purposes of punishment; some he causes indirectly by using creatures instrumentally to bring about his purposes; some evils he simply permits for the sake of a greater good.[10] The problem of evil was intensely debated during the eighteenth century. Leibniz in his *Theodicy* (1710) distinguished among three types of evil: metaphysical, physical, and moral. He propounded the optimist thesis that all is for the best in the best of all possible worlds, a position that Alexander Pope popularized in his poem, *An Essay on Man* (1734). The disastrous earthquake in Lisbon on All Saints Day, 1755, provided Voltaire with an occasion to ridicule the optimist thesis both in a lengthy poem and in his novel *Candide.* While Voltaire effectively rebutted the optimist theology, he failed to explain how he as a deist did account for evil.

David Hume in his *Dialogues Concerning Natural Religion,* Part X, promoted a more skeptical view, casting doubt on the existence of an all-powerful God. He puts in the mouth of one of his interlocutors the dilemma:

Epicurus's old questions are yet unanswered.
Is He (God) willing to prevent evil, but not able? then He is impotent.

6. Augustine, *Enchiridion,* 12.
7. Augustine, *On True Religion,* XII, 23 (Chicago: Henry Regnery, 1964), p. 22.
8. Thomas Aquinas, *Summa theologiae,* especially Part I, questions 48 and 49.
9. Thomas Aquinas, *De Malo,* with facing-page translation, introduction, and notes (New York: Oxford University Press, 2001).
10. Aquinas, *ST,* I, q. 48.

Is He able but not willing? then He is malevolent.
Is He both able and willing? whence, then, is evil?[11]

A new aspect of the problem was raised by Dostoyevsky in his novel *The Brothers Karamazov*. Ivan Karamazov presses the objection that God is to be blamed for creating a universe in which terrible acts of injustice take place, like the torture and slaughter of innocent children by murderous invaders or sadistic masters. No amount of compensation in a future life, Ivan argues, can make up for such evils. Ivan, to be sure, does not represent the point of view of Dostoyevsky himself, who gives a kind of answer to the objection in the remainder of the book, notably in the mysticism of the Staretz Zosima, who sees the whole world as bathed in heavenly glory.[12]

In the twentieth century, with the growing influence of process philosophy, some theologians such as the Protestants Jürgen Moltmann and Dorothee Sölle and the Catholics Jon Sobrino and Elizabeth Johnson have attempted to alleviate the problem of suffering by declaring that God also suffers; that he is, in the famous phrase of Whitehead, "the greatest companion — the fellow sufferer who understands."[13] Rabbi Harold S. Kushner contended in his popular book *When Bad Things Happen to Good People* that God is not an all-powerful ruler; he is a victim rather than a perpetrator of suffering.[14] Recognizing God's limitations, says Kushner, we can love and forgive him. Kushner's book is in many ways helpful, but his view of God is not an option, at least for Catholics, since the Church definitively teaches that God is almighty, unchangeable, and most blessed in himself and from himself.[15]

Within the limits of this essay I cannot take up the complex problem

---

11. David Hume, *Dialogues Concerning Natural Religion* (London: William Blackwood and Sons, 1907), p. 134. Hume wrote this work before 1752, but it was not published until 1779, after the author's death. Frederick Copleston holds that Philo, who speaks the words here quoted, represents approximately the views of Hume himself. See his *A History of Philosophy* (Garden City, N.Y.: Doubleday Image, 1964), vol. 5, Part 2, p. 112.

12. For a contemporary reflection on Dostoyevsky see David Bentley Hart, *The Doors of the Sea* (Grand Rapids: Eerdmans, 2005), pp. 36-44 and passim.

13. Alfred North Whitehead, *Process and Reality* (New York: Free Press, 1979), p. 351.

14. Harold S. Kushner, *When Bad Things Happen to Good People*, 2nd ed. (New York: Schocken Books, 1989).

15. Vatican I, Dogmatic Constitution *Dei Filius*, DS 3001. On the question of God's immutability see Thomas G. Weinandy, *Does God Change?* (Still River, Mass.: St. Bede's Press, 1985).

of whether and in what sense God may be said to suffer. God suffers in the incarnate Son, but does he suffer as God? Leaving this question open, I limit myself to the question of human suffering, which is more than sufficiently complex for our fare this evening.[16]

*   *   *

It may be time to reflect on the results of our biblical and historical survey. As for the optimist thesis, we should note that there is no such thing as a "best possible world." Any world God creates will be finite and therefore surpassable. We cannot demand that God create the best possible world; it is sufficient that he create one that is good. People generally cling to life in this world with the sense that it is good in spite of all sin, suffering, and death. Perhaps, then, we can find an answer to the questions of Epicurus and Hume.

In terms of God's causality it is helpful to distinguish three kinds of evil. First of all, there is physical evil inflicted for purposes of punishment. Secondly, there are natural evils that occur through the regular operation of physical and biological laws. And thirdly, there are moral evils, or sins.

Punishment can be either remedial or retributive. If God inflicts it, he obviously wills it for some reason, either to cure the sinner or to exact reparation for evil that has been done. Hell is the prime instance of retributive punishment. Purgatory would be a clear example of remedial punishment insofar as it purifies the soul of the effects of forgiven sin.

In the Bible and Christian literature, certain historical reverses are seen as punishments for nations or individual persons. If we have a revelation to the effect that they are in fact punishments, we may credit it, but it is dangerous to ascribe particular mishaps to God's punitive will on our own authority. Jesus warned against such rashness in the case of the man born blind (John 9:3).

As a second category I propose natural evils that flow from the regular course of nature, operating according to physical or biological laws. Laws of nature are necessary if there is to be an orderly universe. On the whole these laws produce beneficial effects, making it possible for us to act rationally and prudently. The progress of industry and science depends upon

---

16. On this subject see Thomas G. Weinandy, *Does God Suffer?* (Notre Dame: University of Notre Dame Press, 2000).

the regularity of such laws. Although death is in some respects evil, it prevents the universe from becoming overpopulated. Often people die prematurely by chance. A small child, for example, may wander into the path of a bullet aimed at a different target. But incidents such as this prove nothing against the goodness of God. In willing the order of the universe as a greater good, God may reasonably permit some particular evils to occur by way of exception.

Pain receives a great deal of attention in literature on natural evils. Physical pain is in some ways a benefit, because it deters us from harming our bodies, as we might do if we felt no pain, for example, while holding our hand over a fire. Pain alerts us to illnesses and prompts us to seek appropriate remedies. But because general laws do not always act for the best in particular cases, pain can sometimes be useless or excessive, motivating doctors to invent and prescribe painkillers. These developments may be reckoned as instances of God's providential care.

Natural evils can sometimes be occasions for goods of various orders. Many authors have written about the ways in which people have grown in moral stature by encountering handicaps and setbacks.[17] A world without adversity and suffering would provide less opportunity for compassion, courage, determination, integrity, and heroism. Perhaps God could have created a micromanaged universe in which the virtuous would never suffer, but it would not evidently be better than the world we have, with all the risks involved.

In spite of the philosophical justifications for pain and suffering, there seems to be something like a consensus among contemporary theologians that the world contains more adversity than we would expect from the hands of a beneficent creator. Many attribute this excess of evil to original sin, which not only weakened the human mind and will but also had an impact on the world of nature. St. Thomas in his *De Malo* discusses at some length the influence of original sin and that of the devil. Whatever the contribution of these causes may be, they do not solve our problem so much as complicate it. Why does God allow us to suffer from the sins of our first parents? Why does he allow the devil to tempt and molest certain persons? In the end we shall probably have to admit our inability to account for the terrible afflictions sometimes suffered by persons who seem relatively good and innocent. Perhaps the best we can do is to point to the

17. O'Malley, *Redemptive Suffering* (supra, note 2).

cross of Christ, which offers us the assurance that the righteous are some-times allowed to suffer and that suffering is not the last word; it can lead to glory.

The third category of evil is sin, or moral evil. Unlike punishment and natural evil, sin is absolutely opposed to the will of God, who cannot be supposed to will it either for itself or as a means to a good end. But God in his omnipotence could prevent sin. Why, then, is he not responsi-ble for its occurrence? The best theological answer seems to be that God prefers to leave the human will free either to follow his bidding or to resist it. He wants us to have a choice whether to serve him or reject him. If we choose evil, he is not responsible because he causes only what is good. Sin is a negative thing, a falling away from the good to which God invites us. The failure is attributable not to God, but to the human creature alone.[18] By giving extraordinary graces God could perhaps so confirm persons in grace that they would never fail to love him, but it is not natural for per-sons in this life to rise to such perfection. High and extraordinary gifts cannot be conferred except by miracles of grace, which by their very na-ture must be exceptional.

The problem of evil is essentially the same in the cases of physical and moral evil. God could intervene to prevent any natural mishap or human misdeed, but ordinarily he does not. He evidently prefers to let natural causes take their course in the present life. If he regularly intervened on be-half of those who were virtuous or who were prayed for, we would have a world in which human responsibility would be greatly diminished. It is far from evident that the world would be a better place if it were magically governed, so that the laws of nature were likely to be suspended at any mo-ment. In any case, it would not be the world God actually has made. God is said to write straight with crooked lines. When we see the full picture, as the saints in heaven are thought to do, we may understand better how all the pieces fit together in God's providential plan.

---

18. The question of God's responsibility for the failures of human beings to follow his law has been extensively debated among followers of Thomas Aquinas. My own position is closer to that of Charles Journet, Jacques Maritain, Bernard Lonergan and others than to the position of Domingo Bañez and his modern disciples, who seem to hold that God brings about even the refusal to obey his will. For a recent discussion of this question see the arti-cles by Gilles Emery, Stephen A. Long, and Thomas Joseph White in the English edition of *Nova et Vetera* 4, no. 3 (Summer 2006).

*   *   *

To summarize, then, we may conclude that there are at least seven possible responses to suffering, when it is imposed upon us. The first is rebellion against God, which can lead to blasphemy or atheism. The second is a philosophical resignation, which induces us to accept suffering with a kind of Stoic indifference, typified by the Emperor Marcus Aurelius. The third is moralism, which explains suffering as a punishment for sin, arousing feelings of guilt and contrition and possibly leading to conversion. The fourth holds that suffering, even when undeserved, is a school of patience, and that it can elicit heroic virtue. Higher than all these, I think, is the fifth response, that of Job, who submits to inexplicable suffering with an adoring silence before the majesty of God. Then there are the two responses more characteristic of the New Testament. One of these — the sixth — is confidence that those who suffer patiently in this life will be richly rewarded with blessed immortality in the life to come. The seventh response, the most sublime of all, is that of the saints who suffer with joy because affliction brings them into closer union with their crucified Lord, and enables them to participate in the expiatory sufferings that he accepted for the redemption of the world.

Suffering, then, may have good or bad effects. What makes all the difference is the way we respond to it. We can react with bitterness like the atheist, with grim indifference like the Stoic, with contrition like Azariah in the Book of Daniel, with reverent adoration like Job, with eager hope like the Maccabees, or with loving gratitude like certain Christian saints.

For the Christian believer, the theories of the philosophers, while helpful up to a point, do not give a satisfactory answer, which can be found only in the concrete fact of Jesus Christ. Christ does not provide a speculative answer that clearly explains why God permitted sufferings such as his own. But his life, death, and resurrection provide us with assurance that suffering, in the end, need not be meaningless. In some mysterious way, all human sufferings can have redemptive value when united with his. The real evil is not suffering itself but rather wasted suffering.

Neither philosophy nor theology can unravel the full mystery of suffering. The human mind lacks the capacity to judge why God's providence allows certain crimes and misfortunes, though we can find some hints of an answer in speculations such as I have presented in this paper. Such reflections may be helpful for persons tempted to doubt or disbelieve, but they will be of little value to persons in actual situations of suffering. Rabbi Kushner says very wisely that religious answers of this type often leave people feeling worse than before. "What people going through sorrow need most is consolation, not explanation. A warm hug and a few minutes of patient listening mend more hearts than the most learned theological lecture."[19]

19. Kushner, *When Bad Things Happen*, p. xi.

Select Bibliography

Adams, Marilyn McCord. *Christ and Horrors: The Coherence of Christology.*
   New York: Cambridge University Press, 2006.

————. *Horrendous Evils and the Goodness of God.* Ithaca, N.Y.: Cornell University Press, 1999.

————. "Redemptive Suffering: A Christian Solution to the Problem of
   Evil." In *Rationality, Religious Belief and Moral Commitment,* edited by
   Robert Audi and William J. Wainwright, pp. 248-67. Ithaca & London:
   Cornell University Press, 1986.

*At the Heart of the Real: Philosophical Essays in Honour of Archbishop
   Desmond Connell,* edited by F. O'Rourke. Dublin: Irish Academic Press,
   1992.

Athenagoras. *Legatio.* Edited by W. R. Schoedel. Oxford: Oxford University
   Press, 1972.

Attfield, D. G. "Can God Be Crucified? A Discussion of J. Moltmann," *Scottish Journal of Theology* 30 (1977): 47-56.

Ayres, Lewis. *Nicaea and Its Legacy: An Approach to Fourth-Century Trinitarian Theology.* Oxford: Oxford University Press, 2006.

Baloian, B. E. *Anger in the Old Testament.* New York: Peter Lang, 1992.

Balthasar, Hans Urs von. *The Glory of the Lord: A Theological Aesthetics,* Vol.
   VII: *Theology: The New Covenant.* Translated by Brian McNeil. San
   Francisco: Ignatius Press, 1989.

————. *Mysterium Paschale: The Mystery of Easter.* Translated by Aidan
   Nichols. Grand Rapids: Eerdmans, 1990.

————. *Theo-Drama: Theological Dramatic Theory,* Vol. V: *The Last Act.*
   Translated by Graham Harrison. San Francisco: Ignatius Press, 1998.

Barth, Karl. *Church Dogmatics* IV/1. Translated by Geoffrey Bromiley. London and New York: T. & T. Clark, 2004.

Barth, Karl, and Rudolf Bultmann. *Karl Barth — Rudolf Bultmann: Letters, 1922-1968.* Translated by Geoffrey Bromiley. Grand Rapids: Eerdmans, 1981.

Bauckham, Richard A. *God Crucified: Monotheism and Christology in the New Testament.* Carlisle: Paternoster Press, 1998.

———. "In Defence of *The Crucified God.*" In *The Powers and Weakness of God: Impassibility and Orthodoxy,* edited by Nigel M. de S. Cameron, pp. 93-118. Edinburgh: Rutherford House Books, 1990.

———. "Only the Suffering God Can Help: Divine Passibility in Modern Theology," *Themelios* 3 (1984): 6-12.

———. *The Theology of Jürgen Moltmann.* Edinburgh: T. & T. Clark, 1995.

Bayes, Jonathan. "Divine *Apatheia* in Ignatius of Antioch," *Studia Patristica* 21 (1987): 27-31.

Blocher, Henri. "Divine Immutability." In *The Powers and Weakness of God: Impassibility and Orthodoxy,* edited by Nigel M. de S. Cameron, pp. 1-22. Edinburgh: Rutherford House Books, 1990.

Boespflug, François. "La Compassion de Dieu le Père dans l'Art Occidental (XIII-XVII Siècles. In *Le Supplement, Revue d'Étique et Théologie Morale* 172, pp. 124-59. Paris, 1990.

Bonino, Serge-Thomas. "L'immutabilité de Dieu." In *Istituto San Tommaso: Studi 1997-1998,* edited by Giacomo Grasso and Stefano Serafini, pp. 73-95. Roma: Pontificia Università San Tommaso, 1999.

Borde, Marie-B. "Un Dieu souffrant?" In *Le mystère du mal: Péché, souffrance et rédemption,* edited by Marie-B. Borde, pp. 261-75. Toulouse: Editions du Carmel, 2001.

Brantschen, Johannes B. "Die Macht und Ohnmacht der Liebe. Randglossen zum dogmatischen Satz: Gott ist unveränderlich," *Freiburger Zeitschrift für Philosophie und Theologie* 27 (1980): 224-46.

Brasnett, B. R. *The Suffering of the Impassible God.* New York: Macmillan, 1928.

Brito, Emilio. *La Christologie de Hegel: Verbum Crucis.* Paris: Beauchesne, 1983.

———. "Dieu en mouvement? Thomas d'Aquin et Hegel," *Revue des Sciences Religieuses* 62 (1988): 111-36.

———. *Dieu et l'être d'après Thomas d'Aquin et Hegel.* Paris: Presses Universitaires de France, 1991.

Bruce, Alex B. *The Humiliation of Christ.* Grand Rapids: Eerdmans, 1955.

Bulgakov, Sergius. *The Comforter.* Translated by Boris Jakim. Grand Rapids: Eerdmans, 2004.

――――. *Du Verbe incarné: L'Agneau de Dieu.* Translated by Constantin Andronikof. Lausanne: L'Âge d'Homme, 1982.

――――. *Sophia: The Wisdom of God.* Hudson, N.Y: Lindisfarne Press, 1993.

Burnley, William F. E. "The Impassibility of God," *The Expository Times* 67 (1955): 90-91.

Burns, Charlene P. E. *Divine Becoming: Rethinking Jesus and Incarnation.* Minneapolis: Fortress Press, 2002.

Burrell, David B. *Freedom and Creation in Three Traditions.* Notre Dame: University of Notre Dame Press, 1993.

Cain, C. C. "A Passionate God?" *Saint Luke's Journal of Theology* 25 (1981): 52-57.

Cantalamessa, Raniero. *L'omelia 'In s. Pascha' dello pseudo-Ippolito di Roma.* Milan: Vita e pensiero, 1967.

――――. *The Power of the Cross.* London: Darton, Longman & Todd, 1996.

Chéné, Jean. "Unus de Trinitate passus est," *Recherches de Science Religieuse* 53 (1965): 545-88.

Christiansen, Peter G. "Dieu, sa vie, son œuvre: Jean D'Ormesson's Attack on 'Apatheia' as a Quality of God," *Literature and Theology* 8 (1994): 405-20.

Clark, Kelly James. "Hold Not Thy Peace at My Tears: Methodological Reflection on Divine Impassibility." In *Our Knowledge of God: Essays on Natural and Philosophical Theology.* Studies in Philosophy and Religion, Vol. 16, edited by K. J. Clark. Norwell, Mass.: Kluwer Academic Publishers, 1992.

Clark, W. Norris. "Person, Being, and St. Thomas." *Communio* 19 (1992): 601-18.

――――. "Response to Long's Comments," *Communio* 21 (1994): 165-69.

Coakley, Sarah. "Does Kenosis Rest on a Mistake? Three Kenotic Models in Patristic Exegesis." In *Exploring Kenotic Christology: The Self-Emptying of God,* edited by C. Stephen Evans, pp. 246-64. Oxford: Oxford University Press, 2006.

――――. "*Kenosis* and Subversion: On the Repression of 'Vulnerability' in Christian Feminist Writing." In *Powers and Submissions: Spirituality, Philosophy and Gender,* pp. 3-39. Oxford: Blackwell Publishers, 2002.

Cook, E. David. "Weak Church, Weak God." In *The Powers and Weakness of*

God: Impassibility and Orthodoxy, edited by Nigel M. de S. Cameron, pp. 69-92. Edinburgh: Rutherford House Books, 1990.

Creel, Richard E. *Divine Impassibility.* Cambridge: Cambridge University Press, 1986.

Crousel, Henri. "La Passion de l'Impassible. Un essai apologétique et polémique du IIIe siècle." In *L'Homme devant Dieu: Mélanges offerts au père Henri de Lubac,* pp. 269-79. Paris: Aubier, 1963.

Cyril of Alexandria. *On the Unity of Christ.* Translated by J. A. McGuckin. Crestwood, N.Y.: St. Vladimir's Seminary Press, 1995.

——— *Select Letters.* Edited by L. R. Wickham. Oxford: Clarendon Press, 1983.

Davies, Brian. "God, Time and Change," *Word and Spirit* 8 (1986): 3-12.

Dodds, Michael. "St. Thomas Aquinas and the Motion of the Motionless God," *New Blackfriars* 86 (1987): 233-42.

———. "Thomas Aquinas, Human Suffering, and the Unchanging God of Love," *Theological Studies* 52 (1991): 330-44.

———. *The Unchanging God of Love.* Fribourg: Editions Universitaires, 1985.

Dorner, I. A. *Divine Immutability: A Critical Reconsideration.* Translated by R. R. Williams and C. Welch. Minneapolis: Fortress, 1994.

Driel, Edwin Chr. Van. "Karl Barth on the Eternal Existence of Jesus Christ," *Scottish Journal of Theology* 60 (2007): 45-61.

Edwards, R. B. "Pagan Dogma of the Absolute Unchangeableness of God," *Religious Studies* 14 (1978): 305-13.

Elert, Werner. "Die Theopaschitsche Formel," *Theologische Lehrbücher* 75 (1950): 195-206.

Emery, Gilles. "The Question of Evil and the Mystery of God in Charles Journet," *Nova et Vetera* (English edition) 4, no. 3 (2006): 529-55.

———. *The Trinitarian Theology of St. Thomas Aquinas.* Translated by Francesca Murphy. Oxford: Oxford University Press, 2007.

Erickson, Millard J. *God the Father Almighty: A Contemporary Exploration of the Divine Attributes.* Grand Rapids: Eerdmans, 1998.

Evagrius Ponticus. *The Praktikos and Chapters on Prayer.* Translated and edited by John Eudes Bamberger. Kalamazoo, Mich.: Cistercian Publications, 1981.

Faber, Roland. *Der Selbsteinsatz Gottes: Grundlegung einer Theologie des Leidens und der Veränderlichkeit Gottes.* Würzburg: Broschiert, 1995.

Farley, Edward. *Divine Empathy: A Theology of God.* Minneapolis: Fortress, 1996.

Farrow, D. B. "Review Essay: In the End Is the Beginning: A Review of Jürgen Moltmann's Systematic Contributions," *Modern Theology* 14, no. 3 (1998): 425-47.

Fiddes, Paul S. *Creative Suffering of God.* Oxford: Clarendon Press, 1988.

Foster, Paul. "Divine Passibility and the Early Christian Doctrine of God." In *The Powers and Weakness of God: Impassibility and Orthodoxy,* edited by Nigel M. de S. Cameron, pp. 23-51. Edinburgh: Rutherford House Books, 1990.

Foyle, Anastasia. "Human and Divine Suffering: The Relation Between Human Suffering and the Rise of Passibilist Theology," *Ars Disputandi.* [http://www.ArsDisputandi.org] 5 (2005).

Franks, Robert S. "Passibility and Impassibility." In *Encyclopedia of Religion and Ethics* XI, 658-60. New York: Charles Scribner's Sons, 1917.

Fretheim, Terence E. "The Repentance of God: A Key to Evaluating Old Testament God-Talk," *Horizons in Biblical Theology* 10 (1988): 47-70.

———. "Suffering God and Sovereign God in Exodus," *Horizons in Biblical Theology* 11 (1989): 31-56.

———. *The Suffering of God: An Old Testament Perspective.* Philadelphia: Fortress Press, 1984.

Fritsch, C. T. *The Anti-Anthropomorphisms of the Greek Pentateuch.* Princeton: Princeton University Press, 1943.

Frohnhofen, Herbert. *Apatheia Tou Theou: Über die Affectlosigkeit Gottes in der griechischen Antike und bei den griechischsprachigen Kirchenvätern bis zu Gregorios Thaumaturgos.* New York: Peter Lang, 1987.

Galot, Jean. *Dieu souffre-t-il?* Paris: Lethielleux, 1976.

———. "Le Dieu trinitaire et la passion du Christ," *Nouvelle Revue Théologique* 104 (1982): 70-87.

———. *Libérés par l'Amour: Christologie III.* Paris: Parole et Silence, 2001.

———. *Père, Qui es-tu? Petite catéchèse sur le Père.* Versailles: Editions St.-Paul, 1996.

———. *Notre Père qui est Amour.* St.-Maur: Parole et Silence, 1998.

———. "La Revelation de la souffrance de Dieu," *Science et Esprit* 31 (1979): 159-71.

Garrigou-Lagrange, Reginald. *Predestination: The Meaning of Predestination in Scripture and the Church.* Translated by Dom Bede Rose. Rockford, Ill.: TAN Books and Publishers, Inc., 1998.

Gathercole, Simon. "Pre-existence, and the Freedom of the Son in Creation and Redemption: An Exposition in Dialogue with Robert Jenson," *International Journal of Systematic Theology* 7, no. 1 (2005): 38-51.

Gavrilyuk, Paul L. *The Suffering of the Impassible God: The Dialectics of Patristic Thought.* Oxford and New York: Oxford University Press, 2004.

———. "*Theopatheia:* Nestorius's Main Charge Against Cyril of Alexandria," *Scottish Journal of Theology* 56, no. 2 (2003): 190-207.

———. "Universal Salvation in the Eschatology of Sergius Bulgakov," *Journal of Theological Studies* 57, no. 1 (2006): 110-32.

Gervais, M. "Incarnation et Immutabilité Divine," *Revue des Sciences Religieuses* 50 (1976): 215-43.

Goetz, Ronald. "The Suffering God: The Rise of a New Orthodoxy," *Christian Century* 103 (1986): 385-89.

Gondreau, Paul. *The Passions of Christ's Soul in the Theology of St. Thomas Aquinas.* Münster: Aschendorff Verlag, 2002.

Grant, C. "Possibilities for Divine Passibility," *Toronto Journal of Theology* 4, no. 1 (1988): 8-14.

Gregory Thaumaturgus. *Saint Gregory Thaumaturgus: His Life and Work.* Translated by Michael Slusser. Washington, D.C.: Catholic University of America, 1988.

Gregory of Nazianzus. *Sermons.* NPNF, 2nd ser. 7 (1955).

Gregory of Nyssa. "Address of Religious Instruction." In *Christology of the Later Fathers,* edited by E. R. Hardy. London: SCM, 1972.

———. *Contra Eunomium libri.* Leiden: Brill, 1960.

Guroian, Vigen, "The Suffering God of Armenian Christology: Towards an Ecumenical Theology of the Cross," *Dialog* 32, no. 2 (1993): 97-101.

Hall, Douglas John. *God and Human Suffering: An Exercise in the Theology of the Cross.* Minneapolis: Augsburg Publishing House, 1986.

Hallman, Joseph M. *The Descent of God.* Minneapolis: Fortress, 1991.

———. "Impassibility." In *Encyclopedia of Early Christianity* (1997), I, pp. 566-72.

———. "The Seed of Fire: Divine Suffering in the Christology of Cyril of Alexandria and Nestorius of Constantinople," *Journal of Early Christian Studies* 5 (1997): 369-91.

Hankey, Wayne. "Aquinas and the Passion of God." In *Being and Truth: Essays in Honour of John Macquarrie,* edited by Alistair Kee and Eugene T. Long, pp. 318-33. London: SCM Press, 1986.

Harnack, Adolf von. *History of Dogma,* vols. 1-4. New York: Dover, 1961.

341

Harrington, Wilfrid J. *The Tears of God: Our Benevolent Creator and Human Suffering.* Collegeville, Minn.: Liturgical Press, 1992.

Hart, David Bentley. *The Beauty of the Infinite: The Aesthetics of Christian Truth.* Grand Rapids: Eerdmans, 2003.

———. *The Doors of the Sea: Where Was God in the Tsunami?* Grand Rapids: Eerdmans, 2005.

———. "No Shadow of Turning: On Divine Impassibility," *Pro Ecclesia* 11 (2002): 184-206.

Haughton, Rosemary. *The Passionate God.* New York: Paulist Press, 1981.

Heaney, Robert S. "Toward the Possibility of Impassibilist Pastoral Care," *The Heythrop Journal* 158 (2007): 171-86.

Hector, Kevin W. "God's Triunity and Self-Determination: A Conversation with Karl Barth, Bruce McCormack and Paul Molnar," *International Journal of Systematic Theology* 7, no. 3 (2005): 246-61.

Helm, Paul. *Eternal God: A Study of God Without Time.* Oxford: Clarendon Press, 1988.

———. "The Impossibility of Divine Passibility." In *The Powers and Weakness of God: Impassibility and Orthodoxy,* edited by Nigel M. de S. Cameron, pp. 119-40. Edinburgh: Rutherford House Books, 1990.

Hengel, Martin. *Judaism and Hellenism: Studies in Their Encounter in Palestine in the Early Hellenistic Period.* Philadelphia: Fortress, 1974.

———. *Studies in Early Christology.* Edinburgh: T. & T. Clark, 1995.

Heschel, Abraham J. *The Prophets.* New York: Harper & Row, 1962.

Hilary of Poitiers. *The Trinity.* Translated by Stephen McKenna. FC 25. 1954.

Hill, William J. "Does Divine Love Entail Suffering in God?" In *Search for the Absent God,* edited by Mary Catherine Hilkert, pp. 152-63. New York: Crossroad, 1992.

Hoogland, Mark-Robin. *God, Passion and Power: Thomas Aquinas on Christ Crucified and the Almightiness of God.* Leuven: Peeters, 2003.

House, Francis H. "The Barrier of Impassibility," *Theology* 83 (1980): 409-15.

Hryniewicz, Waclaw. "Le Dieu Souffrant: réflexions sur la notion chrétienne de Dieu," *Eglise et Theologie* 12 (1981): 333-56.

Inbody, Tyron. *The Transforming God: An Interpretation of Suffering and Evil.* Louisville: Westminster John Knox, 1997.

Insole, Christopher. "Anthropomorphism and the Apophatic God," *Modern Theology* 17 (2001): 475-83.

Jacob, Edmond. "Le Dieu souffrant: Un thème théologique vétérotestamentaire," *Zeitschrift für die Alttestamentliche Wissenschaft* 95 (1983): 1-8.

Jenson, Robert. *Systematic Theology,* volume 1: *The Triune God.* New York: Oxford University Press, 1997.

―――. *Systematic Theology,* volume 2: *The Works of God.* New York: Oxford University Press, 1999.

―――. *The Unbaptized God: The Basic Flaw in Ecumenical Theology.* Minneapolis: Fortress Press, 1992.

―――. *The Triune Identity.* Philadelphia: Fortress Press, 1982.

Jonas, Hans. "The Concept of God After Auschwitz: A Jewish Voice?" *The Journal of Religion* 67 (1987): 1-13.

Journet, Charles. *The Meaning of Evil.* Translated by Michael Barry. New York: P. J. Kenedy & Sons, 1963.

Joussard, G. "Impassibilité du Logos et impassibilité de l'âme humaine chez saint Cyrille d'Alexandrie," *Recherches de Science Religieuse* 45 (1957): 209-24.

Jowers, Dennis W. "The Theology of the Cross as Theology of the Trinity: A Critique of Jürgen Moltmann's Staurocentric Trinitarianism," *Tyndale Bulletin* 52, no. 2 (2001): 245-66.

Jüngel, Eberhard. *God as the Mystery of the World: On the Foundation of the Theology of the Crucified One in the Dispute Between Theism and Atheism.* Translated by Darrell L. Guder. Grand Rapids: Eerdmans, 1983.

―――. "Gottes ursprüngliches Anfangen als schöpferische Selbstbegrenzung: Ein Beitrag zum Gespräch mit Hans Jonas über den Gottesbegriff nach Auschwitz." In *Gottes Zukunft — Zukunft der Welt,* edited by H. Deuser and J. Moltmann, pp. 265-75. Munich: Chr. Kaiser, 1986.

―――. *Unterwegs zur Sache: Theologische Bemerkungen.* Munich: Chr. Kaiser, 1972.

Kamp, Jean. "Présence de Dieu Souffrant," *Lumière et Vie* 25 (1976): 54-66.

Kitamori, Kazoh. *The Theology of the Pain of God.* Richmond, Va.: John Knox, 1965.

Kondoleon, T. J. "The Immutability of God: Some Recent Challenges," *The New Scholasticism* 58, no. 3 (1984): 293-315.

Krenski, T. R. *Passio Caritatis: Trinitarische Passiologie im Werk Hans Urs von Balthasar.* Freiburg: Johannes Verlag, 1990.

Kuyper, Lester J. "The Suffering and the Repentance of God," *Scottish Journal of Theology* 22 (1969): 257-77.

Küng, Hans. *The Incarnation of God: An Introduction to Hegel's Theological Thought as Prolegomena to a Future Christology.* Edinburgh: T. & T. Clark, 1987.

LaCugna, Catherine M. "The Relational God," *Theological Studies* 46 (1985): 647-63.

Lee, Jung Young. *God Suffers for Us: A Systematic Inquiry into a Concept of Divine Passibility.* The Hague: Martinus Nijhoff, 1974.

Lonergan, Bernard. *Grace and Freedom: Operative Grace in the Thought of St. Thomas Aquinas.* Toronto: University of Toronto Press, 2000.

Long, Stephen A. "Divine and Creaturely 'Receptivity': The Search for a Middle Term," *Communio* 21 (1994): 151-61.

————. "Providence, Freedom, and Natural Law," *Nova et Vetera* 4, no. 3 (2006): 557-605.

Maas, W. *Unveränderlichkeit Gottes: Zum Verhältnis von griechisch-philosophischer und christlicher Gotteslehre.* Munich: Schönigh, 1974.

Maritain, Jacques. *God and the Permission of Evil.* Translated by Joseph W. Evans. Milwaukee: The Bruce Publishing Co., 1966.

————. "Quelques réflexions sur le savoir théologique," *Revue Thomiste* 69 (1969): 5-27.

Martin, R. *The Suffering Love.* Petersham: St. Bede's Publications, 1995.

Marshall, Bruce. "*Ex Occidente Lux?* Aquinas and Eastern Orthodox Theology," *Modern Theology* 20, no. 1 (2004): 23-50.

————. "The Filioque as Theology and Doctrine," *Kerygma und Dogma* 50, no. 4 (2004): 271-88.

————. "The Trinity," *The Blackwell Companion to Modern Theology,* edited by Gareth Jones, pp. 183-203. Oxford: Blackwell, 2004.

————. *Trinity and Truth.* Cambridge: Cambridge University Press, 2000.

Mascall, E. L. *He Who Is: A Study in Traditional Theism.* London: Longmans, Green & Co., 1945.

Maximus the Confessor. *The Ascetic Life, The Four Centuries on Charity.* Translated by P. Sherwood. Westminster, Md.: The Newman Press, 1955.

————. *Selected Writing.* Translated by G. C. Berthold. New York: Paulist Press, 1985.

McCormack, Bruce. "Barth's grundsätzliche Chalcedonismus?" *Zeitschrift für dialektische Theologie* 18 (2002): 138-73.

————. "Karl Barth's Christology as a Resource for a Reformed Version of Kenoticism," *International Journal of Systematic Theology* 8 (2006): 243-51.

————. *Karl Barth's Critically Realistic Dialectical Theology: Its Genesis and Development, 1909-1936.* New York: Clarendon, 1995.

————. "The Ontological Presuppositions of Barth's Doctrine of the Atonement." In *The Glory of the Atonement: Biblical, Historical and Practical Perspectives,* edited by Charles E. Hill and Frank A. James III, pp. 346-66. Downers Grove, Ill.: InterVarsity Press, 2004.

———. "Participation in God, Yes, Deification, No: Two Modern Answers to an Ancient Question." In *Denkwürdiges Geheimnis: Beiträge zur Gotteslehre. Festschrift für Eberhard Jüngel zum 70. Geburtstag,* edited by Ingolf U. Dalferth, Johannes Fischer, and Hans-Peter Großhans, pp. 347-74. Tübingen: Mohr Siebeck, 2004.

———. "Seek God Where He May Be Found," *Scottish Journal of Theology* 60 (2007): 62-79.

McDermott, John M. "Hilary of Poitiers: The Infinite Nature of God," *Vigiliae Christianae* 27 (1973): 172-202.

McGill, A. *Suffering: A Test of Theological Method.* Philadelphia: Westminster Press, 1982.

McGuckin, John A. *St. Cyril of Alexandria: The Christological Controversy. Its History, Theology, and Texts.* Leiden: Brill, 1994.

McWilliams, Warren. "Divine Suffering in Contemporary Theology," *Scottish Journal of Theology* 33 (1980): 35-53.

———. *The Passion of God: Divine Suffering in Contemporary Protestant Theology.* Macon, Ga.: Mercer University Press, 1985.

Maier, Barbara. "Apatheia bei den Stoikern und Akedia bei Evagrios Pontikos: ein Ideal und die Kehrseite seiner Realität," *Oriens Christianus* 78 (1994): 230-349.

Metz, J.-B. "Suffering unto God," *Critical Inquiry* 20 (1994): 611-22.

Micka, E. F. *The Problem of Divine Anger in Arnobius and Lactantius.* Washington, D.C.: The Catholic University of America Press, 1943.

Melito of Sardis. *On Pascha and Fragments.* Translated by G. S. Hall. Oxford: Oxford University Press, 1979.

Molnar, Paul. *Divine Freedom and the Doctrine of the Immanent Trinity: In Dialogue with Karl Barth and Contemporary Theology.* London: T. & T. Clark, 2002.

———. "The Trinity, Election and God's Ontological Freedom: A Response to Kevin W. Hector," *International Journal of Systematic Theology* 8 (2006): 294-306.

Moore, Sebastian. "God Suffered," *Downside Review* 27 (1959): 122-40.

Moltmann, Jürgen. *The Crucified God: The Cross of Christ as the Foundation and Criticism of Christian Theology.* San Francisco: Harper & Row, 1974.

———. *The Spirit of Life: A Universal Affirmation.* London: SCM Press, 1992.

————. *The Trinity and the Kingdom of God: The Doctrine of God.* London: SCM Press, 1981.

Morard, Martin. "Thomas d'Aquin lecteur des conciles," *Archivum Franciscanum Historicum* 98 (2005): 211-365.

Mozley, J. K. *The Impassibility of God: A Survey of Christian Thought.* Cambridge: Cambridge University Press, 1926.

Mühlen, H. *Die Veränderlichkeit Gottes als Horizont einer zukünftigen Christologie.* Münster: Aschendorff, 1969.

Muller, R. A. "Incarnation, Immutability and the Case for Classical Theism," *Westminster Theological Journal* 45 (1983): 22-40.

Ngien, Dennis. "Chalcedonian Christology and Beyond: Luther's Understanding of the *Communicatio Idiomatum*," *The Heythrop Journal* 45, no. 1 (2004): 54-68.

————. "God Who Suffers: If God Does Not Grieve, Then Can He Love at All? An Argument for God's Emotions," *Christianity Today* 41 (1997): 38-42.

————. "Reaping the Right Fruits: Luther's Meditation on the 'Earnest Mirror, Christ,'" *International Journal of Systematic Theology* 8, no. 4 (2006): 382-410.

————. *The Suffering of God According to Martin Luther's "Theologia Crucis."* Vancouver: Regent College Publishing, 2005.

Nicolas, J.-H. "Aimante et Bienheureuse Trinité," *Revue Thomiste* 73 (1978): 271-91.

————. "La Souffrance de Dieu?" *Nova et Vetera* (French edition) 53 (1978): 56-64.

Nnamani, A. G. *The Paradox of a Suffering God: On the Classical Modern-Western and Third World Struggles to Harmonize the Incompatible Attributes of the Trinitarian God.* Frankfurt am Main: Peter Lang, 1994.

O'Donnell, J. *Trinity and Temporality.* Oxford: Oxford University Press, 1983.

O'Hanlon, G. F. "Does God Change? H. U. von Balthasar and the Immutability of God," *The Irish Theological Quarterly* 53 (1987): 161-83.

————. *The Immutability of God in the Theology of Hans Urs von Balthasar.* Cambridge: Cambridge University Press, 1990.

O'Keefe, J. J. "Cyrus on the Problem of Divine Pathos," *Studia Patristica* 38 (1997): 358-65.

————. "Impassible Suffering? Divine Passion and Fifth Century Christology," *Theological Studies* 58 (1997): 39-60.

————. "Kenosis and Impassibility: Cyril of Alexandria and Theodoret of

Cyrus on the Problem of Divine Pathos," *Studia Patristica* 32, pp. 358-65. Leuven: Peeters, 1997.

Oliphint, K. Scott. "Something Much Too Plain to Say," *Westminster Theological Journal* 68 (2006): 187-202.

Origen. *Homélies sur Ézéchiel*. Edited by Marcel Borret, S.J. Paris: Editions du Cerf, 1989.

Osborne, Thomas M., Jr. "Thomist Premotion and Contemporary Philosophy of Religion," *Nova et Vetera* 4, no. 3 (2006): 607-31.

Pannenberg, Wolfhart. "The Appropriation of the Philosophical Concept of God as a Dogmatic Problem of Early Christian Theology." In *Basic Questions in Theology: Collected Essays*. Translated by George H. Kehm, pp. 119-83. Philadelphia: Westminster Press, 1971.

———. "Eternity, Time, and the Trinitarian God." In *Trinity, Time, and Church: A Response to the Theology of Robert W. Jenson,* edited by Colin E. Gunton, pp. 62-70. Grand Rapids: Eerdmans, 2000.

———. *Jesus — God and Man*. 2nd edition. Translated by Lewis L. Wilkins and Duane A. Priebe. Philadelphia: Westminster Press, 1990.

Pinnock, C. H. *The Most Moved Mover*. Grand Rapids: Baker, 2001.

Placher, William C. "Narrative of a Vulnerable God," *The Princeton Seminary Bulletin* 14 (1993): 134-51.

Pollard, Evan T. "The Impassibility of God," *Scottish Journal of Theology* 8 (1955): 353-64.

Prestige, George L. *God in Patristic Thought*. London: SPCK, 1952.

Quinn, J. "Triune Self-Giving: One Key to the Problem of Suffering," *The Thomist* 44 (1980): 173-218.

Richard, Lucien J. *A Kenotic Christology in the Humanity of Jesus Christ, the Compassion of Our God*. New York: University Press of America, 1982.

———. *Christ: The Self-Emptying God*. Mahwah, N.J.: Paulist Press, 1997.

Robinson, Wheeler H. *Suffering, Human and Divine*. London: SCM, 1940.

Rosse, Ellen M. *The Grief of God: Images of the Suffering Jesus in Late Medieval England*. Oxford: University Press, 1997.

Sanders, John. *The God Who Risks: A Theology of Providence*. Downers Grove, Ill.: InterVarsity Press, 1998.

Sarot, Marcel. "Patripassianism, Theopaschitism and the Suffering of God: Some Historical and Systematic Considerations," *Religious Studies* 26 (1990): 363-75.

Scrutton, Anastasia. "Emotion in Augustine of Hippo and Thomas Aquinas:

A Way Forward for the Im/passibility Debate?" *International Journal of Systematic Theology* 7, no. 2 (April 2005): 169-77.

Sepiere, Marie-Christine. *L'Image d'un Dieu Souffrant, IX-Xe siècle: Aux Origines du Crucifix.* Paris: Editions du Cerf, 1994.

Shanley, Brian J. "Divine Causation and Human Freedom in Aquinas," *American Catholic Philosophical Quarterly* 72, no. 1 (1998): 99-122.

————. *The Thomist Tradition.* Dordrecht: Kluwer, 2002.

Sholl, Brian K. "On Robert Jenson's Trinitarian Thought," *Modern Theology* 18, no. 1 (2002): 27-36.

Slusser, Michael. "The Scope of Patripassianism," *Studia Patristica* 17, no. 1 (1982): 169-75.

Somos, Robert. "Origen, Evagrius Ponticus and the Ideal of Impassibility," *Origeniana Septima,* pp. 365-73. Louvain: Peeters, 1999.

Song, Choan-Seng. *The Compassionate God.* London: SCM, 1982.

Spanneut, M. "L'apatheia Chretienne," *Proche-Orient Chrétien* 52 (2002): 165-302.

Speyr, Adrienne von. *Erde und Himmel: Ein Tagebuch,* Zweiter Teil: *Die Zeit der Grossen Diktate,* edited by Hans Urs von Balthasar. Einsiedeln: Johannes Verlag, 1975.

Stackhouse, John G., Jr. *Can God Be Trusted? Faith and the Challenge of Evil,* new edition. Oxford: Oxford University Press, 2000.

Stålsett, Sturla J. *The crucified and the Crucified: A Study in the Liberation Christology of Jon Sobrino.* Bern: Peter Lang, 2003.

Streeter, Brunett H. "The Suffering of God," *Hibbert Journal* 12 (1913/14): 603-11.

Surin, Kenneth. "The Impassibility of God and the Problem of Evil," *Scottish Journal of Theology* 35 (1982): 97-115.

Swinburne, Richard. *Providence and the Problem of Evil.* Oxford: Oxford University Press, 1998.

Thaler, Anton. *Gott leidet mit: Gott und das Leid.* Frankfurt am Main: J. Knecht, 1994.

Tirelmont, Antonin de. "Apatheia." In *Dictionnaire de spiritualité ascétique et mystique, doctrine et histoire,* I, pp. 727-46. Paris: Beauchesne, 1937.

Vann, Gerald. *The Pain of Christ and the Sorrow of God.* Oxford: Oxford University Press, 1947.

Varillon, François. *La souffrance de Dieu.* Paris: Le Centurion, 1975.

Von Hügel, Baron F. "Suffering and God." In *Essays and Addresses on the Philosophy of Religion,* 2nd series, pp. 165-213. London: Dent & Sons, 1926.

Ware, Kallistos T. "The Meaning of *Pathos* in Abba Isaiah and Theodoret of Cyrus," *Studia Patristica* 20 (1989): 315-22.

Watson, G. "The Problem of the Unchanging in Greek Philosophy," *Neue Zeitschrift für Systematische Theologie und Religionsphilosophie* 27 (1985): 57-70.

Weinandy, Thomas G. *Does God Change?* Still River, Mass.: St. Bede's Publications, 1985.

————. *Does God Suffer?* Notre Dame: University of Notre Dame Press, 2000.

————. *The Father's Spirit of Sonship: Reconceiving the Trinity.* Edinburgh: T & T Clark, 1995.

Wells, Paul. "God and Change: Moltmann in the Light of the Reformed Tradition." In *The Powers and Weakness of God: Impassibility and Orthodoxy,* edited by Nigel M. de S. Cameron, pp. 52-68. Edinburgh: Rutherford House Books, 1990.

Westland, Daniel. "Emotion and God: A Reply to Marcel Sarot." *The Thomist* 60 (1996): 109-21.

White, Thomas Joseph. "The Voluntary Action of the Earthly Christ and the Necessity of the Beatific Vision," *The Thomist* 69, no. 4 (2005): 497-534.

————. "Von Balthasar and Journet on the Universal Possibility of Salvation and the Twofold Will of God." *Nova et Vetera,* English edition, 4, no. 3 (2006): 633-66.

Whitehead, Alfred N. *Process and Reality: An Essay in Cosmology.* Cambridge: Cambridge University Press, 1929.

Witherington, Ben, III. *The Christology of Jesus.* Minneapolis: Fortress Press, 1990.

————. *Jesus the Sage: Pilgrimage of Wisdom.* Minneapolis: Fortress Press, 1994.

————. *The Many Faces of the Christ.* New York: Crossroad, 1998.

Wolf, William. *No Cross, No Crown.* New York: Doubleday, 1957.

Wolterstorff, Nicholas. "Suffering Love." In *Philosophy and the Christian Faith,* edited by Thomas V. Morris. Notre Dame: University of Notre Dame Press, 1988.

Zoffoli, Enrico. *Mistera della Soffrenza di Dio? Il Pensiero di S. Tomaso,* Studi Tomistici 34. Roma: Ed. Vaticano, 1988.

Contributors

GARY CULPEPPER, associate professor of theology at Providence College, is a member of the study group Evangelicals and Catholics Together and has published articles in *The Thomist, Communio,* and other journals.

AVERY CARDINAL DULLES, S.J. (1918-2008), authored numerous articles on theological topics and published twenty-two books, including *Models of Revelation* (New York: Doubleday, 1983), *The Catholicity of the Church* (Oxford: Clarendon Press, 1985), and *The Assurance of Things Hoped For: A Theology of Christian Faith* (Oxford: Oxford University Press, 1994). He was a president of the Catholic Theological Society of America, a member of the International Theological Commission, and a participant in the United States Lutheran/Roman Catholic Dialogue. Until his death in December 2008, he served as a consultant to the Committee on Doctrine of the National Conference of Catholic Bishops. Until his death in December 2008, he was the Laurence J. McGinley Professor of Religion and Society at Fordham University.

GILLES EMERY, O.P., professor of dogmatic theology, University of Fribourg, Switzerland, is a member of the editorial board of the *Revue Thomiste* and a member of the International Theological Commission. His books include *The Trinitarian Theology of Thomas Aquinas* (Oxford: Oxford University Press, 2007) and *Trinity, Church, and the Human Person: Thomistic Essays* (Naples, Fla.: Sapientia Press, 2007).

PAUL L. GAVRILYUK, associate professor and University scholar of historical theology at the University of St. Thomas in St. Paul, Minnesota, is a deacon in the Orthodox Church of America and the author of *The Suffering of the Impassible God: The Dialectics of Patristic Thought* (Oxford: Oxford University Press, 2004) and *Histoire du catéchuménat dans l'Église ancienne* (Paris: Editions du Cerf, 2007). He is the contributing coeditor of *Immersed in the Life of God: The Healing Resources of the Christian Faith. Essays in Honor of William J. Abraham* (Eerdmans, 2008). His scholarly articles have appeared in *The Journal of Theological Studies, Scottish Journal of Theology,* and *Vigiliae Christianae,* among others.

PAUL GONDREAU, associate professor of theology at Providence College, is the author of *The Passions of Christ's Soul in the Theology of St. Thomas Aquinas* (Münster: Aschendorff, 2002), which originated as a doctoral dissertation under Professor Jean-Pierre Torrell, O.P. He has published many articles on theological topics associated with the anthropology and Christology of Thomas Aquinas.

DAVID BENTLEY HART, 2006-07 Robert J. Randall Chair in Christian Culture at Providence College, has previously taught at the University of Virginia; the University of St. Thomas, St. Paul; Duke University Divinity School; and Loyola College, Baltimore. He is Eastern Orthodox, and among his books are *The Beauty of the Infinite: The Aesthetics of Christian Truth* (Grand Rapids: Eerdmans, 2003) and *Atheist Delusions: The Christian Revolution and Its Fashionable Enemies* (Yale University Press, 2009).

ROBERT W. JENSON, senior research fellow at the Center of Theological Inquiry in Princeton, New Jersey, is an ordained minister of the Evangelical Lutheran Church of America and has been the associate director of the Center for Catholic and Evangelical Theology and the co-editor of its journal, *Pro Ecclesia.* He has published numerous books and articles, including his two-volume *Systematic Theology: The Triune God* and *The Works of God* (Oxford: Oxford University Press, 1997 and 1999).

JAMES F. KEATING, associate professor of theology at Providence College, has published articles on fundamental theology in *The Thomist, The Irish Theological Quarterly,* and other journals.

BRUCE L. McCORMACK, Frederick and Margaret L. Weyerhaeuser Professor of Systematic Theology at Princeton Seminary, and a member of the Presbyterian Church (USA), is the author of *Karl Barth's Critically Realistic Dialectical Theology: Its Genesis and Development, 1909-1936* (Oxford: Oxford University Press, 1995). Based on his scholarship in the field of Barthian studies, in 1998, he became the first American to be awarded the Karl Barth Prize by the Board of the Evangelical Church of the Union in Germany.

BRUCE D. MARSHALL, professor of historical theology in the Perkins School of Theology at Southern Methodist University, is the author of many publications, including *Trinity and Truth* (Cambridge: Cambridge University Press, 2000) and *Christology in Conflict: The Identity of a Saviour in Rahner and Barth* (Oxford: Blackwell, 1987), and the editor of *Theology and Dialogue: Essays in Conversation with George Lindbeck* (Notre Dame: University of Notre Dame Press, 1990).

TRENT POMPLUN, associate professor of theology at Loyola College in Maryland, specializes in late medieval and early modern theology and is the author of numerous articles in scholarly journals. His books include *A Jesuit on the Roof of the World: Ippolito Desideri's Mission to Tibet* (Oxford University Press, 2009) and *The Blackwell Companion to Catholicism,* edited with James Buckley and Frederick Bauerschmidt (Oxford: Basil Blackwell, 2007).

THOMAS G. WEINANDY, O.F.M., CAP., is the executive director of the Secretariat for Doctrine of the United States Conference of Catholic Bishops. He has previously lectured in patristic and modern theology at Greyfriars Hall, Oxford University. He is the author of works such as *Does God Suffer?* (Notre Dame: University of Notre Dame Press, 2000) and *Athanasius: A Theological Introduction* (Ashgate, 2007).

THOMAS JOSEPH WHITE, O.P., is an instructor in theology at the Pontifical Faculty of the Immaculate Conception at the Dominican House of Studies in Washington, D.C. He has published articles in *The Thomist, Nova et Vetera,* and *Pro Ecclesia,* and is the author of *Wisdom in the Face of Modernity: A Study in Modern Thomistic Natural Theology* (Naples, Fla.: Sapientia Press, 2009).

Name Index

Albert the Great, 225-28, 235, 239, 241
Alexander of Hales, 210, 225-26, 235
Alvarez, D., 302
Ambrose, 190, 204, 215, 217
Aquinas, 24, 28, 33, 37, 55-75, 79, 86, 95-96, 100, 104-6, 192, 203, 206-38, 240-44, 253-54, 259, 260, 268-81, 285, 297-98, 302, 329, 332
Aristotle, 35, 85, 118, 225, 227, 228, 229
Arius, 28, 180, 182, 183, 222
Athanasius, 28, 143, 215, 217, 219
Augustine, 22, 61, 95, 122, 136, 142, 190, 192, 204, 208, 215, 219, 259, 262, 289, 328, 329
Aurelius, M., 328, 334
Ayres, L., 60

Bach, J. S., 130
Balthasar, H., 23, 32 48-51, 65, 68, 90, 94, 252, 253, 286, 296
Bañez, D., 302, 306, 312
Barth, K., 1, 8-10, 41, 43, 102, 118, 132, 150-86, 284, 286, 288, 392
Bauckham, R., 132
Begbie, J., 122
Benedict XVI, 5
Berdyaev, N., 44
Biedermann, A. E., 176
Bloy, L., 57

Bonaventure, 192, 203, 205-9, 210, 211
Bouyer, L., 48
Bromiley, G., 152, 153, 155, 157, 158, 167
Bulgakov, S., 1, 44-49, 52, 68, 132

Calvin, J., 25, 42, 51
Camus, A., 138
Catherine of Siena, 18
Chrysippus, 328
Claudianus Mamertus, 190
Clement of Alexandria, 187, 197, 198
Cobb, J., 1
Creel, R., 135
Culpepper, G., 16, 18
Cyril of Alexandria, 6-7, 13-14, 29-31, 66, 74, 84, 120, 143, 145, 150-51, 168-69, 173, 179, 184, 196, 215-19, 249, 253-58, 260, 277-86, 297-98

Damascene, J., 32, 65, 66, 215, 217, 219, 223, 224, 225, 238, 241, 259
David of Dinant, 276
Dostoyevsky, F., 330
Dulles, A., 25
Duns Scotus, J., 192, 203, 205, 209-11

Emery, G., 16-19
Ephrem the Syrian, 130
Epicurus, 328, 331

353

Subject Index

Analogy, 8-12, 18-19, 53-57, 63-69, 78, 81-84, 90-96, 137, 142, 145, 257, 307, 312, 317, 323

Analogical interval, 11-12, 19, 311

Anhypostasia, 169

Apatheia, 6, 12-14, 35, 85, 136-37, 144, 187, 198-200, 245, 249, 253, 284, 300-301, 316

Apokatastasis, 23

Arianism, 79, 180, 190, 193, 215, 223, 238

Askesis, 138

Atheism, 39, 43, 320-23, 334

Bañezianism, 22, 303, 309-13, 317-20

Causality, 22-23, 62, 241, 294, 299-311, 321

Christ: dereliction, 26, 49, 51-52, 91, 194-95, 214, 218, 246-308, 316, 318; descent into hell, 42, 51, 74, 94, 145, 247, 262, 270; fear, 194-201, 222-31, 236-53; passions, 65, 202, 226, 235-37, 272; suffering of, 39-42, 51, 54, 88, 93-94, 141-47, 199, 207, 214-45, 272, 328; two natures of, 13-19, 30, 42, 73-75, 77-97, 157, 192, 216-18, 243-52, 281-82

Compassion, 56, 67, 332

Councils: Chalcedon 3, 5, 13-14, 35, 85, 136-37, 144, 187, 198-200, 249, 253, 284, 300-301, 316; Constantinople I, 29; Constantinople II, 13, 31, 229, 249; Constantinople III, 31-32, 223, 228; Ephesus 13, 30, 74, 187, 216, 277-78; Lateran IV, 33-34, 61; Nicea 5, 8, 18, 28, 119, 124; Vatican I, 33, 61, 230

Creation, 1-19, 22-25, 29, 34-40, 45-50, 60, 71-72, 85-93, 99-116, 125, 133-39, 141, 144, 168-70, 174, 216, 229, 285, 296, 300-318

Damnation, 22, 25, 42, 94, 211, 251, 270-73, 307, 310, 318-19

Death of God, 15, 17, 41, 74, 218, 252, 277, 288, 298, 323

Determinism, 22-23, 125

Docetism, 142-43, 190, 197, 217, 226

Election, 11, 88, 153-60, 170-78, 184-85, 191, 202, 224, 312, 318

Enhypostasia, 169

Evil, 1, 3, 9-25, 53-69, 86-99, 100, 107-16, 142-46, 155, 184, 201, 232-37, 290-91, 305-22, 324-44

Exodus, 101, 112-13

Genus majestaticum, 175-76

Genus tapeinoticum, 174-79, 184